CONSUMER GOVERNMENT

VIA

THE ART OF FULL DISCLOSURE

DOUGLAS W. AYRES

O money, money, I'm not necessarily
one of those who think thee holy,
But I often stop to wonder how thou
canst go out so fast when thou
comest in so slowly.
Ogden Nash
Hymn That Makes The Wolf Go

ISBN: 978-1-4669-1114-7 (sc)
ISBN: 978-1-4669-1115-4 (e)

Library of Congress Control Number: 2012900453

Trafford rev. 04/11/2012

 www.trafford.com

North America & international
toll-free: 1 888 232 4444 (USA & Canada)
phone: 250 383 6864 ♦ fax: 812 355 4082

SYNOPSIS

Between 2007 and 2012 the financial viability of U.S. local governments dived from tenuous to near bankruptcy. The "conservative" turn of many elected officials and refusal of most to consider revenue increases left only "cutting", elimination, or starvation into ineffectiveness for virtually all municipal and state programs and projects. The constant kerfuffle between left and right political extremes in non-constructive terms pushed many municipalities and states to the verge of wholesale abandonment of many services and activities. Clearly, discussion of "viable solutions" is required.

Solutions? This book offers solutions based on the business model of service and goods for a price. But such a concept is near heresy in government. However, a start toward matching public willingness to select and pay for government offerings was forced on California on November 6, 1979 by citizen-initiated _California Constitution_ Article XIII B. Decreed defined "costs reasonably borne" must be calculated, and taxes, fees and charges not mixed. But the near demise of local government has prevented significant application of methodologies to identify, fully cost, and offer specific public services for a definitive price, and acceptable level of effectiveness, as intended by the initiative's sponsors. Computerization capability exists, but is underused. The public need-to-know specifically what their government provides, and how much each service or product costs is prevalent, but wholly unfulfilled. Both of knowledge and willingness of public officials, and detail know-how to respond, is absent.

Specificity. Here is a methodical "System" to present every public service, its costs, beneficiaries and quality, for selection of "needs" from a menu. That list informs "customers" how much need be paid for each service, what level, and how – in taxes, fees or charges. And indicates which to reject, if poorly supplied or improperly-priced.

CONSUMER GOVERNMENT might resolve the current major philosophical dilemma, and provide a practical delivery system to prevent wholesale deterioration and/or abandonment of municipal services and community projects. And to surface the negative ramifications society would suffer were local governments to collapse. Or, in the alternative, allow the private sector to attempt to provide substitutes, but outside the inherent control and ultimate responsibility of elected officials, perhaps even without proper quality monitoring and measurement to assure accuracy and fairness.

Importantly, the "MUNICIPAL BUSINESS SYSTEM" described in detail in this Book provides vital taxpayer information about how and where taxes are spent, what services are provided at specific levels, and exposes inappropriate diversion of tax proceeds from broad public needs to subsidize personal choice direct benefit services.

Information for Decision. The determination, budgeting, accounting, presentation, and political and public information and decision process for full implementation of business-emulating CONSUMER GOVERNMENT is provided in detail by this Book.

TABLE OF CONTENTS

CONSUMER GOVERNMENT -- *VIA THE ART OF FULL DISCLOSURE*

TABLE OF CONTENTS – CONTINUED

CONSUMER GOVERNMENT -- VIA THE ART OF FULL DISCLOSURE

ACKNOWLEDGEMENTS

**Eric Johnson** reviewed computer format, content and, in general and specific, assured the accuracy and veracity of this extended version of the Revenue-Cost match-up "System" developed by MSI, now expanded by RCS. As usual for all my books, Eric's input was vital.

**MSI Principals** Albert "Rick" Kermer, CPA; Owen E. Olson, CPA (deceased); Lee Weber, Eric Johnson, and Scott Thorpe, the major elements of MSI, took my ideas and concepts and gave them life. For their detailed work all of local government should forever be grateful.

**Other MSI Staff**, numerous and greatly diversified in backgrounds, and now widely scattered throughout government. They made significant contributions to development of "The System". These recruits were bright, intellectually and academically prepared, energetic, ethical, and had widely varied municipal operational experience. They produced superior results.

**Kansas City, Missouri Chamber of Commerce** that contracted with PAS in 1957 to do what became the first match-up of specific municipal services with revenue sources and program beneficiaries. And wisely actually adopted the majority of the resulting recommendations. And thanks to the Dean of City Managers, L.P. Cookingham, then in Kansas City, who critiqued, accepted and adopted the PAS/Chamber recommendations and the "new System".

**Salem, Oregon Public Works and Utilities Staff** for the 90 years during which those dedicated public employees developed and faithfully executed a major precursor of "_The System_" of public service delivery, budgeting, accounting and disclosure set out herein. Bob Moore, MPA, the Finance Director who made it go, and Utilities Director John Geren, MSCE, MPH, who insisted on cost accuracy and integrity, added materially to the 1960's systemic updates.

**Inglewood, California Staff** who, from April 1968 thru July 1976, allowed and aided me to throw out the "historic and conventional" and develop and install what became the first revenue-cost and computer-driven city government in the United States. And 110 willingly became "service center" managers and effective business-oriented self-motivated entrepreneurs.

**The 300+ Client Jurisdictions** over five decades that countenanced my tinkering with their budgeting and accounting systems seeking greater clarity for consumers of their services and projects, and for elected officials, and staff as to true full costs and service beneficiaries.

**The 2,800+ Graduate Students** at the University of Southern California; California State University, Long Beach; and the University of California, Irvine who listened to and absorbed my attempts to convince them there are five sides to government finance – revenues, expenditures, budgeting, accounting, and personal integrity, thereby producing intelligible full public reporting with fidelity and, ultimately, public understanding and acceptance.

**The 1,000+ Senior Police Executives and newly-elected Sheriffs** who tolerated my rantings about why they must know what specific services they provide their publics, and how much each activity truly costs. And thus supply full information to the tax and fee payers bearing the cost burden and who benefit from properly financed and prioritized public services.

DEDICATION

To **_Elliot G. Falk,_** MPA, and **_James E. Keys,_** CPA, (both deceased), two exceptional intellects and financial systems geniuses and technicians. They both were marvelously ethical people who taught me everything I know about public finance, accounting and "customer" reporting. And especially how to think and work "beyond the conventional envelope", and "how to keep 'em all honest, informed and in the glare of public scrutiny". Each, indeed, was a rare individual of great professional accomplishments, and my highly respected personal mentors.

HISTORICAL BACKGROUND OF THIS BOOK

The 1992 best seller _Reinventing Government_ by Gaebler & Osborne[1] presented the below statement presaging that best-selling book's major point:

"Doug Ayres, whose company helps California governments determine their true costs, says only 4 percent of local governments know the direct cost of each service they provide; 2 percent know the full total cost of each service...and only 10 percent can even tell you what services they provide!"

Progress? Major efforts since made by DWA, Inc. & MSI, Inc. [more about that later] improved the percentages, recognition and acceptance of service pricing for California elected and appointed officials. But not sufficiently to achieve full public understanding and acceptance. This Book will attempt to awaken both of elected and financial types to the realities of the marketplace. Services can and should be recognized for what they are – consumer goods available at a retail price that _excludes_ profit, bonuses, stock options, and extreme salaries and perks. And selection by separation of municipal services into distinct cost-income matched "lines-of-business", with integrity of pricing accounting. But, with far better full disclosure of services, costs, financing, and direct beneficiaries.

The Alaska Experience. In the 1950's the Author was a field consultant for Public Administration Service (PAS), the consulting arm of the University of Chicago's National Governmental Center (NGC). From early 1954 thru February of 1959 NGC/PAS contracted with the Territory of Alaska Statehood Commission to "create the Alaska State government". I participated in all phases of that assignment, from assisting in drafting the _Constitution_, to detailed Statehood implementation. One major task was to be gofer/learner to a financial systems genius, Elliot G. Falk. In the process of designing and installing the State and Territorial purchasing and contracting, budgeting, accounting, reporting, audit, treasury, cash management, and data processing systems I absorbed gobs of learning from this fantastically gifted teacher, designer, and practitioner of financial systems with integrity. "Buddy" spent four years as Finance Director of the State of Kentucky and, after fortuitous financial enlightenment

---

1 _Reinventing Government;_ Ted Gaebler and David Osborne; 1992; Addison-Wesley Publishers; page 217

with him, at age 32 he began eight years in the same role for Pennsylvania. I learned from him between his tenures serving two nationally prominent and very wise Governors.

The Kansas City Process. In late 1957 I again was fantastically fortunate to be assigned by PAS to be a gofer/learner to another superb mentor and human being -- James E. Keys, MBA, CPA, (now deceased) then the immediate Past President of the American Institute of Certified Public Accountants. We two were tasked to fulfill a two phase contract with the Kansas City (Missouri) Chamber of Commerce:

1) Review and determine whether the City Manager (L.P. Cookingham, the "Dean" of City Managers) needs added revenues to provide adequate City services, and if so, how much.

2) If more revenues are necessary, recommend specific amounts twice those determined needed, so the Chamber could select which, if any, it might decide worthy of support.

Keys chose to follow the ***corporate multi-line income vs. costs incurred*** approach, a process with which he was intimately familiar. Thus all City services were separated into as complete units as then-available City accounting information could provide. Taxes, fees, utility rates and all other income sources were isolated and matched to specific activities. All services were identified and beneficiaries of each function identified. Then "actual" costs determined from the limited pre-computerization City accounting records. Tax sources also were appropriately allocated, mainly to police, fire protection, parks & recreation, library, facilities maintenance, and other broad-based public impact services.

The totaled result was a massive shortage of monies to provide "necessary and adequate services". A massive misallocation of taxes to functions provided to limited numbers of "special needs and interest 'customers'" also was discovered. Even after reassignment of some inappropriately strayed taxes, all widely-used public services still suffered from fiscal starvation. Tax diversion to special interest services was endemic.

The case was made and the Chamber selected and supported tax and fee increases to prevent public service deterioration. [A recommendation to secure a professional football team to share Municipal Stadium expenses with the MLB Royals resulted in the Chamber enticing Lamar Hunt to move his AFL Dallas Texans to K.C. as the NFL Chiefs.]

Based on the K.C. and Alaska learning, and service in several cities, this writer places much blame for disdain of local government integrity and economy on the omnipresent all-purpose **General Fund**. Also to blame are those political science theoretician professors who believe the General Fund "provides needed policy flexibility". They wholly ignore that the practical potential "political flexibility" encourages transmogrification into political, personal and corporate corruption, by whatever definition.

Conclusion. There is no reason a municipal government cannot be operated as effectively and efficiently as private corporate entities are alleged to be. But by using the multi-line income vs. costs incurred model. The *only* differences are: 1) being **PUBLIC** and 2) **non-profit, non-dividend, low salary, non-bonus, non-stock-option and non-perk.**

Salem, Oregon. In late 1962 Ayres became Finance Director/Treasurer/Assistant City Manager of Salem, Oregon. Nine months later he was elevated to C-M of the then-85,000 population capital city. He there found a highly competent and well equipped public employee construction force in place, building all water, sewer, street and other public infrastructure. Those efforts were supported and openly reported by a superior, but pre-computer age, project costing system. That accounting masterpiece had been developed over the 90+ years the City had been fulfilling citizen-initiated special improvement assessment projects. **ALL** costs were isolated, allocated, and assessed, with some tax contributions made to selected "vital" major projects. Overheads were known and allocated.

Subsequent detailed analysis of the accounting system and project costs incurred during a two year sanitary sewer expansion to serve 40,000+ annexed population definitively proved accuracy and equitability of City costing. The efficacy of the Salem "system" was proved in head-to-head project construction against privately owned AGC contractors. The framework of Salem's accounting was lifted from that City and transplanted to Inglewood, California when, in 1968, Ayres moved there to be its City Manager.

Inglewood, California. Inglewood was quickly modernized. Ayres also was admitted to the University of Southern California School of Public Administration Ph.D. program. A course allowed development of a new City organizational structure, with a matching accounting and budgeting system for the City. The latest behavioral theory and practices, per delightful learned Professors Bruce Storm and Warren Bennis, were carefully incorporated into the City organization. Total abandonment of the City's ancient financial structure and fractured 'bookkeeping' approaches ensued. The latest computing equipment – an IBM 360/20 mainframe, with dozens of terminals – in 1971 was installed in the new 12-level City Hall/$100 million multi-structure Civic Center. A fortuitous federal grant provided three highly experienced programmers, two operational technicians, and a genius supervisor, all displacees from the local downtrodden aerospace industry.

The updated Salem costing system quickly was programmed with Ayres' fully developed Ph.D.-level budgeting/cost accounting/reporting codes and forms *a la Alaska* (Falk) and *Kansas City* (Keys). Scores of "Service Centers" were catalogued, revenue sources matched to each, specific beneficiaries identified for each service, and detailed monthly revenue-cost reports provided for each of the 110 "service center managers". The General Fund was relegated to central overhead costs, and fully distributed by percentage to each discovered and accounted-for service center. Thus a juggernaut organization was put into motion, providing massive cost-benefit information to the five-member Council and their constituents. Resultant demanded service level increases were financed by citizen *demanded* massive tax, rate and fee increases, with literally each such adoption action accompanied by standing ovations. Service levels were high, known, trusted, and valued by constituents. Full disclosure reigned. Almost everyone was pleased and happy.

Moving On. Mid-1975 the Inglewood City Council decided it had had enough modernization. The five literally declared, in private of course, that they did not want voters to have so much information and choice. Thus Ayres was fired, the IBM equipment quickly replaced with short-lived round-hole Sperry-Rand gear, and the budgeting, accounting, service costing, revenue match-up, and public reporting system programs lost.

Doug became a USC Professor and consultant. Management Services, Incorporated, a subsidiary of his DWA, Inc. corporate "umbrella", was created, by teaming with two CPAs [Albert "Rick" Kermer & Owen Olsen], another ex-PAS analyst and former city manager [Lee Weber], and two talented recent recruits [Scott Thorpe & Eric Johnson]. Clientele wishing to emulate the "constant flow of money Ayres had in Inglewood" quickly came calling.

MSI & RCS. The first revenue-cost studies were for Doug Dunlap, City Manager of Villa Park, California, then Richard Rowe, C-M of La Palma. On assuming his new office, the latter called with: *"I can't make payroll. We are out of money."* [See letter page 84]

Over the next 30 years similar and increasingly more expansive work was performed by MSI and its successor, RCS, for more than one-quarter of California's local governments. [See Appendix B for the expanding list. Many are multiple, repeat and/or continuing clients.] Ayres and Weber retired in the mid-1990's, gradually being phased out. Staff had reached 65 at MSI's high point, but rapidly declined as the 21st century began without Ayres' sales and public explanatory capabilities. The company was renamed Revenue & Cost Specialists [RCS] and additional software developed for sale and client follow up.

Failure. Despite MSI staff's and Ayres' sales and explanatory efforts, the revolutionary informational and public choice capabilities of the *Municipal Business System* were only partially or tentatively embraced by elected officials. There was great reluctance to transfer service cost impacts from taxes to fees, rather choosing to continue subsidizing special interest benefit services with taxes. Costs were laundered through the ubiquitous, monstrous, and seemingly bottomless bonanza, the **General Fund**. But ability to identify the massive tax subsidies for powerful individual or group benefit did, in fact, sufficiently egg on quite a few brave elected officials to raise major amounts of desperately needed fee and charge revenues. They thus unburdened the overtaxed, and in many instances, improperly taxed, by beginning to limit tax subsidies to the powerful and for lobbyists.

Kermer, Johnson, Thorpe and RCS continue the good fight, exposing unwarranted tax subsidies and raising vital revenues. RCS has increased emphasis on a subsidiary, *Government Software Systems*, "to better identify the software side of our business". But much needed local revenue is still needed, and now raised by the MSI, now-updated RCS approach to accounting. [See website, *www.revenuecostspecialists.com.*] Also see Appendix C for targeted specialized articles written by the former MSI, Inc., now RCS Principals.

Despite the good works that have taken place over the three decades of MSI/RCS missionary work, significant diversion of taxes to subsidize services to special interests continues. Maybe, just maybe, the current revenue "crunch", brutal budget cuts and mindless outsourcing will force elected officials to "get it". Reasoned rational options do exist.

Renaissance? The self-assigned task of this book is to inject that rational fact-based business-style information into government, thus taking advantage of the now self-destructing local government financial underpinning. The goal is to "inform and educate" local officials that bankruptcy, destructive cuts, toxic protests thereto, and demands to "do something" can be avoided. Or swift and certain political retribution will be sought and secured. And should be, due to massive misuse of taxes to subsidize those who do not warrant such largesse. The loss of services to those who pay for broad tax-supported public services, but are served at lesser levels, is universal, significant and grossly unfair.

Urgency. Such positive responses are necessary, and soon, as attested by the most respected English language financial journal, *The Economist*. After a mind boggling listing of destructive evidence "dotting the American landscape" that publication concluded:

> *"America's middle class is facing a very uncertain future. Wall Street may have its casino up and running again, but Main Street shows no signs of bouncing back anytime soon. Awful statistics – on bankruptcy, unemployment, home foreclosures – flash warnings that the middle class is under assault, and that America **risks turning into a third world nation...**The evidence is everywhere you look, dotting the American landscape....*[An appalling listing of cuts in city, county and state budgets and elimination or destruction of numerous services follows.]

The conclusion reached is *"America's* leaders *seem unable, or just unwilling, to do anything about it....Americans can't simply sit back and wait for the people they elected to make things better...something needs to be done to stop America's slide into third world status."[2]*

Goal. The goal of this book is to provide the **_Municipal Business System_** to provoke recipients of local, and very likely much of state government, into willingness to pay adequate prices for well-managed public services. To do so through reliable and well-documented fair product pricing data would assure integrity of quality and supply and openness of understandable accurate financial information. Thereby taxes would be recouped for general benefit needs. The unconscionable and mostly hidden massive transfer of general taxes to subsidize the wealthy, powerful, business, corporate, and politically favored in-crowd and inside-traders must be stopped.

Separation of services into distinct entities, and definitive alignment between cost and price for fair retail pricing of government activities hopefully will convince elected officials, and their constituents, that truly there isn't and never has been a "free lunch".

Collectively, the "general citizenry" has had their heads handed to them by those powerful enough to suck up General Fund taxes for personal or corporate subsidy and benefit, rather than utilization for known needed broad public benefit and agreed-to social needs. By whatever devices available: "systemic", loop-hole, political artifice, partisan pressures, benefits, political exactions via contributions or other monetary or asset transfers, insider or front running stock trading, promised future employment, family employ, or other maneuvers "normal hard-working people" would consider evil, self-serving, "corrupt" or improper enrichment. [See Chapter VI for a section detailing Corruption.]

The **_Municipal Business System_** is the preventive for ethical and political corruption.

SPECIAL NOTE ABOUT "CUT 'N PASTE"

and

"The back of the Book"

Numerous Schedules, Tables, Exhibits, forms, cut-out text, and patched together globs of data and writings are included in the pages and pieces comprising this Book. Some are within the text; other "cut 'n paste" pieces are additional Schedules, Tables, and Appendices in the ILLUSTRATIONS, "in the back of the book". All, either directly or indirectly, were written by the Author and/or are from MSI's/RCS's hundreds of client Reports.

Pagination. To hold this Book to a reasonable length, the first page of a run of Schedules is interspersed with explanatory text. Thus the Book Section – ILLUSTRATIONS – "in the back of the book" presents the balance of some Schedules, or single sheets expanding on how the *Municipal Business System* is meticulously and methodically built. In process two practical problems arose which required roundabout technical solution.

First, the original MSI/RCS text and Schedules/Tables used in the Book all were written or compiled on now-obsolete and long-gone software. Thus the "originals" could not be tapped. That left only "cut 'n paste". Some of those did not turn out well, for the below process was not conducive to high quality:

1. Find a non-dog-eared copy of the Report in my personal archives
2. Photocopy the appropriate pages
3. Trim the copies to size, page-by-page
4. Scan into a separate "Illustrations" file
5. Try to get each page as much as possible squared & aligned with Book format
6. Give up "squaring" after the fourth scanner run/attempt
7. Recognize the genius of the *Municipal Business System* as a SYSTEM, despite time passage, and cut 'n trim as best as can be done to illustrate its worth
8. Pick and choose which scanned pages to use within the text; and which to consign to "the back of the book" – in ILLUSTRATIONS
9. Valiantly try to get Word '07 to match up with the "far older than" Word '03 or Volkswriter 3 software spacing and text interspersing within scanned pieces

Second, protect appropriate text, system design, software and all copyrights. This part was difficult, for such was necessary to divulge only the logic by which Service Center costs are assembled, not all details. That "logic" and "process" was achieved by means of several decades of intense personal involvement in the intricacies and full breadth of municipal government operations, both from the "inside" and "outside". While several others have attempted to emulate the *Municipal Business System* as it has evolved, been upgraded and updated, those outputs can only be termed as ranging from "miserable" to "wanting", but all "wholly inaccurate, suspect and unreliable". 'Nuff said.

CHAPTER I

THE STATE OF GOVERNMENT FUNCTIONS

The Great Recession*s* of 2007-2020, when connected to the intransigency of the so-called "Tea Party", acted to reduce dramatically the revenues of all levels of government in the United States. The U.S. Federal government met its expenditure needs by massive issuance of Treasury securities, loans, stock purchases, various Federal Reserve "support mechanisms", and QE 1, QE 2 and QE 2½ provided Wall Street banks and investment bankers, and the international economy. And significant program cutbacks which, in turn, depressed further the national and international economies.

__The Crisis.__ State and local governments, especially schools, have suffered what many economists and governmental financial professionals term a "permanent reduction in revenues and national knowledge"[3]. Due to the decline in revenues – in the vicinity of 30% to 40% for many jurisdictions – cutbacks have been made in state, local and educational programs and facilities. These exercises in "cuts" essentially have fallen into two difficult-to-define categories – **"necessary public services"** and **"vital public services"**. Definition of both categories has become an exercise in combat semantics, with various levels of public reaction by citizens. However, police, fire protection, and EMT services comprise those considered as "vital" by most consumers of state and local governmental activities. Health, welfare, social services, recreation, park, library, and maintenance-related activities, and education have borne the brunt of budget reductions as *desirable, but...*" functions. The latter apparently now have dropped below *"necessary"* level. And even the *"vital"* have suffered significant reductions in force and facilities.

__Reaction.__ Public objection to or support for all types and categories of budgetary reductions and money search schemes has varied greatly. On observing those public reactions one must reflect on the old saw of "beauty is in the eyes of the beholder". In this case, "beauty" is dependent on the CONSUMER of the service or, for some activities, on the actual social need. Identification and definition of terms obviously is needed, a task which this book will attempt, to a probable level of *ad nauseam.* But mainly for cities.

Another measure of differentiation also must be applied. Namely, a basic law of physics – "For every action there is an opposite reaction". Plainly put, for every governmental negative service change, be it "level reduction" or elimination, there will be those who object, and those whose interests or activities are adversely affected.

__Examples.__ Some – a very few -- of the more glaring, and psychiatrically-related actions and commensurate reactions follow.

---

[3] The media has been so copiously filled with "information" there is no attempt here to provide specifics.

Law Enforcement. Police and justice system personnel and capabilities reductions are opposed by and documentation provided to assure "crime will rise" as the reaction. The same argument is put forth where prison populations are being reduced through early release, and parole and probation officer positions and oversight eliminated.

Park Closures. When these local and state governmental activities are threatened and, in many instances actually implemented, a rise in juvenile delinquency and loss of tourist and recreational spending is brought forth as the "direct result". Both predicted results are yet difficult to quantify, as is the loss of historical posterity for shuttering museums.

Fire Station Closure. Some localities have closed fire stations, thereby reducing personnel, equipment and facilities operating expenses. Increase in response and run times eventually will result in losses in life and property that otherwise would not occur. And the inevitable re-rating by the Insurance Services Office [ISO] in effect will transfer the loss of revenue from the totality of the serviced population to those who lose life or property, and/or purchase the resulting more expensive insurance. Such reactions have been quantified copiously for previous such closures and personnel/equipment "cut-backs".

Rest Stop Closure. Two countervailing arguments are made about this cost saving gimmick. It is maintained that inconvenience to and reduction in tourism as an industry results from such closures. But some argue that businesses adjacent to highway interchanges will fill the gap and thereby provide added tax revenue. Once the federal government permits Interstate rest stop privatization all may be happy again. Reaction to the latter is yet to be achieved and fully tested in the vast expanses of the United States.

More Problematic CUTS. Expectations are great that the truly unprecedented huge governmental budgetary reductions from 2008 through 2011-2012, so far, and thus on into the indefinite future, will decimate and effectively eliminate considerable numbers of previously supplied governmental services, activities and personnel, especially so for regulatory and environmental functions. Some of those issues are now raised as exemplars of the action-reaction theme.

Street Maintenance. Elimination of street re-surfacing, and drainage maintenance initially will not be so noticeable, especially in warmer and dryer states. But, engineering personnel repeatedly have decried such actions as being "short term solutions resulting in long term disaster". Arguments contrary to that statement are generally mute, especially in the two-thirds of the nation that is susceptible to considerable snow, ice, rain and other adverse climatological phenomena.

Utility Rate Freezes. Publicly owned and operated water supply and distribution, sewage collection and treatment, storm drainage routing and dispersal and, for some, electric power generation and distribution utilities are susceptible to budgetary exigencies. Some jurisdictions have frozen rates, hoping that "when the economy improves" rate catch-up can occur. Meantime, facilities continue to depreciate and deteriorate, maintenance supplies are pinched, and capital improvements deferred. Whether "catch-up" can or ever will occur is, of course, problematical. Or, as is more likely, system physical deterioration will accelerate unabated to failure. Such full economic "recovery" is improbable.

Recreation Program Reduction. "What do the kids do after school and on weekends" is the common cry when sports facilities are allowed to fall into increasingly lower levels of maintenance or actual closure. Most communities have become dependent on sports leagues for various population ages, virtually all of which take place at and on local government-owned and maintained facilities. When these fields and equipment are no longer available and/or staffed, volunteerism has shown to have dramatic limitations and dangers as backfill. Many fees have been imposed for participation in and use of such activities and facilities, but there are practical limits on such, as considerable experience has shown. The basic fields, buildings, and attendant equipment almost universally are provided by expenditure of public capital. More debt issuance no longer can be relied on to update and/or replace desperately depreciated grounds and attendant infrastructure. Thus the greater question -- is there a realistic non-government alternative? For all of society, or just those who can pay? The reaction and probable results do not seem palatable.

Land Use Controls. These activities can and should be paid for by those requiring/requesting modifications and/or additions. However, there are basics of general public safety and nuisance inspections, routine enforcement, updating of technical requirements, and compliance with mandates by higher levels of government. Who pays for these should activities effectively be eliminated through budgetary reductions? The argument that "Houston has never had zoning" apparently has not flown in virtually all other local governments comprising the United States. Heated public discussions at the neighborhood level have made reaction to cuts in this area highly predictable. Then again, those who rail against "tree huggers" and "environmental nut jobs", and many land developers and realtors, would favor such eliminations and reductions in controls.

Libraries. This highly significant adjunct to the educational system has been supported by local government for more than a century. During the California Proposition 13 local government responses fees were instituted and services restricted to residents. Neither action worked, and both soon were abandoned. Libraries have become a symbol of the intellectual status of municipalities. The literal elimination of public libraries could be foreseen as a direct result to the magnitude of the current lack of supporting local government revenues. The "dumbing down" of society could be a long-term result. Such already appears to be well underway for tax financed "public" education.

Debt Service. Since the 17th century governments have relied on issuance of various types of debt instruments for financing of capital plant additions. General debt service payments reflect only property tax receipts. Revenue debt is just that, repaid by dedicated revenues from some "reliable bankable source". With the current, and projected major reduction in property values, and thus taxes derived therefrom, and in other revenues as well, both types of debt are threatened. Defaults were neither prevalent nor un-common during the 1929-1940 Great Depression. Avoidance of default now seems reliant to a great extent on reductions in or outright elimination of "less volatile services" provided by state and local governments. Also, should deferred maintenance be converted to debt?

Response. A State of Arizona budget shortfall response was to sell $750 million of State buildings, then lease them to the tax-supported General Fund. But, is that not redefining lease payments as debt service? And, to whom are buildings sold, and by what process? If revenue flows require, will the State be evicted from its Capitol? What would be the reaction to that happenstance? Yet the "State Budget Plan" contains a "no debt" pledge and pronouncement. This might well be the ultimate "action-reaction" scenario.

Fear and Loathing. Increasingly the drumbeat of potential municipal bond default has galvanized Wall Street into putting municipal bond debt service on the list of major fears. Bond default insurance companies have all but disappeared, municipal bond interest rates have raised, and income tax exempt bond mutual funds now are characterized as "risky". However, Moody's, Fitch, and Standard & Poor's bond rating services as of this writing have not expressed opinions as pessimistic as those of the underwriters, advisors, attorneys and salespersons whose fees are at risk. Further, discussions in several state legislatures to seek federal legislation permitting states to declare bankruptcy have not aided in solidifying the municipals market. But some modifications to state laws have aided cities.

Public Employees. Public employees and their "benefits" are easy targets for "cut and gut" government critics. Those "lazy bureaucrats" and their "lucrative" retirement and health care programs are being savaged, in bulk. These have become the *de rigueur* scapegoat on which demagogues now heap political animosity. Government employment had long been characterized as "stable". However, the government revenue crunch has resulted in significant lay-offs – 162,400 by October, 2011.[4] Without federal "stimulus" providing significant monies to school systems, scores of thousands more teachers would have been let go. Some states refused to accept "bail-out" monies, fearing a lack of future state funding to replace the federal "stimulus". Ideology then consumed this discussion.

Arizona effectively abandoned Kindergarten and is trying mightily to abandon health care for the elderly and low-income disadvantaged portions of the social strata, even though risking loss of substantial amounts of federal Medicaid funding. The undertone is obvious: "Why should **WE** pay for **THEM** with our taxes?" Thousands of State and local workers will be added to unemployment rolls – as those are being reduced nationwide.

So-called government "vacant positions" have and apparently will remain unfilled and probably ultimately abolished. Those type "budget balancing" techniques are now snowballing, since federal "stimulus" monies are exhausted.

Institutional Losses. Even more problematical in employee reductions, for both the public and private sectors, is the loss of institutional competence and memory. Such has occurred due to each of businesses and public jurisdictions reducing payroll costs by offering early retirement "packages" for those employees with long tenure and resulting higher wage/salary/benefit levels. These losses will be felt for decades.

Furloughs. Other devices, such as mandatory furloughs to reduce payroll costs, or

---

[4] This was the highest rate of the eight employment groups. Source: Challenger Gray & Christmas via *MONEY;* December 2011, page 90

across-the-board pay reductions, as attempted to be instituted by Governor Schwarzenegger of California, resulted in significant problems on the days on which, and spirit by which public services are provided. So the action-reaction process has added unquantifiable social, quality, time loss, and tenor of service impacts.

These and other "savings" evoked a barrage of demands to "reduce public salaries", "limit or eliminate health and retirement benefits", and "fight unions". The anti-government employment mantra has and undoubtedly will decrease flow of "quality" personnel into "public service". What that trend might do to provide a self-fulfilling generation of "lazy bureaucrats, and lousy government service" is thought provoking. But if not employed in government, will corporations and businesses hire those dis-employed and now disgusted former or prospective want-to-be "public servants?

Government Retirement & Health Benefits. Significant questioning of the defined benefit type retirement plans prevalent in government has become rampant. The rationale that resulted in the near universal adoption of this category of retirement plan was "public employment provides neither bonuses nor stock ownership, or salaries and perks like private business". That was accompanied with "public employee salaries generally are significantly lower than those in private enterprise". Yet, per current discussions, such prefatory recruitment enticements for "public service" have not surfaced. And few "pay surveys" reportedly have shown that government employee pay exceeds that of private business, especially when annual bonuses are included. Even more interestingly, the lay-off of public employees has more than offset the alleged increases in industrial hiring. Thus national and most state and regional unemployment rates have remained static. And, in some areas rose due to government employee reductions.

Yet the clamor level rises – "get rid of, reduce the pay and benefits of public employees and 'privatize' public services" has become the cry.

A self-fulfilling prophecy of "poor and inefficient government" is virtually certain. There are no indications that any privatizations will be subjected to cost or effectiveness reviews, or any significant competitive process for granting contracts. As to this trend, it will provide abundant food for academic research to determine to what extent political "contributions" directly precede and/or follow and consistently track outsourcing.

A Horrible Exception. Further, toxic national publicity about salaries and benefits of City of Bell, California officials has acted to throw more fuel on the fire of anti-government "pay and benefits" rhetoric. This isolated aberrational "situation" has fanned the anti-flames and spawned inflammatory public employee criticism.

tions to health plans provided public employees. This economic twist is accompanied by elimination and reduction in pay of employees as increasing losses in contributions to those public retirement and health plans. And, in an increasing number of states, statutory limits on or actual elimination of public employee bargaining rights and unions.

Devolution. In many states cities and counties have been assigned various and numerous so-called "social problems" for response and resolution. Provision of medical care for low income and elderly also is not being spared in the national orgy of state and local government budgetary cutbacks. EMS and paramedic service provided by municipal fire departments has become universal, since the U.S.'s first city-wide paramedic service was provided citizens of Inglewood, California in 1969. By public healthcare cutbacks fire agencies by default have become the first responder, and oftimes the ONLY source of medical emergency aid during familial, personal or social "situations". Thus lay-off of fire/EMS personnel considerably depreciates this *ad hoc* element of any type "national health care system". Fabled "Hometown Doctor" house calls have been replaced by public tax-financed EMS, paramedic and ambulance services.[5]

Senior citizen care, food, and medical facilities are being eliminated and/or closed in wholesale fashion. In Arizona kindergarten and juvenile detention and rehabilitation have been either reduced or eliminated via State budget trimming. Organ transplants for those unable to pay were eliminated, causing the death of several prospective recipients. (The Arizona Governor finally relented and further fatalities avoided – thus far.) So, local governments are by default the source of the unfunded burden of day care for working parents, and/or coping with juvenile crime, bad behavior, and purveyors of vandalism. And even housing State prisoners for up to 12 months, at local expense, rather than in State prisons.

To make matters even more critical, state government "sharing" of revenues with local governments has been severely trimmed if not totally eliminated. The states needed the money to solve their own budgetary problems, thus lower level governments must choose between more drastic expenditure reductions, program eliminations, or raising taxes.

The Two Worst Results. The necessity of elected officials to shoehorn services into considerably smaller boots has given rise to much action and reaction which only can be termed, in British terminology, as "bad behaviour".

First, the basest of ideological urges and demagogic language has found a nest. Those of sufficient economic means, or wholesale ignorance of the facts-of-everyday human life in a "civilized society", are having a field day. A rationale is now seen by some "to relieve the 'overburdened taxpayer' from parting with their 'hard earned dollars' paying for all the 'socialist programs' 'pushed onto the taxpayers' by 'liberal politicians'. And the 'stifling overreaching regulation' of 'American free market enterprise' can be eliminated outright, or budgetarily starved into submission. And the 'millions of illegals' 'infecting' the nation are 'breaking the back of the taxpayer because WE have to pay for THEIR medical care, education, and fighting all the crime THEY have brought into our nation.'" Mexico's 'drug wars' serve as exemplar for demands to 'secure the border', however that might be accomplished -- even if by electrocution by fence?

Second, there is much grousing, disagreement, and even evasion of what the term "adopted budget" means. Separately elected officials, judicial systems, and quasi-public/

---

[5] Even in the Author's up-scale high-value, high-income, high-intellect community of Sedona, Arizona. Here "tea party" loyalists by stealth secured control of the Sedona Fire District and proceeded to eliminate positions, equipment, training, services, facilities, and binged on demeaning and threatening employees.

citizen commission-governed publicly owned utilities and facilities are wont to agree to monetary receipt reductions mandated by "politicians". Matters have gotten so tangled that a publicity-crazed elected Sheriff and the elected County Attorney of one of the most populous U.S counties, together, extensively and repeatedly "investigated" and sought indictment and prosecution of numerous appointed and elected officials who had legal control of the county budget. The two maintained that the County Board and a bevy of "bureaucrats" and judges conducted civil racketeering conspiracies obstructing justice.

The leading opinion is that the fooraw is over the depleted County budget and cutbacks being forced onto the two egomaniacal separately-elected officials. This undoubtedly is an extreme, but to-be-expected, reaction to reduction of central budgets for those "separate agencies". Thus the "separation of powers" supposed to exist by electing numerous administrative officials of the same jurisdiction, appears to be breaking down.

The BIG Question. All the preceding thus raises the issue:

Is there a future for many, if not most, state and local government functions, facilities, programs, activities, and infrastructure projects?

Over the past two decades there seems to have been an ever-rising belief that Ronald Reagan's pronouncement "government is not the solution to our problem; government IS the problem" is a verity. What answer to "the problem" is sought, however, has never been discussed specifically or rationally. Thus circular arguments arise – what should government do? Why are many specific tax-financed services still performed? Why should "it", or "they", be continued? What is the role of government, at any level? And, the base queries – who should pay for these things? And how? Or, even more basically, how is determination made of what "programs" and "facilities" will remain "desirable", "necessary" or even "vital"? Or, out in the wild blue yonder: What is a highly specific definition of "it" as government activity. An apt British anecdote by Baroness Perry cites a situation whereby the question "We should press for *them* to build us a proper road" was responded to with "Who's *them*?

"Them's us".[6]

Then there is the famous Walt Kelly cartoon statement by his alter ego, Pogo Possum:

We have seen the enemy, and he is us!

Basic and, for many, even simplistic definitions of government finance need amplification for every public service. And much full disclosure. Thus full, clear and definitive divisions can be made between "tax-financed" and "fee-charge supported" type activities. Clearly, business pricing methodologies need to be followed by government. Local government thus would not be viewed as "anti-business"; rather seen as "business-like".

Other Questions. Query can be made legitimately as to which governmental services and activities are conducive to "privatization"? And, even more basic, will there be sav-

---

[6] *Financial Times;* December 29, 2010; page 7

ings derived from such "out-sourcing" or will deterioration and/or denial of equal service result? Will quality remain the same, merely adequate, or improved by the contracting business enterprise? And how is quality to be measured? And by whom and at what expense to be absorbed by what agency, if done at all? Or will contractor self-regulation be sufficient? And, probably most controversial, basic and necessary -- How can the expectation or extraction of favors and/or political "contributions" from the contractor be denied to the awarding governing body? Or can/should such prohibition even be examined?

Reverse Privatization.
Municipal literature is littered with tales of outsourcings gone bad. One of the first was a massive Los Angeles County equipment maintenance contract. That one lasted about a year before it imploded due to continual breakdowns and unavailability of equipment which ostensibly had been "maintained and repaired" by the contract mechanics. Of even greater interest are numerous examples of "reverse privatization" that made and still make headlines. These instances earn the Ayres opprobrium:

> *Government services that make a profit ultimately will be given to the private sector, while any "necessary" public service that cannot be profitable will be transferred by business "leaders" to a government -- federal, state or local.*

The service landscape is rife with examples of the above:
1. Amtrak
2. Virtually all ground-bound mass transit in urban and urbanizing areas
3. Golf courses with reasonable fees and availability to the general public
4. Swimming facilities with low fees and availability to the general public
5. Sports facilities, including NFL, MLB, NHL, WNBA, FIFA/MLS stadiums
6. "Second tier" airports

Then there are those services which by their very nature are not conducive or appropriate to be outsourced. Those include, but are not restricted to or universally inclusive:
1. Police protection, including crime investigation
2. Non-volunteer fire protection
3. EMS service for areas not intensely urbanized and geographically isolated
4. Ambulance service in non-urbanized or geographically isolated areas
5. 911 emergency call and dispatch service
6. Storm water drainage and levee construction and maintenance
7. Highway speed control via video camera and private fine collection and fee
8. Sewage collection and treatment   } due to the huge amount of capital
9. Water supply, treatment and distribution } in-ground prior to actual service
10. Administrative, prosecutorial and judicial activities
11. Local street maintenance
12. Property tax assessment and collection

Toward a Solution?
An "*outsourcing level playing field*" ordinance proposed to require answers to the above posed questions prior to, and as a result of contracting, is provided as Appendix **A**. The document was utilized in labor negotiations, which resulted in

the ordinance being suppressed in fear the document would be publicized; not adopted, but merely "made public". And that inquisitive, inherent, and now-pathologically suspicious voters would demand adoption. This was a real, but not unexpected, reaction by elected officials. But well out of public view, or during obscure and unreported court proceedings. And a quarter century prior to the currently much publicized and somewhat warped municipal "financial difficulties" and "tough financial times".

The BASIC Questions. Very basic historical and even constitutional questions somehow seem to go begging when dealing with the "privatization" concept. Namely:

Why should government tax revenues be diverted to private for-profit companies?

Should the utilization of taxes so diverted be made subject to FULL DISCLOSURE?

Should such "disclosure" be to the same level of detail as direct government expenses?

Is Government Necessary? The so-called "conservative" talking heads first peppered and now assault TV and radio listeners with questions about government, and opposition to taxes, fees and charges such that the time now seems ripe to examine EVERYTHING from top to bottom. That there seems to be a troublesome disconnect between government revenues and services and facilities continues unabated. That the so-called "special interests" and lobbyists exercise major influence at all levels of government decisions is a fact that is no longer arguable. But, are *costs, service levels, and quality* any longer germane to the discussion of "What is Government"? The corporate PR machines, especially by the "military-industrial complex" that General of the Armies/President Dwight D. Eisenhower denominated, have changed public perceptions markedly. The Supreme Court decision loosing unlimited and anonymous "***contributions***" to political campaigns and causes holds the possibility of waltzing America off the cliff of organized democratic civilization into full blown corporate oligarchy. Thus a major thesis of this book is:

> **ALL government expenditures, including those outsourced, should be subject to detailed analysis and full public revenue-cost and beneficiary disclosure. And assurances had as to "benefits" thereby secured by government officials.**

Limitation. This book is limited to the Author's field of knowledge and experience in local government. Schools and state activities mostly will be eschewed – or just reported. Others will have to undertake those analyses, hopefully having learned something from the path set out herein. The very thesis upon which this Book is built is that the American **CONSUMER** of local government services should be provided choices. *Choice as to* whether to request, and therefore pay for a service that traditionally has been supplied by township, village, district, county or city, and state governments? And if to pay, for what level of quality or quantity? And by what revenue source or sources?

Glimmers of Self-Help. Understanding about and acceptance of the basic fact that local governments cannot be financed and provide a satisfactory level of service by immediate and un-analyzed privatizing seems to be making headway. Examples are arising, some of which are provided following.

K-12 Education. To avoid Legislative gutting of the State's school systems, in 2009 Arizona voters by a significant margin approved a 1% increase in State sales tax. Despite the Legislature then utilizing extant sales tax receipts to provide major business tax reductions, numerous local school districts since also have voted property tax rises. In 2011 the Arizona Legislature and Governor made a further $500 million reduction in school budgets, followed by yet more major business tax reductions and subsidies. Unfortunately, such breaches of faith appear to have become nationally endemic with a massive displacement of state governors and legislators during the 2010 election cycle.

City Services. The City of Phoenix, and other municipalities across the nation, stuck out the political necks of their governing bodies and increased, broadened and otherwise amplified existing tax sources. These somewhat limited acts of political bravery generally have taken place where specific needs and reductions were well publicized. Yet, the connection between taxes and services appears to not be nearly as murky to the voters and taxpayers as one might assume – erroneously. Fees and rates need to be examined.

Utility Rates. Water, sewer, and public-owned electric system rates also have been rising, despite "the difficult economic times". Realization seems to have set in that with collapse of the housing market and increases in energy costs, utilities' expenses and capital needs have risen sufficiently to warrant rate increases. But with little apparent groundswell of opposition seeming to have occurred if such rises are reasonably incremental.

Local Innovation. Innovative municipal "utility" and infrastructure needs also might well have been at least outwardly accepted. Example: the City of Fairmont, West Virginia reportedly adopted a user fee to pay for street paving. That was on top of an increase of $2 per week for street sweeping.[7] Many cities already have "Assessment Districts" and even recycling pick-up charges atop the now universally-accepted refuse collection fee.

It thus appears that survival instincts and desire for a reasonable level of municipal – local – services is gradually being understood, accepted, and applied. In increasing cases, such has become necessary just to retain extant service levels, due to state retention of massive amounts of previously state-shared revenues with local governments – towns, cities, and schools. Government and public administration professors over the last century repeatedly have reminded students of a basic government legal fact of life --

The states create, control, make and can do and un-make and un-do it's local government structure and powers pretty much as and when it chooses to do so.

Those facts were observed in occasions of municipal deficits and bond defaults during the Great Depression of 1929 -1940, and again during the Great Recessions of 2008-2020. With the municipal bond market now (late 2011) in disarray, local revenues and budgets collapsing, and state governors and legislators plundering local government rev-

---

[7] *USA Today*; April 14, 2001; page 6A

enue sources, anything can, and will happen. And not necessarily any of "desirable", "acceptable" or "adequate" happenings. State constitutions and statutes govern locals.

Municipal Securities and Bankruptcies. The default and bankruptcy merry-go-round has once again begun for municipalities. Fortunately, however, most such occurrences, or rumors thereof, have involved any or all of 1.) corruption, 2.) gross incompetence, 3.) political stupidity, or 4) economic over-exuberance. The first three apparently were involved in the fiasco now [November of 2011] unfolding for each of the capital city of Pennsylvania, Harrisburg; and Montgomery County, Alabama. They share a threefer. Vallejo, California apparently was a victim of both of 2 and 3. Fresno, California and Collingswood, NJ suffer from #4. Glendale, Arizona may not be far behind Fresno if it loses its NHL team. That City's stadium-surrounding commercial area now is in receivership.

Unfortunately for the whole of municipal government in the United States, some of these tales have dragged on for years, gathered volumes of headlines and gory news clips, and spooked the entirety of municipal bond issuers, underwriters/marketers, and purchasers. Most are isolated, but one must be knowledgeable to know so. Examples follow:

> *Big cuts in credit ratings of local governments threaten to give the muni market its own taste of volatility....The downgrades, while a reminder of the fragile health of states and municipalities as revenue shrinks, risk creating a fresh round of uncertainty in the municipal bond market....Because the $2.9 trillion municipal bond market is so fragmented—issuers number in the hundreds of thousands—it can be difficult for investors to do their own detailed assessment of the credit risk of issuers. So investors largely are dependent on ratings firms.* [8]

> *Moody's downgraded Fresno, Calif., last month by three notches. Fresno had built a convention center and baseball stadium when times were flush but suffered when a slowing economy sank the projects' revenue forecasts.* [9]

The same article throws out a generic warning for all municipalities:

> *Moody's Investors Service and Standard and Poor's Ratings Services review local government issuers at least once a year, regardless of size, as well as in the days ahead of a bond offering.* [10]

Other significant difficulties are emerging for all local governments due to continuing lagging of revenues. Fund accounting, a bulwark of honest and open government, is now suffering. [**Note: use of the word "funds" interchangeably with the word "money" is inexcusably erroneous! Money is only one asset component of a fund, NOT all of it!**] As discussed, and heavily encouraged later in this Book, a new and broader usage of "fund accounting" for grouped Service Centers is advocated. Currently, the temptation to raid earmarked funds with dedicated revenues is beginning to overcome good judgment and proper accounting.

---

[8] *The Wall Street Journal;* November 11, 2011, page C4
[9] *Ibid.*, page C4
[10] *Ibid.*, page C4

Full disclosure of finances and fiscal status of cities is beginning to go by the wayside, rather than be broadened, tightened and regularly publicly reported as advocated by this Book. The type of current "full disclosure" cited following might be the facilitating force to entice or force municipal officials to adopt the *Municipal Business System*.

> *Cities and states across the country are using money designated for specific purposes— such as fixing roads or sewers—in order to fill financial holes elsewhere….The moves are exposing municipalities to controversy, as federal regulators and local auditors are more heavily scrutinizing their finances to protect bond buyers and taxpayers.[11]*

Mandated Choices. In 1978 the beginning of formulation of answers to all the difficulties and questions put to the then-significantly closed and publicly unresponsive State and local governing agencies was forcibly imposed on all California governments. That year the California Jarvis Proposition 13 combine again marshaled their forces under Howard Jarvis' compatriot, Paul Gann, and formed a Prop. 13 offshoot, "*Spirit of 13, Inc.*". The goal of this new organization was to further limit taxation in California by defining and restricting tax revenue with specific revenue growth and usage limitations. That initiative went to ballot as Proposition 4 of the November 6, 1979 California election, was adopted and now resides in the *California Constitution* as Article XIIIB. Resultant mandated limits apply to the totality of the revenues of *any and all* governments in California, of whatever type, revenue source or derivation. A clear line was attempted to be drawn between the proceeds of taxes and revenues derived from fees, charges and licenses. Appropriate definitions to that end were provided for each category.

Revenue-Cost Matching. Proposition 4 began the revenue-cost match-up process in California, like it or not. And, eventually, should result in demise of the all-purpose, all encompassing heavenly puddle – the **General Fund.** To be replaced by a series of "retail commercial" **service centers** in **fund groups** offering highly specific defined activities. Of great importance, identification of the beneficiaries of each such service, as well as the full actual cost of each specific service, shall be provided, as anticipated by Prop 4. And, distinction between **cost** and **price** applied. Much more will be provided later in this Book relative to the determination and distinction between those two common terms.

A detailed description of the *Municipal Business System* and its components, definitions, identification techniques, cost distribution processes, and quality determination are contained later in this Book. In detail sufficient to exhibit both "problem" and "solution".

Exemplars. Comprehensive analyses made of two well-known and historically very well-governed cities – Pasadena and Beverly Hills, California -- will be provided in the following chapters. In great and exhaustive detail, both in text and tabular form as Illustrations in the "back of the book". Summaries will be provided in the text, and there explained as to significance. Back-up verification and details are the *Illustrations*.

The City Councils of those two cities, and hundreds of others nationwide, contracted

---

[11] *The Wall Street Journal; November 14, 2011; page C1*

with MSI/RCS to provide FULL PUBLIC DISCLOSURE about its services.

Although the "Reports" utilized in the Book are somewhat dated, the process resulted in disclosing numerous inappropriate tax subsidies. Results were acted on. And the principles and processes remained and can be, and currently are applied daily to numerous public jurisdictions. Those forward-looking governments might well be pioneers in what could, and should become a national desire for open fairness in the use of local taxes.

But first, LEGAL definitions of COSTS, and the many components thereof. California terminology will be provided, but easily could, and should be made universal. More terminology and usages follow in the next Chapter.

Final Summarizing Shots. Specific quotations are here placed, intended to frame the issues to which the ***Municipal Business System*** can provide answers.

"There are great lessons to be learned from history. Political history has shown that a well-financed persistent one-trick pony can destroy anything governmental in its path, without regard to facts, figures, opposition, support, history, cost or income impact, even when the attacked people, policy, or program is "right". That historic fact produced a diabolically evil application by a "one-trick pony", annihilating literally millions of innocent persons – namely by Nazi Propaganda Minister Josef Goebbels' "programs". His guiding thesis was proved correct – 'Tell a big enough lie often enough and it becomes fact.'"[12]

Political operative Karl Rove added Madison Avenue advertising gimmickry, color, slant, imagery, perfidy, misdirection, and intensity to this and several other of Goebbels' proved ideological saturation techniques, and created a new approach to American politics.

But, on the positive side perhaps hope does survive:

Ignorance can be cured by information and education; stupidity is terminal.[13]

Everyone is entitled to his own opinion but not to his own facts.[14]

"...the central conservative truth is that it is culture, not politics, that determines the success of a society. The central liberal truth is that politics can change a culture and save it from itself."[15]

"Ethics is knowing the difference between what you have a right to do and what is right to do."[16]

---

[12] © Ayres, Douglas; *Right In The City – Volume II – More Bizarre Tales;* Trafford; Bloomington, IL; 2010; page 7

[13] © Copyright 1986 by Douglas W. Ayres

[14] *Daniel Patrick Moynihan - A PORTRAIT IN LETTERS OF AN AMERICAN VISIONARY*; edited by Steven R. Weisman; Public Affairs; New York, NY; 2010; "quoted from the political lore of Daniel Patrick Moynihan" on page 2

[15] *Ibid.*; p. 664; Moynihan statement during the month of his death in March 2003

[16] U.S. Supreme Court Justice Potter Stewart; quoted in *Public Management;* October 2011; page 3

As of late 2011 the entire Western world was in economic and personal flux, enmeshed in a global financial quandary, with the United States bound up in political ideological stan-doffs trying to secure an acceptable response to the question:

What do we do now?

Is this to be a permanent fixture for parks and recreation facilities?

Not copyrighted   **Unfortunately this has become standard signage for the Arizona State Parks System**

CHAPTER II

"COSTS REASONABLY BORNE"

The above Chapter title is unique to California, but should not be. And, hopefully, soon will not be unknown and unrecognized nationally. Rather, the major intent of this Book is to imbed the theory behind, definitions of, and the process for determining and dictating recognition of the phrase **COSTS REASONABLY BORNE** spread across the budgeting, accounting and governmental public reporting landscape of America.

__Economic Underpinning.__ In the particular case of California's Proposition 4, through careful research and a highly specific and widely distributed *"Drafters' Intent"* [17] document, little was left to speculation. Such problems still pester the original – Jarvis' Proposition 13. But **not** Proposition 4, the "Spirit of 13" revenue limitation amendment. The Prop. 4 definitional document was masterminded and mostly authored by a brilliant graduate level Professor of Economics at the Claremont Colleges – Dr. Craig Stubblebine. The Author of this book had numerous targeted personal conversations with Dr. Stubbleine, securing considerable insight into the driving thought patterns, reasoning, and theories and intentions of the Initiatives' "Authors", including responses to a lengthy list of specific questions about definitions of, extent of, and intended workings of the phrase *"costs reasonably borne"*. In other words – the definitive *"Constitutional legal intent"*.

There also was opportunity to run my ideas by Peter Drucker, during shared long waits at our mutual urologist in Pomona, California. Professor Drucker was intrigued.

Others signing this *"Drafter's Intent"* document were James P. Kennedy, Director, Taxation Department of the California Chamber of Commerce; Kirk West, Executive Vice President of the California Taxpayers' Association; and Dugald Gilles, Vice President of Governmental Relations of the California Association of Realtors. Daniel G. Nauman was Counsel to the Proposition 4 Drafting Committee.

It is ironic that the behind-the-scenes researcher and ultimate front man for both the Jarvis and Gann organizations was/is Jon Coupal, son of the 1965 President of the International City Managers Association, Joe Coupal, then City Manager of Portland, Maine.

__A Primer.__ Following is a primer of what this pioneering type of highly specific and precisely aimed citizen initiative provides. A basic requirement of the then new approach

---

[17] *Summary of Proposed Implementing Legislation and Drafters Intent with regard to Article XIIIB of the California Constitution (Proposition 4, November 6, 1979);* Spirit of 13, Inc.; 1980, California Chamber of Commerce , P.O. Box 1736, Sacramento, CA 95808; Attention: Tax Department

to setting of tax rates and types, fees, and determination of who pays for what was the dictated determination of "***costs reasonably borne***" for all governmental services, products and projects within California – and still is. Following are the essentials.

The following list of governmental costs is from Prop. 4. The definitions, per the Authors' footnote 17 "***Intent***" document, could and should be applicable to all governmental jurisdictions in all 50 states. Such usage would assure true and full cost compilations, and be especially useful in making decisions relative to "privatization", "out-sourcing", "contracting", service abandonment, or tax or fee/rate increases, thus assuring taxes and other government revenues are not used to subsidize those not explicitly designated to receive such subsidy. These full cost definitions must be applied to both the governmental and private sides to accumulate **full costs** for the delivery of a service, good or project.

A. *"All reasonable costs appropriate for the continuation of the service over time."* (Allocated over all services, goods produced & projects) [18]   (*emphasis supplied*)

   1. Personnel Costs:
      a. salaries and wages   b. employee benefits   c. insurance and retirement
   2. All applicable maintenance and operation costs
   3. Overhead and administration
   4. Start-up costs
   5. Costs for future capacity*   *essentially ignored due to lack of definitional
   6. Capital replacement expenses   terminology – but still open for interpretation
   7. Expansion of services costs*
   8. Repayment of related bond issuances

B. *"Total amount of revenue generated from the fee or charge"*

   1. "To be validly treated as a license, fee or charge, a governmental imposition must be exacted in exchange for a <u>direct</u> benefit received by the payer." [19]
   2. "The charge must be for a service or products provided directly to the payer and not for a service or product generally enjoyed by the community at large." [Pay special attention to this proviso #2, and the following #3.]
   3. "A tax is a general imposition on a broad cross-section of the citizenry for a general governmental purpose."

---

[18] ALL appropriations of the governmental jurisdiction must be allocated to ALL its services, goods produced, and projects. The division between "proceeds of taxes" and revenue from "fees and charges" are specifically enumerated as to category and treatment in the document referenced as footnote 17.

ALL revenues of the jurisdiction must be listed with great specificity to assure it is not a "tax" and does not exceed the "costs reasonably borne" in providing the service, producing the good, or accomplishing the project. The division between "proceeds of taxes "and revenue from "fees and charges" are specifically enumerated as to category and treatment in the document referenced as footnote 17.

[19] All quotations and statements hereinafter in this Chapter are from the document referenced by footnote 17, unless otherwise noted.

A Basic Tenet. The above referenced 69 page document is unique in that the absolute *constitutional intent* of the Authors is clearly provided. Personal conversations with the primary Author of the *Intent* booklet further expanded on and solidified the *Intent* Author's goals and definitions for the writer of this Book. That *Drafter's Intent* treatise specifically was aimed at the Legislature and courts. The document was developed to assure careful implementation and subsequent interpretation guidance for Proposition 4 implementation. That this Constitutional Amendment and its detailed back-up instructions were lost in the contention and mists of the California Gray Davis and Arnold Schwarzenegger era budget deficits and partisan legislative battles is unfortunate. And still is not utilized by the now-third Jerry Brown gubernatorial administration.

Here, for the first time, is a requirement to implement a business-derived basic full costing system for determining the worth of governmentally provided services, goods and projects. But it is yet to be fully understood or implemented. Perhaps this Book will aid in achieving that Spirit of 13, Inc. goal, not only for California governments, but also spread to other jurisdictions and other states. Such is necessary to reach decision points about what array and what level of public services are to be provided, and by whom, and at what TRUE cost and rate. Thus "running government like a business."

More Basics. The basic idea of the total cost and revenue allocation system required by *California Constitution* Article XIIIB is to assure that taxes are exclusively utilized for services provided "the community at large"; and that fee, charge and license revenues are exclusively used to pay for "direct benefit" services, goods and projects. Thus taxation is limited by the definitions and growth formulae contained in Article XIIIB.

An as-yet-not raised and thus un-answered question is whether the term "direct" or "direct benefit" would preclude privatization or out-sourcing for a California governmental service requiring payment via diverting governmental revenues directly to a private, almost universally for-profit organization for a thus indirectly provided former governmentally-supplied service or product. But, to reach that level of honesty and integrity, the disdain of and assumption of ignorance of all those elected officials governing, and all those working in government will have to be overcome and totally eliminated.

As a thought-provoking example, opinion of storied Colonel Carlos R. Putterbaugh, an early but not well-known fictional but noted initial advocate of the absolute privatization of all government into a "military-industrial complex":

> *"Costs are costs, and how they are defined should be the exclusive realm of corporate accountants, not government bean-counting budget analysts."*[20]

The above opinion is well-accepted for, but not necessarily by, government for dealings and contracting with private sources for government-tax-paid-for services and facilities. This definition is eschewed for use in the ***Municipal Business System.***

---

[20] "The Irrationality of Costs"; Putterbaugh, Colonel Carlos Ramirez; in the non-existent *Journal of Aerospace Finance;* El Segundo, California; July, 1956; page 34.

An Update and Assessment. A so-titled for Article XIIIB "interpretation" was widely distributed throughout California in February, 2005, as the latest gospel for the misunderstood "Gann Limit". The definitions and accounting integrity provided by Article XIIIB basically have been ignored. ***The following California Constitutional amendments and their impact are only applicable to Article XIIIB "expenditure limit" computations:***

> *Voters have modified the Gann limit in a series of initiative measures. Proposition 99* (1988) and Proposition 10* (1998) exempted new tobacco taxes from the Gann limit. Proposition 98* (1988) required public schools to receive a share of revenues exceeding the Gann limit. That share was changed to a flat 50% by Proposition 111* (1990). Proposition 111 added three exemptions to the Gann limit: capital outlay spending, appropriations supported by increased gas taxes, and appropriations resulting from national disasters.... Under Proposition 111, the population factor is based on a weighted average of population and K-14 school enrollment growth (instead of population only), and the cost of living factor is based solely on California per capita personal income growth (and no longer takes into account the Consumer Price Index.)* (See footnote 17 for details.)
>
> *The changes to the....Gann limit make it less likely that the limit will be reached in the future* [For the State and school districts only]. *Many observers believe that in its current weakened state the Gann limit has ceased to be a meaningfully constraint on State* [and school district] *spending.* [21]

Missing the Point. The State of California and school district level thus has wholly ignored "costs reasonably borne", and solely focused on "the Gann appropriations limit". As can be learned from the quotes opening this Chapter, concentration should be on applying the provided definitions of component "costs" to services provided. Such definitive calculated knowledge, public service-by-service, must be performed prior to calculation of "the expenditure limit". Apparently that no longer is considered in California, despite the continuing Constitutional requirement to do so.

Obviously, such cost calculations and revenue match-ups are not occurring in the California state government, and apparently considered not appropriate for school districts. But schools have to wrestle with another difficult contentious problem – quality of teaching and resultant level of student education – within their *modified* "Gann limits".

Cities, counties and special districts have no choice but have detailed service-by-activity cost and concomitant matching revenue analyses. Those units of government provide such a vast array of services, and projects, that it is impossible to "compute the Gann limit" without applying the rigor of detailed cost-revenue breakdown and analysis. The ***Municipal Business System*** for doing such is provided by this Book, meticulously. Better, however, is that such publicly disclosed information will allow consumer decisions to be made about quantity, quality and, in fact, the very existence of local services.

---

[21] McMahon, Mike; "Tax and Expenditure Limitation in California: Proposition 13 & Proposition 4; February 2005; Berkeley Library (on line)

A UNIVERSAL LONG-LINGERING PROBLEM

"Capital Replacement Expenses" is the most difficult to pin down of the extensive list of "costs reasonably borne". Each of the private and public sectors of the international economy have studied, experimented with, changed approach to, revised, tinkered with, and "adjusted" but have not yet reached a universally acceptable solution to the definition, valuation of and accounting for assets.

The so-called "financial services industry" still holds financial regulators, regulatory bodies and accounting authorities hostage to the wishes of that "industry" – to minimize the reporting of risk and thus to maximize what are defined to be "profits", paper or real.

Government Accounting. For local, and ostensibly for state governments, a major portion of the above-cited dilemma was enactment of GASB Statement 34 in June of 1999. Prior to that time little information about fixed assets existed within the accounting records of local and state governments. [See Article 8 in Appendix C for more complete information.] **GASB** stands for **G**overnmental **A**ccounting **S**tandards **B**oard, the accounting rule-making body for all levels of government [except most Federal agencies].

MSI Founder/CEO and USC Professor Doug Ayres had been preaching such an accounting change and requirement since 1957 – 42 years. Finally, a two-class USC (Public Finance and Public Budgeting) MPA student of Doug's, Barbara Henderson, a prominent California municipal Finance Director, was appointed to the GASBoard. She soon proposed and achieved adoption of her and Doug's fixed asset accounting ideas, as GASB Statement 34. Unfortunately, the new Board dicta allowed the continuation of "historic cost".

At enactment, fixed asset inventories for local and state governments were rare. Even more difficult was that those cities which had taken the time and made the effort to inventory all their fixed assets had little basis for the establishment of values. A fairly common "entry level" F/A value often was $5,000, but for some municipal utility operations, values as low as $25 were used. Further, even after the inventory is taken and some kind of reasonable values literally created, many asked: What is the use of this data?

Valuations? Major discussions ensued about F/A valuations and use. The Proposition 4 Authors apparently erroneously believed that governmental assets were valued similar to businesses – at current replacement cost. However, that approach was rejected by the GASB. Instead, "historical cost" was adopted, mostly because that definition had been used by those governments that had maintained any semblance of F/A records and values. However, gradually since 1999, the accounting landscape has begun to change, and a groundswell started for shifting to "replacement cost". MSI, and now RCS, has always utilized that definition in costing services. However, since there is no accounting requirement to use that some-times considerably higher number, government remains lumbering dangerously along on the "historic" value path. Such can look really ridiculous for municipal utilities when compared to their private sector counterparts. Such is especially so when much city major utility and street infrastructure is from 50 years to more than a century old. One can understand why so many "major leaks", explosions, "failures", and other disasters befall local municipal utilities, bridges and drainage facilities.

Even more annoying, and lacking in understandability, none of municipally-owned street, sidewalk, storm drainage, curb and gutter, and communications cabling is considered as a "utility", so those assets are not cost recovery items from a rate structure. Thus those accumulating replacement expenses are either 1) ignored until failure, 2) replaced by taxes, or 3) accumulated for insertion into a bond issue, most of which rely on property tax for debt service of interest and principal re-payment. Small wonder America's infrastructure is coming apart, as various associations of engineers regularly call to the attention of the public and its officials. Who then summarily ignore the information.

Private Sector F/A Difficulties. Those who constantly carp that "government should be run like a business" obviously are unaware of one of the current conundrums facing the private sector. Such is especially critical for banks, investment bankers, insurance companies, private equity funds, hedge funds, and other entities within the generic "financial services industry". Several illustrative quotes follow. Apparently, from those excerpts local governments just might be more advanced in their desire to replace "historical" with "replacement" or "current cost" for valuation of fixed assets. However, it should be noted that the vast majority of assets ***valued*** by these paragons of corporate financial risk are "financial paper", supposedly backed by tangible physical properties valued by "certified" appraisers, and reviewed and evaluated by the "trusted" risk-rating firms of Moody's, Standard & Poors, Fitch, or some other similar rating *corporation.*

> *Goldman Sachs Group, Inc. and Morgan Stanley....are discussing whether to reduce their use of mark-to-market accounting.... If executives go through with the change, the two companies would increase their use of so-called historical-cost accounting, where assets generally are held at their original value or purchase price....During the financial crisis, many banks avoided taking losses on loans and other assets until they were forced to sell them. By then, though, some assets were nearly worthless. [22]*

More explicit self-serving reasoning is contained in later paragraphs, following:

> *Banks such as **J.P. Morgan Chase & Co**. and **Wells Fargo & Co**. typically value more than half their assets using the historical-cost method, leaving them far less vulnerable to swings in asset values....[those firms using] mark-to-market accounting, contend that wider use of the method might have stemmed the worst of the crisis by forcing financial firms to reckon with declining values of mortgages, loans and other assets on their balance sheets. If more institutions had been required to recognize their exposures promptly and value them appropriately, they would have been likely to curtail the worst risks.... [23]*

Admission by these holders of trillions of dollars of house and commercial building mortgage-backed "hard assets" synthesizes the industry's rationale and reasoning:

---

[22] "Bank Quandry: Valuing the Assets"; *The Wall Street Journal*; November 10, 2011; page C1
[23] *Ibid*. ; same article, page C2

Since commercial banks don't generally mark loans to market prices, some within Gold-man and Morgan appear to believe they are at a competitive disadvantage. Indeed, back during the crisis, J.P. Morgan reclassified some leveraged loans that had to be marked so that they could be held at cost.[24]

Several days after the above announcement, Goldman's CEO announced its flexibility:

We are not moving away from mark-to-market accounting. The more we work with it the more I wish that everybody else would act in a corresponding way.[25]

The Evasive Definition. The struggle between private and public, and within the dark closets of both groups, rages on as public infrastructure continues its slide into doomsday. Accounting regulatory bodies waffle, seeking protection from reality. More confusion between "business" practices and "wasteful governments" accounting continues.

Much municipal financing, such as COPs (Certificates of Participation) essentially are a series of one year leases on hard assets, strung together for 20 to 30 years. Default causes reversion of the fixed assets to the holder of the Certificates. The dominating and defining financial services industry is now groping with a new proposal by both of national and international accounting standards bodies regarding treatment of leases.

Most American companies [and one can assume municipal governments as well] *are resigned to the centerpiece of the overhaul: treating leases – or the right to use a piece of property or equipment – as a new kind of asset. This asset would be offset on a* company's [and assumedly, municipal] *balance sheets by a corresponding liability, the obligation to pay rent.[26]*

Corporations and local governments confuse each other, and their respective share-holders and taxpayers, with garbled and inappropriate terminology. Here is an extreme example of how NOT to explain finances to one's taxpayers.

MF Global Holdings Ltd. shifted hundreds of millions of dollars in customer **funds** *to its own brokerage accounts....Such moves could violate regulations stipulating that commodities brokers can't mix customer* **funds** *with brokerage* **funds***. Broker-age* **funds** *often are used to back proprietary trading positions.[27]* (emphasis supplied)

Again, **[Use of the word "funds" interchangeably with the word "money" is inexcusably erroneous! Money is only one asset component of a fund, NOT all of it!]** But not in the corporate world?!

Which accounting – corporate or governmental – should be trusted? The so-called "financial services industry" produces nothing tangible; only creates and markets paper "assets". Local government does produce, operate and maintain facilities, services and tang-ible goods. Finally, neither of business nor government should garner the following type of news clips. Unfortunately, financial journals daily are voluminously infected with such self-serving tripe, predominately generated by business, corporate and business services.

---

24 *The Wall Street Journal;* November 11, 2011; page C10
25 *The Wall Street Journal;* November 16, 2011; page C2
26 *The Wall Street Journal;* November 16, 2011; page B5
27 *The Wall Street Journal;* November 8, 2011; page C1

...former CSK Auto Corp. Chairman and CEO Maynard Jenkins has agreed to return $2.8 million in bonus compensation and stock profits he received while the company was committing accounting fraud.[28]

Now What? The lesson learned is "the books can be cooked" within corporate or public sector "legal and accepted accounting standards".[29] It takes an experienced municipal-wise analyst to sort out what is the *best-considered government "TRUTH"*.

Obviously, "historical" values are no longer germane. Honest, full disclosure costing must utilize true, explainable, and openly defendable asset valuations. The MSI and now RCS staff always did and continue to do so, using infrastructure and other asset valuation amounts at **replacement** costs. But, other analysts apparently did not know the difference. Thus both of lesser fee amounts and adverse reactions by clients on occasion have forced RCS to accede to client demands and utilize only the available historic costs afforded RCS. As cited in Appendix C Article 8, the ultimate problem is undervaluing assets, ignoring replacement costs, and under-collecting for services. Then elected officials become critical of staff requests for fee increases. Denial of need for rises, to meet inexorably rising asset replacement costs, soon leads to deterioration of service levels. As suggested in Appendix C Article 8: *"pull out your GASB 34 Report and compare current maintenance expenditures with the annual amount of infrastructure expiration at current cost..."*

Moving On. Now that full "costs reasonably borne" have been divulged, discussed and analyzed in depth, the reader should understand the complexity of and necessity for utilizing "*true costs*" to achieve **full disclosure** to the consumer public. And thus acquire the inherent ability to address the lack of revenue sufficient to deliver the quality and breadth of public services "the public expects". Failure to do so will – for ageing requires that it **must** – be underlaid by those deteriorating assets, be they operational equipment, utility, street, office, building, or other government component physical plant.

But, then there is always the ignorant and resultant stupid factor to be coped with:

Eccentricities can be the result of strong wills with no education or common sense to guide: these people latch onto foolish ideas because they have no way of discriminating between sense and nonsense.[30]

Unfortunately, of late it seems as if eccentricities, strong wills, unalleviated ignorance, and stupidity have overcome the nation. Hopefully, this Book just might alleviate some portion of these inevitable results of the apparent dumbing down of America.

---

[28] *The Wall Street Journal;* November 16, 2011; page D2

[29] Is it this kind of seemingly endemic corporate behavior that is reported in depth daily that set off the "99% vs. 1%" confrontation? Per the latest information "more than 90% of the growth in U.S. wealth since 1983 has gone to the top 10%; the bottom 60% has lost wealth" and the top 5% have gained 81.7% of the total gain in wealth 1983-2009. See *MONEY;* December 2011; page 24. <u>Source:</u> Urban-Brookings Tax Policy Center and Economic Policy Institute.

[30] Follett, Ken; *Night Over Water;* Signet, a division of Penguin Group; William Morrow & Company; New York, NY; 1992; page 34

John C. Fitzgerald
Home: P. O. Box 765
Lake Arrowhead, California 92352
Office: 545 South Figueroa Street
Los Angeles, California 90071

I have spent many years working with Doug and his "The System" with municipal governments throughout California.

My business is working with cities to determine financing needs and then structure tax exempt bond issues and market them to meet their needs. Marketing can take the form of a competitive sale to investors or a negotiated underwriting

When first meeting with a city on a particular capital need, they will usually have a pretty good idea of what they need and some idea of the capital cost. But when it comes to how to pay for it they draw a blank. Although more recently they immediately say they don't want to go to the voters for a tax increase. In most cases the only alternative was a Pay-as-you-Use approach for financing, which meant a long term bond issue.

Doug's "The System" was invaluable in that all related revenues to the project could be identified and analyzed for possible use as a source of annual interest and principal (debt service) payments on the bond issue. Once the sources were determined the bond could be sized to fit project costs and annual revenues identified to cover debt service.

"The System" proved very useful in presenting the entire project and financing to the city councils for approval. Analysis and schedules from "The System" became value source documents for the Preliminary and Final Official Statements for disclosure purposed for the marketplace. And finally "The System" provided the bond rating agencies exactly what they wanted for rating the bond issue. Rating agency analysts loved "The System's" output.

John C. Fitzgerald

Note: The Author provided clients and John with vital highly reliable specific municipal data while John was with Merrill Lynch, then Seidler-Fitzgerald Public Finance. By our joint efforts somewhere north of a billion or five or so of municipal bonds, COPs, other capital instruments, and notes were underwritten over two decades of cooperation. We never paid attention to, or ever totaled the amount, since we were too busy providing vital financing at reasonable and far lower interest rates & fees, than other financiers.

TO: Doug Ayres   October 27, 2011

In the early 1970's, I recall that explaining to citizens our tax and fee policies was not always easy. For example, if we were asked "Why is the rental housing inspection fee $50?" then staff would reply that we need to pay for the cost of the inspection. That was it. The most likely explanation was that the recommendation for this fee amount was based on a short discussion of the Finance Director and Housing Inspector in which the Housing Inspector said "I know that the rental property owners won't accept a fee of more than $50!

That fortunately has changed. When I was City Manager in Redlands, California we were annually faced with budget shortfalls because the community had a small retail base and resulting low sales tax receipts. We could not afford to continue to support special services like building permits with tax dollars. We asked MSI to complete a study to correct this situation.

When we presented the proposal to the City Council, Doug Ayres explained that, for the first time, Council members would receive a report listing all city direct benefit service fees, the total cost of providing those services including overhead, the total revenue provided by existing fees and the amount of tax subsidy being provided to those services.

The major outcome of the study, he explained, is the opportunity for the City Council to review each service fee and decide if, and what percentage of subsidy it would like to provide from tax dollars for that special service. As City Manager, I thought that the opportunity for elected officials to set policy on all fees based on accurate information rather than one at a time with a Yes or No vote on a staff proposal not only was more efficient but it allows the City Council to do what it is supposed to do: SET POLICY!

In the Redlands and Riverside, CA and Coconino County, AZ we raised substantial additional funds for the general benefit of the community by reducing the leakage of tax dollars to special benefit services. We now could now answer questions about any special benefit fee and back it up with detailed information and a Council decision!

John E. Holmes
John Holmes
Retired City/County Manager

CHAPTER III

SERVICE CENTER IDENTIFICATION and COSTING

This Chapter, and following Chapters, Tables, Exhibits and Illustrations provide sufficient detail to prove the potentialities of the ***Municipal Business System***. Only enough tabular material is utilized within the text to illustrate end results. One or two of each type summary and detail back-up materials are provided within the text. The remaining documentation is provided as Illustrations and Exhibits in or "in the back of the Book".

Examples. Classes of services are by functional grouping. The listing of the discovered "Service Centers" of a major, well known U.S. city – **Pasadena** – follows, first with text and summaries, then more details as Illustrations in the back of the book. Other similar, but not as complete Service Center examples for another famous Southern California municipality – **Beverly Hills** -- also are supplied. Although several years apart, both contracted for the detailed application of the copyrighted MSI/RCS cost-revenue analysis. After significant discussions, both City Councils adopted many of the resultant "suggestions". Not all, but these two jurisdictions were in the forefront of electoral bravery – each did, and continue to work diligently on their finances, so as to preserve their traditional and well-managed superior levels of service, infrastructure and property development integrity and, in the process, achieve near-equity in payment for services.

A Less Fortunate. Another California city, **Coachella**, provides data from its 1989-90 MSI rather monumental analyses. Other examples provided through the International/County City Managers Association extracts of MSI work for each of the California cities of **Riverside** and **Chino** are woven into the text. The vast majority of the detailed information for each of **Pasadena, Beverly Hills** and **Coachella** are appropriately ensconced and catalogued in the Illustrations "in the back of the Book".

CITY OF PASADENA, CALIFORNIA

The following extract from the MSI Pasadena *Cost Control System* Report illustrates results of that $200,000 12 month study. More details will be shown and explained in the following pages. The text sums up "municipal financial situations" then, and still confronting not only California, but now the entirety of the 19,000 U.S. local governments.

Concentration on Pasadena. Pasadena examples are utilized more extensively than those for the other four cities for which data is provided in this Book. Pasadena is not only well-known internationally, but its array of public services, and the capabilities of its budgeting and financial and work load accounting systems, provided a better example than would many other jurisdictions. MSI had to re-construct much data for many cities.

__Enticing Details.__ The following seven TABLES from the Pasadena Report provide details of the results of the MSI revenue-cost analysis and match-up. Some details of how these summaries were achieved will be provided, as ILLUSTRATIONS in the back of the book. However, for obvious proprietary reasons such illustrations cumulatively will be insufficient for a would-be "copy cat" to reproduce these results.

The *__Municipal Business__ System* is meticulous in detail, encompasses every dollar the client jurisdiction receives and spends, and involves excruciatingly detailed work by CPA accountants, financial analysts, and technicians who "know what they are doing." Accuracy of results has never been challenged. Client reaction mostly can be termed as awe struck. But universally great concern always was expressed as to the straying of taxes.

__Service Center Group Summaries.__ Brief textual explanations and background on each of the seven Service Center Groups is spliced among the Group Tables. The text location does not always match up with what Table is nearby. Such locational precision always is attempted, but not always achieved. More are in the ILLUSTRATIONS.

As a long-tenured Charter City, Pasadena provides a broad array of public services. Reviewing the spread of programs provides a sense of why Pasadena is held in such national – and on New Year's Day – world-wide well-deserved extraordinary repute.

__Community Development Services.__ This wide swath of land use controls fulfills enforcement of the City's Zoning and Planning Ordinances. Basically, however, in effect those require the City to be the arbiter of potential neighborhood squabbles, and worse.

__Public Safety Services.__ This array of municipal effort usually is the most sought after, being both "vital" and "necessary". Any attempt to mitigate the level of these universally is met with the cry "Protection of the public must be the highest priority." The question never is "how much is enough", or "how do we pay for that", but "why aren't there more police officers, firefighters and paramedics?" Those direct public benefit services are, as they should be, financed by taxes, of whatever category. The most likely tax financing source for these services is property tax. After all, the common nomenclature for Police and Fire Department duties is "protection of people and property".

There are numerous ancillary services which, though protection of people and property is primary, are provided in a limited number of "special situations" to those who are "special". Or, to those who cannot, in the vernacular, "get their act together". TABLE 2 isolates those "specials", their costs, and raises the question as to whether tax monies legitimately should be diverted from the "general public" to these "special services".

__Public Health Services.__ At the time of this analysis of the finances of the City of Pasadena it provided an array of services through its Public Health Department. Some of these, as can be derived from Table 3, may well be inappropriately subsidized by taxes, rather than by fees paid by those specifically benefitting. Or could be financed by a City-wide assessment district for "Mosquito, Fly & Rodent Control".

Pasadena Cost Control Report

Summary of Chapter V

The following Table 8 summarizes the recommendations and suggestions made in this Chapter in detail.

TABLE 8

SUMMARY

SERVICE CENTER	TOTAL REVENUE	TOTAL COST	TOTAL PROFIT (SUBSIDY)	RECOVERY ACTUAL	PERCENT SUGGEST	POSSIBLE NEW REVENUE
COMMUNITY DEVELOPMENT SERVICES	$3,779,386	$6,364,054	($2,584,668)	59.4%	100.0%	$2,926,600
PUBLIC SAFETY SERVICES	$5,606,134	$9,914,685	($4,308,551)	56.5%	65.1%	$849,900
HEALTH DEPARTMENT SERVICES	$4,885,105	$5,894,930	($1,009,825)	82.9%	90.6%	$455,200
LEISURE AND CULTURAL SERVICES	$1,401,425	$4,591,129	($3,189,704)	30.5%	49.1%	$851,200
UTILITY AND ENTERPRISE SERVICES	$155,037,176	$178,920,264	($23,883,088)	86.7%	100.0%	$46,579,500
MAINTENANCE SERVICES	$5,897,859	$15,419,185	($9,521,326)	38.3%	99.8%	$9,494,600
FINANCE AND ADMINISTRATIVE SVCS	$1,321,828	$1,746,004	($424,176)	75.7%	100.0%	$838,200
TOTAL	$177,928,913	$222,850,251	($44,921,338)	79.8%	100.0%	$61,995,200

NOTE:
(1) - The large "Possible New Revenue" in Utility and Enterprise services was calculated including in-lieu charges, although costs of such charges are not shown.

Result of Adoption. If all the recommendations and suggestions made in this Chapter are adopted, the City would raise some $61,995,200 of which $46,579,500 would be from utility and enterprise services and $9,158,000 would be from special assessment revenue increases. With both assessments and utilities removed, the suggested gain in general revenues still amounts to $6,257,700.

Taxpayer Equity Achieved. By taking such positive actions, a deteriorating City financial picture would be improved to the point that a major residential street replacement and improvement program could be implemented, far more equity between taxpayers and fee-payers could be gained, and fairness between property-related and non-property-related services could be secured.

Other Advantages. Further, the City would be free of the blatantly partisan political brinkmanship-type of financial dependency on the whims of the State Legislature and Governor. It would no longer have to rely on the rapidly shrinking Federal resources.

In other words, local control would come through local financial independence from the State government and its political/financial misconceptions and games, and from the Federal budget deficit.

TABLE 1

COMMUNITY DEVELOPMENT SERVICES

MSI #	SERVICE CENTER	TOTAL REVENUE	TOTAL COST	TOTAL PROFIT (SUBSIDY)	RECOVERY ACTUAL	PERCENT SUGGEST	POSSIBLE NEW REVENUE
S-001	Concept Plan Review	$9,600	$104,783	($95,183)	9.2%	100.0%	$57,100 */**
S-002	Preliminary Plan Check	$42,062	$88,858	($46,796)	47.3%	100.0%	$46,800 *
S-003	Tentative Parcel Map Review	$36,315	$31,373	$4,942	115.8%	100.0%	($4,900)
S-004	Tentative Tract Map Review	$58,680	$47,616	$11,064	123.2%	100.0%	($11,100)
S-005	Construction Staging Plan Review	$0	$9,788	($9,788)	0.0%	100.0%	$9,800
S-006	Design Commission Review (Minor)	$3,350	$14,969	($11,619)	22.4%	100.0%	$11,600 *
S-007	Design Commission Review (Major)	$23,750	$99,391	($75,641)	23.9%	100.0%	$75,600 *
S-008	Design Review (Final)	$0	$30,173	($30,173)	0.0%	100.0%	$30,200 *
S-009	Design Review (Seismic)	$0	$5,028	($5,028)	0.0%	100.0%	$5,000 *
S-010	Design Review-City of Gardens	$3,953	$53,665	($49,712)	7.4%	100.0%	$49,700
S-011	Design Review (Consolidated)	$10,780	$31,275	($20,495)	34.5%	100.0%	$20,500 *
S-012	Design Review Extension	$0	$446	($446)	0.0%	100.0%	$400
S-013	Landmark District Review	$0	$8,137	($8,137)	0.0%	100.0%	$8,100
S-014	Historic Building Search	$0	$22,072	($22,072)	0.0%	100.0%	$16,500 **
S-015	Master Development Plan Review	$2,799	$17,602	($14,803)	15.9%	100.0%	$14,800
S-016	Conditional Use Permit Review	$214,350	$244,635	($30,285)	87.6%	100.0%	$21,200 **
S-017	Minor Conditional Use Permit Rvw	$11,480	$36,806	($25,326)	31.2%	100.0%	$17,700 **
S-018	Temporary Conditionl Use Prmt Rvw	$20,020	$26,268	($6,248)	76.2%	100.0%	$4,700 **
S-019	Variance Review	$60,830	$95,105	($34,275)	64.0%	100.0%	$34,300
S-020	Minor Variance Review	$9,515	$34,268	($24,753)	27.8%	100.0%	$24,800
S-021	Use Permit & Variance Extension	$0	$5,115	($5,115)	0.0%	100.0%	$5,100
S-022	Lot Line Adjustment	$13,305	$17,390	($4,085)	76.5%	100.0%	$4,100
S-023	Rezoning Request Rvw (Zone Change)	$8,288	$17,591	($9,303)	47.1%	100.0%	$9,300
S-024	Subdivision Map Extension Prcssng	$6,152	$8,070	($1,918)	76.2%	100.0%	$1,900
S-025	Growth Management Allocation	$32,864	$319,860	($286,996)	10.3%	100.0%	$287,000 *
S-026	Growth Managemnt Allocatn Exemptn	$0	$19,621	($19,621)	0.0%	100.0%	$19,600
S-027	Growth Allocation Appeal	$1,901	$2,064	($163)	92.1%	100.0%	$200
S-028	Growth Mgmnt Conditional Use Prmt	$28,580	$30,359	($1,779)	94.1%	100.0%	$1,800
S-029	Growth Management Time Extension	$0	$4,603	($4,603)	0.0%	100.0%	$4,600
S-030	Initial Environmental Study	$49,692	$96,384	($46,692)	51.6%	100.0%	$46,700
S-031	Environmntl Impact Rprt (Consltnt)	$10,230	$19,236	($9,006)	53.2%	100.0%	$9,000
S-032	Fish & Game Environ. Impact Revw	$2,132	$12,543	($10,411)	17.0%	100.0%	$10,400
S-033	Env. Impact Mitigation Monitoring	$0	$15,317	($15,317)	0.0%	100.0%	$15,300 *
S-034	Monitoring of Conditions	$0	$277,304	($277,304)	0.0%	100.0%	$277,300 *
S-035	Certificate of Appropriateness	$0	$66,722	($66,722)	0.0%	100.0%	$66,700 *
S-036	Replacement Building Prmt Relief	$0	$1,874	($1,874)	0.0%	100.0%	$1,900
S-037	Appeal Processing	$18,130	$93,549	($75,419)	19.4%	100.0%	$37,700 **
S-038	Appeal Processing - Staff Decisn	$0	$3,111	($3,111)	0.0%	100.0%	$1,500 **
S-039	Vesting Map Review	$16,730	$12,222	$4,508	136.9%	100.0%	($4,500)
MSI #	SERVICE CENTER	TOTAL REVENUE	TOTAL COST	TOTAL PROFIT (SUBSIDY)	RECOVERY ACTUAL	PERCENT SUGGEST	POSSIBLE NEW REVENUE
S-040	Final Tract Map Review	$0	$23,095	($23,095)	0.0%	100.0%	$23,100
S-041	Final Parcel Map Review	$0	$5,730	($5,730)	0.0%	100.0%	$5,700
S-042	Eng eering Plan Review	$79,400	$76,644	$2,756	103.6%	100.0%	($2,800)
S-043	Str Occupation Permit	$207,200	$45,403	$161,797	456.4%	100.0%	$0 *
S-044	Public Works Permit	$207,200	$287,508	($80,308)	72.1%	100.0%	$80,300 *
S-045	Street Vacation	$4,144	$45,733	($41,589)	9.1%	100.0%	$41,600
S-046	Grading Plan Check	$4,206	$1,422	$2,784	295.8%	100.0%	($2,800)*
S-047	Hillside Grading Plan Check	$6,718	$1,773	$4,945	378.9%	100.0%	($4,900)*
S-048	Grading Inspection	$4,206	$423	$3,783	994.3%	100.0%	($3,800)*
S-049	Hillside Grading Inspection	$0	$4,785	($4,785)	0.0%	100.0%	$4,800 *
S-050	Construction Plan Check	$794,312	$1,555,280	($760,968)	51.1%	100.0%	$761,000 *
S-051	Construction Review and Inspectn	$1,455,219	$1,141,048	$314,171	127.5%	100.0%	SEE TEXT *
S-052	Misc/Special Bldg Insp Investgtn	$12,183	$8,219	$3,964	148.2%	100.0%	($4,000)
S-053	Condominium Conversion	$0	$1,637	($1,637)	0.0%	100.0%	$1,600
S-054	Relocation Investgtn (House Moves)	$9,324	$7,820	$1,504	119.2%	100.0%	($1,500)
S-055	Address Change	$966	$716	$250	134.9%	100.0%	($300)
S-056	Address Assignment	$1,650	$8,345	($6,695)	19.8%	100.0%	$6,700
S-057	Temporary Certificate f Occupncy	$34,020	$37,007	($2,987)	91.9%	100.0%	$3,000
S-058	Occupancy Inspection	$254,384	$680,584	($426,200)	37.4%	100.0%	$426,200 *
S-059	Certificate of Compliance Invstgn	$1,955	$7,278	($5,323)	26.9%	100.0%	$5,300
S-060	Parkway Usage License Agreement	$3,191	$21,864	($18,673)	14.6%	100.0%	$18,700
S-061	Sidewalk Dining Permit	$0	$889	($889)	0.0%	100.0%	$900
S-062	Building Permit Center	$0	$162,623	($162,623)	0.0%	100.0%	$162,600 *
S-063	Zoning Parking Credit	$2,400	$13,142	($10,742)	18.3%	100.0%	$10,700
S-064	Temporary Street Closure (Events)	$1,219	$30,229	($29,010)	4.0%	100.0%	$14,500 **
S-065	Traffic Impact Review	$0	$75,339	($75,339)	0.0%	100.0%	$75,300 *
S-066	Trip Reduction Plan Review	$0	$71,854	($71,854)	0.0%	100.0%	$71,900 *
S-067	Development Agreement Revw	$0	$9,335	($9,335)	0.0%	100.0%	$0 #
S-068	Legal Description	$0	$4,387	($4,387)	0.0%	100.0%	$4,400
S-069	Planned Development	$0	$4,653	($4,653)	0.0%	100.0%	$0 #
S-070	General Plan Amendment	$0	$4,096	($4,096)	0.0%	100.0%	$0 #
	TOTAL	$3,779,386	$6,364,054	($2,584,668)	59.4%	100.0%	$2,926,600

NOTES:
* - See Text
** - Market Sensitive
# - Frequency of Service Unknown

TABLE 2

PUBLIC SAFETY SERVICES

MSI #	SERVICE CENTER	TOTAL REVENUE	TOTAL COST	TOTAL PROFIT (SUBSIDY)	RECOVERY ACTUAL	PERCENT SUGGEST	POSSIBLE NEW REVENUE	
S-071	Annual Hm Business Occupancy Prmt	$13,000	$24,668	($11,668)	52.7%	100.0%	$11,700	
S-072	Garage Sale Permit	$7,500	$9,990	($2,490)	75.1%	100.0%	$1,900	**
S-073	Special Business Regulation	$0	$63,207	($63,207)	0.0%	100.0%	$63,200	*
S-074	Wide, Overweight, Ovrlng Ld Prmt	$5,594	$3,337	$2,257	167.6%	100.0%	($2,300)	
S-075	Vehicle Code Enforcement	$240,000	$894,037	($654,037)	26.8%	100.0%	SEE TEXT	
S-076	Non-Vehicle Code Enforcement	$0	$425,841	($425,841)	0.0%	50.0%	SEE TEXT	
S-077	Parking Enforcement	$1,625,000	$764,794	$860,206	212.5%	100.0%	SEE TEXT	
S-078	Parking Permits	$85,988	$145,066	($59,078)	59.3%	100.0%	$47,200	**
S-079	Limited Time Parking Permit	$0	$6,888	($6,888)	0.0%	100.0%	$6,900	
S-080	Bicycle Registration	$2,132	$3,666	($1,535)	58.1%	100.0%	$1,500	
S-081	Burglar Alarm Review	$133,500	$34,234	$99,266	390.0%	100.0%	SEE TEXT	
S-082	Police False Alarm Response	$176,554	$1,069,384	($892,830)	16.5%	100.0%	$44,600	*/**
S-083	Clearance Letter Processing	$3,000	$3,366	($366)	89.1%	100.0%	$400	
S-084	Police Report Copying	$100,000	$112,243	($12,243)	89.1%	100.0%	$12,200	
S-085	Police Photograph Reproduction	$3,108	$7,264	($4,156)	42.8%	100.0%	$4,200	
S-086	Police Photo Lab Services	$0	$59,543	($59,543)	0.0%	100.0%	$20,800	*
S-087	Police Tape & Video Duplicatn Svc	$0	$2,817	($2,817)	0.0%	100.0%	$2,800	
S-088	Spcl Police Computer Prnt-Out Svc	$1,400	$5,300	($3,900)	26.4%	100.0%	$3,900	
S-089	Fingerprint Processing	$33,300	$41,531	($8,231)	80.2%	100.0%	$7,000	**
S-090	Vehicle Correction Inspection	$0	$4,658	($4,658)	0.0%	100.0%	$3,000	**
S-091	Remvl of Abnd/Abatd Veh & Release	$0	$91,405	($91,405)	0.0%	100.0%	$9,100	*/**
S-092	Impound Vehicle Release Service	$0	$60,184	($60,184)	0.0%	100.0%	$36,000	**
S-093	DUI Acc. Response, Invest & Rprt	$4,500	$243,933	($239,433)	1.8%	100.0%	$35,900	*/**
S-094	DUI Arrest Procedure/Non-Accident	$0	$346,891	($346,891)	0.0%	100.0%	$52,000	*/**
S-095	Noise Disturbance Respnse Cl-back	$0	$11,584	($11,584)	0.0%	100.0%	$1,700	**
S-096	Public Crosswalk Protection	$0	$195,930	($195,930)	0.0%	100.0%	$0	*
S-097	One-Day Alcohol Permit Processing	$0	$6,041	($6,041)	0.0%	100.0%	$6,000	
S-098	Commercial Foot Patrol	$0	$198,704	($198,704)	0.0%	50.0%	$99,300	*
S-099	Rifle Range Use	$25,000	$40,401	($15,401)	61.9%	100.0%	$15,400	
S-100	Helicopter Pad Landing Use	$4,070	$1,304	$2,766	312.1%	100.0%	$0	*
S-101	I.N.S. Prisoner Housing	$391,500	$384,610	$6,890	101.8%	100.0%	$0	*
S-102	Trustee Housing	$73,650	$83,247	($9,597)	88.5%	100.0%	$9,600	
S-103	V.I.N. Verification	$0	$8,280	($8,280)	0.0%	100.0%	$4,100	**
S-104	Hazardous Materials Permit Insp	$766,640	$719,743	$46,897	106.5%	100.0%	$0	*
S-105	State Mandated Fire Inspection	$159,360	$185,178	($25,818)	86.1%	100.0%	$25,800	*
S-106	Underground Tank Plan Check/Insp	$72,505	$62,984	$9,521	115.1%	100.0%	($9,500)	
S-107	Fire False Alarm Response	$0	$99,790	($99,790)	0.0%	100.0%	$10,000	*/**
S-108	Non-Emergency Service	$0	$19,917	($19,917)	0.0%	100.0%	$5,000	**
S-109	Illegal Burn Response	$0	$11,830	($11,830)	0.0%	100.0%	$11,800	
S-110	Post-Fire Investigation Analysis	$44,556	$76,272	($31,716)	58.4%	100.0%	$31,700	
S-111	Fire Report Copying	$1,125	$3,284	($2,159)	34.3%	100.0%	$2,200	
S-112	Weed Abatement	$33,152	$69,330	($36,178)	47.8%	100.0%	$18,000	**
S-113	Medical Aid Response	$1,600,000	$3,309,171	($1,709,171)	48.4%	100.0%	$256,000	*/**
S-114	Hazard Abatement Services	$0	$2,838	($2,838)	0.0%	100.0%	$800	**
		$5,606,134	$9,914,685	($4,308,551)	56.5%	65.1%	$849,900	

NOTES:

* - See Text

market sensitive

- Frequency of Service Unknown

Complete Data Available. The Pasadena City Council now had each of revenue, cost and benefit data upon which to make decisions as to the division in financing between fees, taxes, and utility charges. Thus full disclosure was achieved, resulting in extensive public discussion and, ultimately decisions, or non-decisions made by the City Council in front of the voting taxpaying public at a public meeting and/or budget "public hearing".

TABLE 3

PUBLIC HEALTH

MSI #	SERVICE CENTER	TOTAL REVENUE	TOTAL COST	TOTAL PROFIT (SUBSIDY)	RECOVERY ACTUAL	PERCENT SUGGEST	POSSIBLE NEW REVENUE
S-115	Health Department Plan Check/Insp	$17,000	$23,755	($6,755)	71.6%	100.0%	$6,800 *
S-116	Environmental Health Inspection	$208,432	$140,573	$67,859	148.3%	100.0%	($67,900)*
S-117	Noise Control Permit	$3,200	$15,087	($11,887)	21.2%	100.0%	$5,900 */*
S-118	Food Sanitation Inspection	$205,368	$240,468	($35,100)	85.4%	100.0%	$35,100 *
S-119	Mosquito, Fly & Rodent Control	$0	$235,799	($235,799)	0.0%	100.0%	$235,800 *
S-120	Animal Control	$116,264	$425,273	($309,009)	27.3%	50.0%	$46,300 *
S-121	Vital Statistics	$255,408	$255,408	$0	100.0%	100.0%	$0 *
S-122	Travel Immmunizations	$181,000	$119,540	$61,460	151.4%	100.0%	$0 *
S-123	Water Examination	$99,840	$94,652	$5,188	105.5%	100.0%	($5,200)*
S-124	Alcoholism & Drug Depndncy Prgrm	$269,354	$362,784	($93,430)	74.2%	100.0%	$46,700 *
S-125	First Offender Program	$75,696	$73,491	$2,205	103.0%	100.0%	$0 *
S-126	Public Health Laboratory	$246,272	$246,272	$0	100.0%	100.0%	$0 *
S-127	Prenatal Clinic	$1,369,582	$1,369,582	$0	100.0%	100.0%	$0 *
S-128	Women, Infants & Childrn Voucher	$399,798	$534,954	($135,156)	74.7%	100.0%	$0 *
S-129	AIDS Program	$243,223	$294,808	($51,585)	82.5%	100.0%	$51,600 *
S-130	SGV, HIV Early Interventn Program	$255,300	$316,296	($60,996)	80.7%	100.0%	$61,000 *
S-131	Child Health Clinic	$424,713	$424,713	$0	100.0%	100.0%	$0 *
S-132	Ambulatory Care Clinic	$16,783	$80,906	($64,123)	20.7%	100.0%	$13,000 *
S-133	Senior Preventive Health Program	$22,427	$112,223	($89,796)	20.0%	100.0%	$9,000 *
S-134	Sexually Transmittd Disease Prgrm	$127,218	$127,218	$0	100.0%	100.0%	$0 *
S-135	Tuberculosis Program	$270,649	$313,777	($43,128)	86.3%	100.0%	$11,000 *
S-136	Flu/Pneumonia Immunization	$19,874	$21,943	($2,069)	90.6%	100.0%	$2,100 *
S-137	Immmunization	$57,704	$65,408	($7,704)	88.2%	100.0%	$4,000 *
		$4,885,105	$5,894,930	($1,009,825)	82.9%	90.6%	$455,200

NOTES:
```
 *  - See Text
**  - Market Sensitive
 #  - Frequency of Service Unknown
```

Leisure and Cultural Services.   This category raises the question as to who truly benefits.   And the concomitant query – should the user pay?   But then when "ability to pay" is viewed, another array of commentary ensues.   Thus it is vital to know, in detail, identity of the "beneficiary" of each specific service.   But with equal specificity.   It is with this category that policy decision makers have the greatest difficulty.

Utility and Enterprise Services.   Theoretically, each of these specific services should be wholly self-supporting from fees and charges made for measurable service.   But the terms "self-supporting", "specific", and "measurable" each has become arguable.   And the totality of this grouping is ideologically charged as to whether the local government should be involved at all.   These services often are targeted for outsourcing or sale, whether appropriate and economically sound or not.   Thus discussions about "socialism" vs. "capitalism" enter the fray.   Great municipal financial damage has resulted from these philosophical and now, ideological arguments and resultant major policy decisions.

Municipal Ownership.   The City of Pasadena was incorporated in 1886.   At that time investor-owned water and electric utilities were rare.   Construction costs and operational expense to provide such services then were, and still are, extremely capital intensive. Major amounts of capital must be expended long prior to the connection of sufficient customers to cover debt service and operational expenses.   That municipalities can borrow vast amounts of money at federal and state income tax exempt rates has made a great difference in meeting the needs of urban dwellers. Pasadena was founded, and remains, what is often termed as "an upscale community". Superior services were demanded, built, maintained and continue to this day. That level of response is invested and expected. And a willingness to pay appropriately also has followed these utilities, their subsidiary services, and other so-called "enterprise activities".

Many cities are in the same position for each of their water, electric, sanitary sewer, and in some instances, storm drainage, and municipal natural gas utilities. Even airports – but only the very largest – are coveted by Private Equity Funds and other corporate investors. Municipal capital borrowing interest costs, and the total lack of stock options, bonuses, lucrative 'perks', corporate jets, shareholder dividends, and typical private industry salaries and expenses cumulatively add up and drive up "costs" such that municipal services have materially lower rates. Or, in the usual alternative, major chunks of the "usual" equivalent shareholder-owned business expenses are not eaten up by the owning municipality. The result is that significant amounts of the above non-municipal expenses are transferred to the general city coffers as in-lieu of tax and realistic "franchise" fees.

Utility Rates. Unfortunately, over the decades most municipal utilities "held down their rates". Problematically, the net result was lack of re-investment in maintenance, plant replacement, and capital additions for purposes of efficiency. Such practice is rampant for water and sewer collection and disposal utilities. But, a century or more on, both of the utility basics and in lieu and property tax expenses have been neglected. True, proper accounting requires each such utility and enterprise to be operated within a wholly self-supporting discreet FUND [**absolutely NOT synonymous with the word "money"**]. Such is akin to a corporate "subsidiary corporation". But, elected policy makers are under constant pressure to "keep rates down". At times utility "enterprise Funds" are "raided' and strict government enterprise accounting guidelines not followed. The summary of the Pasadena Water Fund on a subsequent page somewhat illustrates this result.

Other Enterprises. Cities and counties, especially those habituated by so-called "affluent citizens" are notorious for engaging in a wide variety of beneficial entertainment, sports, and artistic support facilities. So-called "economic development" schemes also have entered the municipal lexicon, some allegedly "self-supporting" by "generating revenues", or not. Thus the definition of "enterprise" has been seriously abused. And results are problematical when factored into annual finances and budgeting. Illustration of the Rose Bowl as exemplar was so documented, following.   At least for fiscal 1992-1993.

The Tournament of Roses & Rose Bowl. The annual Parade was founded by the
Valley Hunt Club in 1890, soon re-named "Tournament of Roses", and taken over by a non-profit Association. The football game has been held annually since 1916. The Rose Bowl was completed in 1923, and an annual "major bowl game" [now BCS] played there annually. It still holds the attendance record of 103,985 for NFL Super Bowl XIV – Steelers vs. Rams – January 20, 1980. A three-year $152 million renovation is underway.

The two events – Parade and Bowl game – respectively, bring 1 million and 100,000+

TABLE 4

LEISURE AND CULTURAL SERVICES

MSI #	SERVICE CENTER	TOTAL REVENUE	TOTAL COST	TOTAL PROFIT (SUBSIDY)	RECOVERY ACTUAL	PERCENT SUGGEST	POSSIBLE NEW REVENUE
S-138	City Youth Sports Programs	$0	$738,658	($738,658)	0.0%	50.0%	$92,000 */**
S-139	City Adult Sports Programs	$47,552	$288,392	($240,840)	16.5%	75.0%	$120,000 */**
S-140	Private Youth Group Fld Rntl Svc	$0	$59,381	($59,381)	0.0%	50.0%	$15,000 */**
S-141	Private Adult Group Fld Rntl Svc	$14,947	$63,639	($48,692)	23.5%	75.0%	$24,000 */**
S-142	Youth Recreation Classes	$18,217	$230,396	($212,179)	7.9%	50.0%	$26,500 */**
S-143	Adult Recreation Classes	$42,372	$72,436	($30,064)	58.5%	75.0%	$11,900 */**
S-144	Youth Special Activities	$0	$23,976	($23,976)	0.0%	50.0%	$2,400 */**
S-145	Summer Day Camp	$40,000	$236,855	($196,855)	16.9%	50.0%	$9,800 */**
S-146	Adaptive Recreation Activities	$21,425	$87,377	($65,952)	24.5%	25.0%	$500 */**
S-147	Senior Citizen Programs	$6,530	$177,083	($170,553)	3.7%	25.0%	$2,000 */**
S-148	Recreational Swimming	$10,464	$167,983	($157,519)	6.2%	50.0%	$5,000 */**
S-149	Swimming Lessons	$21,652	$33,601	($11,949)	64.4%	75.0%	$3,500 */**
S-150	Recreation Facility Rental	$131,490	$105,716	$25,774	124.4%	100.0%	$0 *
S-151	City-Wide Special Events	NA	$489,581	($489,581)	0.0%	10.0%	$10,000 */**
S-152	Tournament of Roses Support	$787,577	$1,255,945	($468,368)	62.7%	100.0%	$468,400 *
S-153	Special Event Set-Up/Clean Up	$4,000	$44,598	($40,598)	9.0%	100.0%	$4,000 *
S-154	Overdue Material Processing	$192,461	$28,456	$164,005	676.3%	100.0%	$0 *
S-155	Replacing Lost Library Items	$12,897	$19,682	($6,785)	65.5%	100.0%	$6,800
S-156	Replacement Of Lost Library Cards	$9,501	$20,448	($10,947)	46.5%	100.0%	$3,800 */**
S-157	Book Reservation Service	$5,115	$206,113	($200,998)	2.5%	100.0%	$5,000 */**
S-158	Inter Library Loan Processing	$2,060	$51,813	($49,753)	4.0%	50.0%	$2,500 */**
S-159	Retrieval & Copyng Of Periodicals	$1,734	$2,083	($349)	83.2%	100.0%	$200 **
S-160	Reproduction Of Photographs	$100	$510	($410)	19.6%	100.0%	$200 **
S-161	Library Media Rental	$5,914	$28,775	($22,861)	20.6%	75.0%	$5,700 */**
S-162	Library On-Line Database Search	$12,411	$21,409	($8,998)	58.0%	100.0%	$5,000 **
S-163	Author Program	$5,505	$25,741	($20,236)	21.4%	100.0%	$17,000 **
S-164	Library Facility Rental	$7,500	$110,482	($102,982)	6.8%	100.0%	$10,000 **
		$1,401,425	$4,591,129	($3,189,704)	30.5%	49.1%	$851,200

NOTES:
* - See Text
** - Market Sensitive
# - Frequency of Service Unknown

persons annually into the City to those events. From a municipal standpoint, the economic activity is massive, but mainly for Southern California, not necessarily the City of Pasadena itself. However, from a purely City position, the following 1992 revenue-cost analysis indicated significant "losses" of varying definitions. One of the major "difficulties" is that the Parade somehow has been defined as "a public event", thus the numerous national and world-wide commercial television and filming enterprises maintain that they cannot be charged for, nor the City derive revenue from the privilege of providing access to, or "selling" the resultant live, tape and other images of various types to the resultant thousands of "business customers" and millions of viewers around the world.

Parade and Bowl Summary. These two are "big time" examples of how "community promotional events" and "cultural and sport venues" can almost literally dominate sensible municipal finance. When such venues and events are municipally owned, sponsored, or tax subsidized, revenue-cost analysis becomes necessary. Such is required to avoid the "tail wagging the dog" syndrome. A considerable amount of taxes can be risked, expected, and/or consumed, without full public knowledge or taxpayer approval. So analysis is required, caution needed, and full disclosure and financial discipline mandatory.

S-152: Tournament of Roses Support One answer to the potential need for greater Rose Bowl revenues would be to merge the costs of the Rose Bowl with those of the Tournament of Roses, thus achieving a broadened revenue base. But, prior to so considering, the costs incurred by the City in accommodating the Tournament must be examined. Those costs are contained in this Report in great detail, and are summarized herein below.

Tournament of Roses City Revenues		$ 787,577
Tournament Costs:		
Parade	$877,995	
Post Parade	58,242	
Game	319,708	
Total Costs		$1,255,945
COSTS IN EXCESS OF REVENUES		$ 468,368

S-204: Rose Bowl Maintenance/Operation. The imbalance between revenues generated and costs incurred by the Rose Bowl is significant. A summary follows. More details are provided in Appendix A and far more data in the supporting documentation and microcomputer data bases.

Gross Rose Bowl Revenues	$3,850,292
Total Rose Bowl Costs	6,456,755
Net Loss	($2,606,463)

Maintenance Services. Table 6 lists municipal efforts rarely referred to as "vital". But after intervening Table 5, accompanying text being provided on earlier pages. Thus proving that there are more Tables with numbers than explanatory words. The "story" told in this Book about the unwitting and devious manner in which taxes are diverted from community benefit to personal and/or corporate gain should by now be evident.

Maintenance can be deferred, and in times of "fiscal crisis" usually are. That practice most often results in rapid decline in the integrity of underlying infrastructure and the consequent major increase in ultimate longer term expense.

The old saying "Pay me now or pay me *more* later" here applies. Deferral of maintenance can, will, and should be exposed by the simple application of full costing, matched against supporting revenue streams. Be those monies derived from taxes, fees or charges.

TABLE 5

UTILITY AND ENTERPRISE SERVICES

MSI #	SERVICE CENTER	TOTAL REVENUE	TOTAL COST	TOTAL PROFIT (SUBSIDY)	RECOVERY ACTUAL	PERCENT SUGGEST	POSSIBLE NEW REVENUE
S-165	Electrical Power Service	$112,168,115	$117,999,638	($5,831,523)	95.1%	100.0%	$23,859,376 *
S-166	In-Field Service Spots	$0	$62,944	($62,944)	0.0%	100.0%	$62,900
S-167	New Vaults >200 Amps.	$484,334	$147,917	$336,417	327.4%	100.0%	$0 *
S-168	Trouble Shooter Service	$0	$252,008	($252,008)	0.0%	100.0%	$252,000
S-169	Power Credit Turn Off/On	$35,812	$71,416	($35,604)	50.1%	100.0%	$35,600
S-170	Damaged Meter Repair or Replcmnt	$13,350	$49,078	($35,728)	27.2%	100.0%	$35,700
S-171	Restore Service Wire Cuts	$2,500	$13,038	($10,538)	19.2%	100.0%	$10,500
S-172	Restore Bucket/Underground Cut	$900	$764	$136	117.8%	100.0%	$0 *
S-173	Same Day Service Turn-On	$25	$126	($101)	19.8%	100.0%	$100
S-174	Electric Meter Test	$490	$22,329	($21,839)	2.2%	100.0%	$21,800
S-175	Electric Meter Removal & Repl.	$4,150	$52,299	($48,149)	7.9%	100.0%	$48,100
S-176	Power Service Relocation	$1,150	$2,478	($1,328)	46.4%	100.0%	$1,300
S-177	Power Service Installation	$155,400	$127,120	$28,280	122.2%	100.0%	$0 *
S-178	Street Marking for Utility	$0	$163,283	($163,283)	0.0%	100.0%	$163,300
S-179	Water Service	$19,126,816	$22,875,219	($3,748,403)	83.6%	100.0%	$7,318,924 *
S-180	Water Service Installation	$152,100	$174,888	($22,788)	87.0%	100.0%	$22,800
S-181	Water Service Cut Off At Street	$200	$537	($337)	37.2%	100.0%	$300
S-182	Water Credit Turn Off/On	$19,516	$15,271	$4,245	127.8%	100.0%	$0 *
S-183	Replacemnt Of Curb Stop 3/4" & 1"	$11,100	$21,162	($10,062)	52.5%	100.0%	$10,100
S-184	Repl. Of 1-1/2" Wheel Gate Valve	$900	$1,708	($808)	52.7%	100.0%	$800
S-185	Meter Test/Field (5/8" & 1")	$240	$3,784	($3,544)	6.3%	100.0%	$3,500
S-186	Water Meter Removal and Replcmnt	$5,200	$8,438	($3,238)	61.6%	100.0%	$3,200
S-187	Water Meter Equipment Upgrade	$0	$21,164	($21,164)	0.0%	100.0%	$21,200
S-188	Water Quality Test	$0	$17,192	($17,192)	0.0%	100.0%	$17,200
S-189	Flow Test (Low/Leak/Frozen Valve)	$0	$18,158	($18,158)	0.0%	100.0%	$18,200
S-190	Hydrant Flow Test	$0	$13,855	($13,855)	0.0%	100.0%	$13,900
S-191	Hydrant Portable/Constructn Meter	$0	$2,776	($2,776)	0.0%	100.0%	$2,800
S-192	Hydrant Installation	$14,112	$4,524	$9,588	311.9%	100.0%	$0 *
S-193	Backflow Device Installation	$48,000	$293,726	($245,726)	16.3%	100.0%	$245,700
S-194	Utility Billing	$675,000	$524,771	$150,229	128.6%	100.0%	$0 *
S-195	Bill Investigation	$0	$16,093	($16,093)	0.0%	100.0%	$27,900
S-196	Sewer & Storm Drain Operatn & Mtc	$2,598,642	$11,675,856	($9,077,214)	22.3%	100.0%	$9,077,200 *
S-197	Sewer Stoppage Investigation	$0	$5,422	($5,422)	0.0%	100.0%	$5,400
S-198	Utility Excavation Permit	$14,620	$70,448	($55,828)	20.8%	100.0%	$55,800
S-199	Residential Refuse Collection	$6,844,500	$7,067,644	($223,144)	96.8%	100.0%	$223,100 *
S-200	Commercial Refuse Service	$1,400,000	$1,423,072	($23,072)	98.4%	100.0%	$23,100 *
S-201	Special Requested Refuse Pick-Up	$45,000	$32,678	$12,322	137.7%	100.0%	$0 *
S-202	Street Sweeping	$636,206	$825,836	($189,630)	77.0%	100.0%	$189,600 *
S-203	Right-of-Way Clean-up	$0	$35,777	($35,777)	0.0%	100.0%	$0 *
S-204	Rose Bowl Maintenance/Operation	$3,850,292	$6,456,756	($2,606,464)	59.6%	100.0%	$2,606,500 *
S-205	Golf Course Maintenance/Operation	$1,948,129	$1,367,058	$581,071	142.5%	100.0%	$0 *
S-206	Old Pasadena Parking District	$2,492,648	$3,274,759	($782,111)	76.1%	100.0%	$782,100 *
S-207	South Lake Parking District	$135,203	$346,662	($211,459)	39.0%	100.0%	$211,500 *
S-208	Plaza Las Fuentes Parking	$1,950,075	$2,756,310	($806,235)	70.7%	100.0%	$806,200 *
S-209	City Parking Lot Service	$202,451	$604,282	($401,831)	33.5%	100.0%	$401,800 *
		$155,037,176	$178,920,264	($23,883,088)	86.7%	100.0%	$46,579,500

NOTES:
    * - See Text
   ** - Market Sensitive
    # - Frequency of Service Unknown

```
+-------------------------------------------------------------------------------+
|                              TABLE 5.2                                        |
|        REVENUE & COSTS REASONABLY BORNE FOR WATER SALES                       |
|                        CITY OF PASADENA                                       |
|                       FISCAL YEAR 1992-93                                     |
|                                                                               |
|  Element of Revenue/Cost                            Amount                    |
|  ----------------------------                       ------------              |
|         TOTAL WATER UTILITY REVENUES.............................. $19,126,816 |
|                                                                               |
|  Water Utility Costs........................ $22,875,219                       |
|  In-Lieu Property Tax a 1%..................   3,187,985                       |
|  In-Lieu Franchise Fee a 2%.................     382,536                       |
|                                              ------------                      |
|         TOTAL COSTS.............................................. $26,445,740  |
|                                                                               |
|  NET WATER UTILITY INCOME/BALANCE TO WATER RESERVE............... $(7,318,924) |
+-------------------------------------------------------------------------------+
```

The Maintenance listing literally is "where the rubber meets the road." Since the nation discovered the Canadian-developed MacAdam asphaltic process, paved streets have become not only a status symbol, but an absolute necessity for commerce and reasonable and enjoyable personal travel. Potholes are anathema; constant smoothness costs money. But fuel taxes for road maintenance do not produce anywhere near enough dollars for each of the State, counties, and cities to "do the job properly", as the public is wont to remark, other than to complain.

Of late both Federal and State highway monies have become limited. Nationally, Congressional gridlock and resultant inability to extend the long-standing federal highway program is limiting projects. Numerous States have used various accounting and other devious and questionable devices to divert allegedly "earmarked" highway monies to depleted General Fund purposes. The net result is local government at risk at the financial bottom, thus lacking road & street monies.

Some cities, admittedly a very few, have reverted to the *original* financing for roads. Namely, by assessments against abutting benefitting properties. Or, more likely and generalized, an annual "street utility" charge on a per-vehicle, front foot, or some other calculable basis. Fairmont, West Virginia has pioneered in this "new" revenue source.

Also, a great number of counties, and an increasing number of cities, have changed the scope of their storm drainage programs from tax-supported to a "utility" charge basis.

Administrative and Finance Services. Even the much berated "overhead" operations are capable of producing services for the demanding public. Almost all these fall into the category of "convenience", although some have been re-defined into "public disclosure" legally-required acts. Following Table 7 lists those being provided by Pasadena.

Sufficient details of how these and all other costs were developed are included as Tables and Illustrations in "the back of this Book". Those curious enough, or sufficiently technically capable, very likely can figure out how these analyses were performed. But likely lack the depth of municipal knowledge to allow for full faith public disclosure.

Such details are subject to two major limitations as to accuracy. *First*, the analysts "really have to know government and what they are doing". And, *Second* this procedure is complex, and copyrighted, applicable to all of process, forms, and software.

Service Units. The following eight pages of "Summary of Revenues, Costs and Subsidies by Service Unit" for the Pasadena 1992-1993 Budget are revealing. Those Tables, titled as "Schedule 10" for Pasadena, are extracted from the full two-volume Pasadena Report. They are presented to illustrate how important public fairness was to the City.

First, the complete name of all 235 "Services" which the City provides its taxpayers, residents, businesses and citizens. These encompass the entirety of the City's local governmental activities.

Second, nomenclature of each unit.

Third, the number of each such specific "service" requested or needed, and provided.

Fourth, the per unit revenue identified as being generated by that service – total revenue divided by the number of units delivered.

Fifth, the cost of providing each unit -- total accumulated costs divided by the number of units. These numbers are the highlight of the *Municipal Business System*.

Results. The following eight Tables provide the process by which 100% of the City's revenues are determined, 100% of the City's total costs distributed, and thus actual analytically-determined cost per unit is determined. These numbers are backed up by highly detailed revenue and cost distribution "sheets". Only a few examples of these latter will be shown in the Illustrations section of this Book.

The real "secret sauce" of the MSI/RCS devised and fully developed and applied "System" is the deep and intimate knowledge of and understanding of municipal government by all its founders, employees and component system parts designers. And the totality thereof. And the background, knowledge, capabilities, understanding, and grace of the quality municipal employees and officials with whom we worked.

Hope. It is the fervent hope of this writer, who devoted his entire life from age 20 to now age 81 to the betterment of local government, that the *Municipal Business System* will aid all of America. Thus far one-jurisdiction at a time. Hopefully, then hundreds; up to thousands a year will adopt and utilize the *Municipal Business System*. The results illustrated in this Book can be replicated, spread and, yes, bettered. [See Appendix C]

"Per Unit" Exemplars. The next eight Pasadena Schedule 10 "Schedules" are shown to pique the curiosity of those reading this Book. The revenues and costs compiled composing costs cumulatively add up to 100% of the current budget, but also include costs NOT then recovered, especially fixed assets at replacement cost. [See Chapter II, page 19] Also note "**subsidy per unit**" is the amount of tax monies being shifted from the requestor/user/beneficiary of this service onto the taxpayer -- **not** the special service fee-payer.

The latter usually are undercharged. But, on rare occasion, a profit has been realized. As a result of "profit", rates must be adjusted to secure recovery of "costs reasonably borne" ONLY. And, if necessary and appropriate, employees laid off and other costs cut to reach equitable balance between revenues and costs. "Costs" are defined by the Authors of Proposition 4, *California Constitution* Article XIIIB, per footnote 17 on pages 15 and 16.

TABLE 6

MAINTENANCE SERVICES

MSI #	SERVICE CENTER	TOTAL REVENUE	TOTAL COST	TOTAL PROFIT (SUBSIDY)	RECOVERY ACTUAL	PERCENT SUGGEST	POSSIBLE NEW REVENUE
S-210	Utility St. Usage (Gas & CATV)	$1,350,000	$1,432,182	($82,182)	94.3%	100.0%	$82,200 *
S-211	Street Light & Signal Mntc & Optn	$3,900,000	$6,493,336	($2,593,336)	60.1%	100.0%	$2,593,300 *
S-212	Median & Parkway Maintenance	$0	$440,333	($440,333)	0.0%	100.0%	$440,300 *
S-213	Street Tree Maintenance	$0	$2,218,643	($2,218,643)	0.0%	100.0%	$2,218,600 *
S-214	Tree Mntc Contractor Permit Rvw	$320	$1,070	($750)	29.9%	100.0%	$800
S-215	Barricade Installation	$10,000	$14,253	($4,253)	70.2%	100.0%	$3,000 **
S-216	Barricade Rental	$2,000	$5,085	($3,085)	39.3%	100.0%	$1,500 **
S-217	Hazardous Materials Clean-up	$0	$39,269	($39,269)	0.0%	100.0%	$9,800 **
S-218	Special Business Services	$0	$238,377	($238,377)	0.0%	100.0%	$238,400 *
S-219	Business Improvement District	$0	$51,033	($51,033)	0.0%	100.0%	$51,000 *
S-220	Alley Maintenance	$0	$440,289	($440,289)	0.0%	100.0%	$440,300 *
S-221	Special Curb Marking	$1,500	$18,169	($16,669)	8.3%	100.0%	$16,700
S-222	Neighborhood Park Maintenance	$0	$3,227,138	($3,227,138)	0.0%	100.0%	$3,227,100 *
S-223	Gasoline Charges	$576,286	$747,615	($171,329)	77.1%	100.0%	$171,300 *
S-224	Smog Check	$1,040	$1,360	($320)	76.5%	100.0%	$300 *
S-225	City Property Damage	$56,713	$51,033	$5,680	111.1%	100.0%	$0 *
		$5,897,859	$15,419,185	($9,521,326)	38.3%	99.8%	$9,494,600

NOTES:
   * - See Text
   ** - Market Sensitive
   # - Frequency of Service Unknown

TABLE 7

ADMINISTRATIVE AND FINANCE SERVICES

MSI #	SERVICE CENTER	TOTAL REVENUE	TOTAL COST	TOTAL PROFIT (SUBSIDY)	RECOVERY ACTUAL	PERCENT SUGGEST	POSSIBLE NEW REVENUE
S-226	New/Moved Business Applicatn Rvw	$0	$161,773	($161,773)	0.0%	100.0%	$161,800 *
S-227	Business License Renewal	$0	$462,875	($462,875)	0.0%	100.0%	$462,900 *
S-228	Returned Check (NSF) Processing	$30,000	$47,877	($17,877)	62.7%	100.0%	$8,900 *
S-229	Research Of City Records	NA	NA	NA	NA	100.0%	NA */**
S-230	Document Printing and Copying	NA	NA	NA	NA	100.0%	NA */**
S-231	Document Certification Charges	$58	$190	($132)	30.7%	100.0%	$100 **
S-232	Agenda/Minute Mailing Service	$3,289	$2,975	$314	110.6%	100.0%	($300)
S-233	Facility Rental and Maintenance	$70,000	NA	NA	NA	100.0%	NA *
S-234	Film Permit	$599,480	$246,549	$352,931	243.1%	100.0%	$0 *
S-235	Services to Housing & Comm. Dev	$619,000	$823,765	($204,765)	75.1%	100.0%	$204,800 *
		$1,321,828	$1,746,004	($424,176)	75.7%	100.0%	$838,200

NOTES:
* - See Text
** - Market Sensitive
# - Frequency of Service Unknown

Greater details as to how these analyses were performed are ILLUSTRATIONS "in the back of the Book".

Other more detailed Illustrations for each of Pasadena, Beverly Hills, and Coachella also are provided "in the back of the book", such that any reader should be able to divine the intricate and exquisite [and copyrighted] process by which highly experienced specialist municipal analysts accumulate detailed data which ultimately results in divulging the totality of revenues, costs and beneficiaries for all services provided. The end result accounts for 100% of City costs of service matched against 100% of the City's revenues, service-by-service.

Achieving Reality. The only solution available to municipalities to achieve secure financing is to subject all its services and activities to the strenuous impartial revenue-cost analysis illustrated herein. Approaching absolute diminution or abolition of "expected and usual" municipal service levels, and potential bankruptcy or bond default, might well be necessary to force such analyses. Thus, ***each and every*** municipal activity must be identified, then minutely examined and matched against a revenue source and a group of benefitting "customers".

The general tenor of voters during The Great Recession is to "destroy all government" and then start over to see what we really "need" and/or "want". Which, when viewed rationally, might not be a totally insane concept. But quite financially risky in the process. Thus the *Municipal Business System* is, and will continue to be vitally needed.

CITY OF PASADENA   Schedule 10

SUMMARY OF REVENUES, COSTS AND SUBSIDIES BY SERVICE UNIT

FISCAL YEAR 1992–1993 BUDGET

MSI # (1)	SERVICE CENTER (2)	UNIT TYPE (3)	NO. UNITS (4)	REVENUE PER UNIT (5)	COST PER UNIT (6)	PROFIT (SUBSIDY) PER UNIT (7)
	COMMUNITY DEVELOPMENT SERVICES					
S-001	Concept Plan Review	Application	40	$240.00	$2,619.58	($2,379.58)
S-002	Preliminary Plan Check	Application	200	$210.31	$444.29	($233.98)
S-003	Tentative Parcel Map Review	Application	15	$2,421.00	$2,091.53	$329.47
S-004	Tentative Tract Map Review	Application	20	$2,934.00	$2,380.80	$553.20
S-005	Construction Staging Plan Review	Application	20	$0.00	$489.40	($489.40)
S-006	Design Commission Review (Minor)	Permit	50	$67.00	$299.38	($232.38)
S-007	Design Commission Review (Major)	Permit	50	$475.00	$1,987.82	($1,512.82)
S-008	Design Review (Final)	Permit	40	$0.00	$754.33	($754.33)
S-009	Design Review (Seismic)	Permit	30	$0.00	$167.60	($167.60)
S-010	Design Review–City of Gardens	Application	24	$164.72	$2,236.04	($2,071.32)
S-011	Design Review (Consolidated)	Permit	20	$539.00	$1,563.75	($1,024.75)
S-012	Design Review Extension	Application	10	$0.00	$44.60	($44.60)
S-013	Landmark District Review	Application	22	$0.00	$369.86	($369.86)
S-014	Historic Building Search	Request	360	$0.00	$61.31	($61.31)
S-015	Master Development Plan Review	Application	3	$933.00	$5,867.33	($4,934.33)
S-016	Conditional Use Permit Review	Application	150	$1,429.00	$1,630.90	($201.90)
S-017	Minor Conditional Use Permit Review	Application	20	$574.00	$1,840.30	($1,266.30)
S-018	Temporary Conditional Use Permit Rvw	Application	70	$286.00	$375.26	($89.26)
S-019	Variance Review	Application	55	$1,106.00	$1,729.18	($623.18)
S-020	Minor Variance Review	Application	20	$475.75	$1,713.40	($1,237.65)
S-021	Use Permit & Variance Extension	Request	20	$0.00	$255.75	($255.75)
S-022	Lot Line Adjustment	Application	15	$887.00	$1,159.33	($272.33)
S-023	Rezoning Request Rvw (Zone Change)	Application	4	$2,072.00	$4,397.75	($2,325.75)
S-024	Subdivision Map Extension Prcssng	Request	8	$769.00	$1,008.75	($239.75)
S-025	Growth Management Allocation	Application	20	$1,643.20	$15,993.00	($14,349.80)
S-026	Growth Management Allocation Exemptn	Application	50	$0.00	$392.42	($392.42)
S-027	Growth Allocation Appeal	Project	20	$95.05	$103.20	($8.15)
S-028	Growth Mgt. Conditional Use Permit	Permit	20	$1,429.00	$1,517.95	($88.95)
S-029	Growth Management Time Extension	Application	20	$0.00	$230.15	($230.15)
S-030	Initial Environmental Study	Study	82	$606.00	$1,175.41	($569.41)
S-031	Environmental Impact Report (Consltnt)	Study	3	$3,410.00	$6,412.00	($3,002.00)
S-032	Fish & Game Environ. Impact Revw	Application	82	$26.00	$152.96	($126.96)
S-033	Env. Impact Mitigation Monitoring	Project	24	$0.00	$638.21	($638.21)
S-034	Monitoring of Conditions	Project	350	$0.00	$792.30	($792.30)
S-035	Certificate of Appropriateness	Permit	50	$0.00	$1,334.44	($1,334.44)
S-036	Replacement Building Permit Relief	Application	8	$0.00	$234.25	($234.25)
S-037	Appeal Processing	Application	25	$725.20	$3,741.96	($3,016.76)

CITY OF PASADENA   Schedule 10

SUMMARY OF REVENUES, COSTS AND SUBSIDIES BY SERVICE UNIT

FISCAL YEAR 1992–1993 BUDGET

MSI # (1)	SERVICE CENTER (2)	UNIT TYPE (3)	NO. UNITS (4)	REVENUE PER UNIT (5)	COST PER UNIT (6)	PROFIT (SUBSIDY) PER UNIT (7)
S-038	Appeal Processing – Staff Decision	Application	5	$0.00	$622.20	($622.20)
S-039	Vesting Map Review	Application	5	$3,346.00	$2,444.40	$901.60
S-040	Final Tract Map Review	Map	15	$0.00	$1,539.67	($1,539.67)
S-041	Final Parcel Map Review	Map	6	$0.00	$955.00	($955.00)
S-042	Engineering Plan Review	Plan	47	$1,689.36	$1,630.72	$58.64
S-043	Street Occupation Permit	Permit	448	$462.50	$101.35	$361.15
S-044	Public Works Permit	Permit	1,400	$148.00	$205.36	($57.36)
S-045	Street Vacation	Application	8	$518.00	$5,716.63	($5,198.63)
S-046	Grading Plan Check	Plan	8	$525.77	$177.75	$348.02
S-047	Hillside Grading Plan Check	Plan	4	$1,679.50	$443.25	$1,236.25
S-048	Grading Inspection	Permit	8	$525.75	$52.88	$472.88
S-049	Hillside Grading Inspection	Permit	4	$0.00	$1,196.25	($1,196.25)
S-050	Construction Plan Check	Plan	2,934	$270.73	$530.09	($259.36)
S-051	Construction Review and Inspection	Permit	8,847	$164.49	$128.98	$35.51
S-052	Misc/Special Building Inspection Invstgn	Inspection	120	$101.53	$68.49	$33.04
S-053	Condominium Conversion	Application	2	$0.00	$818.50	($818.50)
S-054	Relocation Investigation (House Moves)	Permit	12	$777.00	$651.67	$125.33
S-055	Address Change	Request	6	$161.00	$119.33	$41.67
S-056	Address Assignment	Project	75	$22.00	$111.27	($89.27)
S-057	Temporary Certificate of Occupancy	Application	160	$94.50	$102.80	($8.30)
S-058	Occupancy Inspection	Inspection	8,408	$30.25	$80.94	($50.69)
S-059	Certificate of Compliance Investigation	Application	5	$391.00	$1,455.60	($1,064.60)
S-060	Parkway Usage License Agreement	Application	15	$212.73	$1,457.60	($1,244.87)
S-061	Sidewalk Dining Permit	Application	5	$0.00	$177.80	($177.80)
S-062	Building Permit Center	Permit/App	13,403	$0.00	$12.13	($12.13)
S-063	Zoning Parking Credit	Application	8	$300.00	$1,642.75	($1,342.75)
S-064	Temporary Street Closure (Events)	Permit	52	$23.45	$581.33	($557.88)
S-065	Traffic Impact Review	Study	30	$0.00	$2,511.30	($2,511.30)
S-066	Trip Reduction Plan Review	Plan	25	$0.00	$2,874.16	($2,874.16)
S-067	Development Agreement Revw	Project	1	$0.00	$9,335.00	($9,335.00)
S-068	Legal Description	Project	5	$0.00	$877.40	($877.40)
S-069	Planned Development	Application	1	$0.00	$4,653.00	($4,653.00)
S-070	General Plan Amendment	Application	1	$0.00	$4,096.00	($4,096.00)

CITY OF PASADENA   Schedule 10

SUMMARY OF REVENUES, COSTS AND SUBSIDIES BY SERVICE UNIT

FISCAL YEAR 1992–1993 BUDGET

MSI # (1)	SERVICE CENTER (2)	UNIT TYPE (3)	NO. UNITS (4)	REVENUE PER UNIT (5)	COST PER UNIT (6)	PROFIT (SUBSIDY) PER UNIT (7)
	PUBLIC SAFETY SERVICES					
S-071	Annual Hm Business Occupancy Prmt	Permit	589	$22.07	$41.88	($19.81)
S-072	Garage Sale Permit	Permit	1,000	$7.50	$9.99	($2.49)
S-073	Special Business Regulation	Application	704	$0.00	$89.78	($89.78)
S-074	Wide, Overweight, Overlong Ld Prmt	Permit	196	$28.54	$17.03	$11.52
S-075	Vehicle Code Enforcement	Citation	45,077	$5.32	$19.83	($14.51)
S-076	Non-Vehicle Code Enforcement	Citation/Insp.	1,300	$0.00	$327.57	($327.57)
S-077	Parking Enforcement	Citation	115,000	$14.13	$6.65	$7.48
S-078	Parking Permits	Permit	2,900	$29.65	$50.02	($20.37)
S-079	Limited Time Parking Permit	Request	24	$0.00	$287.00	($287.00)
S-080	Bicycle Registration	License	490	$4.35	$7.48	($3.13)
S-081	Burglar Alarm Review	Permit	1,500	$89.00	$22.82	$66.18
S-082	Police False Alarm Response	Incident	9,414	$18.75	$113.60	($94.84)
S-083	Clearance Letter Processing	Letter	300	$10.00	$11.22	($1.22)
S-084	Police Report Copying	Report Copy	10,000	$10.00	$11.22	($1.22)
S-085	Police Photograph Reproduction	Photo	300	$10.36	$24.21	($13.85)
S-086	Police Photo Lab Services	NA	NA	NA	NA	NA
S-087	Police Tape & Video Duplication Service	Tape	60	$0.00	$46.95	($46.95)
S-088	Spec. Police Computer Print-Out Service	Request	175	$8.00	$30.29	($22.29)
S-089	Fingerprint Processing	Card	3,700	$9.00	$11.22	($2.22)
S-090	Vehicle Correction Inspection	Inspection	900	$0.00	$5.18	($5.18)
S-091	Removal of Aband/Abated Veh & Release	Vehicle	1,200	$0.00	$76.17	($76.17)
S-092	Impound Vehicle Release Service	Vehicle	1,000	$0.00	$60.18	($60.18)
S-093	DUI Acc. Response, Invest. & Report	Incident	525	$8.57	$464.63	($456.06)
S-094	DUI Arrest Procedure/Non-Accident	Arrest	1,000	$0.00	$346.89	($346.89)
S-095	Noise Disturbance Response Call-back	Call-back	100	$0.00	$115.84	($115.84)
S-096	Public Crosswalk Protection	Crosswalk	10	$0.00	$19,593.00	($19,593.00)
S-097	One-Day Alcohol Permit Processing	Permit	125	$0.00	$48.33	($48.33)
S-098	Commercial Foot Patrol	Business	297	$0.00	$669.04	($669.04)
S-099	Rifle Range Use	Customer	4,900	$5.10	$8.25	($3.14)
S-100	Helicopter Pad Landing Use	Permit	10	$407.00	$130.40	$270.00
S-101	I.N.S. Prisoner Housing	Prisoner	5,220	$75.00	$73.68	$1.32
S-102	Trustee Housing	Prisoner Day	982	$75.00	$84.77	($9.77)
S-103	V.I.N. Verification	Request	400	$0.00	$20.70	($20.70)
S-104	Hazardous Materials Permit Insp	Inspection	5,000	$153.33	$143.95	$9.38
S-105	State Mandated Fire Inspection	Inspection	392	$406.53	$472.39	($65.86)

CITY OF PASADENA   Schedule 10

SUMMARY OF REVENUES, COSTS AND SUBSIDIES BY SERVICE UNIT

FISCAL YEAR 1992–1993 BUDGET

MSI # (1)	SERVICE CENTER (2)	UNIT TYPE (3)	NO. UNITS (4)	REVENUE PER UNIT (5)	COST PER UNIT (6)	PROFIT (SUBSIDY) PER UNIT (7)
S-106	Underground Tank Plan Check/Insp.	Plan Ck/Insp	1,434	$50.56	$43.92	$6.64
S-107	Fire False Alarm Response	Incident	1,000	$0.00	$99.79	($99.79)
S-108	Non-Emergency Service	Incident	208	$0.00	$95.75	($95.75)
S-109	Illegal Burn Response	Response	50	$0.00	$236.60	($236.60)
S-110	Post-Fire Investigation Analysis	Investigation	224	$198.91	$340.50	($141.59)
S-111	Fire Report Copying	Report	150	$7.50	$21.89	($14.39)
S-112	Weed Abatement	Parcel	440	$75.35	$157.57	($82.22)
S-113	Medical Aid Response	Avg. Incident	9,500	$168.42	$348.33	($179.91)
S-114	Hazard Abatement Services	Incident	10	$0.00	$283.80	($283.80)

HEALTH DEPARTMENT SERVICES

MSI # (1)	SERVICE CENTER (2)	UNIT TYPE (3)	NO. UNITS (4)	REVENUE PER UNIT (5)	COST PER UNIT (6)	PROFIT (SUBSIDY) PER UNIT (7)
S-115	Health Department Plan Check/Insp	Plan	60	$283.33	$395.92	($112.58)
S-116	Environmental Health Inspection	Inspection	8,178	$25.49	$17.19	$8.30
S-117	Noise Control Permit	Permit	92	$34.78	$163.99	($129.21)
S-118	Food Sanitation Inspection	Inspection	6,949	$29.55	$34.60	($5.05)
S-119	Mosquito, Fly & Rodent Control	Parcel	35,602	$0.00	$6.62	($6.62)
S-120	Animal Control	License	5,666	$20.52	$75.06	($54.54)
S-121	Vital Statistics	Certfict/Prmt	25,939	$9.85	$9.85	$0.00
S-122	Travel Immmunizations	Patient	3,120	$58.01	$38.31	$19.70
S-123	Water Examination	Specimen	2,424	$41.19	$39.05	$2.14
S-124	Alcoholism & Drug Depndncy Prgrm	Contact	8,592	$31.35	$42.22	($10.87)
S-125	First Offender Program	Client	295	$256.60	$249.12	$7.47
S-126	Public Health Laboratory	Varies	NA	NA	NA	NA
S-127	Prenatal Clinic	Delivery	1,500	$913.05	$913.05	$0.00
S-128	Women, Infants & Childrn Voucher	Recipient	49,000	$8.16	$10.92	($2.76)
S-129	AIDS Program	Patient/Contact	4,735	$51.37	$62.26	($10.89)
S-130	SGV, HIV Early Intervention Program	Client	100	$2,553.00	$3,162.96	($609.96)
S-131	Child Health Clinic	Patient	6,525	$65.09	$65.09	$0.00
S-132	Ambulatory Care Clinic	Patient	1,922	$8.73	$42.09	($33.36)
S-133	Senior Preventive Health Program	Patient	1,500	$14.95	$74.82	($59.86)
S-134	Sexually Transmitted Disease Program	Patient	4,160	$30.58	$30.58	$0.00
S-135	Tuberculosis Program	Patient	13,280	$20.38	$23.63	($3.25)
S-136	Flu/Pneumonia Immunization	Patient	4,091	$4.86	$5.36	($0.51)
S-137	Immmunization	Patient	5,500	$10.49	$11.89	($1.40)

CITY OF PASADENA   Schedule 10

SUMMARY OF REVENUES, COSTS AND SUBSIDIES BY SERVICE UNIT

FISCAL YEAR 1992–1993 BUDGET

MSI # (1)	SERVICE CENTER (2)	UNIT TYPE (3)	NO. UNITS (4)	REVENUE PER UNIT (5)	COST PER UNIT (6)	PROFIT (SUBSIDY) PER UNIT (7)
	LEISURE & CULTURAL SERVICES					
S-138	City Youth Sports Programs	Participant	2,000	$0.00	$369.33	($369.33)
S-139	City Adult Sports Programs	Team	318	$149.54	$906.89	($757.36)
S-140	Private Youth Group Fld Rental Srvc	Hour	11,374	$0.00	$5.22	($5.22)
S-141	Private Adult Group Fld Rental Svc	Hour	5,132	$2.91	$12.40	($9.49)
S-142	Youth Recreation Classes	Participant	3,000	$6.07	$76.80	($70.73)
S-143	Adult Recreation Classes	Participant	7,000	$6.05	$10.35	($4.29)
S-144	Youth Special Activities	Participant	NA	NA	NA	NA
S-145	Summer Day Camp	Participant	400	$100.00	$592.14	($492.14)
S-146	Adaptive Recreation Activities	Participant	145	$147.76	$602.60	($454.84)
S-147	Senior Citizen Programs	Total Partcpnt	1,258	$5.19	$140.77	($135.57)
S-148	Recreational Swimming	Swimmer	17,150	$0.61	$9.79	($9.18)
S-149	Swimming Lessons	Student	9,030	$2.40	$3.72	($1.32)
S-150	Recreation Facility Rental	Hour	14,691	$8.95	$7.20	$1.75
S-151	City-Wide Special Events	Participant	NA	NA	NA	NA
S-152	Tournament of Roses Support	Est.Attend	1,000,000	$0.79	$1.26	($0.47)
S-153	Special Event Set-Up/Clean Up	Request	25	$160.00	$1,783.92	($1,623.92)
S-154	Overdue Material Processing	NA	NA	NA	NA	NA
S-155	Replacing Lost Library Items	Item	575	$22.43	$34.23	($11.80)
S-156	Replacement Of Lost Library Cards	Card	3,800	$2.50	$5.38	($2.88)
S-157	Book Reservation Service	Reservation	29,979	$0.17	$6.88	($6.70)
S-158	Inter Library Loan Processing	Request	3,678	$0.56	$14.09	($13.53)
S-159	Retrieval & Copying Of Periodicals	Request	150	$11.56	$13.89	($2.33)
S-160	Reproduction Of Photographs	Photograph	50	$3.33	$12.33	($9.00)
S-161	Library Media Rental	Item	5,150	$1.15	$5.59	($4.44)
S-162	Library On-Line Database Search	Request	350	$35.46	$61.17	($25.71)
S-163	Author Program	Ticket	1,092	$5.04	$23.57	($18.53)
S-164	Library Facility Rental	Rental	1,315	$5.70	$84.02	($78.31)

CITY OF PASADENA   Schedule 10

SUMMARY OF REVENUES, COSTS AND SUBSIDIES BY SERVICE UNIT

FISCAL YEAR 1992–1993 BUDGET

MSI # (1)	SERVICE CENTER (2)	UNIT TYPE (3)	NO. UNITS (4)	REVENUE PER UNIT (5)	COST PER UNIT (6)	PROFIT (SUBSIDY) PER UNIT (7)
	UTILITY & ENTERPRISE SERVICES					
S-165	Electrical Power Service	Customers	57,084	$1,964.97	$2,067.12	($102.16)
S-166	In-Field Service Spots	Incident	217	$0.00	$290.06	($290.06)
S-167	New Vaults >200 Amps.	Vault	60	$8,072.23	$2,465.28	$5,606.95
S-168	Trouble Shooter Service	Incident	3,640	$0.00	$69.23	($69.23)
S-169	Power Credit Turn Off/On	Credit Off/On	2,941	$12.18	$24.28	($12.11)
S-170	Damaged Meter Repair or Replacemnt	Meter	267	$50.00	$183.81	($133.81)
S-171	Restore Service Wire Cuts	Incident	100	$25.00	$130.38	($105.38)
S-172	Restore Bucket/Underground Cut	Incident	6	$150.00	$127.33	$22.67
S-173	Same Day Service Turn-On	Incident	1	$25.00	$126.00	($101.00)
S-174	Electric Meter Test	Meter	14	$35.00	$1,594.93	($1,559.93)
S-175	Electric Meter Removal & Repl.	Meter	166	$25.00	$315.05	($290.05)
S-176	Power Service Relocation	Project	10	$115.00	$247.80	($132.80)
S-177	Power Service Installation	Installation	777	$200.00	$163.60	$36.40
S-178	Street Marking for Utility	Request	2,340	$0.00	$69.78	($69.78)
S-179	Water Service	Customer	36,234	$527.87	$631.32	($103.45)
S-180	Water Service Installation	Incident	169	$900.00	$1,034.84	($134.84)
S-181	Water Service Cut Off At Street	Incident	2	$100.00	$268.50	($168.50)
S-182	Water Credit Turn Off/On	Credit Off/On	1,583	$12.33	$9.65	$2.68
S-183	Replacement Of Curb Stop 3/4" & 1"	Incident	185	$60.00	$114.39	($54.39)
S-184	Repl. Of 1-1/2" Wheel Gate Valve	Incident	12	$75.00	$142.33	($67.33)
S-185	Meter Test/Field (5/8" & 1")	Test	24	$10.00	$157.67	($147.67)
S-186	Water Meter Removal and Replacement	Meter	104	$50.00	$81.13	($31.13)
S-187	Water Meter Equipment Upgrade	Meter	148	$0.00	$143.00	($143.00)
S-188	Water Quality Test	Test	90	$0.00	$191.02	($191.02)
S-189	Flow Test (Low/Leak/Frozen Valve)	Test	200	$0.00	$90.79	($90.79)
S-190	Hydrant Flow Test	Test	52	$0.00	$266.44	($266.44)
S-191	Hydrant Portable/Construction Meter	Meter	79	$0.00	$35.14	($35.14)
S-192	Hydrant Installation	Hydrant	1	$14,112.00	$4,524.00	$9,588.00
S-193	Backflow Device Installation	Device	2,000	$24.00	$146.86	($122.86)
S-194	Utility Billing	Varies	204,040	$3.31	$2.57	$0.74
S-195	Bill Investigation	Investigation	2,788	$0.00	$5.77	($5.77)
S-196	Sewer & Storm Drain Operation & Mtc	City H20 Cust	29,839	$87.09	$391.30	($304.21)
S-197	Sewer Stoppage Investigation	Request	20	$0.00	$271.10	($271.10)
S-198	Utility Excavation Permit	Permit	450	$32.49	$156.55	($124.06)
S-199	Residential Refuse Collection	Account	26,740	$255.96	$264.31	($8.34)

CITY OF PASADENA   Schedule 10

SUMMARY OF REVENUES, COSTS AND SUBSIDIES BY SERVICE UNIT

FISCAL YEAR 1992–1993 BUDGET

MSI # (1)	SERVICE CENTER (2)	UNIT TYPE (3)	NO. UNITS (4)	REVENUE PER UNIT (5)	COST PER UNIT (6)	PROFIT (SUBSIDY) PER UNIT (7)
S-200	Commercial Refuse Service	Customer	1,343	$1,042.44	$1,059.62	($17.18)
S-201	Special Requested Refuse Pick-Up	Pick-up	918	$49.02	$35.60	$13.42
S-202	Street Sweeping	Power Custmr	57,084	$11.15	$14.47	($3.32)
S-203	Right-of-Way Clean-up	Power Custmr	57,084	$0.00	$0.63	($0.63)
S-204	Rose Bowl Maintenance/Operation	Varies	NA	NA	NA	NA
S-205	Golf Course Maintenance/Operation	Round	190,000	$10.25	$7.20	$3.06
S-206	Old Pasadena Parking District	Space	1,450	$1,719.07	$2,258.45	($539.39)
S-207	South Lake Parking District	Space	750	$180.27	$462.22	($281.95)
S-208	Plaza Las Fuentes Parking	Space	850	$2,294.21	$3,242.72	($948.51)
S-209	City Parking Lot Service	Space	1,753	$115.49	$344.71	($229.22)

MAINTENANCE SERVICES

MSI #	SERVICE CENTER	UNIT TYPE	NO. UNITS	REVENUE PER UNIT	COST PER UNIT	PROFIT (SUBSIDY) PER UNIT
S-210	Utility St. Usage (Gas & CATV)	Miles R-O-W	330	$4,090.91	$4,339.95	($249.04)
S-211	Street Light & Signal Maint & Op'n	Power Custmr	57,084	$68.32	$113.75	($45.43)
S-212	Median & Parkway Maintenance	Parcel	35,602	$0.00	$12.37	($12.37)
S-213	Street Tree Maintenance	Parcel	35,602	$0.00	$62.32	($62.32)
S-214	Tree Maintenence Contractor Permit Rvw	Permit	20	$16.00	$53.50	($37.50)
S-215	Barricade Installation	Request	40	$250.00	$356.33	($106.33)
S-216	Barricade Rental	Request	40	$50.00	$127.13	($77.13)
S-217	Hazardous Materials Clean up	Incident	15	$0.00	$2,617.93	($2,617.93)
S-218	Special Business Services	Various	NA	NA	NA	NA
S-219	Business Improvement District	Parcel	3,231	$0.00	$15.79	($15.79)
S-220	Alley Maintenance	Parcel	2,400	$0.00	$165.43	($165.43)
S-221	Special Curb Marking	Request	105	$14.29	$173.04	($158.75)
S-222	Neighborhood Park Maintenance	Resd'l Parcel	20,649	$0.00	$156.29	($156.29)
S-223	Gasoline Charges	Gallons	NA	NA	NA	NA
S-224	Smog Check	Certificate	40	$26.00	$34.00	($8.00)
S-225	City Property Damage	Incident	NA	NA	NA	NA

CITY OF PASADENA   Schedule 10

SUMMARY OF REVENUES, COSTS AND SUBSIDIES BY SERVICE UNIT

FISCAL YEAR 1992–1993 BUDGET

MSI # (1)	SERVICE CENTER (2)	UNIT TYPE (3)	NO. UNITS (4)	REVENUE PER UNIT (5)	COST PER UNIT (6)	PROFIT (SUBSIDY) PER UNIT (7)
	ADMINISTRATIVE & FINANCE SERVICES					
S-226	New/Moved Business Applicatn Rvw	Application	1,797	$0.00	$90.02	($90.02)
S-227	Business License Renewal	Business	10,621	$0.00	$43.58	($43.58)
S-228	Returned Check (NSF) Processing	Check	3,000	$10.00	$15.96	($5.96)
S-229	Research Of City Records	NA	NA	NA	NA	NA
S-230	Document Printing and Copying	Page	NA	NA	NA	NA
S-231	Document Certification Charges	Document	16	$3.65	$11.88	($8.23)
S-232	Agenda/Minute Mailing Service	Subscription	25	$131.57	$119.00	$12.57
S-233	Facility Rental and Maintenance	Hour/Reservtn	36	$1,944.44	NA	$1,944.44
S-234	Film Permit	Permit	360	$1,665.22	$684.86	$980.36
S-235	Services to Housing & Comm. Dev	Varies	NA	NA	NA	NA

Tax Subsidies. The previous Pasadena "Schedules" illustrate with exactitude where tax monies are being "leaked" to, and consumed by those services received by few with justification, predominately those who could be termed as "privileged". Or, as referred to in the Beverly Hills Report, next, the locally dubbed "Personal Choice Public Services".

The following two listings show where the City of Pasadena secures its tax revenues. Supposedly, and theoretically, those revenues are to be used for "Community-Supported Public Services". Those generally are considered as financing Fire and Police Protection, Parks Maintenance, Library, Recreation facilities and some Recreation programs.

PASADENA MAJOR TAX SOURCES

Tax Revenue Group	Pct.
Sales & Use Tax	22.29%
Property Taxes	22.12%
Utility Users Tax	16.91%
Contributions from Enterprise Funds	10.00%
Motor Vehicle In-Lieu	4.70%
Intergovernmental Revenue	4.23%
TOTAL	**80.25%**

The above, and following Schedules 12 and 13, and attendant text are repeated in the Chapter "Revenue Sources for Local Government Services". Other data and examples are there provided about "sources".

Schedule 12

CITY OF PASADENA
SCHEDULE OF TAX REVENUES
FISCAL YEAR 1992–93

MSI REF	SOURCE	BUDGET 1992–93	PER CAPITA
TAX–1	SALES AND USE TAX	$21,760,015	$166.11
TAX–2	PROPERTY/TRANSFER/EXEMPTION TAX	$21,592,812	$164.83
TAX–7	UTILITY USERS TAX	$16,502,260	$125.97
TAX–15	CONTRIBUTIONS FROM ENTERPRISE FUNDS	$9,765,387	$74.54
TAX–4	MOTOR VEHICLE IN–LIEU	$4,587,525	$35.02
TAX–10	INTERGOVERMENTAL REVENUE	$4,352,324	$33.22
TAX–5	INVESTMENT EARNINGS	$3,900,000	$29.77
TAX–11	BUSINESS TAX	$3,250,000	$24.81
TAX–3	STATE & FEDERAL STREET & HWY GRANTS	$3,148,015	$24.03
TAX–6	TRANSIENT OCCUPANCY TAX	$2,900,000	$22.14
TAX–14	UNDERGROUND UTILITIES TAX	$2,747,407	$20.97
TAX–13	CONSTRUCTION TAX	$1,630,800	$12.45
TAX–9	INTERGOVTL CAPITAL PROJECTS REVENUE	$1,575,000	$12.02
TAX–12	OTHER FUND REVEN!	$125,000	$0.95
TAX–8	OTHER MISCELLANEOUS REVENUES	$6,810	$0.05
	TOTAL	$97,843,355	$746.90

========

NOTES:

The various Tax categories include a number of different revenue accounts.

The per capita amounts are calculated by using the approximated City population of 131,000.

Schedule 13

CITY OF PASADENA
SCHEDULE OF TAX SUPPORTED SERVICES
FISCAL YEAR 1992–93

MSI REFERENCE	SERVICE PROVIDED	TOTAL	PER CAPITA
S–236	STATUS OF WOMEN ISSUES COORDINATION	$183,548	$1.40
S–237	CHILD CARE ISSUES COORDINATION	$191,706	$1.46
S–238	CHILD & YOUTH ISSUES COORDINATION	$193,837	$1.48
S–239	SENIOR CITIZEN ISSUES COORDINATION	$97,899	$0.75
S–240	HUMAN RELATIONS & MISCELLANEOUS ISSUES COORDINATION	$141,652	$1.08
S–241	PASADENA VOLUNTEER PROGRAM	$120,287	$0.92
S–242	COMMUNITY CENTER SERVICES	$921,018	$7.03
S–243	NEIGHBORHOOD CONNECTIONS	$201,690	$1.54
S–244	PROSECUTION–PUBLIC SAFETY	$927,493	$7.08
S–245	FIRE SUPPRESSION & INVESTIGATION	$13,958,621	$106.55
S–246	DISASTER PREPAREDNESS	$98,087	$0.75
S–247	CRIME PREVENTION & INTERDICTION	$4,788,816	$36.56
S–248	PATROL SERVICES	$17,135,612	$130.81
S–249	CRIMINAL INVESTIGATION & ANALYSIS	$4,933,676	$37.66
S–250	CRIME PREVENTION & INVST SUPPORT	$1,382,143	$10.55
S–251	GRAFFITI REMOVAL PROGRAM	$111,093	$0.85
S–252	CURRENT PLANNING PROGRAM	$1,459,953	$11.14
S–253	GENERAL PLAN UPDATE	$783,269	$5.98
S–254	URBAN CONSERVATION & HISTORIC PRESERVATION	$289,348	$2.21
S–255	GROWTH MANAGEMENT INITIATIVE ADMN PROGRAM	$19,734	$0.15
S–256	PUBLIC ARTS PROGRAM	$582,539	$4.45
S–257	LIBRARY SERVICES & SPECIAL PROGRAMS	$7,793,489	$59.49
S–258	CAREER SERVICES PRORAMS	$2,191,539	$16.73
S–259	PROJECT D.A.Y. SUPPPORT	$54,757	$0.42
S–260	GENERAL & NEEDS–TARGETED RECREATION	$681,433	$5.20
S–261	CAPITAL PROJECTS PROGRAM	$52,041,599	$397.26
S–262	GENERAL ENGINEERING PROJECTS	$589,043	$4.50
S–263	TRANSPORTATION PLANNING	$1,868,429	$14.26
S–264	TRAFFIC SERVICES–SIGN/STRIPE/SIGNAL	$1,307,570	$9.98
S–265	GENERAL STREET/BRIDGE/CURB MAINTENANCE	$15,094,832	$115.23
S–266	CITY PARK & CULTURAL FACILITY MAINTENANCE	$1,442,980	$11.02
S–267	TOBACCO CONTROL PROGRAM	$179,019	$1.37
S–268	PUBLIC HEALTH EDUCATION & DISEASE PROGRAM	$527,514	$4.03
S–269	NON–DEPARTMENTAL DEBT/CONTRIBUTIONS/OBLIGATIONS	$16,156,326	$123.33
S–270	ELECTIONS PROGRAM	$398,752	$3.04
S–271	NORTHWEST ISSUES COORDINATION	$865,754	$6.61
	SUBTOTAL --- TAX SERVICES	$149,714,855	$1,142.86
	TAX SUBSIDIES TO FEE & CHGE SVCS (SCHEDULE 11)	$44,921,338	$342.91
	TOTAL --- TAX SUPPORT	$194,636,193	$1,485.77

NOTES:
The Detail for the Tax Services is found in Appendix C.
The per capita amounts are caliuated by using the approximated City population of 131,000.

Page 171

Pasadena Cost Control Report
_____

Tax Service Costs

As shown on Schedule 13, MSI divided the City's general benefit/tax services into thirty-six service centers that cost a total of $149,714,855. In addition to these direct tax and non-fee supported services, taxes are needed to cover the shortfall in fee-supported services by $44,921,338. Although the fee-supported services of Chapter V are "private goods" in the sense that the user is identifiable, there will be a social purpose in continuing some subsidies. Together, the two components currently require the use of $194,636,193 in taxes. This final figure is the 1992-93 fiscal year, full, businesslike cost of the City's services. The detail for each of these general benefit/tax services is found in Appendix C.

As discussed in Chapter II, MSI identified two major categories of service for costing purposes: Special Benefit Services and General Benefit Services. A third category, Limited Benefit Services, also exists. Since these services normally receive general tax dollar subsidies in addition to grants or restricted revenues, they have been included with the Special Benefit Services for simplification.

Tax Vs. Fee

If a revenue is a "tax," then it becomes part of the City's "Proceeds of Taxes" amount for comparison with the Proposition 4 Appropriation Limit. At the point that the Limit is reached, the City may have to refund some of its taxes. However, when a revenue is a "fee," the Council may establish the fee at whatever level the costs are and the revenue becomes part of the "Non-Proceeds of Taxes." Nevertheless, calling any revenue a "fee," including franchise fees and maintenance assessments, would require that it be used for the service charged.

The General Theory. The basics of American democracy hold that those who are able to pay should not only pay for the services which they receive from government for the general good, but also for those special benefit services which they receive. However, as the array of services demanded and provided to citizens and businesses by government have multiplied, the basics have been lost sight of. The broad and ubiquitous municipal "General Fund" containing most revenues, coupled with the demand for service has led city councils into the death spiral of attempting to be all things to all people, without examining either the cost or benefits.

The Specifics. The MSI Revenue/Cost match-up system, for which data is provided and summarized in this Report, enables the City Council to bridge the "Ignorance Gap" to determine specifically who pays what and how much and what they receive from the City in return for the payment.

Chapter VI - Tax Revenues and Services

The Results. This Report shows definitively, and in exact amount, what revenues finance each and every City service, who benefits, the dollar value of the benefit, and a quantification of the benefits. Further, to the extent that any tax monies are utilized in the provision of Special Benefit Services, that amount is given. Thus the City Council will have the information upon which to base decisions as to whether a narrowly based specific service benefitting specific beneficiaries should be subsidized by general tax monies or financed in whole or major part by fees or special charges or taxes paid by targeted beneficiaries.

Utilization of the Categories. Schedule 14, which follows, can be utilized by the City Council in its quest to maximize fairness and equity in the payment for services provided by the City, to attempt to assure that there is as close a relationship as possible between payment and benefit as the City Council chooses.

Division as Assistance. The divisions contained in Schedule 14 may further assist the City Council in its policy deliberations as it decides both level of service which can be afforded, and the extent that costs incurred will be met by taxes paid by all or by fees paid in direct relationship to benefits derived, or some balance between the two and, if so, on what basis should the balance be measured.

The hereinabove, and more data to follow, definitively show why the "expenditure control" feature of the Gann Proposition 4 Article XIIIB was adopted by California's voters. But not, at least not yet [late 2011], truly enforced. Local self-enforcement is required.

Wrong Concentration. It is little wonder that such groups as the "Tea Party" and "Occupy Wall Street" have evolved. There is a national sense that tax monies are being "misused". That term, of course, is both judgmental and subject to great personal interpretation. However, by reviewing the information provided in the foregoing Tables, one could quite easily reach the conclusion that "something is wrong here". And force an answer to the now overarching questions: ***"Where do my tax monies go?"*** And, ***"Should they go there?"*** Asked at the local level, and perhaps even of each State government.

It is time to examine from top to bottom all municipal functions and activities as to their need, beneficiaries, financing sources, effectiveness, and efficiency. Those last two terms are similar to the expression "Beauty is in the eyes of the beholder". In this instance a great argument can be made for the type of examination promoted by this Book. But performed by capable, well-trained, ethical, diversified-in-knowledge and absolutely unbiased local government experienced and attuned analysts. Not 'pure' CPAs, accountants, proverbial "bean counters", or "analysts" without basic technical knowledge of the extreme complexities, great nuances and at times bewilderingly wide array of local government services. Many "business types" have tried; most have failed. They talk a great and costly game, but expire by half-time. Their knowledge has run out. Again, 'nuff said.

"Costs Reasonably Borne" is constitutional law in California. That analysis process should be implemented fully in that State, and emulated across the United States by all local, and perhaps even State governments. The **business principles of "profit-center accounting" are applied by** the **Municipal Business System,** but while similar, the terminology, technology, and settings are hugely dissimilar from the so-called "private sector". The services illustrated in this Book are "public" governmental service offerings.

CITY of BEVERLEY HILLS, CALIFORNIA

This well known haunt and residence of the Stars, the *uber*-wealthy, the self-promoted or unearned "celebrities", and sometimes notorious, are always well-cared for by its City government. The City continually seeks municipal improvement and systems betterment.

Thus, in 2006 the City Council, on recommendation of the City Manager and Finance Director, contracted with Revenue Cost Specialists [corporate successor to Management Services, Inc. [**MSI**]] to identify, catalogue, and analyze the revenues and detail the costs for each of its "Personal Choice" and "Community [Tax] Supported Public Services".

Summarized Results. The following Tables are extracted from the **Cost of Services Study for the City of Beverly Hills,** dated and copyrighted April 2007. [31] These provide yet another listing of municipal services, their costs, and the revenues utilized to finance those identified services, and their beneficiaries. It is especially revealing that development, modification, and normally nit-picky changes to property have such overwhelming attention provided by the City. Its beauty and reputation thus is quite well protected.

The in-text "Tables" and "Illustrations" are not as extensive as those provided for Pasadena. Beverly Hills provides a wide variety of services, but it is neither as large as nor as old as Pasadena. Beverly Hills was not incorporated until 1914. However, the respective Reports illustrate the same tax-subsidy pattern was seen for Beverly Hills as existed in Pasadena. Purposefully, this Book does not delve into what has transpired in any of the five cities illustrated herein since the respective MSI/RCS Studies performed. However, each of the five did adopt many of the recommendations and recovered diverted taxes back to basic community-wide services.

Taxes. To anyone who has read this far, and who might be taking the message seriously, **_the message_** about improper and unfair utilization of taxes for Private Goods and Services should have gotten across. If not, their constituents will soon so inform.

Following Table 6 summarizes the six Service Group Tables which follow. That new revenue of $2.7 million was recognized by Beverly Hills. Of greater import, however, is that much of that money would come from those relatively few who are enjoying heavily tax-subsidized "Personal Choice" services. Tax-starved "Community Tax Supported Ser-

---

[31] The name "Beverly Hills" is copyrighted by the City and here is used due to its inclusion in the RCS Report, which document was contracted by, paid for by, and received and approved, and many recommendations adopted by the City Council, and implemented by the City Manager and departmental staff.

vices" are now being reduced, in most jurisdictions, far beyond what could be termed "reasonable and prudent". Both of the Pasadena and Beverly Hills City Councils adopted many of the MSI/RCS recommendations, thus retrieving taxes from Personal Choice Services to be used for Community Tax-Supported Services. And stabilizing their finances.

Summary of Personal Choice Public Services

The following Table 6 summarizes the recommendations and suggestions made in this Chapter.

Table 6
Summary

SERVICE GROUP	Revenue	Cost	Profit (Subsidy)	Percent Recovery Current	Percent Recovery Suggest	Possible New Revenue
DEVELOPMENT SERVICES	$6,668,549	$8,114,733	($1,446,184)	82.2%	VAR.	$1,255,100
PUBLIC SAFETY SERVICES	$2,300,934	$5,911,204	($3,610,270)	38.9%	VAR.	$1,129,450
LEISURE & CULTURAL SERVICES	$2,790,562	$6,927,012	($4,136,450)	40.3%	VAR.	$44,050
MAINT & ENTERPRISE SERVICES	$14,510,767	$16,755,176	($2,244,409)	86.6%	VAR.	$269,600
ADMINISTRATIVE SERVICES	$795	$165,565	($164,770)	0.5%	VAR.	$90,900
TOTAL	$26,271,607	$37,873,690	($11,602,083)	69.4%		$2,789,100

__Usual Array of Services.__ Following Tables 1 through 5 provide another listing of the service array provided by cities. Column 5 divulges the drainage of tax monies from "*Community-Supported* Public Services" to listed "*Personal Choice* Public Services". That diversion should be reviewed for virtually ___all___ taxes, save for the few chosen by affected governing bodies after full public disclosure and debate as to merit at public meetings. Each of Pasadena and Beverly Hills did so, and adjusted rates to recover previously-unknown tax diversions. Such policy decisions are difficult. Yet the City Councils of both cities did retrieve unwittingly diverted taxes, and annually continue to review and update revenue-to-cost match-ups and equity. Those two are extraordinary.

Explanatory text from the original *Beverly Hills Cost of Services Study Report* are included, thereby providing the "bean counting logic" instilled in the MSI, now RCS analytical personnel. Even more materials will be provided in the numbered and labeled ILLUSTRATIONS grouped within the text and in the back of the Book. When read in context with this text, these should complete the acquisition of sufficient knowledge by the reading municipal policy makers, staff and critics alike to make decisions as to acquisition of staff, software, or consulting aid to conduct revenue-cost matchup studies.

__Fit.__ As is the case for Pasadena in-text tables, transfer of these 8½" x 11" Tables from the Report to fit within this 7½" x 9¼ " smaller book was not easy, or "clean". The original text and Tables have been "lost" in the constant upgrade of software all competent business and governments periodically accomplish. So please excuse.

Table 1
Community Development Services
(Continued)

Ref #	Service Title	Revenue	Cost	Profit (Subsidy)	Percent Recovery		Possible New Revenue	
					Current	Suggest		
(1)	(2)	(3)	(4)	(5)	(6)	(7)	(8)	
S-030	ENV. IMPACT ASSMNT (NEG DEC)	$39,613	$20,301	$19,312	195.1%	100.0%	$(19,300)	
S-031	NEG DECLAR RECIRCULATION	$1,277	$677	$600	188.6%	100.0%	$0	#
S-032	ENVIRONMENTAL IMPACT REPORT	NA	NA	NA	NA	100.0%	$0	
S-033	TENTATIVE PARCEL MAP REVIEW	$6,646	$10,577	$(3,931)	62.8%	100.0%	$3,900	
S-034	TENTATIVE TRACT MAP REVIEW	$6,646	$11,849	$(5,203)	56.1%	100.0%	$5,200	
S-035	VESTING TENTATIVE MAP REVIEW	$3,969	$10,808	$(6,839)	36.7%	100.0%	$0	#
S-036	CONDOMINIUM CONVERSION	$4,119	$12,811	$(8,692)	32.2%	100.0%	$0	#
S-037	BOUNDARY LINE ADJUSTMENT	$1,561	$1,485	$76	105.1%	100.0%	$0	#
S-038	MASTER PLAN OF STRTS AMEND	$7,755	$9,695	$(1,940)	80.0%	100.0%	$0	#
S-039	CONFORMITY REVIEW	$69,239	$232,337	$(163,098)	29.8%	100.0%	$163,100	
S-040	TREE REMOVAL REVIEW	$635	$6,392	$(5,757)	9.9%	100.0%	$0	#
S-041	TELECOMM/SAT. DISH ANTENNA	$1,000	$6,716	$(5,716)	14.9%	100.0%	$0	#
S-042	OUTDOOR VENDING PERMIT	$254	$4,706	$(4,452)	5.4%	100.0%	$0	#
S-043	TEMPORARY USE PERMIT	$0	$4,444	$(4,444)	0.0%	100.0%	$0	#
S-044	PUBLIC NOTICING	$43,774	$43,860	$(86)	99.8%	100.0%	$100	
S-045	PUBLIC NOTICE SIGN PROCESSING	$23,331	$23,686	$(355)	98.5%	100.0%	$400	
S-046	EXTENSION OF TIME	$8,178	$7,036	$1,142	116.2%	100.0%	$(1,100)	
S-047	PLANNING DECISION AMENDMENT	$5,500	$5,849	$(349)	94.0%	100.0%	$300	
S-048	APPEAL TO PLANNING COMM.	$151	$3,468	$(3,317)	4.4%	100.0%	$0	#
S-049	APPEAL TO THE CITY COUNCIL	$302	$4,732	$(4,430)	6.4%	100.0%	$0	#
S-050	TRAFFIC ANALYSIS REVIEW	$77,500	$120,556	$(43,056)	64.3%	100.0%	$43,100	
S-051	CONSULTANT SERVICES	NA	NA	NA	NA	100.0%	$0	
S-052	GENERAL PLAN MAINTENANCE	$80,000	$100,018	$(20,018)	80.0%	100.0%	$20,000	
S-053	FINAL PARCEL MAP	$7,088	$4,269	$2,819	166.0%	100.0%	$(2,800)	
S-054	FINAL TRACT MAP	$7,088	$6,814	$274	104.0%	100.0%	$(300)	
S-055	LOT LINE ADJUSTMENT	$0	$509	$(509)	0.0%	100.0%	$0	#
S-056	PUBLIC IMPROVE PLAN CHECK	$6,652	$4,569	$2,083	145.6%	100.0%	$0	
S-057	MINOR PLAN CHECK REVISION	$0	$127	$(127)	0.0%	100.0%	$0	#
S-058	EASEMENT PROCESSING	$0	$1,273	$(1,273)	0.0%	100.0%	$0	#
S-059	PUBLIC WORKS INSPECT/REINSP	$50	$110	$(60)	45.5%	100.0%	$0	#
S-060	SUBSEQ. SUBMITTAL OF PLANS	$0	$127	$(127)	0.0%	100.0%	$0	#
S-061	COVENANT AND AGREEMENT	$0	$2,545	$(2,545)	0.0%	100.0%	$0	#
S-062	STORMWATER POLL PREV PLAN	$0	$3,951	$(3,951)	0.0%	100.0%	$4,000	
S-063	STAND URBAN S/W MITIG PLAN	$0	$1,097	$(1,097)	0.0%	100.0%	$1,100	
S-064	BUSINESS NPDES INSPECTION	$0	$59,241	$(59,241)	0.0%	100.0%	$59,200	
S-065	DRILLING PERMIT	$14,120	$18,516	$(4,396)	76.3%	100.0%	$0	#
S-066	DEVEL OF OIL, GAS, & MINERALS	$6,184	$8,229	$(2,045)	75.1%	100.0%	$0	#

Table 1
Community Development Services
(Continued)

Ref #	Service Title	Revenue	Cost	Profit (Subsidy)	Percent Recovery Current	Suggest	Possible New Revenue	
(1)	(2)	(3)	(4)	(5)	(6)	(7)	(8)	
S-067	APPROVAL EXPLOR BOUNDARY	NA	NA	NA	NA	100.0%	$0	#
S-068	MINING & EXTRACTION APPL.	$3,263	$1,018	$2,245	320.5%	100.0%	$0	#
S-069	HOUSING MOVE PERMIT	$0	$776	$(776)	0.0%	100.0%	$0	#
S-070	TREE REPLACEMENT	$0	$943	$(943)	0.0%	100.0%	$900	
S-071	REQUEST FOR TRAFFIC MARKINGS	$0	$13,427	$(13,427)	0.0%	100.0%	$0	**
S-072	RES. STREET ADDR NUM PAINT	$0	$547	$(547)	0.0%	100.0%	$0	**
S-073	MAP COPYING SERVICE	$3,500	$3,742	$(242)	93.5%	100.0%	$0	
S-074	DRIVEWAY APPR STREET USE	$15,535	$43,951	$(28,416)	35.3%	100.0%	$28,400	
S-075	SIDEWALK REPLACE STREET USE	$4,040	$1,993	$2,047	202.7%	100.0%	$(2,000)	
S-076	CURB & GUTTER STREET USE	$3,680	$5,237	$(1,557)	70.3%	100.0%	$1,600	
S-077	CURB DRAIN STREET USE PERMIT	$36,780	$58,942	$(22,162)	62.4%	100.0%	$22,200	
S-078	SURFACE ENCROACH PERMIT	$558	$780	$(222)	71.5%	100.0%	$200	
S-079	SUBSURFACE ENCROACH PERMIT	$3,262	$6,054	$(2,792)	53.9%	100.0%	$2,800	
S-080	SUBSURFACE LATRL SUPP ENCR	$7,280	$7,360	$(80)	98.9%	100.0%	$0	
S-081	SHORT-TERM STRT LANE CLOSE	$12,900	$12,328	$572	104.6%	100.0%	$(600)	
S-082	LONG TERM STRT LANE CLOSURE	$129	$1,255	$(1,126)	10.3%	100.0%	$0	#
S-083	STREET/R-O-W VACATION	$0	$6,020	$(6,020)	0.0%	100.0%	$0	#
S-084	BORING EXCAVATION PERMIT	$220	$1,781	$(1,561)	12.4%	100.0%	$1,600	
S-085	UTILITY ENCROACHMENT PERMIT	$20,200	$15,241	$4,959	132.5%	100.0%	$(5,000)	
S-086	PAVING REPLACEMENT INSPECT	$0	$45,778	$(45,778)	0.0%	100.0%	$45,800	
S-087	SEWER LATERAL INSTALL PERMIT	$33,008	$26,915	$6,093	122.6%	100.0%	$(6,100)	
S-088	HEAVY HAUL PERMIT	$419,240	$300,162	$119,078	139.7%	100.0%	$(119,100)	
S-089	DUMPSTER PERMIT	$12,900	$12,252	$648	105.3%	100.0%	$0	
S-090	PERMANENT ENCROACH PERMIT	$17,000	$18,059	$(1,059)	94.1%	100.0%	$1,100	
S-091	LOADING/UNLOAD STREET USE	$322,500	$306,300	$16,200	105.3%	100.0%	$0	
S-092	MOTORCOACH LOAD/UNLOAD	$7,280	$21,441	$(14,161)	34.0%	100.0%	$14,200	
S-093	MOVING TRUCK STREET USE	$51,668	$88,125	$(36,457)	58.6%	100.0%	$36,500	
S-094	SURVEYING STREET USE PERMIT	$0	$409	$(409)	0.0%	100.0%	$400	
S-095	SPECIAL EVENT ENCROACHMENT	$3,870	$3,676	$194	105.3%	100.0%	$0	
S-096	SPEC EV VALET PARK STRT USE	$14,144	$24,657	$(10,513)	57.4%	100.0%	$10,500	
S-097	PARK METER HEAD REMOVE/INST	$2,632	$3,556	$(924)	74.0%	100.0%	$900	
S-098	TRAFF/PARK SIGN & POST REMOV	$162	$514	$(352)	31.5%	100.0%	$400	
S-099	CONSTR BARR/FENCE STRT USE	$6,450	$7,211	$(761)	89.4%	100.0%	$800	
S-100	COMM. STRT LGHT RELOCATION	$0	$1,264	$(1,264)	0.0%	100.0%	$1,300	
S-101	RES. STREET LIGHT RELOCATION	$0	$2,367	$(2,367)	0.0%	100.0%	$2,400	
S-102	NEWSRACK ENCROACHMENT	$5,761	$34,948	$(29,187)	16.5%	50.0%	$3,200	
S-103	AMEND TO STREET USE PERMIT	$0	$23	$(23)	0.0%	100.0%	$0	

Table 1
Community Development Services
(Continued)

Ref # (1)	Service Title (2)	Revenue (3)	Cost (4)	Profit (Subsidy) (5)	Percent Recovery Current (6)	Percent Recovery Suggest (7)	Possible New Revenue (8)	
S-104	BUILDING PERMIT/INSPECTION	$2,593,686	$2,015,429	$578,257	128.7%	100.0%	$0	*
S-105	ELECTRICAL PERMIT/INSPECTION	$240,608	$146,535	$94,073	164.2%	100.0%	$0	*
S-106	MECHANICAL PERMIT/INSPECTION	$164,639	$102,950	$61,689	159.9%	100.0%	$0	*
S-107	PLUMBING PERMIT/INSPECTION	$159,988	$96,622	$63,366	165.6%	100.0%	$0	*
S-108	BUILDING PLAN CHECK	$1,192,414	$1,954,643	$(762,229)	61.0%	100.0%	$0	*
S-109	ELECTRICAL PLAN CHECK	$72,834	$102,440	$(29,606)	71.1%	100.0%	$0	*
S-110	MECHANICAL PLAN CHECK	$50,094	$79,649	$(29,555)	62.9%	100.0%	$0	*
S-111	PLUMBING PLAN CHECK	$40,342	$44,861	$(4,519)	89.9%	100.0%	$0	*
S-112	DEMOLITION PERMIT	$38,600	$50,696	$(12,096)	76.1%	100.0%	$12,100	
S-113	SANDBLASTING PERMIT	$2,036	$9,383	$(7,347)	21.7%	100.0%	$7,300	
S-114	RESTAURANT NEW ENCROACH	$129	$226	$(97)	57.1%	100.0%	$100	
S-115	MODIF/ALT MAT'L/DESIGN/METH	$3,448	$27,189	$(23,741)	12.7%	100.0%	$11,850	**
S-116	TREE REMOVAL	$255	$2,232	$(1,977)	11.4%	100.0%	$2,000	
S-117	BOND PROCESSING/REFUND	$58,992	$76,418	$(17,426)	77.2%	100.0%	$17,400	
S-118	SEWER CONNECTION PROCESSING	$0	$19,252	$(19,252)	0.0%	100.0%	$19,300	
S-119	COVENANT PROC RECORDATION	$0	$424	$(424)	0.0%	100.0%	$0	#
S-120	TEMP. CERT. OF OCCUPANCY	$15,325	$30,308	$(14,983)	50.6%	100.0%	$15,000	
S-121	BLDG ADDRESS CHANGE REQ	$78	$551	$(473)	14.2%	100.0%	$0	#
S-122	STREET NAME CHANGE REQUEST	$0	$551	$(551)	0.0%	100.0%	$0	#
S-123	GARAGE/ESTATE SALE PERMIT	$2,858	$3,207	$(349)	89.1%	100.0%	$300	
S-124	DUPLICATE INSPECTION CARD	$867	$1,148	$(281)	75.5%	100.0%	$300	
S-125	DUPLICATE CERT OF OCCUPANCY	$124	$610	$(486)	20.3%	100.0%	$500	
S-126	CONDITION MONITOR ANNL INSP	$0	$12,853	$(12,853)	0.0%	100.0%	$12,900	
S-127	RENT CONTROL ENFORCE/ADMIN	$0	$170,265	$(170,265)	0.0%	100.0%	$170,300	*
		$6,668,549	$8,114,733	$(1,446,184)	82.2%		$1,255,100	

Key to Symbols:
    # - Occurs Infrequently
    ** - Market Sensitive
    * - See Text

__City As Impartial Arbiter of Land Use.__ The City staff, Planning Commission and the City Council require the processes enumerated in the above list as the price of community review, input and ultimate acceptance by neighboring properties of land development. Such municipal review is basically required by State law, assigning the role of impartial arbiter of land use decisions to local government -- cities and counties.

City of Beverly Hills Cost of Services Study

Public Safety Services

These service centers are identified for those who use the City public safety services disproportionately from others. Comments on specific service centers are made following Table 2.

Table 2
Public Safety Services

Ref # (1)	Service Title (2)	Revenue (3)	Cost (4)	Profit (Subsidy) (5)	Percent Recovery		Possible New Revenue (8)	
					Current (6)	Suggest (7)		
S-128	POLICE FALSE ALARM RESPONSE	$0	$487,961	$(487,961)	0.0%	100.0%	$0	**
S-129	SECOND RESPONSE CALL-BACK	$0	$327,735	$(327,735)	0.0%	100.0%	$32,770	**
S-130	DUI COLLISION EMERGENCY RESP	NA	NA	NA	NA	100.0%	$0	
S-131	SPECIAL EVENT POLICE SERVICE	NA	NA	NA	NA	100.0%	$0	
S-132	SPECIAL RESP. TEAM CALL-OUT	NA	NA	NA	NA	100.0%	$0	
S-133	VEHICLE IMPOUND RELEASE	$195,261	$408,602	$(213,341)	47.8%	100.0%	$213,300	
S-134	VEHICLE REPOSSESS PROCESS	$2,250	$4,677	$(2,427)	48.1%	100.0%	$0	
S-135	CONCEALED WEAPONS PERMIT	$0	$1,833	$(1,833)	0.0%	100.0%	$0	#
S-136	BACKGROUND INVESTIGATION	$1,182	$2,477	$(1,295)	47.7%	100.0%	$1,300	
S-137	ADULT ENTERTAIN BUSINESS PMT	$0	$1,258	$(1,258)	0.0%	100.0%	$0	#
S-138	ADULT ENTERTAINER PERMIT	$0	$824	$(824)	0.0%	100.0%	$0	#
S-139	**PRIVATE CLUB BUSINESS PERMIT**	$3,573	$1,282	$2,291	278.7%	100.0%	$0	#
S-140	ESCORT BUREAU PERMIT	$1,200	$1,258	$(58)	95.4%	100.0%	$0	#
S-141	FORTUNE TELLER PERMIT	$1,200	$1,258	$(58)	95.4%	100.0%	$0	#
S-142	DATING SERVICE PERMIT	$1,200	$1,258	$(58)	95.4%	100.0%	$0	#
S-143	PUBLIC DANCING PERMIT	$1,623	$1,282	$341	126.6%	100.0%	$0	#
S-144	**MASSAGE PARLOR PERMIT**	$873	$1,258	$(385)	69.4%	100.0%	$0	#
S-145	MASSAGE TECHNICIAN PERMIT	$169	$393	$(224)	43.0%	100.0%	$0	#
S-146	PAWNSHOP PERMIT	$3,986	$28,925	$(24,939)	13.8%	100.0%	$24,900	
S-147	SECONDHAND DEALER PERMIT	$1,436	$10,696	$(9,260)	13.4%	100.0%	$9,300	
S-148	FIREARM SALES PERMIT	$299	$917	$(618)	32.6%	100.0%	$600	
S-149	**PRIVATE POLICE PATROL PERMIT**	$559	$393	$166	142.2%	100.0%	$0	#
S-150	PROFESS SALES PROMOTE PRMT	$335	$393	$(58)	85.2%	100.0%	$0	#
S-151	PEDDLER PERMIT	$170	$287	$(117)	59.2%	100.0%	$100	
S-152	TOW SERVICE BUSINESS PERMIT	$567	$1,269	$(702)	44.7%	100.0%	$0	#
S-153	TOW DRIVER PERMIT	$0	$192	$(192)	0.0%	100.0%	$0	#
S-154	FINGERPRINTING ON REQUEST	$40,750	$71,100	$(30,350)	57.3%	100.0%	$30,400	
S-155	POLICE RECORD SEAL REQUEST	$0	$78,239	$(78,239)	0.0%	100.0%	$78,200	
S-156	ARREST VERIFICATION	$0	$669	$(669)	0.0%	100.0%	$700	
S-157	LOCAL CRIMINAL HISTORY RPRT	$5,360	$9,105	$(3,745)	58.9%	100.0%	$3,700	
S-158	**IMMIGRATION CLEARANCE LETTER**	$1,190	$1,077	$113	110.5%	100.0%	$(100)	
S-159	NON-STATE MANDATE RPRT GEN	$0	$58,260	$(58,260)	0.0%	100.0%	$5,830	**
S-160	POLICE REPORT/DOC. REPROD.	$718	$1,705	$(987)	42.1%	100.0%	$0	
S-161	PHOTO REPRODUCTION	$10,303	$35,819	$(25,516)	28.8%	100.0%	$12,750	**
S-162	POLICE DISPATCH TAPE COPY	$200	$540	$(340)	37.0%	100.0%	$0	
S-163	**POLICE AUDIO TAPE COPY**	$67	$56	$11	119.6%	100.0%	$0	

Table 2
Public Safety Services
(Continued)

| Ref # | Service Title | Revenue | Cost | Profit (Subsidy) | Percent Recovery | | Possible New Revenue |
| | | | | | Current | Suggest | |
(1)	(2)	(3)	(4)	(5)	(6)	(7)	(8)
S-164	POLICE VIDEO TAPE COPY	$3,990	$6,169	$(2,179)	64.7%	100.0%	$2,200
S-165	COMPUTER/DATABASE RESEARCH	$0	$0	$0	0.0%	100.0%	$0
S-166	BUSINESS ENGINE COMPANY INSP	$10,000	$244,119	$(234,119)	4.1%	100.0%	$0
S-167	MFR ENGINE COMPANY INSPECT	$5,000	$99,196	$(94,196)	5.0%	100.0%	$0
S-168	AMBULANCE RESPONSE SERVICES	$1,658,000	$1,763,126	$(105,126)	94.0%	100.0%	$105,100
S-169	FIRE FALSE ALARM RESPONSE	$0	$603,926	$(603,926)	0.0%	100.0%	$0
S-170	NEGLIGENT INCIDENT RESPONSE	NA	NA	NA	NA	100.0%	$0
S-171	HAZARD MATERIAL INCID RESP	NA	NA	NA	NA	100.0%	$0
S-172	ARSON INVESTIGATION	$0	$65,061	$(65,061)	0.0%	100.0%	$0
S-173	VEGETATION MANAGE PROGRAM	$0	$596,936	$(596,936)	0.0%	100.0%	$0
S-174	FIRE SPRINKLER PLAN CHCK/INSP	$83,442	$361,006	$(277,564)	23.1%	100.0%	$277,600
S-175	FIRE ALARM PLAN CHECK/INSP	$42,400	$181,621	$(139,221)	23.3%	100.0%	$139,200
S-176	FIRE HOOD PLAN CHECK/INSPECT	$24,150	$44,546	$(20,396)	54.2%	100.0%	$20,400
S-177	FIRE PERMIT PLAN CHECK	$33,000	$35,739	$(2,739)	92.3%	100.0%	$0
S-178	STATE MANDATE FIRE INSPECTION	$0	$17,865	$(17,865)	0.0%	100.0%	$17,900
S-179	HI-RISE FIRE INSPECTION	$42,798	$88,431	$(45,633)	48.4%	100.0%	$22,800
S-180	TANK INSTALL/REMOVAL INSPECT	$4,050	$8,039	$(3,989)	50.4%	100.0%	$4,000
S-181	TENT/CANOPY FIRE PERMIT	$45,089	$65,449	$(20,360)	68.9%	100.0%	$20,400
S-182	FIRE CODE PERMIT	$24,899	$48,387	$(23,488)	51.5%	100.0%	$23,500
S-183	FIRE PREVENTION INSPECTION	$48,745	$131,306	$(82,561)	37.1%	100.0%	$82,600
S-184	FIRE ALARM PERMIT PROCESSING	$0	$5,427	$(5,427)	0.0%	100.0%	$0
S-185	FIRE INCIDENT REPORT COPY	$300	$1,242	$(942)	24.2%	100.0%	$0
S-186	FIRE DEPARTMENT STAND-BY	$600	$615	$(15)	97.6%	100.0%	$0
		$2,300,934	$5,911,204	$(3,610,270)	38.9%		$1,129,450

Key to Symbols:
- Occurs infrequently
** - Market Sensitive
* - See Text

Table 3
Leisure and Cultural Services

Ref #	Service Title	Revenue	Cost	Profit (Subsidy)	Percent Recovery		Possible New Revenue
					Current	Suggest	
(1)	(2)	(3)	(4)	(5)	(6)	(7)	(8)
S-187	PRESCHOOL PROGRAM	$374,434	$977,163	($602,729)	38.3%	60.0%	See Text
S-188	PARENT AND ME CLASSES	$167,443	$394,627	($227,184)	42.4%	60.0%	See Text
S-189	ADVENTURE CAMP PROGRAM	$293,891	$933,735	($639,844)	31.5%	50.0%	See Text
S-190	SUMMER CAMP PROGRAM	$409,409	$968,499	($559,090)	42.3%	55.0%	See Text
S-191	YOUTH RECREATION CLASSES	$555,658	$619,229	$(63,571)	89.7%	100.0%	See Text
S-192	ADULT RECREATION CLASSES	$95,068	$677,927	$(582,859)	14.0%	20.0%	See Text
S-193	ADULT SPORTS PROGRAM	$343,385	$749,594	($406,209)	45.8%	70.0%	See Text
S-194	FARMERS MARKET	$93,500	$410,850	($317,350)	22.8%	30.0%	See Text
S-195	RECREATION REGISTR. PROC	$0	$240,087	$(240,087)	0.0%	100.0%	See Text
S-196	PARK BBQ/TABLE RENTAL	$12,625	$15,401	$(2,776)	82.0%	100.0%	See Text
S-197	COMM GROUP/SCHOOL BALLFLD	$0	$401,279	$(401,279)	0.0%	100.0%	See Text
S-198	FILM PERMIT	$234,813	$113,211	$121,602	207.4%	Market	See Text
S-199	STUDENT FILM PERMIT	$0	$7,325	$(7,325)	0.0%	20.0%	$750
S-200	STILL PHOTO PERMIT	$36,292	$12,176	$24,116	298.1%	Market	See Text
S-201	SPECIAL EVENT PERMIT - SMALL	$29,898	$50,567	$(20,669)	59.1%	100.0%	$20,700
S-202	SPECIAL EVENT PERMIT - LARGE	$77,821	$74,304	$3,517	104.7%	100.0%	$0
S-203	INTER-LIBRARY LOAN PROCESS	$2,250	$126,455	($124,205)	1.8%	10.0%	$0
S-204	LIBRARY ITEM RESERV SERVICE	$5,775	$46,354	$(40,579)	12.5%	15.0%	$0
S-205	REPLACE LOST LIBRARY CARD	$11,000	$12,430	$(1,430)	88.5%	100.0%	$0
S-206	REPL LOST/DAMG LIBRARY MAT.	$12,600	$35,220	$(22,620)	35.8%	100.0%	$22,600
S-207	LIBRARY COLL PHOTO/CD REPR	NA	NA	NA	NA	100.0%	$0
S-208	PASSPORT PROCESSING	$34,700	$60,579	($25,879)	57.3%	100.0%	$0
S-209	FACIL RENT AFTER-HR MONITOR	NA	NA	NA	NA	100.0%	$0
		$2,790,562	$6,927,012	($4,136,450)	40.3%		$44,050

The services in the above table suggest that the reader refer to the text before passing judgement on any of the fees. This is because leisure and cultural services are market sensitive and any fee increases without an appropriate market analysis could "kill" the services. This comment does not mean to imply that additional revenues are unavailable. It just means that determining the appropriate fees should be left to the recreation professionals unless the City Council is indifferent toward continuing a particular service.

This group of services can be viewed as being ways in which the City can raise monies equitably, legally, properly, and in significant amounts, as needed. A case can be made for each that all should be done, otherwise certain segments of the public and/or certain property owners are being subsidized by the taxes paid by others.

Table 4
Maintenance and Enterprise Services

Ref #	Service Title	Revenue	Cost	Profit (Subsidy)	Percent Recovery		Possible New Revenue
					Current	Suggest	
(1)	(2)	(3)	(4)	(5)	(6)	(7)	(8)
S-210	PREFERENTIAL PARKING PERMIT	$231,859	$364,238	$(132,379)	63.7%	100.0%	$132,400
S-211	OVERNIGHT PARKING PERMIT	$392,971	$406,578	$(13,607)	96.7%	100.0%	$13,600
S-212	VALET SHORT TERM PARK PRMT	$70,556	$93,502	$(22,946)	75.5%	100.0%	$22,900
S-213	COMM. VALET PARKING APPL	$1,130	$8,192	$(7,062)	13.8%	100.0%	$7,100
S-214	COMM. VALET PARK TRANSFER	$2,033	$2,345	$(312)	86.7%	100.0%	$300
S-215	6 MNTH COMM. VALET PARK PMT	$7,747	$10,388	$(2,641)	74.6%	100.0%	$2,600
S-216	ANNL COMM. VALET PARK PMT	$40,775	$50,862	$(10,087)	80.2%	100.0%	$10,100
S-217	MODIF. TO COMM. VALET PERMIT	$0	$4,970	$(4,970)	0.0%	100.0%	$5,000
S-218	VALET PARKING ATTEND PRMT	$11,710	$24,369	$(12,659)	48.1%	100.0%	$12,700
S-219	TAXICAB BUSINESS PERMIT.	NA	NA	NA	NA	100.0%	$0
S-220	TAXICAB OPERATOR PERMIT	$6,426	$13,494	$(7,068)	47.6%	100.0%	$7,100
S-221	ANNUAL TAXICAB VEHICLE PRMT	$92,586	$122,069	$(29,483)	75.8%	100.0%	$29,500
S-222	TAXI VEHICLE PERMIT REPLACE	$360	$743	$(383)	48.5%	100.0%	$400
S-223	VALET ATTD/TAXI DRIVE APPEAL	$0	$10,405	$(10,405)	0.0%	100.0%	$5,200 **
S-224	NURSE/CAREGIVER PARK PRMT	$0	$2,461	$(2,461)	0.0%	35.0%	$900
S-225	WATER SERVICE INSTALLATION	$100,000	$104,646	$(4,646)	95.6%	100.0%	$0
S-226	FIRE FLOW TEST	$12,000	$12,919	$(919)	92.9%	100.0%	$0
S-227	WATER METER TEST	$422	$4,306	$(3,884)	9.8%	100.0%	$0
S-228	WATER DELINQ. TURN-OFF/ON	$5,340	$14,472	$(9,132)	36.9%	100.0%	$9,100
S-229	CUSTOMR REQ WATER TURN-OFF	$5,340	$14,472	$(9,132)	36.9%	100.0%	$9,100
S-230	UNAUTHOR TURN ON OF WATER	$2,164	$3,618	$(1,454)	59.8%	100.0%	$1,500
S-231	TEMP. METER RENTAL SERVICE	$800	$861	$(61)	92.9%	100.0%	$100
S-232	EMERG. SEWAGE SPILL RESP	NA	NA	NA	NA	100.0%	$0
S-233	PARKING STRUCT. OPERATIONS	$13,526,548	$15,485,159	$(1,958,611)	87.4%	100.0%	See Text
S-234	PRIV TREE REMOVAL IN R-O-W	$0	$107	$(107)	0.0%	100.0%	$0
		$14,510,767	$16,755,176	$(2,244,409)	86.6%		$269,600

Key to Symbols:
    ** - Market Sensitive

Table 5
Administrative Services

| Ref # | Service Title | Revenue | Cost | Profit (Subsidy) | Percent Recovery | | Possible New Revenue |
| | | | | | Current | Suggest | |
(1)	(2)	(3)	(4)	(5)	(6)	(7)	(8)
S-235	NEW BUSINESS TAX PROCESS	$0	$14,180	$(14,180)	0.0%	100.0%	$14,200
S-236	BUSINESS TAX RENEW PROC.	$0	$76,560	$(76,560)	0.0%	100.0%	$76,600
S-237	PUBLIC RECORDS REQUEST	$0	$73,826	$(73,826)	0.0%	100.0%	$0
S-238	RECORDS RESEARCH	NA	NA	NA	NA	100.0%	$0
S-239	CITY CLERK CERTIFICATION	$22	$45	$(23)	48.9%	100.0%	$0
S-240	AGENDA MAILING SERVICE	$474	$554	$(80)	85.6%	100.0%	$100
S-241	MINUTE MAILING SERVICE	$93	$152	$(59)	61.2%	100.0%	$0
S-242	ACTION MINUTE MAILING SRVC	$93	$152	$(59)	61.2%	100.0%	$0
S-243	CD COPY REQUEST	$0	$8	$(8)	0.0%	100.0%	$0
S-244	MEETING AUDIO TAPE COPY	$24	$35	$(11)	68.6%	100.0%	$0
S-245	DVD COPY SERVICE	$89	$53	$36	167.9%	100.0%	$0
		$795	$165,565	$(164,770)	0.5%	$11	$90,900

Result of Adoption. If all the recommendations and suggestions made in this Chapter and in Appendix A are adopted, the City would raise about $2.8 Million on an annual basis.

Taxpayer Equity Achieved. By taking such positive actions, the City's financial picture would be improved, far more equity between taxpayers and fee-payers could be gained, and fairness between property-related and non-property-related services could be secured.

The above table shows that the City is subsidizing PERSONAL CHOICE PUBLIC SERVICES with $11,602,083 in tax dollars. Should the City Council feel that tax dollars are insufficient, this chapter has shown that there are many opportunities to either increase the fee or lower the cost of PERSONAL CHOICE PUBLIC SERVICES.

Schedule of Revenues & Costs in Sequence by Possible New Revenue

The following schedule lists all of the services in sequence by possible new revenue or grouped by the special conditions that exist for the services.

CITY OF BEVERLY HILLS
SUMMARY OF REVENUES, COSTS, AND SUBSIDIES BY ORDER OF POSSIBLE NEW REVENUE
FISCAL YEAR 2006-2007

REF #	SERVICE TITLE	REVENUE	COST	PROFIT/ (SUBSIDY)	PERCENT RECOVERY CURRENT	SUGGEST	POSSIBLE NEW REVENUE	
S-002	ARCHITECTURAL REVIEW	$108,049	$386,532	($278,483)	28.0%	100.0%	$278,500	
S-174	FIRE SPRINKLER PLAN CHECK/INSPECT	$83,442	$361,006	($277,564)	23.1%	100.0%	$277,600	
S-133	VEHICLE IMPOUND RELEASE	$195,261	$408,602	($213,341)	47.8%	100.0%	$213,300	
S-003	DESIGN REVIEW	$67,032	$256,424	($189,392)	26.1%	100.0%	$189,400	
S-127	RENT CONTROL ENFORCEMENT/ADMIN	$0	$170,265	($170,265)	0.0%	100.0%	$170,300	*
S-039	CONFORMITY REVIEW	$69,239	$232,337	($163,098)	29.8%	100.0%	$163,100	
S-175	FIRE ALARM PLAN CHECK/INSPECTION	$42,400	$181,621	($139,221)	23.3%	100.0%	$139,200	
S-210	PREFERENTIAL PARKING PERMIT	$231,859	$364,238	($132,379)	63.7%	100.0%	$132,400	
S-168	AMBULANCE RESPONSE SERVICES	$1,658,000	$1,763,126	($105,126)	94.0%	100.0%	$105,100	
S-183	FIRE PREVENTION INSPECTION	$48,745	$131,306	($82,561)	37.1%	100.0%	$82,600	
S-155	POLICE RECORD SEALING REQUEST	$0	$78,239	($78,239)	0.0%	100.0%	$78,200	
S-236	BUSINESS TAX RENEWAL PROCESSING	$0	$76,560	($76,560)	0.0%	100.0%	$76,600	
S-064	BUSINESS NPDES INSPECTION	$0	$59,241	($59,241)	0.0%	100.0%	$59,200	
S-086	PAVING REPLACEMENT INSPECTION	$0	$45,778	($45,778)	0.0%	100.0%	$45,800	
S-008	DEVELOPMENT PLAN REVIEW	$33,026	$77,461	($44,435)	42.6%	100.0%	$44,400	
S-050	TRAFFIC ANALYSIS REVIEW	$77,500	$120,558	($43,058)	64.3%	100.0%	$43,100	
S-007	OPEN AIR DINING PLAN REVIEW	$7,401	$47,364	($39,963)	15.6%	100.0%	$40,000	
S-093	MOVING TRUCK STREET USE PERMIT	$51,668	$88,125	($36,457)	58.6%	100.0%	$36,500	
S-004	R-1 SINGLE FAMILY REVIEW	$95,266	$128,614	($33,348)	74.1%	100.0%	$33,300	
S-129	SECOND RESPONSE CALL-BACK	$0	$327,735	($327,735)	0.0%	100.0%	$32,770	**
S-154	FINGERPRINTING ON REQUEST	$40,750	$71,100	($30,350)	57.3%	100.0%	$30,400	
S-221	ANNUAL TAXICAB VEHICLE PERMIT	$92,586	$122,069	($29,483)	75.8%	100.0%	$29,500	
S-074	DRIVEWAY APPROACH STREET USE PERMIT	$15,535	$43,951	($28,416)	35.3%	100.0%	$28,400	
S-146	PAWNSHOP PERMIT	$3,986	$28,925	($24,939)	13.8%	100.0%	$24,900	
S-182	FIRE CODE PERMIT	$24,899	$48,387	($23,488)	51.5%	100.0%	$23,500	
S-212	VALET SHORT TERM PARKING PERMIT	$70,556	$93,502	($22,946)	75.5%	100.0%	$22,900	
S-179	HI-RISE FIRE INSPECTION	$42,798	$88,431	($45,633)	48.4%	100.0%	$22,800	
S-206	REPLACE LOST/DAMAGED LIBRARY MAT.	$12,600	$35,220	($22,620)	35.8%	100.0%	$22,600	
S-077	CURB DRAIN STREET USE PERMIT	$36,780	$58,942	($22,162)	62.4%	100.0%	$22,200	
S-029	ENVIRON. CATEGORICAL EXEMPTION	$8,242	$29,325	($21,083)	28.1%	100.0%	$21,100	
S-201	SPECIAL EVENT PERMIT - SMALL	$29,898	$50,567	($20,669)	59.1%	100.0%	$20,700	
S-176	FIRE HOOD PLAN CHECK/INSPECTION	$24,150	$44,546	($20,396)	54.2%	100.0%	$20,400	
S-181	TENT/CANOPY FIRE PERMIT	$45,089	$65,449	($20,360)	68.9%	100.0%	$20,400	
S-052	GENERAL PLAN MAINTENANCE	$80,000	$100,018	($20,018)	80.0%	100.0%	$20,000	
S-118	SEWER CONNECTION PROCESSING	$0	$19,252	($19,252)	0.0%	100.0%	$19,300	
S-178	STATE MANDATED FIRE INSPECTION	$0	$17,865	($17,865)	0.0%	100.0%	$17,900	
S-117	BOND PROCESSING/REFUND	$58,992	$76,418	($17,426)	77.2%	100.0%	$17,400	
S-120	TEMPORARY CERTIFICATE OF OCCUPANCY	$15,325	$30,308	($14,983)	50.6%	100.0%	$15,000	
S-092	MOTORCOACH LOAD/UNLOAD STRT USE PMT	$7,280	$21,441	($14,161)	34.0%	100.0%	$14,200	
S-235	NEW BUSINESS TAX PROCESSING	$0	$14,180	($14,180)	0.0%	100.0%	$14,200	
S-010	MINOR ACCOMMODATION REVIEW	$18,609	$32,168	($13,559)	57.8%	100.0%	$13,600	
S-211	OVERNIGHT PARKING PERMIT	$392,971	$406,578	($13,607)	96.7%	100.0%	$13,600	
S-126	CONDITION MONITORING ANNUAL INSPECT	$0	$12,853	($12,853)	0.0%	100.0%	$12,900	
S-161	PHOTO REPRODUCTION	$10,303	$35,819	($25,516)	28.8%	100.0%	$12,750	**
S-218	VALET PARKING ATTENDANT PERMIT	$11,710	$24,369	($12,659)	48.1%	100.0%	$12,700	
S-112	DEMOLITION PERMIT	$38,600	$50,696	($12,096)	76.1%	100.0%	$12,100	
S-115	MODIF/ALTERNATE MAT'L/DESIGN/METHOD	$3,448	$27,189	($23,741)	12.7%	100.0%	$11,850	**
S-096	SPEC EVENT VALET PARK STRT USE PMT	$14,144	$24,657	($10,513)	57.4%	100.0%	$10,500	
S-009	VARIANCE PROCESSING	$15,243	$25,579	($10,336)	59.6%	100.0%	$10,300	
S-216	ANNUAL COMMERCIAL VALET PARKING PMT	$40,775	$50,862	($10,087)	80.2%	100.0%	$10,100	
S-020	IN-LIEU PARKING REVIEW	$7,621	$17,663	($10,042)	43.1%	100.0%	$10,000	
S-147	SECONDHAND DEALER PERMIT	$1,436	$10,696	($9,260)	13.4%	100.0%	$9,300	
S-228	WATER DELINQUENT TURN-OFF/ON	$5,340	$14,472	($9,132)	36.9%	100.0%	$9,100	
S-011	CONCEPT REVIEW	$53,601	$71,277	($17,676)	75.2%	100.0%	$8,850	**
S-113	SANDBLASTING PERMIT	$2,036	$9,383	($7,347)	21.7%	100.0%	$7,300	
S-213	COMMERCIAL VALET PARKING APPL.	$1,130	$8,192	($7,062)	13.8%	100.0%	$7,100	
S-220	TAXICAB OPERATOR PERMIT	$6,426	$13,494	($7,068)	47.6%	100.0%	$7,100	
S-006	SECOND UNIT REVIEW	$14,354	$20,559	($6,205)	69.8%	100.0%	$6,200	
S-159	NON-STATE MANDATE REPORT GENERATION	$0	$58,260	($58,260)	0.0%	100.0%	$5,830	**
S-001	CONDITIONAL USE PERMIT	$56,574	$61,867	($5,293)	91.4%	100.0%	$5,300	
S-034	TENTATIVE TRACT MAP REVIEW	$6,646	$11,849	($5,203)	56.1%	100.0%	$5,200	
S-223	VALET ATTENDANT/TAXI DRIVER APPEAL	$0	$10,405	($10,405)	0.0%	100.0%	$5,200	**
S-217	MODIFICATION TO COMM. VALET PERMIT	$0	$4,970	($4,970)	0.0%	100.0%	$5,000	

CITY OF BEVERLY HILLS
SUMMARY OF REVENUES, COSTS, AND SUBSIDIES BY ORDER OF POSSIBLE NEW REVENUE
FISCAL YEAR 2006-2007

REF #	SERVICE TITLE	REVENUE	COST	PROFIT/ (SUBSIDY)	PERCENT RECOVERY CURRENT	PERCENT RECOVERY SUGGEST	POSSIBLE NEW REVENUE
S-005	R-4 MULTI FAMILY REVIEW	$6,104	$11,028	($4,924)	55.4%	100.0%	$4,900
S-062	STORMWATER POLLUTION PREV PLAN	$0	$3,951	($3,951)	0.0%	100.0%	$4,000
S-180	TANK INSTALLATION/REMOVAL INSPECT	$4,050	$8,039	($3,989)	50.4%	100.0%	$4,000
S-033	TENTATIVE PARCEL MAP REVIEW	$6,646	$10,577	($3,931)	62.8%	100.0%	$3,900
S-157	LOCAL CRIMINAL HISTORY REPORT	$5,360	$9,105	($3,745)	58.9%	100.0%	$3,700
S-102	NEWSRACK ENCROACHMENT PERMIT	$5,761	$34,948	($29,187)	16.5%	50.0%	$3,200
S-079	SUBSURFACE ENCROACHMENT PERMIT	$3,262	$6,054	($2,792)	53.9%	100.0%	$2,800
S-215	6 MONTH COMMER. VALET PARKING PMT	$7,747	$10,388	($2,641)	74.6%	100.0%	$2,600
S-101	RES. STREET LIGHT RELOCATION PRMT	$0	$2,367	($2,367)	0.0%	100.0%	$2,400
S-164	POLICE VIDEO TAPE COPY	$3,990	$6,169	($2,179)	64.7%	100.0%	$2,200
S-116	TREE REMOVAL	$255	$2,232	($1,977)	11.4%	100.0%	$2,000
S-076	CURB & GUTTER STREET USE PERMIT	$3,680	$5,237	($1,557)	70.3%	100.0%	$1,600
S-084	BORING EXCAVATION PERMIT	$220	$1,781	($1,561)	12.4%	100.0%	$1,600
S-230	UNAUTHORIZED TURN ON OF WATER	$2,164	$3,618	($1,454)	59.8%	100.0%	$1,500
S-100	COMM. STREET LIGHT RELOCATION PRMT	$0	$1,264	($1,264)	0.0%	100.0%	$1,300
S-136	BACKGROUND INVESTIGATION	$1,182	$2,477	($1,295)	47.7%	100.0%	$1,300
S-063	STANDARD URBAN S/W MITIGATION PLAN	$0	$1,097	($1,097)	0.0%	100.0%	$1,100
S-090	PERMANENT ENCROACHMENT PERMIT	$17,000	$18,059	($1,059)	94.1%	100.0%	$1,100
S-070	TREE REPLACEMENT	$0	$943	($943)	0.0%	100.0%	$900
S-097	PARK METER HEAD REMOVE/INSTALL PRMT	$2,632	$3,556	($924)	74.0%	100.0%	$900
S-224	NURSE/CAREGIVER PARKING PERMIT	$0	$2,461	($2,461)	0.0%	35.0%	$900
S-099	CONSTR BARRICADE/FENCE STRT USE PMT	$6,450	$7,211	($761)	89.4%	100.0%	$800
S-199	STUDENT FILM PERMIT	$0	$7,325	($7,325)	0.0%	20.0%	$750
S-156	ARREST VERIFICATION	$0	$669	($669)	0.0%	100.0%	$700
S-024	RESOLUTION OF CONVENIENCE & NECESS.	$4,073	$4,648	($575)	87.6%	100.0%	$600
S-148	FIREARM SALES PERMIT	$299	$917	($618)	32.6%	100.0%	$600
S-125	DUPLICATE CERTIFICATE OF OCCUPANCY	$124	$610	($486)	20.3%	100.0%	$500
S-045	PUBLIC NOTICE SIGN PROCESSING	$23,331	$23,686	($355)	98.5%	100.0%	$400
S-094	SURVEYING STREET USE PERMIT	$0	$409	($409)	0.0%	100.0%	$400
S-098	TRAFF/PARK SIGN & POST REMOVAL PRMT	$162	$514	($352)	31.5%	100.0%	$400
S-222	TAXI VEHICLE PERMIT REPLACEMENT	$360	$743	($383)	48.5%	100.0%	$400
S-047	PLANNING DECISION AMENDMENT	$5,500	$5,849	($349)	94.0%	100.0%	$300
S-123	GARAGE/ESTATE SALE PERMIT	$2,858	$3,207	($349)	89.1%	100.0%	$300
S-124	DUPLICATE INSPECTION CARD	$867	$1,148	($281)	75.5%	100.0%	$300
S-214	COMMERCIAL VALET PARKING TRANSFER	$2,033	$2,345	($312)	86.7%	100.0%	$300
S-078	SURFACE ENCROACHMENT PERMIT	$558	$780	($222)	71.5%	100.0%	$200
S-044	PUBLIC NOTICING	$43,774	$43,860	($86)	99.8%	100.0%	$100
S-114	RESTAURANT NEW ENCROACHMENT PERMIT	$129	$226	($97)	57.1%	100.0%	$100
S-151	PEDDLER PERMIT	$170	$287	($117)	59.2%	100.0%	$100
S-231	TEMPORARY METER RENTAL SERVICE	$800	$861	($61)	92.9%	100.0%	$100
S-240	AGENDA MAILING SERVICE	$474	$554	($80)	85.6%	100.0%	$100
	SUBSIDY SUBTOTAL	$4,246,676	$7,634,555	($3,387,879)	55.6%		$2,945,500
S-158	IMMIGRATION CLEARANCE LETTER PROC.	$1,190	$1,077	$113	110.5%	100.0%	($100)
S-054	FINAL TRACT MAP	$7,088	$6,814	$274	104.0%	100.0%	($300)
S-081	SHORT-TERM STREET LANE CLOSURE PMT	$12,900	$12,328	$572	104.6%	100.0%	($600)
S-046	EXTENSION OF TIME	$8,178	$7,036	$1,142	116.2%	100.0%	($1,100)
S-075	SIDEWALK REPLACE STREET USE PERMIT	$4,040	$1,993	$2,047	202.7%	100.0%	($2,000)
S-053	FINAL PARCEL MAP	$7,088	$4,269	$2,819	166.0%	100.0%	($2,800)
S-085	UTILITY ENCROACHMENT PERMIT	$20,200	$15,241	$4,959	132.5%	100.0%	($5,000)
S-087	SEWER LATERAL INSTALLATION PERMIT	$33,008	$26,915	$6,093	122.6%	100.0%	($6,100)
S-030	ENVIRON IMPACT ASSESSMENT (NEG DEC)	$39,613	$20,301	$19,312	195.1%	100.0%	($19,300)
S-088	HEAVY HAUL PERMIT	$419,240	$300,162	$119,078	139.7%	100.0%	($119,100)
	PROFIT SUBTOTAL	$552,545	$396,136	$156,409	139.5%		($156,400)
S-233	PARKING STRUCTURE OPERATIONS	$13,526,548	$15,485,159	($1,958,611)	87.4%	100.0%	See Text
S-108	BUILDING PLAN CHECK	$1,192,414	$1,954,643	($762,229)	61.0%	100.0%	$0 *
S-189	ADVENTURE CAMP PROGRAM	$293,891	$933,735	($639,844)	31.5%	50.0%	See Text
S-169	FIRE FALSE ALARM RESPONSE	$0	$603,926	($603,926)	0.0%	100.0%	$0
S-187	PRESCHOOL PROGRAM	$374,434	$977,163	($602,729)	38.3%	60.0%	See Text
S-173	VEGETATION MANAGEMENT PROGRAM	$0	$596,936	($596,936)	0.0%	100.0%	$0 *
S-192	ADULT RECREATION CLASSES	$95,068	$677,927	($582,859)	14.0%	20.0%	See Text

CITY OF BEVERLY HILLS
SUMMARY OF REVENUES, COSTS, AND SUBSIDIES BY ORDER OF POSSIBLE NEW REVENUE
FISCAL YEAR 2006-2007

REF #	SERVICE TITLE	REVENUE	COST	PROFIT/ (SUBSIDY)	PERCENT RECOVERY CURRENT	SUGGEST	POSSIBLE NEW REVENUE	
S-190	SUMMER CAMP PROGRAM	$409,409	$968,499	($559,090)	42.3%	55.0%	See Text	
S-128	POLICE FALSE ALARM RESPONSE	$0	$487,961	($487,961)	0.0%	100.0%	$0	**
S-193	ADULT SPORTS PROGRAM	$343,385	$749,594	($406,209)	45.8%	70.0%	See Text	
S-197	COMM. GROUP/SCHOOL BALLFIELD USE	$0	$401,279	($401,279)	0.0%	100.0%	See Text	
S-194	FARMERS MARKET	$93,500	$410,850	($317,350)	22.8%	30.0%	See Text	
S-195	RECREATION REGISTRATION PROCESSING	$0	$240,087	($240,087)	0.0%	100.0%	See Text	
S-166	BUSINESS ENGINE COMPANY INSPECTION	$10,000	$244,119	($234,119)	4.1%	100.0%	$0	
S-188	PARENT AND ME CLASSES	$167,443	$394,627	($227,184)	42.4%	60.0%	See Text	
S-203	INTER-LIBRARY LOAN PROCESSING	$2,250	$126,455	($124,205)	1.8%	10.0%	$0	
S-187	MFR ENGINE COMPANY INSPECTION	$5,000	$99,196	($94,196)	5.0%	100.0%	$0	
S-237	PUBLIC RECORDS REQUEST	$0	$73,826	($73,826)	0.0%	100.0%	$0	
S-172	ARSON INVESTIGATION	$0	$65,061	($65,061)	0.0%	100.0%	$0	
S-191	YOUTH RECREATION CLASSES	$555,658	$619,229	($83,571)	89.7%	100.0%	See Text	
S-204	LIBRARY ITEM RESERVATION SERVICE	$5,775	$46,354	($40,579)	12.5%	15.0%	$0	
S-109	ELECTRICAL PLAN CHECK	$72,834	$102,440	($29,606)	71.1%	100.0%	$0	*
S-110	MECHANICAL PLAN CHECK	$50,094	$79,649	($29,555)	62.9%	100.0%	$0	*
S-208	PASSPORT PROCESSING	$34,700	$60,579	($25,879)	57.3%	100.0%	$0	
S-012	ZONE CHANGE	$28,580	$53,862	($25,282)	53.1%	100.0%	$0	#
S-071	REQUEST FOR TRAFFIC MARKINGS	$0	$13,427	($13,427)	0.0%	100.0%	$0	**
S-027	HISTORIC RESOURCE NOMINATION	$0	$8,832	($8,832)	0.0%	100.0%	$0	#
S-036	CONDOMINIUM CONVERSION REVIEW	$4,119	$12,811	($8,692)	32.2%	100.0%	$0	#
S-026	EXTENDED HOURS PERMIT	$318	$8,832	($8,514)	3.6%	100.0%	$0	#
S-035	VESTING TENTATIVE MAP REVIEW	$3,969	$10,808	($6,839)	36.7%	100.0%	$0	#
S-023	OVERNIGHT STAY PERMIT	$4,318	$11,030	($6,712)	39.1%	100.0%	$0	#
S-083	STREET/R-O-W VACATION PROCESSING	$0	$6,020	($6,020)	0.0%	100.0%	$0	#
S-040	TREE REMOVAL REVIEW	$635	$6,392	($5,757)	9.9%	100.0%	$0	#
S-041	TELECOMM/SATELLITE DISH ANTENNA REV	$1,000	$6,716	($5,716)	14.9%	100.0%	$0	#
S-028	CHARACTER CONTRIBUTING STRUCT. REV.	$0	$5,711	($5,711)	0.0%	100.0%	$0	#
S-184	FIRE ALARM PERMIT PROCESSING	$0	$5,427	($5,427)	0.0%	100.0%	$0	
S-021	PARKING COVENANT AMENDMENT REVIEW	$3,652	$8,832	($5,180)	41.3%	100.0%	$0	#
S-225	WATER SERVICE INSTALLATION	$100,000	$104,646	($4,646)	95.6%	100.0%	$0	
S-022	JOINT DAYTIME/NIGHTTIME PARKING REV	$4,252	$8,832	($4,580)	48.1%	100.0%	$0	#
S-111	PLUMBING PLAN CHECK	$40,342	$44,861	($4,519)	89.9%	100.0%	$0	*
S-042	OUTDOOR VENDING PERMIT	$254	$4,706	($4,452)	5.4%	100.0%	$0	#
S-043	TEMPORARY USE PERMIT	$0	$4,444	($4,444)	0.0%	100.0%	$0	#
S-049	APPEAL TO THE CITY COUNCIL	$302	$4,732	($4,430)	6.4%	100.0%	$0	#
S-065	DRILLING PERMIT	$14,120	$18,516	($4,396)	76.3%	100.0%	$0	#
S-015	SPECIFIC PLAN AMENDMENT	$4,287	$8,677	($4,390)	49.4%	100.0%	$0	#
S-227	WATER METER TEST	$422	$4,306	($3,884)	9.8%	100.0%	$0	
S-019	DENSITY BONUS PERMIT	$2,784	$6,392	($3,608)	43.6%	100.0%	$0	#
S-048	APPEAL TO THE PLANNING COMMISSION	$151	$3,468	($3,317)	4.4%	100.0%	$0	#
S-196	PARK BBQ/TABLE RENTAL	$12,625	$15,401	($2,776)	82.0%	100.0%	See Text	
S-177	FIRE PERMIT PLAN CHECK	$33,000	$35,739	($2,739)	92.3%	100.0%	$0	
S-061	COVENANT AND AGREEMENT	$0	$2,545	($2,545)	0.0%	100.0%	$0	#
S-134	VEHICLE REPOSSESSION PROCESSING	$2,250	$4,677	($2,427)	48.1%	100.0%	$0	
S-066	DEVELOPMENT OF OIL, GAS, & MINERALS	$6,184	$8,229	($2,045)	75.1%	100.0%	$0	#
S-038	MASTER PLAN OF STREETS AMENDMENT	$7,755	$9,695	($1,940)	80.0%	100.0%	$0	#
S-135	CONCEALED WEAPONS PERMIT	$0	$1,833	($1,833)	0.0%	100.0%	$0	#
S-205	REPLACEMENT OF LOST LIBRARY CARD	$11,000	$12,430	($1,430)	88.5%	100.0%	$0	
S-058	EASEMENT PROCESSING	$0	$1,273	($1,273)	0.0%	100.0%	$0	#
S-137	ADULT ENTERTAINMENT BUSINESS PERMIT	$0	$1,258	($1,258)	0.0%	100.0%	$0	#
S-082	LONG TERM STREET LANE CLOSURE PRMT	$129	$1,255	($1,126)	10.3%	100.0%	$0	#
S-160	POLICE REPORT/DOCUMENT REPRODUCTION	$718	$1,705	($987)	42.1%	100.0%	$0	
S-185	FIRE INCIDENT REPORT COPY	$300	$1,242	($942)	24.2%	100.0%	$0	
S-226	FIRE FLOW TEST	$12,000	$12,919	($919)	92.9%	100.0%	$0	
S-138	ADULT ENTERTAINER PERMIT	$0	$824	($824)	0.0%	100.0%	$0	#
S-069	HOUSING MOVE PERMIT	$0	$776	($776)	0.0%	100.0%	$0	#
S-149	TOW SERVICE BUSINESS PERMIT	$607	$1,300	($709)	44.7%	100.0%	$0	#
S-122	STREET NAME CHANGE REQUEST	$0	$551	($551)	0.0%	100.0%	$0	#
S-072	RES. STREET ADDRESS NUMBER PAINTING	$0	$547	($547)	0.0%	100.0%	$0	**
S-055	LOT LINE ADJUSTMENT	$0	$509	($509)	0.0%	100.0%	$0	#
S-121	BUILDING ADDRESS CHANGE REQUEST	$78	$551	($473)	14.2%	100.0%	$0	#
S-119	COVENANT PROCESSING RECORDATION	$0	$424	($424)	0.0%	100.0%	$0	#
S-144	MASSAGE PARLOR PERMIT	$873	$1,258	($385)	69.4%	100.0%	$0	#

CITY OF BEVERLY HILLS
SUMMARY OF REVENUES, COSTS, AND SUBSIDIES BY ORDER OF POSSIBLE NEW REVENUE
FISCAL YEAR 2006-2007

REF #	SERVICE TITLE	REVENUE	COST	PROFIT/ (SUBSIDY)	PERCENT RECOVERY CURRENT	SUGGEST	POSSIBLE NEW REVENUE	
S-162	POLICE DISPATCH TAPE COPY	$200	$540	($340)	37.0%	100.0%	$0	
S-073	MAP COPYING SERVICE	$3,500	$3,742	($242)	93.5%	100.0%	$0	
S-145	MASSAGE TECHNICIAN PERMIT	$169	$393	($224)	43.0%	100.0%	$0	#
S-153	TOW DRIVER PERMIT	$0	$192	($192)	0.0%	100.0%	$0	#
S-057	MINOR PLAN CHECK REVISION	$0	$127	($127)	0.0%	100.0%	$0	#
S-060	SUBSEQUENT SUBMITTAL OF PLANS	$0	$127	($127)	0.0%	100.0%	$0	#
S-234	PRIVATE TREE REMOVAL IN PUBLIC ROW	$0	$107	($107)	0.0%	100.0%	$0	
S-080	SUBSURFACE LATERAL SUPP ENCROACH	$7,280	$7,360	($80)	98.9%	100.0%	$0	
S-059	PUBLIC WORKS INSPECTION/REINSPECT	$50	$110	($60)	45.5%	100.0%	$0	#
S-241	MINUTE MAILING SERVICE	$93	$152	($59)	61.2%	100.0%	$0	
S-242	ACTION MINUTE MAILING SERVICE	$93	$152	($59)	61.2%	100.0%	$0	
S-140	ESCORT BUREAU PERMIT	$1,200	$1,258	($58)	95.4%	100.0%	$0	#
S-141	FORTUNE TELLER PERMIT	$1,200	$1,258	($58)	95.4%	100.0%	$0	#
S-142	DATING SERVICE PERMIT	$1,200	$1,258	($58)	95.4%	100.0%	$0	#
S-150	PROFESSIONAL SALES PROMOTER PERMIT	$335	$393	($58)	85.2%	100.0%	$0	#
S-025	CERTIFICATE OF COMPLIANCE REVIEW	$1,448	$1,485	($37)	97.5%	100.0%	$0	#
S-103	AMENDMENT TO STREET USE PERMIT	$0	$23	($23)	0.0%	100.0%	$0	
S-239	CITY CLERK CERTIFICATION	$22	$45	($23)	48.9%	100.0%	$0	
S-186	FIRE DEPARTMENT STAND-BY	$600	$615	($15)	97.6%	100.0%	$0	
S-244	MEETING AUDIO TAPE COPY	$24	$35	($11)	68.6%	100.0%	$0	
S-243	CD COPY REQUEST	$0	$8	($8)	0.0%	100.0%	$0	
S-165	COMPUTER/DATABASE RESEARCH	$0	$0	$0	0.0%	100.0%	$0	
S-163	POLICE AUDIO TAPE COPY	$67	$56	$11	119.6%	100.0%	$0	
S-245	DVD COPY SERVICE	$89	$53	$36	167.9%	100.0%	$0	
S-037	BOUNDARY LINE ADJUSTMENT	$1,561	$1,485	$76	105.1%	100.0%	$0	#
S-149	PRIVATE POLICE PATROL PERMIT	$559	$393	$166	142.2%	100.0%	$0	#
S-095	SPECIAL EVENT ENCROACHMENT PERMIT	$3,870	$3,676	$194	105.3%	100.0%	$0	
S-143	PUBLIC DANCING PERMIT	$1,623	$1,282	$341	126.6%	100.0%	$0	#
S-031	NEGATIVE DECLARATION RECIRCULATION	$1,277	$677	$600	188.6%	100.0%	$0	#
S-089	DUMPSTER PERMIT	$12,900	$12,252	$648	105.3%	100.0%	$0	
S-056	PUBLIC IMPROVEMENT PLAN CHECK	$6,652	$4,569	$2,083	145.6%	100.0%	$0	
S-018	PLANNED DEVELOPMENT REVIEW	$10,979	$8,832	$2,147	124.3%	100.0%	$0	#
S-068	MINING & EXTRACTION APPLICATION	$3,263	$1,018	$2,245	320.5%	100.0%	$0	#
S-139	PRIVATE CLUB BUSINESS PERMIT	$3,573	$1,282	$2,291	278.7%	100.0%	$0	#
S-202	SPECIAL EVENT PERMIT - LARGE	$77,821	$74,304	$3,517	104.7%	100.0%	$0	
S-014	SPECIFIC PLAN REVIEW	$28,580	$22,684	$5,896	126.0%	100.0%	$0	#
S-013	GENERAL PLAN AMENDMENT	$16,245	$9,349	$6,896	173.8%	100.0%	$0	#
S-091	LOADING/UNLOADING STREET USE PERMIT	$322,500	$306,300	$16,200	105.3%	100.0%	$0	
S-200	STILL PHOTO PERMIT	$36,292	$12,176	$24,116	296.1%	100.0%	See Text	
S-106	MECHANICAL PERMIT/INSPECTION	$164,639	$102,950	$61,689	159.9%	100.0%	$0	*
S-107	PLUMBING PERMIT/INSPECTION	$159,988	$96,622	$63,366	165.6%	100.0%	$0	*
S-105	ELECTRICAL PERMIT/INSPECTION	$240,608	$146,535	$94,073	164.2%	100.0%	$0	*
S-198	FILM PERMIT	$234,813	$113,211	$121,602	207.4%	100.0%	See Text	
S-104	BUILDING PERMIT/INSPECTION	$2,593,686	$2,015,429	$578,257	128.7%	100.0%	$0	*
S-016	ANNEXATION REQUEST	NA	NA	NA	NA	100.0%	$0	#
S-017	DEVELOPMENT AGREEMENT REVIEW	NA	NA	NA	NA	100.0%	$0	#
S-032	ENVIRONMENTAL IMPACT REPORT REVIEW	NA	NA	NA	NA	100.0%	$0	
S-051	CONSULTANT SERVICES	NA	NA	NA	NA	100.0%	$0	
S-067	APPROVAL OF EXPLORATORY BOUNDARY	NA	NA	NA	NA	100.0%	$0	#
S-130	DUI COLLISION EMERGENCY RESPONSE	NA	NA	NA	NA	100.0%	$0	
S-131	SPECIAL EVENT POLICE SERVICE	NA	NA	NA	NA	100.0%	$0	
S-132	SPECIAL RESPONSE TEAM CALL-OUT	NA	NA	NA	NA	100.0%	$0	
S-170	NEGLIGENT INCIDENT RESPONSE	NA	NA	NA	NA	100.0%	$0	
S-171	HAZARDOUS MATERIAL INCIDENT RESP.	NA	NA	NA	NA	100.0%	$0	
S-207	LIBRARY COLLECTION PHOTO/CD REPROD.	NA	NA	NA	NA	100.0%	$0	
S-209	FACILITY RENTAL AFTER-HOURS MONITOR	NA	NA	NA	NA	100.0%	$0	
S-219	TAXICAB BUSINESS PERMIT	NA	NA	NA	NA	100.0%	$0	
S-232	EMERGENCY SEWAGE SPILL RESPONSE	NA	NA	NA	NA	100.0%	$0	
S-238	RECORDS RESEARCH	NA	NA	NA	NA	100.0%	$0	

SPECIAL CIRCUMSTANCES SUBTOTAL	$21,472,386	$29,842,999	($8,370,613)	72.0%		$0
GRAND TOTAL	$26,271,607	$37,873,690	($11,602,083)	69.4%		$2,789,100

CITY OF BEVERLY HILLS
SCHEDULE OF TAX COSTS
FISCAL YEAR 2006-2007

Schedule 4
Tax-Supported Services

REF #	SERVICE TITLE	TOTAL COSTS	PER CAPITA COSTS
TAX-01	POLICE SERVICES	$40,617,978	$1,202.28
TAX-02	FIRE SUPPRESSION SERVICES	$14,724,793	$435.85
TAX-03	EMERGENCY MEDICAL SERVICES	$6,353,406	$188.06
TAX-04	FIRE PREVENTION SERVICES	$246,589	$7.30
TAX-05	URBAN SEARCH AND RESCUE	$2,066,580	$61.17
TAX-06	CERT VOLUNTEER PROGRAM	$141,291	$4.18
TAX-07	CPR/FIRST AID CLASSES	$43,143	$1.28
TAX-08	ASPHALT POTHOLE REPAIR	$727,091	$21.52
TAX-09	CONCRETE MAINTENANCE	$788,444	$23.34
TAX-10	PAINT & SIGN MAINTENANCE	$870,005	$25.75
TAX-11	SIGNAL & LIGHTS MAINTENANCE	$1,610,491	$47.67
TAX-12	STREET & PARK TREE MAINTENANCE	$1,729,702	$51.20
TAX-13	TREE REMOVAL/INSTALLATION	$203,414	$6.02
TAX-14	PARK MAINTENANCE	$3,879,146	$114.82
TAX-15	STREETSCAPE MAINTENANCE	$411,457	$12.18
TAX-16	STORM DRAIN MAINTENANCE	$1,440,102	$42.63
TAX-17	NPDES STORMWATER PROGRAM	$171,452	$5.07
TAX-18	WATER SERVICES	$18,992,863	$562.19
TAX-19	SEWER SERVICES	$6,256,707	$185.20
TAX-20	SOLID WASTE SERVICES	$12,721,946	$376.57
TAX-21	TRANSIT SERVICES	$1,448,270	$42.87
TAX-22	CAPITAL PROJECT ADMIN.	$1,107,045	$32.77
TAX-23	TRAFFIC ENGINEERING	$187,511	$5.55
TAX-24	TRANSPORTATION PLANNING	$331,039	$9.80
TAX-25	ADVANCED PLANNING	$2,004,785	$59.34
TAX-26	CDBG PROGRAMS	$329,741	$9.76
TAX-27	CODE ENFORCEMENT	$988,451	$29.26
TAX-28	BUSINESS TRIANGLE MAINTENANCE	$37,483	$1.11
TAX-29	PARKING ENFORCEMENT	$4,102,813	$121.44
TAX-30	PARKING METER COLLECTIONS	$1,005,255	$29.76
TAX-31	LIBRARY SERVICES	$8,993,325	$266.20
TAX-32	CITY SPECIAL EVENTS	$421,857	$12.49
TAX-33	COMMUNITY EVENTS/PROGRAMS	$803,230	$23.78
TAX-34	CULTURAL PROGRAMS	$764,331	$22.62
TAX-35	HUMAN SERVICES PROGRAMS	$8,950,633	$264.94
TAX-36	RESIDENT EDUCATION PROGRAM	$114,996	$3.40
TAX-37	CITY-WIDE VOLUNTEER PROGRAM	$152,147	$4.50
TAX-38	PUBLIC ARTS/FINE ARTS COMMISSION	$201,190	$5.96
TAX-39	AFTERSCHOOL CHILDCARE PROGRAM	$583,114	$17.26
TAX-40	TEEN PROGRAMS	$177,667	$5.26
TAX-41	SENIOR ADULT LEISURE SERVICES	$217,434	$6.44
TAX-42	COMMUNITY CENTER STAFFING	$855,245	$25.32
TAX-43	PARK FACILITY RENTAL	$247,430	$7.32
TAX-44	PARK RANGERS	$1,023,453	$30.29
TAX-45	SCHOOL DISTRICT JPA	$455,950	$13.50
TAX-46	PROMOTIONS/TOURISM	$3,431,015	$101.56
TAX-47	REVENUE ADMINISTRATION	$845,972	$25.04
TAX-48	NON-DEPARTMENTAL EXPENSES	$2,805,000	$83.03

		$1,xx,xxx,xxx	$x,xxx.xx

SUBSIDIZED PERSONAL CHOICE PUBLIC SERVICES	$11,602,083	$343.42

	$168,185,065	$4,978.25

Per Capita Costs are based on a City population of 33,784

CITY OF COACHELLA, CALIFORNIA

In early 1989 the Coachella City Manager called MSI for help, he just having been elevated to his position from Assistant City Manager. A supportive alert City Council had replaced his predecessor and assigned the new Manager "to do something", not knowing "what was wrong." But they knew "something was 'messed up'". Although it never became common knowledge, the City's CPA firm had submitted a "Draft Audit" with a "going concern" statement. That meant Federal Bankruptcy Court and inability to pay vendors and employees, and possible multiple bond defaults were imminent.

Response. The initial MSI response was simple, following:

MSI CEO Douglas Ayres and Owen Olsen, CPA, will spend Friday questioning the City Manager and Finance Director, and learning City systems. The two will spend Saturday and Sunday in the Finance Department, including the City vault, accompanied by the Finance Director. On Monday morning Ayres & Olson will provide a written Report to a City Council executive [closed] session, with the City Manager and Finance Director in attendance. A Proposal assuring that the City remains "a going concern" and will not file for bankruptcy, and divulging how, will be supplied. Once reviewed, the Proposal may be accepted or rejected. If accepted the resultant MSI Report will provide the City information for utilization as Council might see fit to avoid default.

The Result. The City Council accepted each the "Problem/Solution Report" and Proposal, and the "Final Report(s)". Causal factors, systems difficulties, and procedural problems in abundance were discovered and corrected and/or modified. More about the specific processes, solutions and ultimate recommendations are presented in the following pages. They are exemplars of what could, and should be performed for all government.

As a direct result bankruptcy not only was avoided, but a Plan whereby the City recovered financial equilibrium was proposed, accepted, and implemented. Within one year the Annual Audit was "clean". Although today times are still "difficult", such status currently is due solely to the national economy and the budgetary response of most states.

Enigmatically, the City's problems could be traced to the enormous amount of very expensive mapping and engineering work done "on the come" for a major national "figure" and his wife, designing and preparing to implement their proposed "City of God". Since recovery, the City has not been in danger of financial "difficulties" to any degree. And, better yet, the causal factors of the "going concern" opinion were eliminated and positive revenue-cost systems put in place. That City now shares in the physical and financial growth of the Palm Springs area. And, none of Pasadena, Beverly Hills or Coachella are in, or anticipated to be "in financial distress", despite "these difficult times".

Table 6, following, is extracted from an analytical analysis developed in 1989 for the City of Coachella, California. Although dated, the very fact of the study and development of the circumstances relative to the City's financial naivetè and misconceptions, lit-

TABLE 6
SUMMARY

SERVICE GROUP	TOTAL REVENUE	TOTAL COST	TOTAL SUBSIDY (PROFIT)	PERCENTAGE SUBSIDY		POSSIBLE NEW REVENUE
				SUBSIDY	SUGGEST	
Community Development Services	$457,050	$465,434	$8,384	2%	0%	$157,700
Public Safety Services	$196,817	$612,925	$416,108	68%	54%	$87,700
Utility and Enterprise Services	$1,565,940	$2,156,559	$590,619	27%	7%	$449,400
Maintenance Services	$116,920	$1,359,846	$1,242,926	91%	22%	$945,900
Administrative and Finance Services	$7,915	$17,444	$10,329	61%	0%	$9,800
TOTALS	$2,344,642	$4,612,208	$2,268,366	49%	13%	$1,650,500

erally prevented the City from being forced to declare bankruptcy.

Nationally, in 2011, such conditions are far more prevalent and egregious than 22 years ago; and steadily deteriorating as elected officials continue to cling to the misconception that "the economy and revenues will come back". Yes, probably, but not very likely to anywhere near the roaring pumped-up times between 2000 and 2008.

Specific Systems Recommendations. The following text, interspersed with detailed information providing a peek into Coachella's "situation", provides answers to the question always asked at the completion of a revenue-cost analysis.

What do we do now?

The answer is simple – develop a step-by-step "Plan" and inexorably implement it. MSI and the predominately Hispanic-American City of Coachella did so -- together. MSI *always* provided implementing documents, but usually not as extensive as for Coachella.

Budgeting & Accounting Systems Revisions. The next several pages provide *only portions of the specifics proposed, supplied to staff and City Council, and implemented* by and for Coachella. These were the actions that had to be done to take the City out of the risk pattern into which it had allowed itself to descend over the past decade.

These specific recommendations as to accounting revisions could, and should, be applied to any municipal organization [or state] which has allowed its financial status to descend into near chaos and potential bankruptcy. Politics aside, such actions are absolutely required if there is any level of desire to continue as a "going concern". These are BUSINESS SYSTEMS, but in a government organization and atmosphere.

1. Sick Leave & Vacation Accrual. The cost of employee leave hours being accrued should be accumulated in a special fund as earned. The "accrual" benefit recognizes the cost of those benefits earned in prior years but not "taken" by the employee until a subsequent year, when paid off, at a higher salary cost, and in recognition that the payoff amount might prevent filling the position were adequate monies not set aside as a reserve.

CITY OF COACHELLA   Schedule 9

SUMMARY OF REVENUES, COSTS AND SUBSIDIES

FISCAL YEAR 1988-1989 BUDGET

MSI #	SERVICE CENTER	TOTAL REVENUE	TOTAL COST	TOTAL SUBSIDY (PROFIT)	PERCENT SUBSIDY
	Community Development				
S-1	Plan Checking	$66,170	$18,270	($47,900)	NA
S-2	Building Review and Inspection	$181,732	$55,722	($126,010)	NA
S-3	Demolition Review	$50	$6,872	$6,822	99%
S-4	Special Building Inspection Rev.	$180	$14,274	$14,094	99%
S-5	Certificate of Occupancy	$0	$35,345	$35,345	100%
S-6	Building/Zoning Enforcement	$0	$15,348	$15,348	100%
S-7	Zone Change Review	$9,000	$15,152	$6,152	41%
S-8	Zone Variance Review	$3,600	$16,187	$12,587	78%
S-9	Zone/Subdivision Ord. Amend. Rev.	$1,100	$3,142	$2,042	65%
S-10	Annexation Review	$1,000	$12,307	$11,307	92%
S-11	Conditional Use Review	$3,075	$7,076	$4,001	56%
S-12	General Plan Review & Revision	$2,800	$10,074	$7,274	72%
S-13	Preliminary Project Review	$0	$832	$832	100%
S-14	Specific Development Plan Review	$13,000	$11,163	($1,837)	NA
S-15	Tentative Parcel Review	$4,000	$12,195	$8,195	67%
S-16	Tentative Parcel Map Ext. Review	$500	$642	$142	22%
S-17	Tentative Tract Map Review	$3,500	$21,259	$17,759	84%
S-18	Tentative Tract Map Ext. Review	$2,165	$2,663	$498	19%
S-19	Environmental Review	$9,300	$31,404	$22,104	70%
S-20	Categorical Exempt. Assess. Rev.	$675	$2,012	$1,337	67%
S-21	EIR Report Review	$3,750	$10,318	$6,568	64%
S-22	Modifications to EIR Review	$500	$2,422	$1,922	79%
S-23	CUP Time Extension Review	$300	$772	$472	61%
S-24	Sign Review	$0	$80	$80	100%
S-25	Lot Line Adjustment Review	$3,000	$3,268	$268	8%
S-26	Compliance Review	$425	$113	($312)	NA
S-27	Minor Lot Line Adjustment Review	$375	$336	($39)	NA
S-28	Architectual Plan Review	$20,039	$51,477	$31,438	61%
S-29	Parcel Merger Review	$375	$322	($53)	NA
S-30	Reversion to Acreage Processing	$450	$558	$108	19%
S-31	Williamson Act Cancell. Review	$1,900	$3,676	$1,776	48%
S-32	Development Agreement Review	$10,000	$6,805	($3,195)	NA
S-33	Appeal Processing	$300	$106	($194)	NA
S-34	Planned Unit Development Review	$1,500	$3,517	$2,017	57%
S-35	EIR Appeal Review	$125	$1,276	$1,151	90%
S-36	AR/Grading Permit & Inspection	$6,574	$11,538	$4,964	43%
S-37	Subdivision Grading Permit & Insp	$500	$1,309	$809	62%
S-38	Subdivision Parcel Map Check	$1,380	$1,557	$177	11%
S-39	Subdivision Tract Map Check	$750	$2,277	$1,527	67%
S-40	AR/Improvement Plan Checking	$6,071	$1,760	($4,311)	NA
S-41	Subdivision Engr. Plan Checking	$72,638	$39,236	($33,402)	NA
S-42	Street Cuts Review and Inspection	$1,100	$15,168	$14,068	93%
S-43	AR/Permit and Inspection	$2,174	$1,759	($415)	NA

CITY OF COACHELLA   Schedule 9

SUMMARY OF REVENUES, COSTS AND SUBSIDIES

FISCAL YEAR 1988-1989 BUDGET

MSI #	SERVICE CENTER	TOTAL REVENUE	TOTAL COST	TOTAL SUBSIDY (PROFIT)	PERCENT SUBSIDY
S-44	Subdivision Engr. Permit & Insp.	$20,977	$13,845	($7,132)	NA
	Public Safety Services				
S-45	Municipal Ordinance Enforcement	$53,997	$56,126	$2,129	4%
S-46	Parking Enforcement	NA	$20,617	$20,617	100%
S-47	Traffic Code Enforcement	$113,276	$297,978	$184,702	62%
S-48	Police False Alarm Response	$0	$14,507	$14,507	100%
S-49	Vehicle Inspection	$0	$6,675	$6,675	100%
S-50	Accident Investigation	$2,105	$40,702	$38,597	95%
S-51	Fingerprint Processing	$875	$1,878	$1,003	53%
S-52	Regulation of Special Events	$100	$125	$25	20%
S-53	Crime Report Copying	$700	$1,307	$607	46%
S-54	Animal Control	$2,508	$45,238	$42,730	95%
S-55	DUI Investigation	$1,510	$5,196	$3,686	71%
S-56	Abandoned Vehicle Removal	$0	$18,064	$18,064	100%
S-57	Abandoned Shopping Cart Removal	$4,900	$3,013	($1,887)	NA
S-58	Notification of Vehicle Storage	$0	$1,633	$1,633	100%
S-59	Immigration/Verif. Ltr. Process.	$600	$1,102	$502	46%
S-60	Loud Party Second Response	$0	$5,672	$5,672	100%
S-61	Reproduct. of Crime Scene Photos	$125	$215	$90	42%
S-62	Temporary Alcohol Use Review	$0	$352	$352	100%
S-63	Water/Flood Pumping & Clean-Up	$120	$637	$517	81%
S-64	Special Fire Suppression Services	$410	$530	$120	23%
S-65	Private Water Flow Testing	$480	$1,002	$522	52%
S-66	Burn Regulation Enforcement	$4,000	$17,025	$13,025	77%
S-67	Special Use Fire Regulation	$200	$274	$74	27%
S-68	Fire Report Copying	$128	$420	$292	70%
S-69	Hazardous Material Review & Insp.	$90	$13,442	$13,352	99%
S-70	Haz. Mat. Negligent Fire Response	$1,140	$526	($614)	NA
S-71	Fire False Alarm Response	$20	$28	$8	29%
S-72	Weed/Trash Abatement Insp/Removal	NA	$21,030	$21,030	100%
S-73	Medical Assistance Response	$6,688	$28,925	$22,237	77%
S-74	Fire Suppression Stand-By	$210	$249	$39	16%
S-75	Fire Protect. Sys. Plan Chk/Insp.	$500	$874	$374	43%
S-76	Special Services	$1,000	$1,296	$296	23%
S-77	CPR Class	$1,135	$6,267	$5,132	82%
	Utility and Enterprise Services				
S-78	Utility Sign-Up Processing	$5,445	$3,273	($2,172)	NA
S-79	Water Service	$774,000	$780,438	$6,438	1%
S-80	Utility Line Location	$0	$7,171	$7,171	100%
S-81	Water Service Installation	NA	$819	$819	100%
S-82	Water Delinquent Turn On/Off	$11,635	$22,924	$11,289	49%
S-83	Water Meter Test	$0	$193	$193	100%
S-84	Utility Availability Research/Rev	$0	$661	$661	100%
S-85	Sewer Service	$469,000	$797,767	$328,767	41%

CITY OF COACHELLA   Schedule 9

SUMMARY OF REVENUES, COSTS AND SUBSIDIES

FISCAL YEAR 1988-1989 BUDGET

MSI #	SERVICE CENTER	TOTAL REVENUE	TOTAL COST	TOTAL SUBSIDY (PROFIT)	PERCENT SUBSIDY
S-86	Thermal Sanitary District Service	$22,436	$26,415	$3,979	15%
S-87	CVWD Sanitary Service	$15,000	$16,826	$1,826	11%
S-88	Sewer Leak Testing	$0	$260	$260	100%
S-89	Sewer Stoppage Investigation	$390	$777	$387	50%
S-90	Refuse Collection	$268,034	$502,732	$234,698	47%
	Maintenance Revenues				
S-91	Utility Street Use	$50,143	$367,199	$317,056	86%
S-92	Street Light Maintenance	$0	$150,809	$150,809	100%
S-93	R.O.W Landscaping	$58,591	$39,823	($18,768)	NA
S-94	Parks Maintenance	$0	$644,782	$644,782	100%
S-95	Street Sweeping	$0	$95,976	$95,976	100%
S-96	Storm Drain Maintenance	$0	$41,965	$41,965	100%
S-97	State Highway Sweeping	$8,186	$6,830	($1,356)	NA
S-98	State Highway Landscaping	$0	$12,462	$12,462	100%
	Administrative and Finance Services				
S-99	New Bus. License Review & Insp.	$4,550	$11,587	$7,037	61%
S-100	Returned Check Processing	$1,450	$599	($851)	NA
S-101	Agenda/Minute Mailing Service	$0	$3,966	$3,966	100%
S-102	Council Chamber Mtce. & Ops.	$315	$1,292	$977	76%
S-103	Printed Material Production/Sale	$800	NA	NA	NA
S-104	Copying of Document	$800	NA	($800)	NA
S-105	Clerk Certification	$0	NA	$0	NA
S-106	Research Activities	$0	NA	$0	NA
	TOTALS	$2,344,642	$4,612,208	$2,268,366	49%

CITY OF COACHELLA   Schedule 10

SUMMARY OF REVENUES, COSTS AND SUBSIDIES BY SERVICE UNIT

FISCAL YEAR 1988-1989 BUDGET

MSI #	SERVICE CENTER	UNIT TYPE	NO. UNITS	REVENUE PER UNIT	COST PER UNIT	SUBSIDY (PROFIT) PER UNIT
	Community Development					
S-1	Plan Checking	Plan	223	$296.73	$81.93	($214.80)
S-2	Building Review and Inspection	Permit	3,000	$60.58	$18.57	($42.00)
S-3	Demolition Review	Permit	2	$25.00	$3,436.00	$3,411.00
S-4	Special Building Inspection Rev.	Request	12	$15.00	$1,189.50	$1,174.50
S-5	Certificate of Occupancy	Certificate	18	$0.00	$1,963.61	$1,963.61
S-6	Building/Zoning Enforcement	Inspection	248	$0.00	$61.89	$61.89
S-7	Zone Change Review	Application	9	$1,000.00	$1,683.56	$683.56
S-8	Zone Variance Review	Application	9	$400.00	$1,798.56	$1,398.56
S-9	Zone/Subdivision Ord. Amend. Rev.	Application	1	$1,100.00	$3,142.00	$2,042.00
S-10	Annexation Review	Request	2	$500.00	$6,153.50	$5,653.50
S-11	Conditional Use Review	Application	4	$768.75	$1,769.00	$1,000.25
S-12	General Plan Review & Revision	Application	2	$1,400.00	$5,037.00	$3,637.00
S-13	Preliminary Project Review	Application	2	$0.00	$416.00	$416.00
S-14	Specific Development Plan Review	Application	3	$4,333.33	$3,721.00	($612.33)
S-15	Tentative Parcel Review	Application	8	$500.00	$1,524.38	$1,024.38
S-16	Tentative Parcel Map Ext. Review	Application	1	$500.00	$642.00	$142.00
S-17	Tentative Tract Map Review	Application	7	$500.00	$3,037.00	$2,537.00
S-18	Tentative Tract Map Ext. Review	Application	3	$721.67	$887.67	$166.00
S-19	Environmental Review	Application	35	$265.71	$897.26	$631.54
S-20	Categorical Exempt. Assess. Rev.	Application	9	$75.00	$223.56	$148.56
S-21	EIR Report Review	Application	1	$3,750.00	$10,318.00	$6,568.00
S-22	Modifications to EIR Review	Application	1	$500.00	$2,422.00	$1,922.00
S-23	CUP Time Extension Review	Application	1	$300.00	$772.00	$472.00
S-24	Sign Review	Application	1	$0.00	$80.00	$80.00
S-25	Lot Line Adjustment Review	Application	4	$750.00	$817.00	$67.00
S-26	Compliance Review	Request	1	$425.00	$113.00	($312.00)
S-27	Minor Lot Line Adjustment Review	Application	1	$375.00	$336.00	($39.00)
S-28	Architectual Plan Review	Project	26	$770.73	$1,979.88	$1,209.15
S-29	Parcel Merger Review	Application	1	$375.00	$322.00	($53.00)
S-30	Reversion to Acreage Processing	Application	1	$450.00	$558.00	$108.00
S-31	Williamson Act Cancell. Review	Application	2	$950.00	$1,838.00	$888.00
S-32	Development Agreement Review	Application	2	$5,000.00	$3,402.50	($1,597.50)
S-33	Appeal Processing	Application	3	$100.00	$35.33	($64.67)
S-34	Planned Unit Development Review	Application	1	$1,500.00	$3,517.00	$2,017.00
S-35	EIR Appeal Review	Application	1	$125.00	$1,276.00	$1,151.00
S-36	AR/Grading Permit & Inspection	Permit	5	$1,314.80	$2,307.60	$992.80
S-38	Subdivision Parcel Map Check	Map	3	$460.00	$519.00	$59.00
S-39	Subdivision Tract Map Check	Map	3	$250.00	$759.00	$509.00
S-40	AR/Improvement Plan Checking	Plan	4	$1,517.75	$440.00	($1,077.75)
S-41	Subdivision Engr. Plan Checking	Plan	4	$18,159.50	$9,809.00	($8,350.50)
S-42	Street Cuts Review and Inspection	Permit	43	$25.58	$352.74	$327.16
S-43	AR/Permit and Inspection	Permit	3	$724.67	$586.33	($138.33)

CITY OF COACHELLA   Schedule 10

SUMMARY OF REVENUES, COSTS AND SUBSIDIES BY SERVICE UNIT

FISCAL YEAR 1988-1989 BUDGET

MSI #	SERVICE CENTER	UNIT TYPE	NO. UNITS	REVENUE PER UNIT	COST PER UNIT	SUBSIDY (PROFIT) PER UNIT
S-44	Subdivision Engr. Permit & Insp.	Permit	2	$10,488.50	$6,922.50	($3,566.00)
	Public Safety Services					
S-45	Municipal Ordinance Enforcement	Citation	936	$57.69	$59.96	$2.27
S-46	Parking Enforcement	Citation	1,412	$0.00	$14.60	$14.60
S-47	Traffic Code Enforcement	Citation	5,512	$20.55	$54.06	$33.51
S-48	Police False Alarm Response	Response	436	$0.00	$33.27	$33.27
S-49	Vehicle Inspection	Inspection	500	$0.00	$13.35	$13.35
S-50	Accident Investigation	Report	421	$5.00	$96.68	$91.68
S-51	Fingerprint Processing	Card	175	$5.00	$10.73	$5.73
S-52	Regulation of Special Events	Hour	4	$25.00	$31.25	$6.25
S-53	Crime Report Copying	Reports	140	$5.00	$9.34	$4.34
S-54	Animal Control	License	229	$10.95	$197.55	$186.59
S-55	DUI Investigation	Accident	16	$94.38	$324.75	$230.38
S-56	Abandoned Vehicle Removal	Vehicle	520	$0.00	$34.74	$34.74
S-57	Abandoned Shopping Cart Removal	Cart	980	$5.00	$3.07	($1.93)
S-58	Notification of Vehicle Storage	Letter	125	$0.00	$13.06	$13.06
S-59	Immigration/Verif. Ltr. Process.	Letter	120	$5.00	$9.18	$4.18
S-60	Loud Party Second Response	Incident	50	$0.00	$113.44	$113.44
S-61	Reproduct. of Crime Scene Photos	Request	5	$25.00	$43.00	$18.00
S-62	Temporary Alcohol Use Review	Request	18	$0.00	$19.56	$19.56
S-63	Water/Flood Pumping & Clean-Up	Response	4	$30.00	$159.25	$129.25
S-64	Special Fire Suppression Services	Incident	1	$410.00	$530.00	$120.00
S-65	Private Water Flow Testing	Request	12	$40.00	$83.50	$43.50
S-66	Burn Regulation Enforcement	Permit	400	$10.00	$42.56	$32.56
S-67	Special Use Fire Regulation	Permit	10	$20.00	$27.40	$7.40
S-68	Fire Report Copying	Report	16	$8.00	$26.25	$18.25
S-69	Hazardous Material Review & Insp.	Permit	3	$30.00	$4,480.67	$4,450.67
S-70	Haz. Mat. Negligent Fire Response	Incident	1	$1,140.00	$526.00	($614.00)
S-71	Fire False Alarm Response	Response	1	$20.00	$28.00	$8.00
S-72	Weed/Trash Abatement Insp/Removal	Parcel	NA	NA	NA	NA
S-73	Medical Assistance Response	Response	1,040	$6.43	$27.81	$21.38
S-74	Fire Suppression Stand-By	Hour	1	$210.00	$249.00	$39.00
S-75	Fire Protect. Sys. Plan Chk/Insp.	Plan	7	$71.43	$124.86	$53.43
S-76	Special Services	Call	40	$25.00	$32.40	$7.40
S-77	CPR Class	Person	227	$5.00	$27.61	$22.61
	Utility and Enterprise Services					
S-78	Utility Sign-Up Processing	Customer	363	$15.00	$9.02	($5.98)
S-79	Water Service	Customer	2,750	$281.45	$283.80	$2.34
S-80	Utility Line Location	Request	75	$0.00	$46.32	$46.32
S-81	Water Service Installation	Connection	1	$0.00	$819.00	$819.00
S-82	Water Delinquent Turn On/Off	Turn On/Off	625	$18.62	$36.68	$18.06
S-83	Water Meter Test	Request	10	$0.00	$19.30	$19.30
S-84	Utility Availability Research/Rev	Request	20	$0.00	$33.05	$33.05
S-85	Sewer Service	Customer	2,700	$173.70	$295.47	$121.77

CITY OF COACHELLA

SUMMARY OF REVENUES, COSTS AND SUBSIDIES BY SERVICE UNIT

FISCAL YEAR 1988-1989 BUDGET

MSI #	SERVICE CENTER	UNIT TYPE	NO. UNITS	REVENUE PER UNIT	COST PER UNIT	SUBSIDY (PROFIT) PER UNIT
S-86	Thermal Sanitary District Service	Customer	225	$99.72	$117.40	$17.68
S-87	CVWD Sanitary Service	Customer	147	$102.04	$114.46	$12.42
S-88	Sewer Leak Testing	Request	1	$0.00	$260.00	$260.00
S-89	Sewer Stoppage Investigation	Request	2	$195.00	$388.50	$193.50
S-90	Refuse Collection	Customer	2,750	$97.47	$182.81	$85.34
	Maintenance Revenues					
S-91	Utility Street Use	Mile of ROW	60	$835.72	$6,119.98	$5,284.27
S-92	Street Light Maintenance	Parcel	3,468	$0.00	$43.49	$43.49
S-93	R.O.W Landscaping	Parcel	3,468	$16.89	$11.48	($5.41)
S-94	Parks Maintenance	Parcel	3,468	$0.00	$185.92	$185.92
S-95	Street Sweeping	Miles	30	$0.00	$3,199.20	$3,199.20
S-96	Storm Drain Maintenance	Parcel	3,468	$0.00	$12.10	$12.10
S-97	State Highway Sweeping	Mile	8	$1,023.25	$853.75	($169.50)
S-98	State Highway Landscaping	Contract	1	$0.00	$12,462.00	$12,462.00
	Administrative and Finance Services					
S-99	New Bus. License Review & Insp.	Application	91	$50.00	$127.33	$77.33
S-100	Returned Check Processing	Check	100	$14.50	$5.99	($8.51)
S-101	Agenda/Minute Mailing Service	Subscriber	80	$0.00	$49.58	$49.58
S-102	Council Chamber Mtce. & Ops.	Reservation	17	$18.53	$76.00	$57.47
S-103	Printed Material Production/Sale	Page	160	$5.00	$0.00	($5.00)
S-104	Copying of Document	Page	800	$1.00	$0.00	($1.00)
S-105	Clerk Certification	Document	0	NA	NA	NA
S-106	Research Activities	Hour	200	$0.00	$0.00	$0.00

2. Employee Benefits Fund. It was recommended the City create an Employee Benefits Fund in which to accumulate, and from which to pay all employee fringe benefits. This would simplify the City's accounting for its employee benefits and program costs.

3. Equipment Maintenance and Replacement Fund. The City should modify its Equipment Maintenance Replacement (internal service) Fund to distribute the full costs of equipment maintenance, operation, and replacement among its several funds, budgetary programs, and the newly established "Cost Centers" or better named, "Service Centers". For purposes of this Study, an analysis of the full costs which should be charged was conducted by MSI. This analysis resulted in a 58% increase in charges ($170,771), which were added to the operating budgets in proportion to those budgeted for 1988-89.

4. General and Departmental Overhead. "Overhead" can be defined as coordinative and analytical capability of a level necessary to research and respond to City policy and operation issues, and then to execute those City Council policies quickly, and report the results accurately. Such research, execution, and reporting capabilities would not exist were it not for the recognition of overhead as the vital glue that holds an organization together rather than it being a loose, uncoordinated confederation of expensive parts. Although overhead is a well-established, recognized and necessary expense item in business, it is only recently that governments even considered adopting business techniques. MSI's costing systems began "pushing & educating" about overheads in 1981. The history of the Consumer Government experience of the MSI Founder, Author of this Book, and originator of the *Municipal Business System*, understood and applied overhead rates to cities starting in 1957 for Kansas City, Missouri, then in 1963, in Salem, Oregon. The "educational" effort to get governments to recognize the facts of inventorying and fully expensing services gradually grew from there. A more detailed genesis outline is provided in the **HISTORICAL BACKGROUND OF THIS BOOK** starting on page v.

"Government is no different than a good corporation – the adage was and still is 'Buy Good Management'".

5. Two Levels of Overhead. In a mid-sized business, or governmental organization, there usually are two levels of overhead – general and departmental. Larger organizations, such as the City of Pasadena, add a third – division. To determine those *all* costs must be identified, isolated and computed. And then applied to the "cost centers" when those expenses are accumulated service-by-service.

These tables show the reduction of both levels of overhead to a percentage. Application of those rates to each appropriate expense grouping is easily accomplished by use of the MSI-based, now RCS, integrated costing and budget software.

6. Other Accounting Modifications. Due to the nature of the assignment, the Coachella Report turned out to be almost a textbook example of "**how to re-design and re-build a municipal accounting and budgeting system.**" The following paragraphs provide snippets or listings of the materials provided in the Report, and resultant full installation. Some employee reductions did occur, but with great empathy and care, to mitigate the expected and known adverse economic and psychological impacts.

1. Federal Grant Allocations were developed following FMC 74-4, the U.S. Office of Management and Budget A-87 process. Meeting those requirements was easily accomplished through use of the MSI-developed overhead process, with a few simple deletions.

2. Application of the two level overhead rates to all Assessment or Mello-Roos (Special Improvement) Districts, and the Redevelopment Agency was accomplished. Appropriate supporting accounting documents were easily derived from the MSI "System".

3. Overhead rates were applied to all Capital Budget and Fund projects.

CITY OF COACHELLA   SCHEDULE 8B

GENERAL GOVERNMENT OVERHEAD

FISCAL YEAR 1988--1989 BUDGET

DEPARTMENT/PROGRAM	SALARIES (1)	FRINGE BENEFITS (2)	OPERATING EXPENSE (3)	BUILDING OCCUPANCY CHARG (4)	FIXED ASSET CHARGE (5)	SUBTOTAL (6)	DEDUCT DIRECT CHARGES (7)
City Council	$28,021	$26,035	$19,111	$10,263	$7,710	$91,140	$1,026
City Clerk	$20,629	$7,696	$9,046	$2,877	$1,680	$41,928	$0
City Manager	$71,122	$25,794	$145,068	$4,186	$570	$246,740	$1,495
Economic Development	$0	$0	$636	$0	$0	$636	$636
Personnel	$74,330	$26,172	$218,065	$17,262	$0	$335,829	$1,926
Legal	$0	$0	$150,500	$0	$0	$150,500	$0
Finance	$189,534	$75,206	$31,052	$8,734	$6,310	$310,836	$100,893
General Government	$0	$0	$67,929	$0	$0	$67,929	$0
Data Processing	$0	$0	$31,000	$0	$0	$31,000	$10,230
TOTALS	$355,615	$134,868	$653,296	$33,059	$1,193,958	$1,300,578	$1,185,398

CITY OF COACHELLA   SCHEDULE 8A

DEPARTMENTAL OVERHEAD

FISCAL YEAR 1988--1989 BUDGET

DEPARTMENT	SALARIES (1)	FRINGE BENEFITS (2)	OPERATING EXPENSES (3)	BUILDING OCCUPANCY CHARGE (4)	FIXED ASSET CHARGE (5)	TOTAL (6)
Community Development	$27,437	$9,138	$9,449	$1,252	$879	$48,155
Public Works	$57,995	$19,468	$19,396	$5,893	$1,413	$104,165
Police	$74,733	$35,872	$21,625	$2,424	$6,029	$140,683
Fire	$44,889	$20,319	$8,215	$6,348	$3,534	$83,305
TOTALS						

CITY OF COACHELLA   SCHEDULE 7
OVERHEAD RATES
FISCAL YEAR 1988-1989 BUDGET

	TOTAL (1)	GENERAL GOVERNMENT (2)	COMMUNITY DEVELOPMENT (3)	PUBLIC WORKS (4)	POLICE (5)	FIRE (6)
			D E P A R T M E N T S			
CITY BUDGET	$9,450,069					
REDEVELOPMENT PROJECTS	$1,238,694					
	$10,688,763					
BUDGET ADJUSTMENTS	($2,960,356)					
ADJUSTED BUDGET	$7,728,407	$1,026,946	$850,971	$3,404,045	$1,769,916	$676,529
COSTING ADJUSTMENTS	$1,355,006	$1,240,524	$12,785	$30,898	$32,953	$37,846
OVERHEAD BASE	$9,083,413	$2,267,470	$863,756	$3,434,943	$1,802,869	$714,375
LESS, OVERHEAD:						
GENERAL	$1,185,398	$1,185,398				
DEPARTMENTAL	$376,308		$48,155	$104,165	$140,683	$83,305
DIRECT COST OF TAX & FEE SUPORTED SERVICES	$7,521,707	$1,082,072	$815,601	$3,330,778	$1,662,186	$631,070
APPLIED OVERHEAD:						
COST	$1,185,398		$48,155	$104,165	$140,683	$83,305
RATE:						
GENERAL	16%					
DEPARTMENTAL			6%	3%	9%	13%
COMPOSITE RATE	21%					

===========================
NOTES TO SCHEDULE:
 "BUDGET ADJUSTMENTS" -- deductions for capital outlay, contingency appropriations,
      appropriations estimated to be unspent, transfers, and depreciation
      & debt service not included in the overhead base.

 "COSTING ADJUSTMENTS" -- additions for costs related to fixed assets in
      overhead and building occupancy charges.

4. Both levels of overheads also were recommended to be added to any bills rendered by the City to any outside agency or party for services rendered, damage recovery, or the like, inasmuch as these two rates are true costs reasonably borne in doing City business.

5. To secure monies to pay the $1 million in Council-approved warrants built up over a year's time that could not be released due to lack of money, a GAAP Opinion was developed. The two level overhead calculations backed up and implemented that Opinion. That justification was provided Bond Counsel and Underwriter Counsel for each of the City's recent Water, Sewer and CRA Refunding issues. This Opinion was accepted in writing by all for recovery of applicable overhead amounts from the securities issues.

6. The several special assessment and bond counsel firms involved in any capital or operational assessments opined that the overhead calculations provided by above Schedules 7, 8A and 8B justified inclusion of those expenses in any District or assessment.

7. Addition of the positions of Administrative Services Director, Financial Analyst, and a Revenue Specialist to City staff was recommended, justified, and implemented.

8. The calculated overhead rate of 16% for Coachella admittedly was higher than the then 74 cities MSI had served. Those rates averaged 10.4%, with a median of 10.0%. However, the Report justified 16% and related that it would come down to near the overall city average once Coachella resumed capital projects and re-established and resuscitated several programs that had been savaged due to the unexpected un-funded cutbacks.

9. Numerous expositions were provided relative to the dangers of "low" overhead vs. inadequate administration; future financial planning; researched and informed vs. on-the-spot policy making by the City Council; and cessation of diversion of water and CRA revenues to meet General Fund shortfalls. Only "in lieu" 'franchise' fees were applied.

THE Major System Change. Abandonment of the General Fund for use other than calculation of and provision of overhead rates was accomplished. Creation of Special Funds for each of the following was put into place:

1. General Fund – overhead only
2. Police Fund
3. Fire Fund
4. Streets Fund – for State and Federal-funded activities
5. Parks and Recreation Fund
6. Public Works Fund – City-financed maintenance
7. Community Development Fund
8. Water Fund
9. Sewer Fund
10. Refuse Fund
11. Capital Projects Fund
12. Community Redevelopment Agency Fund – and one for each 'project'
13. Various Internal Service Funds -- previously enumerated
14. Any Special Project or Capital Funds – needed to fulfill grant or aid restrictions

Service Centers and Managers. Each Fund contained assigned "Service Centers" and allied revenues. The MSI software package has a "Manager" designated for each Service Center, backed by monthly costing reports. A number of Service Centers were grouped into the appropriate above Funds. It was recognized, and the ***Municipal Business System*** allowed for, creation of such Special Purpose Funds as might be necessary. However, anti-proliferation cautions were spread throughout the instructions for Fund creation.

Fortuitous Circumstance. The then-Coachella City Council Members were the first to realize "something was wrong" with the City's finances. Thus the MSI initial findings and resultant need for a creative rescue came as no surprise. That body was in a quite receptive frame of mind when the Final Report arrived. They particularly appreciated, and reacted quite positively, to one particular section of the Report text, following.

> *"The City Council has four clear alternatives available to them regarding its policy as to the revenue/cost mix of each identified and costed Service:*
>
> 1. *Continue any tax subsidy which might be found.*
>
> 2. *Eliminate the tax subsidy by increasing fees to cover all Prop. 4 'costs reasonably borne', as computed.*
>
> 3. *Reduce costs by reducing the level of service.*
>
> 4. *Decide on an appropriate level of tax subsidy, being aware that taxes are now limited in rate, base and, consequently, in amounts yielded, and thus availability."*

This elected body took the news well. They were pleased it had not "gotten out" that the City literally was on the verge of bankruptcy, and that a viable "Recovery Plan" had not only been made available, but the Plan was now known, specific and, even better, actually achievable and being implemented. And that "installation" was without "fuss and feathers". The quiet professionalism of MSI staff was greatly appreciated, and praised.

Subsequently. Numerous other cities, counties, special districts, and even a major Arizona Indian Tribe ultimately "got wind" of what had been accomplished for Coachella, resulting in much additional work for MSI, and many now-continuing relationships for RCS. The hallmark of the Coachella "experience" was unexpected. Namely, that a terrible situation had been evaded, seemingly effortlessly and highly professionally. But, far better, specific solutions not only were offered but actually implementable, and installed.

More "Good Stuff". A listing of the paragraph/section headings of the balance of the MSI Report to the Coachella City Council tells the balance of the story, in few words:

Fees Relate to Services.

Diversification of City Revenue Base.

Prop. 4 Offsets.

Policy Guidance.

Understanding of Equitable Charging for Government.

Application of Business Principles.*

   *Provided in detail after this listing

Reversing Past Practices. [each in great explanatory detail]
1. Inflation
2. Lack of tax monies to provide requested services
3. Increase fees to limit tax subsidies
4. Lack of realistic information from staff ^

Basic Services Have Suffered.

General Comment Regarding Police and Fire Services.

Police and Fire Department Awareness.

Specific Service Center by Service Center Commentary.

---

*Report: "As business people, there is no reason for the City Council members either individually or collectively to part with their 'good business sense' when they enter the Council chambers. Thus the costing and equity principles intended by the Authors of Proposition 4 (*California Constitution* Article XIIIB), and as analyzed and applied by the MSI staff as a constitutional control system, should be both familiar to and acceptable by the City Council members, individually and as a body."

^Report: "The last difficulty was inability or unwillingness, or both, of the then-City Manager, City Finance Director, and budgeting/accounting 'systems' to provide realistic and accurate estimates of and recordation of revenues and expenses being incurred by the City. The City Council heard only the 'good news'; the 'bad news' either was not known, ignored, or suppressed. Which was the case is not known."

A Universal "Special Benefit" Service. The following text from the Coachella *Cost Control System (**Municipal Business System**)* Report can be repeated for almost every government jurisdiction in the United States which has a law enforcement responsibility. The "lesson" here is that any technological advance will have some level of impact – both positive and negative – on local government. "Police False Alarm Response" is one of the most annoying, dangerous, and expensive for local police and sheriff departments. These following comments were applicable to each City for which data is provided in this Book. And most others, as well. This identified Service Center is the poster child for diversion of tax monies away from "Public Benefit" to "Private Benefit" services.

"**S-48: Police False Alarm Response.** The City makes no charge for false alarm responses. Many cities do, but wholly inadequately. Costs of response to these police-oriented calls average [in 1988 costs] $33.27 for the 436 annual [Coachella 1988] responses, for a total diversion from more normal police duties amounting to $14,507 in tax monies.

An unknown element of 'cost' is the degradation of service elsewhere in the City, and the risk to the officer responding to a "real" alarm when false alarms are so common.

Given no current revenue return and the major on-going tax subsidy, consideration of a policy permitting only two free calls within any twelve month period, with a $50 charge kicking in on the third response within any 12 month period seems in order. Thus some of the calls would be charged out slightly above actual cost, but the net result should be to reduce substantially the total subsidy for this service and encourage the alarm users to pick the desired option from among:

1. Learn how to operate the system properly.
2. Failing 1, remove the system.
3. Failing 1 and 2, pay the full cost of special police service when provided if the alarm is a false one.

An 'escalating fine' process should be implemented with the 'fine' increasing to $75 on the 4th call, and $100 on the 5th call and beyond. In other cities this process acts to reduce significantly the numbers of false alarms, and to produce income for this special service. The estimate of additional revenue from this source would be another $5,000 annually, against a cost that undoubtedly would decline from the current $14,507."

Marketing of Public Services.   Over the next several years the "smaller government" movement undoubtedly will continue to secure some of its goals. Some reductions and considerable tightening is needed. Hopefully, such will be secured by utilization of the ***Municipal Business System (MBS)*** which, if performed properly and by those who are not ideologically involved, sound local government can be assured. However, some municipal reductions will be secured by scare techniques, untruths, exaggerations, and other means. In those jurisdictions where the ***Municipal Business System*** is applied, full disclosure will require more than producing Exhibits, Tables and Illustrations as provided in this Book. MARKETING of municipal services will be required. Such is required to inform the CONSUMER of local government services, whether paying fees, charges or taxes. The clear delineation of all activities, and their customers and costs, is vital. Expectantly, by such full disclosure some measure of rationality will overcome raw ideology. Also to be overcome is the shibboleth *"Private business can do it better than government"*. By applying the ***Municipal Business System*** the private sector can have a shot, but only on a level playing field. Here, once again, review Appendix A.

Do or Die.   Superior service, economically and impartially delivered and paid for can secure a 'market'. Poor service either will be upgraded, outsourced, or abandoned. Local government is 180° different from the largest of the private sector – the Financial Services Industry. The latter produces nothing tangible. Local government, when operated properly, can, does, and must deliver physically tangible and vital human services.

TWO OTHER CALIFORNIA CITIES

The three following Exhibits are transplanted from a Management Information Service booklet produced by the International City/County Management Association. Both cities' Tables were produced as part of MSI studies for these two cities.

EXHIBIT 1–Service Center Worksheet for Cost Detail (Riverside, California)

SERVICE PROVIDED	CITY	REF. NO.
SENIOR NUTRITION PROGRAM		UNITS

KEY TO COST COLUMNS	FILE	DEPARTMENT	SECTION
A	PR 427	PARKS & RECREATION	Sr. Nutrition Program (427 & 428)
B	REC 424	PARKS & RECREATION	Recreation (424 & 426)
C	REC 421	PARKS & RECREATION	Administration (421)
D			
E			
F			
G			

EXPENSE TYPE	TOTAL	A	B	C	D	E	F	G
SALARIES & WAGES	$169,763	$138,377	$16,687	$4,789				
FRINGES	$21,548	$14,297	$5,623	$1,628				
MAINTENANCE & OPERATION	$449,082	$441,213	$7,000	$869				
BUILDING OCCUPANCY	$163,313	$152,409	$657	$247				
SECTION OVERHEAD	$1,869		$1,869					
DEPARTMENT OVERHEAD	$31,348	$29,852	$1,195	$301				
GENERAL OVERHEAD	$54,859	$52,241	$2,091	$527				
FIXED ASSET REPLACEMENT	$33,498	$32,940	$368	$190				
OTHER COST								
TOTAL	$905,270	$851,329	$36,390	$8,661				

EXPENSE TYPE	PER UNIT	A	B	C	D	E	F	G
SALARIES & WAGES	$236.66	$205.00	$24.57	$7.09				
FRINGES	$31.92	$21.18	$8.33	$2.41				
MAINTENANCE & OPERATION	$665.31	$653.65	$10.37	$1.29				
BUILDING OCCUPANCY	$227.13	$225.79	$0.97	$0.37				
DEPARTMENT OVERHEAD	$46.45	$44.23	$1.77	$0.45				
GENERAL OVERHEAD	$81.27	$77.39	$3.10	$0.78				
FIXED ASSET REPLACEMENT	$49.63	$48.80	$0.65	$0.28				
OTHER COST								
TOTAL BY UNIT	$1,341.14	$1,276.04	$52.43	$12.67				

© Management Services Institute, Inc., Anaheim, California, March, 1990.

26   Management Information Service

EXHIBIT 2—Service Center Worksheet for Fees and Charges (Riverside, California)

SERVICE PROVIDED	CITY	REF. NO.
SENIOR NUTRITION PROGRAM		

SERVICES PRIMARILY PERFORMED BY	FUND	EXP. ACCT.
Recreation	General	01–427 & 01–428

REVENUE RECEIVED (Actual—Potential)	FUND	REV. ACCT.
SENIOR NUTRITION PROGRAM FEES	General	01–378 & 01–574

REVENUE AUTHORIZATION	
Administrative Authority	DATE LAST REVISED: 2/88
	SUBSIDY RATIONALE: Unable to Pay

DESCRIPTION OF SERVICE	REVENUE COLLECTION SCHEDULE:
To conduct a nutrition lunch program for senior citizens in the City.	Donation at Meal
	REVENUE COLLECTED BY: Recreation
	UNIT OF SERVICE DESIGNATION: Participant

CURRENT FEE STRUCTURE

Donations by Seniors of $1.25 per meal generated $154,600.
The balance of the revenue ($493,218) is from a Federal Grant.

FISCAL YEAR 1989–1990 REVENUE AND COST COMPARISON

TOTAL EST. REVENUE	:	$647,818	UNIT REVENUE	:	$959.73
TOTAL COST	:	$905,271	UNIT COST	:	$1,341.14
PROFIT (SUBSIDY)	:	< $257,453 >	PROFIT (SUBSIDY)	:	< $381.41 >
% OF COST RECOVERED	:	71.6%	UNITS OF SERVICE	:	675

SUGGESTED % RECOVERY AND FEE STRUCTURE

PERCENT: 75%   SPECIAL CONDITIONS: See Text

Donation of $1.50 per meal.

[Note: In this area, staff must balance need for additional revenue with social needs and market constraints. Decreasing costs of service and increasing numbers of participants will achieve the same financial goal.]

20   Management Information Service

EXHIBIT 2—Portion of Summary Data Table Prepared for City Council Consideration (Chino, California)

		Service		(1)			(2) Subsidy Level Proposed % of Cost Not Recovered By City	(3) Total Annual Revenue Increase
			User Pays (Current Fee)	& City Pays	= Actual Cost of Service	Proposed Fee		
S-1	Building Inspection		*	*	*	*	0.0%	$0
S-2	Plumbing Inspection		*	*	*	*	0.0%	$0
S-3	Electrical Inspection		*	*	*	*	0.0%	$0
S-4	Heating & A/C Inspection		*	*	*	*	0.0%	$0
S-5	Grading Plan Review/Inspection		*	*	*	*	0.0%	$12,200
S-6	Curb Cut Rvw/Insp-Combined W/S-34		---	---	---	---	---	---
S-7	Annexation Processing Svc		$483	$817	$1,300	$650	50.0%	$167
S-8	Tentative Subdivision Map Rvw		*	*	*	*	.0.0%	$31,700
S-9	Final Subdivision Map Review		*	*	*	*	0.0%	$0
S-10	Environmental Assessment Rvw		$120	$400	$520	$520	0.0%	$37,200
S-11	Environmental Impact Review		$10,000	$3,380	$13,380	$13,380	0.0%	$3,380
S-12	Building Plan Review		*	*	*	*	0.0%	$0
S-13	Engineering Plan Review		*	*	*	*	0.0%	$56,400
S-14	Revision of Engineering Plans		$0	$307	$307	$307	0.0%	$15,350
S-15	Occupancy Inspection		$0	$27	$27	$27	0.0%	$30,726
S-16	Public Improvement Inspection		*	*	*	*	0.0%	$55,000
S-17	General Plan Amendment		$1,450	$110	$1,560	$1,560	0.0%	$990
S-18	Conditional Use Review		$543	$407	$950	$950	0.0%	$19,536
S-19	Variance Fees—Regular Appl.		$301	$304	$605	$605	0.0%	$1,520
S-19	Variance Fees—Ownr/Occ S F Res		$301	$304	$605	$30	95.0%	($271)
S-20	Appeal Processing—Non-Res. Applican		$60	$757	$817	$817	0.0%	$3,785
S-20	Appeal Proc—Non-Appl Res/Bus Ownr		$60	$757	$817	$0	100.0%	($60)
S-20	Appeal Proc—Ownr/Occ S F Res Appl		$60	$757	$817	$41	95.0%	($538)
S-21	Development Time Ext Review		$0	$110	$110	$110	0.0%	$1,210
S-22	Home Occupation Permit		$60	$81	$141	$141	0.0%	$7,290
S-23	Zone Change Review		$725	$188	$913	$913	0.0%	$2,444
S-24	Zoning Ordinance Amendmt Review		$0	$1,750	$1,750	$1,750	0.0%	$12,250
S-25	Sign Review		$0	$63	$63	$63	0.0%	$13,545
S-26	Site Approval Review		$422	$518	$940	$940	0.0%	$23,310
S-27	Sign Ordinance Amendment		$0	$543	$543	$543	0.0%	$543
S-28	Sign Ordinance Variance		$195	$372	$567	$567	0.0%	$372
S-29	Developer Agreement Processing		$0	$491	$491	$491	0.0%	$491

(1) Current fee and actual cost of services is based on one unit of service.
(2) Proposed fee and proposed level of subsidy are based on one unit of service.
(3) Annual revenue increase is based on the total number of units of service during a one year period multiplied by any increase in the unit fee. For those with a 0% subsidy level proposed, the increase in the unit fee will eliminate the dollar amount which is currently being paid by the City.

* Fees cannot be listed as one charge for one unit of service because the calculations are made either on a sliding scale or because the type of service has many different levels, each with a different fee. Examples would be recreation classes, building and engineering fees based on percentages of other fees, sanitation fees, and other fees with a variable used to calculate actual charges.
Refer to description of each service for fee amounts.

Source for all three above Exhibits: *Establishing the Cost of Services,* a Management Information Service (MIS) Report of the International City/County Management Association (ICMA); (Volume 22, Number 5, May 1990). See following footnote in next Chapter for full reference.
Note: At the time the population of Riverside was approximately 226,000 and Chino 60,000. Other cities herein had the following populations: Pasadena 135,000, La Palma 16,000, Beverly Hills 32,000 and Coachella 17,000. Pasadena and Beverly Hills each day are invaded by thousands of persons who work in and commute to those communities.

Date: November 15, 2011

To: Doug Ayres

After Proposition 13 passed in California, cities were searching for additional revenue since property tax, a principal source of revenue for most cities, was seriously reduced. Focus began to center on fees for service. However, City Council policy decisions about those fees that did exist often reflected a rate that would not raise significant political opposition or controversy. These rates often reflected poor documentation. They were "sold" to the community as an attempt to recover the costs of a particular service. Additionally, no comprehensive effort had been made to draw a distinction between those services that provided a general benefit to all constituents such as basic police and fire services and the costs of those that provided a special benefit such as inspection services for which fees could be charged the customer.

As the new City Manager of La Palma, California I struggled in assembling my first budget wherein I inherited a small general fund carry over from the previous year. La Palma is principally a residential community with property tax being the principle source of funds. Small neighborhood shopping centers did not produce substantial sales tax revenue. La Palma was in serious financial peril.

Douglas Ayres of Management Services Institute came to my rescue. Doug prepared a report and delivered a presentation to the City Council with the legal and practical reasons for and a description of the difference between general benefit services and special services. His report developed a methodology which included a narrative description of all special services, the full cost of such services including overhead, recommendations regarding the percentage of costs to be recovered for these services and the revenue to be received based upon the historical volume of the delivered special services.

The City Council could now make policy decisions regarding the setting of special service fees with a clear understanding of the full costs associated with them, the amount of revenue to be recovered or the amount of subsidy that resulted with the established fee. The Council accepted the recommendations as presented. Over time the percentage of recovery for a few of the special service fees were modified but with that clear understanding.

In La Palma the additional revenue that was generated through the levy of special service fees gave the city "breathing room" to get its other finances in order. Both in La Palma and later in Chino, California thousands of additional funds were generated and most importantly taxes that were collected for general benefit services would not be diverted to support special services.

Richard Rowe
City Manager (Retired)

CHAPTER IV

REVENUE SOURCES for LOCAL GOVERNMENT SERVICES

The array of revenue sources available to local governments is vast. But to secure those "available" requires much study, political understanding and support and, it is hoped, supporting data and information made available by means of this Book.

The following Tables illustrate what one middle-sized, but fairly affluent city secures from the various types of taxes. The array will vary widely throughout the United States, but the first two – Sales and Property -- taxes predominate for local government. The base issue being addressed by this Book is the fact that taxes, by definition, are levied on some property or economic activity that is not necessarily connected to the municipal services which the tax is utilized to finance. That misguidance of monies could be significantly modified by use of the *Municipal Business System.*

The Basics. The overarching goal of cost identification data accumulation is to have capability to determine the closest match between payers and beneficiaries of taxes. The term "GENERAL PUBLIC BENEFIT" denotes, or at least it should, that taxes are utilized to finance services for "the community at large". PERSONAL CHOICE SERVICES should be paid for by fees charged to those securing direct benefit from or are specifically targeted for utilization of a non-tax supported service. Tax monies should not be diverted to these PERSONAL CHOICE SERVICES from GENERAL PUBLIC BENEFIT SERVICES. Such diversion is a major inequitable burden on taxpayers and unwarranted subsidy to a limited number of individuals or limited number groups.

Diversion. The following Exhibits, Tables and Schedules show the taxes secured by several jurisdictions. Schedule 13 definitively shows the array of "General Benefit Services" financed by taxes. However, carried over from the detailed identification and analysis of the "Personal Choice Services" indicates that $44,921,338 in taxes were being diverted to the imposing list of "Personal Choice Services".

The result is astounding. Of the $97,843,355 in tax revenues $44,921,338, or 46%, was diverted away from "General Benefit Services" to subsidize "Personal Choice Services". The question that must be asked is: *Is such diversion of taxes to the benefit of "Personal Choice Services" users justified and defendable?*

Is this REALLY how the City Council wants to spend its tax monies? Information upon which a decision, or a series of decisions, are provided by an analysis such as this can provide elected officials data which they can support, to secure equity.

EXHIBIT 1—Revenue Sources for Local Government Services

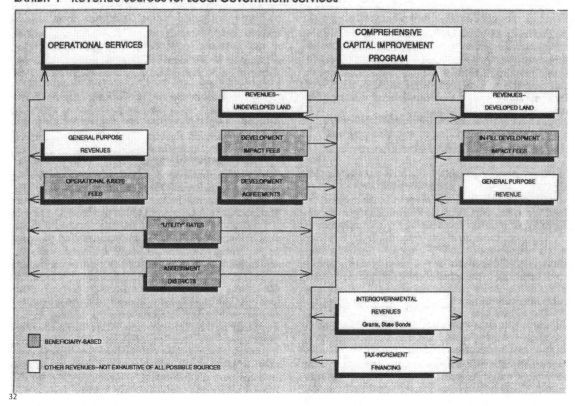

32

Exhibit 1 is from *Establishing the Cost of Services*, a Management Information Service (MIS) Report of the International City/County Management Association (ICMA), (Volume 22, Number 5, May 1990). This issue was instigated by work being performed by Management Services, Inc., (MSI) (now Revenue and Cost Specialists, LLC). At that time Douglas W. Ayres was the Chairman/CEO of MSI and, as a long time ICMA Member and former City Manager of several cities, had convinced ICMA staff that the future lie in matching revenues with costs, and assuring the accuracy and completeness of those "costs".

Each of Mary O'Neil, Director of Management Services and Treasurer for the City of Chino, California; and Barbara Steckel, Finance Director and Treasurer of the City of Riverside, California, contributed articles to the MIS Report. Each were clients of MSI; O'Neill in her second City (La Palma, CA being the first) where she and City Manager Richard Rowe had MSI analyze their City's operations and determine costs and revenues, and match the two. Analysis of Chino then transpired.

The twinned articles are entitled "Cost Recovery Analysis in Two California Cities". Douglas Weiford was then City Manager of Riverside, several years later John Holmes became Riverside City Manager.

Exhibit 1 was prepared by O'Neill to illustrate the mixture and use of revenue sources utilized by the two cities she served for which MSI had conducted its Revenue and Cost Studies.

Unfortunately for the progress of municipal government, "good economic times" arrived, revenues rose dramatically, and desire and necessity to ascertain full costs withered. And dedication to knowing costs ended due to lack of both political interest, and cost accounting personnel.

City of Pasadena, California
1992-1993

Tax Revenue Group	Pct.
Sales & Use Tax	22.29%
Property Taxes	22.12%
Utility Users Tax	16.91%
Contributions from Enterprise Funds	10.00%
Motor Vehicle In-Lieu	4.70%
Intergovernmental Revenue	4.23%
TOTAL	80.25%

Schedule 12

CITY OF PASADENA
SCHEDULE OF TAX REVENUES
FISCAL YEAR 1992-93

MSI REF	SOURCE	BUDGET 1992-93	PER CAPITA
TAX-1	SALES AND USE TAX	$21,760,015	$166.11
TAX-2	PROPERTY/TRANSFER/EXEMPTION TAX	$21,592,812	$164.83
TAX-7	UTILITY USERS TAX	$16,502,260	$125.97
TAX-15	CONTRIBUTIONS FROM ENTERPRISE FUNDS	$9,765,387	$74.54
TAX-4	MOTOR VEHICLE IN-LIEU	$4,587,525	$35.02
TAX-10	INTERGOVERMENTAL REVENUE	$4,352,324	$33.22
TAX-5	INVESTMENT EARNINGS	$3,900,000	$29.77
TAX-11	BUSINESS TAX	$3,250,000	$24.81
TAX-3	STATE & FEDERAL STREET & HWY GRANTS	$3,148,015	$24.03
TAX-6	TRANSIENT OCCUPANCY TAX	$2,900,000	$22.14
TAX-14	UNDERGROUND UTILITIES TAX	$2,747,407	$20.97
TAX-13	CONSTRUCTION TAX	$1,630,800	$12.45
TAX-9	INTERGOVTL CAPITAL PROJECTS REVENUE	$1,575,000	$12.02
TAX-12	OTHER FUND REVENUE	$125,000	$0.95
TAX-8	OTHER MISCELLANEOUS REVENUES	$6,810	$0.05
	TOTAL	$97,843,355	$746.90

NOTES:

The various Tax categories include a number of different revenue accounts.

The per capita amounts are calculated by using the approximated City population of 131,000.

Schedule 13

CITY OF PASADENA
SCHEDULE OF TAX SUPPORTED SERVICES
FISCAL YEAR 1992–93

MSI REFERENCE	SERVICE PROVIDED	TOTAL	PER CAPITA
S–236	STATUS OF WOMEN ISSUES COORDINATION	$183,548	$1.40
S–237	CHILD CARE ISSUES COORDINATION	$191,706	$1.46
S–238	CHILD & YOUTH ISSUES COORDINATION	$193,837	$1.48
S–239	SENIOR CITIZEN ISSUES COORDINATION	$97,699	$0.75
S–240	HUMAN RELATIONS & MISCELLANEOUS ISSUES COORDINATION	$141,652	$1.08
S–241	PASADENA VOLUNTEER PROGRAM	$120,287	$0.92
S–242	COMMUNITY CENTER SERVICES	$921,018	$7.03
S–243	NEIGHBORHOOD CONNECTIONS	$201,690	$1.54
S–244	PROSECUTION–PUBLIC SAFETY	$927,493	$7.08
S–245	FIRE SUPPRESSION & INVESTIGATION	$13,958,621	$106.55
S–246	DISASTER PREPAREDNESS	$98,087	$0.75
S–247	CRIME PREVENTION & INTERDICTION	$4,788,818	$36.56
S–248	PATROL SERVICES	$17,135,612	$130.81
S–249	CRIMINAL INVESTIGATION & ANALYSIS	$4,933,876	$37.66
S–250	CRIME PREVENTION & INVST SUPPORT	$1,382,143	$10.55
S–251	GRAFFITI REMOVAL PROGRAM	$111,093	$0.85
S–252	CURRENT PLANNING PROGRAM	$1,459,953	$11.14
S–253	GENERAL PLAN UPDATE	$783,269	$5.98
S–254	URBAN CONSERVATION & HISTORIC PRESERVATION	$289,346	$2.21
S–255	GROWTH MANAGEMENT INITIATIVE ADMN PROGRAM	$19,734	$0.15
S–256	PUBLIC ARTS PROGRAM	$582,539	$4.45
S–257	LIBRARY SERVICES & SPECIAL PROGRAMS	$7,793,489	$59.49
S–258	CAREER SERVICES PRORAMS	$2,191,539	$16.73
S–259	PROJECT D.A.Y. SUPPPORT	$54,757	$0.42
S–260	GENERAL & NEEDS–TARGETED RECREATION	$681,433	$5.20
S–261	CAPITAL PROJECTS PROGRAM	$52,041,599	$397.26
S–262	GENERAL ENGINEERING PROJECTS	$589,043	$4.50
S–263	TRANSPORTATION PLANNING	$1,868,429	$14.26
S–264	TRAFFIC SERVICES–SIGN/STRIPE/SIGNAL	$1,307,570	$9.98
S–265	GENERAL STREET/BRIDGE/CURB MAINTENANCE	$15,094,832	$115.23
S–266	CITY PARK & CULTURAL FACILITY MAINTENANCE	$1,442,980	$11.02
S–267	TOBACCO CONTROL PROGRAM	$179,019	$1.37
S–268	PUBLIC HEALTH EDUCATION & DISEASE PROGRAM	$527,514	$4.03
S–269	NON–DEPARTMENTAL DEBT/CONTRIBUTIONS/OBLIGATIONS	$16,156,326	$123.33
S–270	ELECTIONS PROGRAM	$398,752	$3.04
S–271	NORTHWEST ISSUES COORDINATION	$865,754	$6.61
	SUBTOTAL -- TAX SERVICES	$149,714,855	$1,142.86
	TAX SUBSIDIES TO FEE & CHGE SVCS (SCHEDULE 11)	$44,921,338	$342.91
	TOTAL -- TAX SUPPORT	$194,636,193	$1,485.77

=========
NOTES:
The Detail for the Tax Services is found in Appendix C.
The per capita amounts are caluated by using the approximated City population of 131,000.

Page 171

Pasadena Cost Control Report

Tax Service Costs

As shown on Schedule 13, MSI divided the City's general benefit/tax services into thirty-six service centers that cost a total of $149,714,855. In addition to these direct tax and non-fee supported services, taxes are needed to cover the shortfall in fee-supported services by $44,921,338. Although the fee-supported services of Chapter V are "private goods" in the sense that the user is identifiable, there will be a social purpose in continuing some subsidies. Together, the two components currently require the use of $194,636,193 in taxes. This final figure is the 1992-93 fiscal year, full, businesslike cost of the City's services. The detail for each of these general benefit/tax services is found in Appendix C.

As discussed in Chapter II, MSI identified two major categories of service for costing purposes: Special Benefit Services and General Benefit Services. A third category, Limited Benefit Services, also exists. Since these services normally receive general tax dollar subsidies in addition to grants or restricted revenues, they have been included with the Special Benefit Services for simplification.

Tax Vs. Fee

If a revenue is a "tax," then it becomes part of the City's "Proceeds of Taxes" amount for comparison with the Proposition 4 Appropriation Limit. At the point that the Limit is reached, the City may have to refund some of its taxes. However, when a revenue is a "fee," the Council may establish the fee at whatever level the costs are and the revenue becomes part of the "Non-Proceeds of Taxes." Nevertheless, calling any revenue a "fee," including franchise fees and maintenance assessments, would require that it be used for the service charged.

The General Theory. The basics of American democracy hold that those who are able to pay should not only pay for the services which they receive from government for the general good, but also for those special benefit services which they receive. However, as the array of services demanded and provided to citizens and businesses by government have multiplied, the basics have been lost sight of. The broad and ubiquitous municipal "General Fund" containing most revenues, coupled with the demand for service has led city councils into the death spiral of attempting to be all things to all people, without examining either the cost or benefits.

The Specifics. The MSI Revenue/Cost match-up system, for which data is provided and summarized in this Report, enables the City Council to bridge the "Ignorance Gap" to determine specifically who pays what and how much and what they receive from the City in return for the payment.

Chapter VI - Tax Revenues and Services

The Results. This Report shows definitively, and in exact amount, what revenues finance each and every City service, who benefits, the dollar value of the benefit, and a quantification of the benefits. Further, to the extent that any tax monies are utilized in the provision of Special Benefit Services, that amount is given. Thus the City Council will have the information upon which to base decisions as to whether a narrowly based specific service benefitting specific beneficiaries should be subsidized by general tax monies or financed in whole or major part by fees or special charges or taxes paid by targeted beneficiaries.

Utilization of the Categories. Schedule 14, which follows, can be utilized by the City Council in its quest to maximize fairness and equity in the payment for services provided by the City, to attempt to assure that there is as close a relationship as possible between payment and benefit as the City Council chooses.

Division as Assistance. The divisions contained in Schedule 14 may further assist the City Council in its policy deliberations as it decides both level of service which can be afforded, and the extent that costs incurred will be met by taxes paid by all or by fees paid in direct relationship to benefits derived, or some balance between the two and, if so, on what basis should the balance be measured.

City of Coachella, California
1988-1989

The woes, process, and recovery of this relatively small predominately Hispanic city at the southeast end of the famous Palm Springs area was covered in the prior Chapter. The following tables illustrate that "save" from several poor choices and limited staff capabilities. The woes of Coachella generally were identical to, but 'worse' than most of those for which MSI worked. But, by experience gathered from engagements in states other than California, to the Author's satisfaction, such self-inflicted difficulties afflict to a major degree virtually every American city, county, town, village, township, special district and virtually all 50 of the United States.

Simply put – "Personal Choice Services" are being heavily subsidized by taxes which more properly should be utilized to finance "General Benefit Services".

The Solution – **Universal application of the *Municipal Business System* and its requirement of "full disclosure" as set out in this Book, and citizen insistence on a severe limitation on utilization of taxes for other than clearly defined "General Benefit Services", must be secured.** Current levels of taxpayer disgust are absolutely valid.

TABLE 7
BUDGET/ACTUAL TAX REVENUES -- 1988-89

		REVISED BUDGET 1988-89	UNAUDITED REPORT 1988-89
TAX 1	Property Taxes	$416,000	$394,127
TAX 2	Redevelopment Income	$1,048,000	$740,747
TAX 3	Motor Vehicle In-Lieu Tax	$448,576	$540,734
TAX 4	General Sales and Use Taxes	$553,000	$689,950
TAX 5	Business License	$60,000	$60,808
TAX 6	Community Development Block Grants	$126,300	$20,762
TAX 7	Cigarette Tax	$28,000	$27,061
TAX 8	Special Police Tax	$0	$0
TAX 9	Special Fire Tax	$0	$0
TAX 10	Property Transfer Tax	$2,000	$6,433
TAX 11	Construction Development Tax	$82,500	$50,723
TAX 12	Gas Taxes	$203,600	$225,173
TAX 13	Other State Grants	$59,881	$65,131
TAX 14	County Grants	$0	$6,500
TAX 15	Homeowners Property Tax Relief	$8,800	$2,815
TAX 16	Miscellaneous State Subventions	$10,000	$9,827
TAX 17	Miscellaneous Revenue	$165,064	$341,114
TAX 18	Property Tax - Water Debt Service	$58,950	$47,673
TAX 19	Property Tax - Sewer Debt Service	$124,300	$121,652
		$3,394,971	$3,351,230

Explanation of Schedule 12. Each of the 13 tax-supported services, starting with the current tax subsidy to fee services, are listed on the following Schedule 12.

SERVICE PROVIDED is the service which is financed by taxes, "non-taxes" of grants, bond issuances, and state and federal restricted grants. These amounts are contained on Schedule 1, Revenue History.

TOTAL COST is the total "costs reasonably borne" of the service provided. Due to financing by taxes and non-fee revenues, as previously explained, the tax supported "service centers" are far broader in definition than fee-supported service centers.

TOTAL -- TAX SUPPORTED is the total "costs reasonably borne" of the of the 12 wholly or partially tax-supported service centers and is $6,493,131. To understand fully the implications of this amount one should re-read in Chapter III, the definitions of "costs reasonably borne", the Constitutional derivation of the elements of costs, and the way which MSI, Inc. has applied those definitions and arrived at these total costs.

<u>TOTAL -- FEE AND CHARGE SUPPORTED</u> represents the revenue received for the provision of the 106 previously discussed fee-based service centers based on the City's current fee structure.

<u>TOTAL RESOURCES REQUIRED.</u> The City needs a total of $8,837,773 of taxes and fees, expressed in 1988-89 dollars, with which to continue, in perpetuity, to finance the City's services it currently offers.

CITY OF COACHELLA -- SCHEDULE 12
SUMMARY OF OPERATING TAX EXPENDITURES

FISCAL YEAR 1988-89 BUDGET

REFERENCE #	SERVICE PROVIDED	TOTAL
Refer to Sch. 9	Fee and Charge Service Cost	$4,612,208
Refer to Sch. 9	Fee and Charge Service Revenue	$2,344,642
Refer to Sch. 9	Centers with Cost "NA" 's	$1,600
	* TOTAL -- FEE AND CHARGE SUPPORTED	$2,265,966
Tax Service 101	* Tax Supported Fee & Charge Services	$2,265,966
102	Business Licenses	$15,022
103	Community Promotion	$163,566
104	Economic Development	$8,087
105	General Planning	$85,038
106	Redevelopment	$353,245
107	General Engineering	$131,158
108	Police Operations	$1,198,496
109	Police Investigation	$90,664
110	Police Support Services	$253,171
111	Fire Prevention	$110,085
112	Fire Suppression	$620,586
113	General Street Maintenance	$1,198,047
	TOTAL -- TAX SUPPORTED SERVICES	$6,493,131
	TOTAL -- FEE & CHARGE SUPPORTED	$2,344,642
	TOTAL RESOURCES REQUIRED	$8,837,773

__The Shortfall.__ From the above the City's plight can be seen:

TOTAL *__TRUE__* COST OF ALL SERVICES................ **$8,837,773**

Tax and Grant Revenues.......................................$3,351,230
Fee and Charge Revenues...................................... $2,344,642
       TOTAL REVENUES................................... $5,695,872

       SHORTFALL..$3,141,901

The above boxed text, repeated here, states the case rather succinctly:

__The City needs $8,837,773 of taxes and fees, expressed in 1988-89__
__dollars, with which to continue, in perpetuity, to finance the City's__
__services it currently offers."__

MSI proceeded to issue supplemental action Reports showing exactly how costs could be reduced and controlled, and revenues increased. But over time. Gently. Politically wisely. But precisely. All recommendations were then installed. Subsequently Coachella was "discovered" during the "Great Palm Springs Expansion" from the early 1990's until the real estate financing crash in 2007-08. Its recovery base thus became increasingly firm.

All involved in the 1989 "rescue" learned one big lesson: ***When confronted with truly open minds, without ideological paralysis, difficulties in extremis can be resolved.*** However, a major key to resolution is the act of legislative confrontation, open and fully honest transparency, professional explanation, and a step-by-step process to absolution.

__Recognition.__ All governing bodies need to recognize a basic fact of governmental, business, and corporate fiscal life:

Revenues can be used only once, for a service within one of the following:

       1. Tax-supported Services
              OR
       2. To Subsidize Fee-Financed Services

Past "standard and traditional public finance" has been based on the assumption that when facilities and assets must be replaced one of two things would occur:

       1. Property taxes will be increased
              OR
       2. Property tax-financed General Obligation Bonds will be voted.

The former is now either constitutionally or statutorily prohibited or seriously limited in many states. If not, then the political winds and economic turbidity is such that few elected officials are sufficiently hardy to even try to increase property taxes.

Number 2 also has been limited in many states, and/or the mind-set of the electorate is such that "It just ain't gonna happen!"

The importance of the utilization of extant tax monies exclusively to finance tax-supported ***General Benefit Public Services*** thus can be seen. And NOT to use taxes to subsidize ***Special Private Benefit Services***. *Taxes need to be repatriated and recaptured.*

Academic Legitimacy. In 1977 Dr. Robert Biller, Dean of the School of Public Administration of the University of Southern California, enticed Ayres to be a non-tenured Professor in his School. In 1981 he astutely wrote his observations of "the phenomena" Ayres was in the process of developing.

> *It is through the variable delivery of public services that the unique needs or preferences of a heterogeneous population can best be addressed. The decision rule becomes basically doing as little as possible commonly and as much as possible variably...We should act to associate benefits and costs as closely as possible...The public sector should work hard to establish charges wherever possible on the variable services that unique citizens wish....In the same vein, the public sector should work to establish benefit assessment districts for groups of citizens who want particular enhanced service levels for particular geographic areas or because of functional preferences.*[33]

Ayres had been teaching at USC in Adjunct status since January of 1975, rising to full Professor in 1978. As can be surmised, Biller and Ayres were philosophically of the same mind, as can be surmised from the piece Bob wrote in 1981. The two had mutual effects on one another about "government benefits" and how/who should pay.[34]

That same year the MSI ***Municipal Business System*** [MBS] was being perfected, partner/shareholders acquired, more employees recruited, and several of the newly introduced 35 pound "luggable" Compaq computers purchased. Then MSI custom MBS software was programmed for those by Rick Kermer, CPA, and later, by Eric Johnson. The then-leading spread sheet software Lotus 1-2-3 formed a customizing idea.

The Author continued teaching Public Finance, Public Budgeting, Public Personnel, Public Administration, and various workshops, seminars, in-service CPA sessions, and other special interest classes "spreading the gospel" until retirement from USC mid-1990. Promotion and explanation of the MSI MBS approach continued throughout Ayres' CSULB, USC and UCI sequential 15 year academic run. Students were, and became clients, having been [some claimed] "brainwashed" into understanding the GASB-required accounting standards and then determining how their current or future employer was far out of compliance. And removed from reality as to the cost of services and uses of revenues. Thus the Professor Ayres USC-assigned duty of "outreach" into the local government constituency for the Graduate School of Public Administration led to yet more converts and clients and more intertwining of teaching, consulting, and academic expansion.

---

[33] Biller, Robert P., former Dean of the School of Public Administration, University of Southern California (then University Provost); "Making a More Direct Democracy Work; The Opportunity of Shrinking Resources", Los Angeles, March, 1981; pages 12 and 13.

[34] See "How I Became a Professor" in Ayres, Douglas W.; *Right In the City – Volume II - More Bizarre Tales*; Trafford Publishing, Victoria, BC, Canada (now Bloomington, Indiana); 2010; pages 131-140; available at Trafford.com and Amazon.com

No one on either side of the equation -- being taught or devising the need for financial analysis – ever complained. To them, and more important, to the Author, these two efforts were a continuum of local government improvement. One favorite saying, repeated in varying forms to each and every class and workshop each day was simple and direct:

> *There is absolutely no reason why government cannot be as effective and efficient as private business and corporations are alleged to be.*

<u>***Political Conclusion.***</u> Absolute confrontation of a "financial crisis" of *any* nature, when proclaimed by professionally astute analysis, is vital for both of organizational and political survival. The very word "political" shares a common Greek root with the word "tooth", thus deeply and historically infers biting into the problem and resolving it by policy development. But, as those of us who have spent decades within definitively political environments, experiencing and then having to implement policy decisions, yet another important lesson has to be learned, because it is <u>absolute dicta</u>:

> *Politically developed and adopted policies are useless and/or wholly ineffective unless and until fully and impartially implemented by professional "bureaucrats".[35] ©*

So now we former bureaucrats, now business owners, have developed a workable emulation of the corporate approach to products, costs and profits –

The Municipal Business System

But we were loyal bureaucrats, and all our governmental clients did and still will do without any of profit, high salaries, bonuses, stock options, jets, limousines, traveling first or business class, multiple cumulative retirement plans, expensive office art works, unlimited expense accounts, outlandish job or 'position' perquisites, up-scale country club memberships, and lavish birthday parties. All those are considered to be "basic costs of doing *corporate business*", thus are untaxed, being legitimate "business expenses".

We had NO possibility of selling the municipal corporation or spinning off any portion thereof to secure either of personal or group capital gain. Yet most of we "public servants" see ourselves as just that, despite the comparative fact that many of us literally are responsible for lives, property and budgets valued from hundreds of millions to scores of billions of dollars. And our top salaries were and are no more than five or six times that of the lowest paid employee for whom we have empathy and responsibility, not a factor of 1>80 or far more as in scores of corporations, private equity and hedge funds, partnerships, LLCs, and various other forms of for-profit private businesses.

And the corporate lobbied tax loopholes, exemptions, and subsidies, both for their corporation and executives, are plot how to provide millions of campaign dollars to those political candidates who will not only continue, but expand those corporate benefits.

So, the "public servants" labor on, as First Responders.

---

[35] Repeatedly used in various speeches, lectures and articles by Douglas W. Ayres

To Whom it May Concern: December 10, 2011

I was the City Manager of the City of Porterville from 1977 until 2002. During my first ten (10) years the population of the city increased 51%. During that ten year period the City Council was confronted with the monumental task of maintaining an acceptable level of service to the citizens, while at the same time dealing with severe financial constraints. The financial constraints were brought about in part because of the passage of Proposition 13, the Federal Governments' elimination of general revenue sharing and the City's significant population growth.

The City of Porterville was like most other California Cities, searching for additional revenue sources, not only to finance the day to day operations of the City, but to address the immediate and long term capital improvements needs.

We began to focus on fees for services. However, the City did not possess the appropriate methodology to identify and fully cost special services such as conditional use permits, building permits, recreation activities, ad infinitum. This data was important for the City Council to have in order to make sound policy decisions relating to setting fees.

In 1987 the City Council retained the services of Doug Ayres, President of Management Services Institute (MSI) to analyze the City operation for alternate and equitable ways to finance the City's services and capital improvements.

In early 1988 Doug Ayres presented the comprehensive report to the City Council. The report described in detail the difference between tax supported general benefit services and special services. The report developed the methodology and description of all special services, the full cost of providing those services (including overhead), the total revenue generated by existing fees (if a fee was charged) and the amount of tax subsidy being provided for those services. The report enabled the City Council, for the first time, to set policy on all fees based on knowledge of costs, revenues to be generated, or the the amount of subsidy.

In addition, the report addressed alternatives for financing capital improvements. In late 1988, the City Council approved bonding through Certificates of Participation in the amount of $20.6 million. The monies were secured for a new police facility, a new fire substation, expansion of City Hall, water and sewer projects. The water projects included the purchase of three private water companies that were integrated into the City's water system. The City Council established adequate user fees based on methodology recommended in Management Services Institutes report. It is felt we received a favorable bond rating because of documentation created by the report.

Initially we were interested in retaining Doug Ayres and Management Services to enhance City revenues. This was accomplished. During my tenure hundreds of thousands of dollars were generated through applying special user fees. However, an extremely important result of the report is that it created a business model to do City business in a business like manner.

Guy Huffaker
City Manager, retired

CHAPTER V

WHO CONSUMES LOCAL GOVERNMENT SERVICES?

The first situation to be confronted by any serious study of the status and viability of local government is an enumeration of the services currently provided by the government unit, and the facilities within and by which such activities are supplied. Without an extensive and exhaustive listing of "what" is being provided, choices cannot be made. And, that choice should be made by the ultimate consumer – 1) either the requester or 2) the direct beneficiary of the activity. These two categories are not necessarily the same groups, although for some services such can and should be put forth and argued as to applicability.

__Categorization.__   Of necessity there are two very broad categories of public service that need be enumerated.

First, discretionary services.

Second, mandatory services.

Now, some degree of discernment between the two will be provided.

Immediately, an argument – not discussion – over semantics raises its ugly head. This brouhaha morphs into: Why are some services considered mandatory?

For example, the petroleum industry argues that their work is environmentally sound, safe and thus should not be subject to the "intense regulation and controls" implemented after the Gulf of Mexico BP Macondo Well explosion, deaths and resultant damage.

Other similar discussions surround drug approvals by new medicines put forth by the industry labeled as "Big Pharma". The recent salmonella infestation of roughly 1% of the national egg supply had three results: 1) demand for more testing, inspections and regulation. 2) claims of governmental interference with maximization of food production. 3) need for an alternate system of industry self-monitoring.

__Conflicts.__ The self-immolation of the housing industry and its supporting financial markets resulted in Congress eking out a much-compromised "regulatory protocol" referred to by non-partisan economic sources as "inadequate" and "ineffective".[36]

The above are national and state issues, but well-publicized. Thus examples of "discussions" to come, but viewed in light of the above *pro* and *con* circumstances. These philosophical "for" and "against" discussions are held regularly at the local and state

---

[36] *Financial Times* and *The Economist;* various articles at various times, repeatedly, in excruciatingly detailed text and tabular form, with intensely researched data back-up by internationally-renowned institutions and experts, including several Nobel Laureates.

levels "in these trying economic times". Unfortunately, most "consumers" of local government services have no idea or even concept of what they secure from their local government(s); what jurisdiction, business or who provides it; or even worse, the process by which the functions are delivered. "They just happen."

This most basic of understandings was brought into this Author's world in a mind-boggling quite revelational manner, This event literally formed the absolute need to provide some framework, with as much detail and as open as functionally and linguistically/grammatically possible, to inform local government tax and rate payers of **what** they get, **how** and from **whom**, and for **how much**, and through **what form of fiscal exaction.**

Situation. In the 1960's the City of Salem, Oregon, where the Author was City Manager, was growing rapidly. The area was hilly, those scenic uprisings being solid limestone, loosely covered by soil, trees and grass. Thousands of dwellings, with commercial interstices, State Capital buildings, and housing for 85,000 persons, were sprawled across and around the magnificent landscaping made possible by the copious rainfall, hills and mild weather of the Willamette Valley. But, another 35,000 souls, and some businesses, populated a similar immediately adjacent unincorporated area, titled South Salem.

Regular, and increasing numbers of complaints were being lodged with the Marion County Health Department about "green slime sliding down the hill into my backyard". Resultingly, scary reports of diseases feared to be emanating from the slippery stuff in which children played, it having invaded many backyards. Investigation proved beyond doubt that the slime was produced by septic tank seepage from "uphill homes". These facts and factors quickly combined to demand the installation of sanitary sewers. And discovery that the only financially feasible way to do such was by means of annexation to the fully-sewered and fiscally solid City of Salem. That the City had just begun constructing what then was to be the largest primary and secondary sewage treatment plant in the Pacific Northwest was a salient driving force to the drumbeat demanding joining Salem to secure sewers and sewage relief.

The election was held and South Salem overwhelmingly opted to join the City, driven specifically to secure sewers to remove the slime. To the north Keizer opted out.

Revelation. Plans were prepared, assessment districts formed, costs estimated and neighborhood information meetings scheduled. City staff prepared attractive, informative graphics and beautiful slide presentations. Meetings were to be led by the Mayor and a Councilman at each of the nine Ward conclaves. Staff was prepared to assure "full information about the costs and their distribution" now that the demanded and petitioned-for construction was to begin soon. Each meeting had two parts. First, the magnificent well-documented and prepared articulate presentation by elected officials and City staff. Then, free-wheeling audience participation question and unlimited-length answer period.

The first part of the first meeting went well, but audience eyes seemed glazed, with mouths up tight and faces indicating confusion. Staff knew we were "bombing", but had no idea why. "Things just weren't going well."

Then **IT** happened. The first question was from a lady who appeared to be in her 60's, but she was quite articulate and determined. She simply said:

> *I'm confused. I have no idea what you're talking about. And what's so expensive? I go into the bathroom, sit and do my thing, flush, and IT just goes. What's all this stuff you're talking about? IT just goes!*

With that we folded up our easels, collected the remaining hand-outs, and retired, a beaten bunch of equally confused politicians, administrators, financial types, and engineers. Next day we recovered and each, individually, had our own *EUREKA* moments. After my personal epiphany, I immediately convened a staff meeting to reconstruct reality. All agreed that we had assumed far too much; that any discussion of any details about bodily functions simply would go nowhere. The level of constituent ignorance was unexpected and, obviously, had been unsuspected. So each of the graphics and presentations, and the entire underlying belief system was recast.

Subsequent far more simplistic illness-centric and mechanistic presentations proceeded well. We only emphasized "green slime" and generalized "public health". And physically how and where IT went. Ample compliments rained down, as did mother nature, and South Salem and numerous additional properties adjacent to Salem were duly annexed and sewered. The ubiquitous green slime thereby was removed, effluent treated, and the Willamette River made pure again.

And at least one public administrator was duly educated about levels of public knowledge and understanding.

Conclusion. By utilizing this Book a broadly-informed municipal finance analyst should be able to sift through all activities of the jurisdiction and develop the following:

1   *Services provided*
2   *Division into "General Public Benefit Services" provided to the Community-at-large*
3   *"Personal Choice Services" that are of direct benefit to the recipient*
4   *Source of income for each service*
5   *Beneficiary of each service*
6   *True and full documented cost of each and every service*
7   *Creation of a fund structure and service center cost distribution accounting system*
8   *Assignment of each Service Center to the appropriate fund*
9   *Designation of "Service Center Managers"*
10   *Allocation of Service Centers to appropriate revenue sources*
11   *Assurance that each Service Center Manager and Fund is appropriately supervised*
12   *Development of service measurement standards and reporting*
13   *Transparent fully disclosed reporting of revenues, costs and service beneficiaries*
14   *Development of and preparation of annual budgets based on* the herein outlined **Municipal Business System**

From there the detailed work ascertaining and developing each item in the above simplified list begins.

REDUCING COSTS BY IMPROVING EMPLOYEE MORALE

In 1972, while City Manager of Inglewood, California, a "great and noble experiment" was launched, with the goal of reducing employee costs while simultaneously increasing employee morale. This major change in organizational culture occurred immediately following full implementation of what a few years later acquired the title of *Municipal Business System.*

Flexible Employee Hours. The following described employee work hour revisions have been attempted in numerous jurisdictions and companies, under several names. In Inglewood it was "Flexible Employee Hours". The elements and organizational implementation were simple.

1.   Review the hours "normally" worked by each of the 940 employees
2.   Determine what positions are, and are not conducive to conversion to Flexible Hours
3.   Exclude those positions – primarily sworn Police, certified Fire and EMS, Refuse and some utilities plant operations personnel – that were not conducive to the program
4.   Include item 3 personnel whose duties are neither shift nor public contact sensitive
5.   Establish, then review the proposed "protocol" with all employee representatives, all Service Center Managers, and all Project Team Leaders
6.   Make appropriate individual and organizational adjustments to meet the needs of as many as possible of the public receiving each municipal service
7.   Create and publish the protocol by presenting it to several all-employee meetings

The Protocol. While some referred to "The Rules", that term quickly died, killed by skyrocketing employee morale and huge cost reductions. The following process was quite straight forward and immediately embraced by all involved.

A.   All affected employees would work 80 hours within each two week pay period, utilizing personal schedules that best satisfied individual *and* organizational needs
B.   The general hours-worked structure of each employee would be provided by that individual to each supervisor affecting that employee
C.   Any daily special hours deviations would be worked out between those involved
D.   Public office hours were extended to 7:00 a.m. to 6:00 p.m. for all facilities save Libraries, which would extend hours to those which best met the needs of users
E.   A "specialist" in each field of public service must be available during open hours, which schedule will be worked out between employees and supervisors

Results. It became obvious very quickly that the new "work schedules" were highly popular with both of covered employees and the publics they served. As important, however, was the dramatic rise in morale, and cost and employee time savings:

1.)   Use of "sick" and "bereavement" leave plummeted, employees now being able to make required appointments, including with/for family members, and other revisions needed
2.)   Overtime, even for "crash projects", was eliminated for all but a very few "situations"
3.)   Use of "vacation" time now must be used for that, not "frittered" away hour-by-hour
4.)   Tardiness was totally eliminated, by the work hours flexibility
5.)   Direct, Indirect and Employee Benefit *costs* (not available benefits) were reduced by around 10%, without gripes or grumps, thus willingly
6.)   Payroll accounting and budgeting was greatly simplified

Soon it was discovered that around ⅓ liked to arrive early; ⅓ late; and ⅓ were totally flexible. And that ability to have greater control over work and personal time had value greater than $$$.

CHAPTER VI
SERVICE MEASUREMENT

Over the last decade "performance measurement" has become *de rigueur*. Almost cult-like, much has been written about, many "studies" have been performed by numerous local governments, but Rolling Stones-like, little "Satisfaction" has been achieved.

Measurement Elements. To this analyst, from reading and reacting to much of these published "research results", it seems that a logical progression of study generally has only begun to take place. This sequence is offered and explained in this Chapter. To secure *reliable* measurement the following steps would be necessary:

1. Definition of the service to be measured
2. Determination of customers/clientele served
3. Definition of all costs for each service
4. Determination of each and every cost incurred in service delivery
5. Revenue source(s) proposed to be used in delivery of each service
6. Match up of costs and revenues for each and every service
7. Assignment of ALL revenues and ALL costs such that the two balance for the jurisdiction's services being measured
8. Development and installation of an appropriate fund, revenue and service center accounting system
9. Assurance of a valid measurement of quality and quantity
10. Full disclosure of all revenues, costs, services, beneficiaries, and quality

Various Chapters of this book develop each of these needed elements for adequate measurement, but not necessarily in the order above listed.

Commentary on Appendix A. This addendum to this Book, "in the back of the book" provides a legal base for assuring non-corrupt implementation of some inevitable responses to cost finding. The referred-to Ordinance has variously been referred to as:

1. The Level Playing Field Ordinance

2. The Outsourcing Guidelines Ordinance

3. The Anti-Corruption Ordinance

Actually, that document acts in all three capacities. The adoption of and full application of corporate line-of-business, or corporate profit-center income-matched-to-cost-and-quality approach provides much data. Among the potential results is the possibility of contracting out activities which could do any number of things, following:

1. Profit a private party which, by the very nature of the activity, the governmental jurisdiction could not accomplish.

2. Provide Service Center Managers incentives to reduce costs, increase revenues or improve quality. Preferably all three.

3. Assure governing bodies and service users that the least possible costs and the highest quality of service is being provided.

4. Assure both of governmental and private business interests that provision of the specific service by a government is directly comparable, both in quality and in cost, to what the private sector could provide.

5. Assure all involved that outsourcing aspirants could not and would not provide jobs, monies, contributions, political support or other suspect or illicit, improper or inappropriate gains or benefits to any of elected or appointed officials or employees.

6. Assure that any attempt at privatizing would assure same for same, for each of quality, charge for, and cost of service.

7. Numerous other benefits of assuring transparency and full disclosure of service cost, level, quality, and process.

___*Variances.*___ Applicable Code references will change in each state and, since this Ordinance was first drafted, utilized and effective 20 years ago, each of situations, law, and corporate/business/political/government morality have markedly changed. However, the basic assertion remains well intact. The "taxpaying citizens" want their "hard earned money" to be utilized in the provision of "cost effective services", not corruptly leaking into the campaigns or income of either of elected or appointed officials. Even more vitally, the inherent corruption of awarding tax-paid outsourcing "deals" to favored political "contributors" in return for any of past, current, or future employment, benefits, political purposes or anything not made absolutely public to the media and public in all respects, is inherently and patently dishonest. And should be unequivocally illegal.

___*Admonition.*___ This Ordinance, if adopted and even marginally enforced, would stop such practices aborning. And assure level playing fields when the full costs of public services are honestly analyzed and determined -- and charged. "Outsourcing" is NOT the panacea for all that is "bad" in local government. Blindly contracting out, without any real and substantial comparative data as to both of costs and quality, is foolish. Giving away tax monies and the "municipal business" in no way is capable of solving "municipal problems" without considerable preceding knowledgeable honest analysis.

And worse, handing out those "hard earned tax dollars" without justification or documentation can literally be a criminal act. In many states that process would qualify as outright theft and be a recordable felony upon conviction. But not in other states.

Elected and appointed officials, and all employees of any and all levels of government, have a sworn fiduciary duty to ___*not*___ award public monies to ___*anyone*___ without written proved justification and documentation to absolutely justify and do so. Honestly applied.

Another View. Another, more practical way to view the proposed "Outsourcing Ordinance" provided as ***Appendix A*** is openly to re-title it as "The Anti-Corruption Ordinance". If successfully placed on the agenda of a public body, and **NOT** embraced and adopted, that tells something about the beliefs, morality, expectations, and reliability of those serving on the governing body – regardless of size. On reading this Ordinance, several well-motivated elected officials termed it "a nuclear device". That reference is germane, for in context, honesty and "fairness" would be institutionalized were it adopted. And enforced. Non-adoption immediately casts suspicion on the refusing elected officials. By **not** adopting they are inherently admitting that they will NOT utilize fair and equal costs, and are announcing that each would accept jobs, political and personal "contributions", payments and favors from those who would profit from and benefit from the outsourcing of municipal activities to profit-making business concerns.

Contrariwise, adoption of ***Appendix A*** as local law supplements State and federal legislation that of necessity is broader in nature. Passage acts to "immunize" those voting in favor of the Ordinance as pledging to remain "clean".   If anyone reading this believes the Author is being unduly harsh on elected and high-level appointed officials, all one must do is to read and/or observe the daily news to see a constant flow of horrible examples of WHY this Ordinance MUST be adopted, and rigidly enforced. Any public official who takes umbrage at the brashness, please realize that more than 60 years of intimate involvement at the highest levels of literally hundreds of local and state governments has provided the Author with adequate exposure to the crimes, peccadilloes, and outright perfidy of some, not all, elected and some, few, higher level appointed public officials. Further, attendance at in excess of 4,000 meetings of public bodies provided significant "education" in and to all manifestations of corruption. So much so I can "smell a rotten deal from a considerable distance". All public officials not operating under coverage of such an anti-corruption regime should be personally terrified.

CORRUPTION

A Flat-Out Statement. Corruption is rampant and controlling in the outsourcing of governmental activities. And that is "**CORRUPTION**" in all its ramifications and permutations. Everywhere. In government and especially for corporate and business government contract aspirants, and those seeking monumental tax dodges. The "problem" is that most is hidden under the term "lobbying" and "public interest informational" advertising. And now fully legal per the January 21, 2010 *Citizens United v. Federal Election Commission* [case 08-205] U.S. Supreme Court 5 to 4 decision. And virtually capable of being anonymous as to "contributory source". A constitutional amendment is needed, and soon, before the corrupters push their monetary and benefit tsunami over democracy.

Arizona, where the Author has lived for two decades, has quickly degenerated into the exemplar of how what by many is considered "CORRUPTION". The Governor, encouraged and aided by a two-thirds majority in both houses of the Legislature, even removed the Chair of the citizen-initiated constitutional Redistricting Commission. Why? Because a preliminary re-districting map achieved partisan and racial balance.

A recent run of exposès regarding outsourcing of the State of Arizona penal system has not resulted in any outburst of taxpayer disgust. Rather, NO adverse public reaction has been illustrated for this fiasco or the one following. One recent article contained the following revelations, now considered to be "normal and accepted", at least in Arizona.

> *Corrections Corp. of America, the country's largest private-prison operator, says it thrives by offering better service at a lower cost than state-run prisons....But when it comes to other ways of winning business, such as employing platoons of lobbyists, doling out campaign contributions and working through political connections, CCA stands head and shoulders above its competitors....'They spend a lot of money, and clearly, they spend it because it benefits their interest....*[37]

The article then relates how State offices, notably that of the current Governor, are populated by former CCA personnel, who regularly rotate between CCA and State government. Is this corruption, or has it now become the norm for government decision-making? Where is the line between partisanship and corruption; moral or monetary?

National Examples. Circumstances such as the above, and carefully worded revelations, are becoming not only common, but accepted. A major industry is very active:

> *U.S. coal companies have pumped $1.5 million into House Speaker John Boehner's political operation this year, a sign of the industry's beefed-up efforts to fight new and proposed regulations from the Obama administration....The coal industry now ranks as one of the top sources of cash for the Ohio Republican, rivaling such perennial GOP donors as Wall Street and the real-estate industry....**Donations** (sic-emphasis added) from coal-industry interests account for more than 10% of the $12.5 million Mr. Boehner collected from Jan. 1 to June 30....*"[38]

However, it must be stated here that such "contributions" are neither illegal nor "corrupt", despite the definitions some give those terms. The U.S. Congress and the U.S. Supreme Court decreed such revisions to the previously "standard" understood and now apparently inappropriate previous morality-based definitions.

Another perhaps even worse case, which was in fact found to be both of illegal and corrupt, was the case of two Pennsylvania judges who *"took more than $2 million in bribes from the builder"* of several contract juvenile detention centers. The judges had found hundreds of youths guilty, and ordered them incarcerated in the for-profit centers. Even the judge who sentenced the two *"spoke of the deep-rooted political culture that produced him, one in which corruption is tacitly accepted."*[39]

---

[37] *The Arizona Republic*; September 4, 2011, page A1
[38] "Coal Industry Backs Boehner"; *The Wall Street Journal;* September 13, 2011; page A4
[39] "Court sentences ex-judges to prison in kickbacks case"; *The Arizona Republic;* September 24, 2011; page A3

Thus it appears that what once was considered to be, and was legally defined as corruption, has undergone a transformation into a "perhaps it is O.K." A final shot opines:

> *A policy is a guiding principle, agreed upon values, which in local governments are established by the elected body.*[40]

In fulfillment of the latter *possibly and hopefully* "agreed upon values" the Ordinance proposed in Appendix A is offered as a way to seek and, again, *possibly and hopefully,* agree upon values for each specific local government.

Crony Capitalism & Redistricting. Per the November 13, 2011 CBS *60 Minutes* segment on serving in Congress is a certain way to become a multi-millionaire. The major point made by the broadcast was that Congress has managed to permit legislative "insider stock trading". Such is patently illegal when done by non-members of Congress, but entirely legal and prevalent for the members of the U.S. House of Representatives and the U.S. Senate. Are local government elected officials immune from such temptations?

The purpose of the following blurbs is to emphasize to those who naively might decide to outsource as to what kind of a garbage pit they might be falling into. Without a highly detailed and properly executed revenue-cost and effectiveness analysis as a precedent to any contract. Although some will say such safeguard methodologies are "unneeded", "wasteful" and "inappropriately accusatory", merely read the daily newspapers and view detailed newscasts for responses. All this raw knowledge & revelations direly infect local governments and their taxpaying constituencies. Two instances here follow, in addition to those provided just above.

> Many of America's major banks are too big to fail, so they can privatize profits while socializing risk….financial institutions boost leverage in search of super-size profits and bonuses. Banks pretend that risk is eliminated because it's securitized. Rating agencies accept money to issue an imprimatur that turns out to be meaningless. The system teeters, and then the taxpayer rushes in to bail bankers out. Where's the accountability? ….further, excessive inequality[which Lawrence Katz a Harvard economist states currently exists *in extremis*] can have two perverse consequences: first, the very wealthy lobby for favors, **contracts** and bailouts that distort markets; and, second, growing inequality undermines the ability of the poorest to invest in their own education.[41]

A more nefarious and indirect, but greatly impactful consequence and product of "corruption" has been cited as "Congressional Redistricting", following:

> Redistricting is the most political endeavor lawmakers ever undertake. It's also expensive. But it's money well spent if you're a partisan politician because redistricting is, at its core, a battle over which party will control the

---

[40] Nanni, Robert; The GovKnowledgeNetwork.org of the International City/County Management Association; e-mailed to the Author September 10, 2011

[41] Nicholas Kristof in *The Las Vegas Sun;* October 30, 2011; page 6

> political landscape for the next decade....Despite the fact that redistricting
> will influence the outcome of elections for the next decade, the Federal
> Elections Commission [FEC] found that redistricting is not an effort to
> influence a specific federal election...."The courts and Congress both have
> held for decades that writing huge checks to public officials can corrupt
> public officials"...." This entails allowing huge checks to be written to political
> parties. We've had laws on the books for decades to limit that threat and
> all that was thrown out the window." [42]

Thus it appears that it does not take an economics Nobel Laureate to realize that the private sector of the economy will attempt to dominate redistricting and other legislation enactments such that more taxpayer monies will be provided to outsourcing contractors.

The financial news media daily reports new corruption developments and forms in all of business and corporate governance, accounting, financial issues, and other forms of what only can be termed as improper, dubious, unethical and inherently illegal self-enrichment at the expense of others.[43] "Bet" is a key word for the self-titled financial services industry. That phrase has been added to the "immune category" count, to assure the governed that all is not well in America; that more bank "bail outs" are inevitable.

The Conundrum. A possible aid in appraising the value of local services outsourcing has been provided recently in Chicago; namely "managed competition" between government and corporate employees, equipment and procedures.   This effort reaches one known conflict and dilemma:

> *Each company has been allocated similar areas of the city to service, and*
> *their cost and performance will be compared with that of the public sector.*
> *The idea reflects an eternal dilemma for governments everywhere. While the*
> *private sector ought to be cheaper at providing services, often after the con-*
> *tract is won either the price goes up, or the quality of the service down;*
> *sometimes both.[44]*

Serious Questions. The Author challenges the above assumptions as being outlandish and based on total ignorance of work experience in the public sector at the local and state level. There is no reason for, and many reasons and examples why, the statement "the private sector ought to be cheaper" is untrue and absolutely unsupportable. There are numerous activities, such as refuse collection and disposal, that have other bases for remaining wholly "public". Public health is the usual citation. Additionally, street maintenance due to numerous free-ranging heavy refuse trucks remains public, so limiting the number and size of such generally overweight vehicles is proper. Such damage often is intense on residential streets.

---

[42] Anjeanete Damon in *The Las Vegas Sun; October 30, 2011; page 3*
[43] *Wall Street Journal; The Economist; Financial Times; Fortune; Money;* various national and local newspapers and other journals; national and local TV news via CBS, NBC, ABC, Fox, CNN, HLN, CNBC *et al*
[44] "Rubbish Competition"; *The Economist; October 22, 2011; page 36*

As further justification for public services is a simple reason previously cited: Why should tax monies be collected by a government merely to be cycled into the private sector"? Are such transfers fully legal and in consonance with the basics of the U.S. version of democracy? If the ideological desire of some groups is secured to "make government smaller" and tax transfers to private corporations are the vehicle, then is government really being made smaller? Or just services made fewer and worse in quality?

Run It Like a Business? This Book provides the ***Municipal Business System*** to "run it like a business". But that phrase merely is a mocking metaphor aimed at those who believe that all government is incompetent, unnecessary, too expensive, and should be "privatized". If the definition of "government" is accepted as non-profit, subject to election and thus regularly scheduled democratic inputs, and openly regulated by often-expressed public opinion, and annually budgeted and audited, then should government truly be "run like a business"? Certainly not like many of the businesses that have generated all the gory headlines of the past decade, for fraud, shoddy and non-existent paperwork, sloppy internal controls, and other violations of both human dignity and financial propriety. (See footnote 42 on the prior page)

Government must be an honest, ethical and open "business". Not like those disciples of the corporate world whose exploits often is the subject of demeaning headlines. The multi-line profit center business model is here applied to local units – and potentially – could be effective in state government. All that is needed is the political and personal integrity to recognize that the goal of government is NOT to transfer tax monies into the pockets of private enterprise and those individuals with "influence". Rather, the ONLY goal of government should be to provide effective and efficient services to the tax and fee-paying public. By the most cost effective and highest quality supplier, public or private. This Book shows in detail how to do that. But, also by means of an honest non-corrupt [*by **any** definition*] "business" approach. Hopefully, via adoption of the ***Municipal Business System***. Thereby local government can be "business-like" without slipping or falling into the morally wanting pit apparently many businesspersons have slid into.

Help Is Available. Once one gets past the epiphany of avoiding corruption, performance measurement of services needs to be provided, be those in-house or outsourced. Appropriate high quality help to assure the quality of government services is available. That aid can assure proper, desired, and appropriate levels of performance. The International City/County Management Association founded, supports, maintains, and offers Performance Management assistance thru its **Center for Performance Management**.

Center Offerings. A visit to the appropriate ICMA website can be quite fulfilling. Call up www.icma.org/en/results/center_for_performance_measurement/home and a cornucopia of quality measurement and how to achieve such will be revealed. The Performance Measurement program is backed by a "Knowledge Network" whereby ideas, successes, failures, remedies, and all types of information can be gathered and shared. On skimming through numerous pages, it readily can be seen that the much vaunted and *private* "private sector" does not have a monopoly on either of good management or quality control. And, even better – or worse, depending on one's viewpoint – failure in quality in government is open and transparent and, oftimes painfully remedied if not immediately corrected. A similar lack in the private sector many times is revealed only when people get very ill, die, or the offender is revealed and punished. Few federal and state agencies that are statutorily assigned to assure quality in private enterprise offerings have actual sufficient authority to seek major remedy or, if needed, evoke criminal filings.

Center Benefits. Following are random snippets from the numerous pages of information provided by merely scanning the ICMA Center for Performance Measurement (CPM) website cited previously. More than 150 peer governments in North America provide data to the Center.

1. Investigate and apply practices found to contribute to high performance in CPM communities

2. Have data mined by CPM staff in an effort to find high performers and interview them on the strategies they used to achieve exceptional results

3. Identify the agencies that are "the best in the business" for a specific component of a particular service area

4. Access a list of participants' names and contact information so that you may contact key staff in particular service areas and learn

5. Receive training on data collection and performance management thru individualized introductory training and a series of web workshops

Consistent Definitions & Comparisons. The ICMA/CPM performance measurement program provides consistent definitions for comparative data. Such vital information is necessary to assure apples-to-apples comparisons once service centers and their costs are developed per the earlier Chapters in this Book. The listing of service areas evaluated under the CPM program includes:

1. Code Enforcement
2. Facilities Management
3. Fire and EMS
4. Fleet Management
5. Highway and Road Maintenance
6. Housing
7. Human Resource
8. Information Technology
9. Library Services
10. Obesity Prevention
11. Parks and Recreation
12. Permits, Land Use, and Plan Review
13. Police Services

14. Procurement
15. Risk Management
16. Solid Waste
17. Sustainability
18. Youth Services

The list is completed with this very important note: "CPM has identified several hundred *performance indicators* and descriptors for each service area."

How to Measure. Another valuable tool also is provided: "CPM offers electronic tools that allow participants to review the performance and their peers and develop customized comparisons based on population, climate, service provision method, and other characteristics. Annual updates have provided for precise definitions and adaptation to changed tasks or technology, while at the same time maintaining the continuity necessary for year to year comparisons."

Several examples are provided in various portions of the ICMA/CPM website that illustrate a "New System to Display Real-time Performance Data to the Public". As the subtitle of this Book infers, meaningful and effective ***Consumer Government*** can only be achieved *via The Art of Full Disclosure* utilizing the **Municipal Business System** set out in excruciating and probable emulatable detail in this Book.

More Is Available. The efforts and results achieved by ICMA/CPM provide pages and pages of important information. Just a few of those 'knowledge nuggets' are quoted or paraphrased above. Any municipal organization aspiring to assure quality, prior to even considering any type of outsourcing, has a need to draw upon the assets and advantages of the ICMA Center for Performance Management. The vital "level playing field" can be assured only by making valid cost AND quality comparisons. Here is the way to do so. Membership in the International City/County Management Association secures all the measurement benefits and assurances offered in this Chapter. See www.icma.org

Other Developments. Recent major activity by computer sellers and service companies potentially can provide performance data at a low cost. "Outsourcing" of this nature just might rehabilitate that approach to provision of government services:

> *"With no end in sight to shrinking budgets, state and local governments are shoring up aging tech systems and relying more on delivering crucial public services over the internet cloud. Computer maker Dell recently helped Gaston County, N.C. consolidate its data storage for a $500,000 savings. Dell also helped the City of St. Petersburg, Fla. realize a $150,000 savings by equipping office workers with virtualized PCs that run on a central server instead of issuing specific desktop machines to each one."[45]*

---

[45] "Governments cut computing costs"; *USA Today;* August 30, 2011; page B1

Not to be bested by Dell, IBM is running full page ads promoting its "Smarter Lessons from our Smarter Cities" program. That corporation's claim is far broader:

> *"Forward-thinking leaders are connecting core city systems, eliminating operational silos, and pinpointing which departments, agencies and communities are crucial to coordinate. By analyzing the vast quantities of data their cities generate, they can remain prosperous and sustainable in the face of unprecedented urban growth, economic and technological change, and increasing social mobility."*[46]

So it appears that low cost computer capacity and capabilities on which revenue-cost matchups in Service Centers, as overseen by Service Center Managers, operating under Performance Management standards, gradually are becoming the "new standard". Thus "the taxpaying public" can be far more informed about the public services they receive. And who pays and who benefits. Full disclosure appropriately is becoming necessary.

Staffing Improvements. Unfortunately, government finance functions usually are the first to suffer budget cuts and employee layoffs. The rationale is –"these people are producing nothing for the public". That statement, of course, is untrue. Not true IF – a very big "if" -- the husbanding of taxes and increasing efficiency and effectiveness of the jurisdiction's operations are valued and proved. Provably able to produce sufficient savings to pay for the costing and quality measurement processes several times over.

Unfortunately many jurisdictions have neither the desire nor capabilities to inventory, cost, and then measure their service outputs. One direct cause and result is as follows:

> *"Local and state governments axed more than 200,000 jobs in 2010....".*[47]

Even more revealing about the plight of local and state governments as to capabilities to "be like a business" are some recent statistics provided by the U.S. Department of Labor.

> *States cut 49,000 jobs over the past year and localities 210,000....There are 30,000 fewer federal workers now than a year ago....By contrast, private-sector jobs have increased by 1.6 million over the past 12 months....All told since the recession began local governments have bled 405,000 jobs, State governments 50,000....*[48]

Another statistic quoted in the same article also sheds more information about the apparent current political jousting between "government" and "corporate America".

> *The number of people earning $1 million a year or more increased in 2010 by nearly 20 percent.*[49]

A subsequent additional Associated Press piece provided further financial elucidation:

---

[46] *The Wall Street Journal;* August 29, 2011; page A18
[47] Reuters website; August 30, 2011
[48] Associated Press via *The Arizona Republic;* October 25, 2011; page A1
[49] "Government job losses add strain on recovery"; Associated Press via *The Arizona Republic;* October 25, 2011; page A1

After-tax income for the top 1 percent of U.S. households almost tripled, up 275 percent, from 1979 to 2007, the Congressional Budget Office found. For people in the middle of the economic scale, after-tax income grew by just 40 percent. Those at the bottom experienced an 18 percent increase. The Report, based on IRS and Census Bureau data.... CBO Director Doug Elmendorf stated "The distribution of after-tax income in the United States was substantially more unequal in 2007 than in 1979....The share of income accruing to higher-income households increased whereas the share accruing to other households declined."[50]

Importance. The import of the above revealing statistics is that apparently the massive re-arrangement of tax burden and resultant impacts in the United States at each of the federal, state and local levels might well be that increasingly greater amounts of special benefit services are being financed by diversion of general benefit taxes to wealthier households. And, assumedly, such diversion is due to increasingly greater political influence by those benefitting from special benefit services. They thus secure ever greater diversion of taxes to their services, and away from services provided "the community at large".[51] Among the latter obviously are police/fire/EMS services, parks and recreation, libraries, local street maintenance, and more, per cited exemplars throughout this Book.

Salvation or Retribution? Those who maintain that public employee salaries and benefits are "too high and need to be cut" perhaps might now being overrun. Read on:

The House Financial Services Committee approved legislation Tuesday that would suspend tens of millions in Fannie and Freddie executive compensation packages, stop future bonuses and align their salaries with other federal employees who make much less. The vote was 52-4, with strong support from both parties.[52] Note: Fannie and Freddie were private for-profit entities until bailed out and taken over by the Federal government.

Differentiation between "private/corporate" employee and "public employee" requirements is clear. The former do not have to follow the three basics that separate private profit-making employment from government duty:

> **SWORN DUTY** -- **MUST** be done = All public employees take an "oath of office"
>
> **MISFEASANCE** -- **a duty** not well or improperly performed
>
> **MALFEASANCE** – must **NOT** be done = *"wholly wrongful and unlawful"*[53]

All should take their employ as a fiduciary duty, with all implications thereof. The above does not necessarily infer that government employment is more demanding than what is required of private sector employees, but these are the stark facts of **public** employee life.

---

[50] "Rich are getting much richer"; Associated Press by Andrew Taylor; via *The Arizona Republic;* October 27, 2011; page A4

[51] *Op.Cit.*; "Intent Document" expounding on *California Constitution* Article XIIIB, "the Gann Proposition 4 Initiative" See footnote 17

[52] *The Arizona Republic ,*November 16, 2011; page D4

[53] *Black's Law Dictionary*; West Publishing Company

SWORN DUTY, MALFEASANCE AND FIDUCIARY DUTY

(A MORALITY TALE)

The mixing and melding of municipal debt with corruption and "standard corporate business practices" now unfolds daily in Jefferson County (Birmingham), Alabama. The largest municipal bankruptcy in U.S. history is being dissected as it is being flushed out.

The bankruptcy was filed November of 2010, due to "inability" to pay. That plea followed several indictments for alleged "arrangements" with financiers who underwrote and marketed $4.2 billion of County sewer revenue warrants, bonds, derivatives and swaps. The County's attorneys argue *"holders of $3 billion in debt used to finance a sewer project should be forced to wait for their money along with other creditors."* [54]

"The parlous finances of America's state and local governments represent 'the largest threat' to the country's economy. Defaults totaling hundreds of billions of dollars are possible, enough to rattle America's $3.7 trillion municipal bond market." [55]

The Birmingham Mayor, who was President of the five member Jefferson County Commission at the time of the financings, was convicted of 60 counts of various forms of "public corruption", removed from office and sentenced to 15 years in prison.

"J.P. Morgan Securities agreed to a settlement with the Securities & Exchange Commission regarding the bank's alleged involvement in a 'pay-to-play' scheme...." [56]

None of the County Commissioners who participated in the bond deals now serve. The episode earned various headlines:

Bond Debacle Sinks Jefferson County (Bloomberg Business Week)

Sewers, Swaps and Bachus (New York Times)

Serious Financial Problems for Alabama's Largest County to Continue Into 2012 (AP)

How Jefferson County Trips Up National Reporters (Reuters)

Various bankers and political operatives were indicted, convicted, or smeared with the offal of bad publicity or smelly fallout from the "Sewer Debt Problem". The most appalling conclusion one can reach from even barely skimming over the thousands of pages of news, pleadings, opinions and whatever can only be:

1. The financial services industry is predatory on public officials. The fiduciary capacity of that industry is owed to the corporate employer, not to clients or customers.

2. Government elected and appointed officials and employees rarely break their oaths of office, commit indictable acts of malfeasance, or violate their fiduciary capacities, thus get prosecuted.

3. Binding oaths, and fiduciary capacity to "outsiders", like customers and clients, are NOT "common practice" for corporate officers and employees, as they are for public officials and employees.

4. Unlimited amounts of corporate money can be utilized to influence government and its officials.

---

[54] *The Wall Street Journal;* November 29, 2011; page C4

[55] *The Economist;* December 3, 2011; page 89

[56] *Bloomberg Business Week;* November 8, 2009

CHAPTER VII

BUDGETING

This arcane subject is assiduously evaded by most non-financially oriented students of government, be they practitioner or policy wonk. Most "government types" have been brainwashed into believing politics and policy make up the whole of government. Those who labor day-to-day in the administrative/management trenches of governance, especially employees coping with local level activities, are painfully aware of two dicta:

1. **It is difficult if not impossible to budget without revenues.**

2. **If you do not have sufficient monies appropriated in the budget for your program or project you are in deep trouble.**

The Budget. This word is to most governmental officials and employees alike, an abomination. It is to be avoided and evaded. And insulted. The budget is the harbinger of tests of will and doom. And, in general and specifically, despised and feared. But, by definition, a **BUDGET** is a financial plan for the subsequent fiscal period.

Due essentially to the dictates of elected bodies and officials, and their appointed minions, it is always wise for serious government executives to prepare **two budgets**. Such a procedure admittedly is self-defensive. But, recent court decisions, especially as highlighted by the discharge of the Chief of the U.S. Park Police, such double preparation evidently is encouraged and legally allowed under the *U.S. Constitution* 1st Amendment. Further, such redundant preparation falls into the category of "the right thing to do." Thus the advice of this Author as to budget preparation is simple, following.

Two Budgets. This maverick advice is vitally important for self-protection in these times of mindless budget cuts, extreme doctrinaire partisanship, and non-analyzed privatization, and politically and financially suspect outsourcing.

Every fiscal year each executive charged with budget preparation should prepare TWO budgets

One: strictly following instructions of the person/organization/edict providing budget guidelines, restrictions, orders, and dictates.

Two: a well-documented budget that will fulfill all legal duties and requirements assigned the organizational unit for which the budget is applicable. Appropriate statutes, court orders, judicial decisions, binding dictates, executive orders, and other such documentation must be inserted and referenced as appropriate. Any "social justice", "fairness", "humane", "medically necessary" or other similar judgmental terms must be eschewed, absent quoting any distinct legal references in these *verboten* areas.

The following lengthy chapter is an update and, as necessary, an expurgation, expansion and/or editing of a 20 page booklet written early on during the Author's 15 year tenure as an Adjunct, then Full Professor of Public Finance in the Graduate School of Public Administration of the University of Southern California. Sadly, on re-reading the document in early 2011 it was realized that little had changed in the intervening 34 years. That fact is adequate testimony to the total inadequacy of the present (2011 - 2012) financial condition of American state and local budgets and budgeting, and the level of information provided to the tax and fee-paying and service expecting/consuming public.

First published in April of 1977, demand required a 2nd printing in February 1978. More than 6,000 copies were sold and mailed at $3/each. The title was:

INTEGRATIVE BUDGETING SYSTEM
A NEW APPROACH FROM OLD FAILURES [57]

ABSTRACT

Current governmental budgeting systems do not provide specific answers to the taxpayer's question, *"What do I get for my taxes?"* Theorists seek budgetary policy flexibility by advocating placement of as much revenue as possible in the General Fund. This Fund then becomes the battleground of opposing economic, functional and special interest forces. Such contention obscures, if not totally destroying, any relationship between revenues raised and services provided.

A new budgetary approach, **I**ntegrative **B**udgeting **S**ystem [IBS] was developed and installed in one mid-sized American city. [And, subsequently, during the 1980's, several more.] Its main features: 1) use of specifically designated revenues by narrowly defined funds to finance specified services, 2) use of the General Fund to finance support and central staff services *only*, 3) distribution of such central costs to all programs by formula, usually percentage, 4) assignment of program responsibilities to program managers, and 5) use of a merit pay plan to reward or disallow performance recognition to those managers.

An extension of IBS to the neighborhood level by a Matrix Budgeting process (subsequently provided in detail) can be utilized to devolve local government and to further secure more citizen and voter confidence and guidance as to levels of services, taxes, fees and charges with which to finance those specifically desired by those willing to pay. The full capabilities of revenue-service cost match-ups also is provided earlier in the Book in which this former booklet is now subsumed. [This "System" ultimately morphed into the *Municipal Business System* explained in and hyped by this Book.]

---

[57] *Integrative Budgeting System – A New Approach From Old Failures©;* Douglas W. Ayres; 1977 & 1978; School of Public Administration of the University of Southern California. [All this Chapter of **Consumer Government** is verbatim from and/or a partial updating or limited expansive re-write of *Integrative Budgeting System.*] Self-published with USC School of Public Administration *imprimatur;* San Juan Capistrano, California.

The purpose of IBS is to connect directly all governmental revenues to specific services. In that way the political leadership and the tax and rate-payer both will know the specific answer to: "What do I get for my taxes and fees that I pay to this government?"

Preface. An omnipresent phrase is heard throughout all levels of government today [1976]: "budget crunch". Two years of double digit inflation accompanied by a problem economy and mushy revenues then raised a fearful double specter: the prospect of constantly rising taxes and a consistent lowering of service levels. Today [late 2011] both threats still exist, but with constantly *lowering* of tax and fee receipts.

These phenomena are happening today, and will continue until governmental jurisdictions re-arrange financial and taxation/charging structures and their concomitant accounting and reporting reports to answer that one basic question which MUST be answered:

"What am I getting for my taxes?"

THE SETTING

For centuries most governmental functions have been, and still are financed from the ubiquitous General Fund. Economists and other budgetary theoreticians have argued compellingly and effectively that by so doing policy makers have maximum flexibility to make policy determinations based on studies indicating the greatest needs. Unfortunately, with the explosive growth of citizen and interest group demands and the political response in the form of added services and facilities, the General Fund took on the illusion of a bottomless pit with ill-defined edges. But it was – and still is – only an illusion, for suddenly and increasingly we have found the bottom, and a shallow one it is.

Policy Analysis. The policy analysts appropriately developed analytical tools to assist legislators to make the "hard choices". The operations and Management By Objectives (MBO) types thought they could make government capable of adopting evaluative and goal-setting techniques. Yet the money kept getting more and more scarce. Citizen demands for economizing grew more shrill, and cries of elected officials and citizenry alike for greater "economy and efficiency" became more strident. Constant attempts were made to apply the stop-watch technology of Frederick W. Taylor and the Gilbreths to the non-production line services of government, such as police patrol, zoning revision application processing, 911 call priority, medical and welfare assistance, and especially of any other "soft" social and protective services of government.

Productivity? How, for example, can the "response time and productivity" of a firefighter with EMS training be improved? But computerization and networks suffer at the hands of minimally educated and thus ill-prepared low-paid clerks that cause office procedure glitches. If she/he never looks up at an applicant for anything, how can productivity possibly be increased by from 30 to 40 reviews per hour? But what about the time loss of the applicant? And for the EMS firefighter, amid the now-basic revelation that he/she is now the primary public health and medical care provider for many?

Then, the resultant seeming "governmental bureaucratic non-responsiveness" reaches criticality. Complaints of inefficiency and employee ineptitude and crass behavior then swamp the offices of appointed, and then elected officials. While these are limited examples of local government functions, they do serve as exemplars of the inherent problems of government "service to clients".

Privatization of many processes, with few noted exceptions, has simply failed in those few governments who have sincerely and honestly tried. Or, simply DONE, without analysis, cost considerations, or adequate arrangements for measurement of effectiveness and service acceptability. Or prevention of "corruption", under all definitions thereof. So, we find ourselves back to the accusation of gross inefficiency of ALL government, generally, without much specificity, only complaints, ideology and a steady flow of exposès filling the media time and space between commercials and advertisements.

Next? Then came the siren song of former Speaker of the House Newt Gingrich, Ph.D.: There is not necessarily any connection between government revenues and expenditures; both of taxes and services must be reduced, but not necessarily in an interrelated manner. That disconnect now is base dicta for the increasingly strident "conservatives", who truly believe that tax cuts can be self-financing, without incurring debt.

Then in 2010 the entire analytical and thought process was overwhelmed by the so-called "tea party", and the obscure message of the "Occupy Wall Street" movements. Hard line ideology triumphed over reasoned fact-based thought and behavior, destroying all considerate political dynamics. The Great Recession provided fertile ground for even grosser usage of Josef Goebbels' propaganda techniques melded into Karl Rove's Madison Avenue "message" expertise. The result thus is considerable seemingly legitimate but massive disinformation by use of Goebbel's "labeling" and "scapegoat" processes. The basic message is: Label your opponents as the cause of all problems. And hang the most blame on one group or person. "They" did, and still do. "Good politics" quickly died.

Advertising sophistication, broadening media, and social networking have impacted life decisively, including all levels of government. Thus bitter partisan outbursts, rampant disrespect, and the label of "socialism" destroyed any remnants of fact-based reasoned impartial policy analysis. Pure ideology has prevailed. Research-based thought has died.

What Now? So here we are – falling revenues, increasing demands for service, deteriorating infrastructure, and anti-government fixations. Local government is dying.

Government officials rarely have bothered to explain government services; rationale, derivation, operation, objectives and, more basically, financing and effects on levels of worth. "Something" has to be done, radically, rapidly, and decisively. Otherwise many local government services will self-destruct into extinction. The intensive fogging of information provided by "impartial" highly biased "commentators" and voices of authority has warped to partisan and ideological ends the theoretical First Amendment safeguards.

A NEW SYSTEM IS NEEDED

Clearly, if public acceptance of lower service levels or higher taxes and charges are taken as criteria, a new look and system is needed with which to explain and "sell", if you will, the services of local government. Elected officials are understandably loath to risk the loss of love by the electorate and reduce or eliminate public services. The "compromise" is to demand "increased productivity" and to order bureaucrats to "cut the fat and the frills", reduce salaries and other costs, "become more effective and efficient by doing more with less," and "eliminate unnecessary programs".

Other Demands. Yet, "the public", and elected officials, somehow fail to recognize that while inflation is relatively minor, it still exists and constantly and continually eats away at public budgets and their inherent costs. Too, adding new services, and the increase in demand for more and better responses with fewer employees to respond, seems to creep into even the most restrictive and depleted of budgets. There also seems to be a belief that "jobs will be created by reducing taxes, [including the lay-off of employees] thereby releasing tax money for businesses to expand". So, the cry "to do more with less" and "run it like a business". Assumedly, "it" includes all local government.

Results. Consumer-taxpayers are confused, distraught and rebellious. Those in local government have yet to provide intelligible, reliable, and trustworthy information in an orderly way for revenues, expenditures, in financial plans, budgets, and definitively productive outputs. The time has come for local government to explain itself in detail if its services are to survive and government to continue to be able to provide those impartial things which simply are not conducive to corporate absorption. The following pages sketch a new budgeting concept and methodology which may assist to divert citizen demands into desirable and productive directions. Marketing of municipal services is called for. Debating over budgetary theology is no longer germane.

DROPPING THE WORST

Since the turn of the 19th century into the 21st, five "systems" of governmental budgeting have been developed, expounded on, publicized, praised, and implemented. Each has its strong and weak points. Each system has been like the phoenix, rising out of the ashes of its predecessor. Unfortunately, in most cases the succeeding system has been superimposed atop its precursor, rather than supplanting it. Accounting suffered, and eventually became worse than impossible – dangerously non-reliable or perverted.

The worst elements of each of the first four systems need to be peeled off and discarded, so the fifth might evolve. That fifth type is the **Integrative Budgeting System (IBS),** which is based on the ***Municipal Business System***. The balance of this Chapter will develop that system of budgeting and its underlying organization and accounting. Such is necessary by which to institute and implement CONSUMER GOVERNMENT. How IBS evolved and works will be exhibited and explained, in some detail. But first –

Review. The first step is to review, evaluate and identify the jettisonable parts of each of the four preceding "systems" of governmental budgeting. Each is still in current usage, in "modified" form somewhere, for no "pure" system exists.[58]

---

58 *Ibid.,* p.5; and massive amounts of critical books, papers, research and daily media outpourings from a wide variety of sources

LINE-ITEM BUDGET SYSTEMS

By far the most prevalent of budget systems is that accountants' dream, the line-item form. Concentrating on the objects and services purchased, no significant thought is possible as to what services or outputs are secured with the goods and services acquired.

Individual line-items are superbly capable of three things: detailed management information, absolute expenditure control by accounting technicians, and total expenditure by the using agency.

Avoiding Evasion. The IBS approach retains many line-item accounts and detailed management information, but not for control purposes. Any experienced middle manager long since has mastered the myriad ways of evading accounting controls. In fact, mastering of evasion techniques is often the reason the manager made it to management.

PERFORMANCE BUDGET SYSTEMS

The obvious need for some type of output identification within government budgets gave rise to adoption of performance budgeting, a derivation of "scientific management". Thus performance budgeting matches the line-items to pre-set performance standards against which workers are measured as to efficiency. But two problems become immediately obvious to those who work with performance budgets.

First, the gathering and assessment of the mountains of performance data assumes awesome proportions, soon tending to degenerate into what has been fondly referred to as "a numbers castle". Computerization has helped, but not solved the massiveness.

Second, and probably more vitally, Roethlisberger and Mayo, and the subsequent thousands of behavioralists since the Hawthorne studies, have irrefutably shown that performance standards into which those workers to be measured have little or no input, and those which are not rather flexible, almost instantaneously become meaningless and counter-productive. The involved employees simply do not buy it.

Extensive use of the then-latest [but still recognized as highly valid] in management behavior derived from Professors Bruce Storm and Warren Bennis of USC, and the writings of Peter Drucker, a self-styled "social ecologist" and behavioralist of world-wide influence, are applicable. [For years Drucker and I were patients of the same Urologist. I was fortunate to have engaged Prof. Drucker in conversations while waiting for our M.D. I asked, then listened intently.]

Data Handling. However, since the development of the currently awesome capabilities of computers, the massive compilation and usage of data accumulation has been mostly resolved. Thus a type of Performance Budgeting such as the herein advocated IBS/MBS is possible. And accurate and irrefutable distribution of costs to the wide variety of revenue-matched services and funds is feasible, without perversion. There was much in the preceding pages of this Book, and more about these match-ups following.

PROGRAM BUDGET SYSTEMS

In the late 1940's several local governments began developing a simplified program budgeting system. It then was called "lump-sum" budgeting. Abandoning the imposing list of line-items which required vast data handling capacity, the new "system" instead concentrated on the three major objects of 1) personal services, 2) services and supplies, and 3) capital outlay and improvement, each within a large number of individual "programs". The program structure followed organizational lines, with each person who supervised any small group of workers or otherwise identifiable sub-function, having a budget for the activity for which they could be held responsible.

One major difficulty plagued this early attempt at program budgeting –loss of vital line-item data felt necessary on which operating personnel could base day-to-day decisions. Despite that flaw, two major advantages surfaced, both now incorporated into the cumulatively eclectic Integrative Budgeting System (IBS w/MBS). Those components are: First, capability to hold one person responsible for an identifiable program and its measurable effectiveness, and Second, concentration on outputs rather than dollar inputs.

Profit Center Marketing. The private sector has long utilized "profit center" and "product line" budgeting and accounting, and consequent matching of decentralized authority and responsibility. There is no reason government cannot and should not do so. Corporate business has now decentralized marketing for many profit centers, while the schools of public administration don't even recognize marketing, much less teach it. One obvious goal of this Book is to incorporate such "profit centers" into budgeting, accounting, responsibility, performance, public disclosure reporting, and marketing of the local government service delivery system. Such an advanced approach has been accomplished in several jurisdictions, each of which are noted for their viable revenue structure, effective service delivery, and depth of public acceptance. (Such as Pasadena and Beverly Hills.)

PLANNING, PROGRAMMING, BUDGETING SYSTEM (PPBS)

The long-ago-dead-but-still-worshiped Rand/Robert McNamara/DOD/PPBS was abandoned by the federal government in 1972. PPBS suffered from several faults.

First, massive analytical capacity applied by beady-eyed "unbiased independent" analysts comparing the cost/benefit ratios of every possible alternative approach to problem solution to all other possibilities. Such expectations and demands were unrealistic. Those crashed and burned with the awesome advent of B-52 carpet bombing.

Second, line-item data generally is abandoned in favor of broad-sweep programs cutting across functional departments, thereby losing vital information needed by responsible supervisors, if indeed they were at all to be held accountable. Last, multi-year planning was to be programmed into each sub-function. Unfortunately, or fortunately, the political structure of the United States and the resultant public responsiveness being as it is, governments have not become known for adopting multi-year plans and adhering to them. Rather, program planning and budgeting execution has all the appearances of the tracks of a lame horse with the blind staggers. The transfer of this type of "pure" analysis proved to be wholly inappropriate and incapable at the local level. And at the DOD.

However, highly selective cost/benefit and alternative analysis, including integrating capital projects into the operating budget as alternatives, and selective multi-year financial projections, are viable and are retained in the Integrative Budgeting System (IBS) to secure effective and open CONSUMER GOVERNMENT.

TWO OTHER BUDGETING CONSIDERATIONS

To achieve **Consumer Government** two more major items were incorporated into the design of IBS/MBS: data handling capacity, and behavioral opportunities and constraints.

1. Data Handling Equipment. Until development of high speed "electronic data processing" (EDP) equipment in the 1960's, most governmental budgetary and accounting systems were limited to multi-column addition and subtraction. But with development of massive data storage, retrieval and computational equipment coupled with reliable programming languages in the 1980's, a new era of almost limitless possibilities dawned. Unfortunately, most governments have not recognized and utilized the vast potentialities.

HISTORY OF BUDGETING, EQUIPMENT, INPUT & BEHAVIOR*

APPROXIMATE ERA	BUDGET SYSTEM	DATA HANDLING SYSTEM	PUBLIC INPUT & DECISIONS	BEHAVIORIAL APPROACH
Pre-1910	Functional Line-Item	Hand-posting by ink in multiple ledgers^	Little to none- some business	Authoritarian/ political spoils
1910-1925	Line-Item	Hand-cranked mechanical	Little to none - some public	Authoritarian/ political Spoils
1925-1940	Line-Item	Start of electro-mechanical	Minor public & business	Administrative Management
1940-1955	Performance	Advanced electro-mechanical	WWII/Korea – little input	Scientific Management
1955-1965	Classical Program	Unit-record ADP	Era of "Sound Communities"	Human Relat'ns Sensitivity
1965-1975	PPBS	Data-base/data communic'tns Electronic Data Processing	Expanding Business Lobbying	Participative; increasing unionization
1977-1981 & faded fast	Zero-Based	Varied	Little was constructive	Authoritative & highly naïve
1975-1990	Integrative Budgeting	On-line remote terminal solid state w/PC innovations	Anti-tax limitations	Job-enriched self-actualizing
1990-2005	Return to Line-item	On-line remote terminal solid state PC/EDP networks	Anti-govern't movement	Unions become defensive
1995-2005	Variable as to & by Jurisdiction	High-speed EDP/DB/DC and PC networks	Anti-govern't forces grow	Rationality disappears
2005-2015	Disassembled to respond to massive cuts	Same, but w/reduced staff & inadequate equipment	Anti-govern't forces securing program cuts	Negative – loss of institutional memory
2015-future	**IBS w/ *The System***	Purchased software & training with leased software use & unlimited CLOUD storage	Public chooses Service Ctrs. & Svc. levels	Reinstatement of self-actualizing behavior

*Double entry self-balancing accounting was not in common use until the turn of 19th to 20th century

^Use of warrants and reliance on elected Treasurer and/or Finance Official remains despite inherent systemic dangers and inability to integrate into double entry self-balancing accounting and basic budgeting

Those virtually unlimited capabilities can, and should be in place to inform, educate and advise administrators, program managers, workers, policy makers, elected officials and, more important, consumers/citizens/taxpayers. Unfortunately, such public information-related publicity remains mostly unrecognized and not implemented.

Integrative Budgeting, resulting in **Consumer Government,** is possible due to computerized data managing and sharing, and the resultant communication and informational exchange capabilities of the internet, via **www.***whateve*r**.com** .gov or .org.

Table 1 – History. The table on the previous page traces the evolution of budgeting systems and the inherent constraints and limitations, and how each successive capability allowed the accurate match-up of budgetary allocations with tax and ratepayer/consumer by providing meaningful but previously opaque government "accounting data".

The goal of Integrative Budgeting is to provide such information sufficient to obviate the use of any but the most basic of "top down" controls, relying rather on Abraham Maslow's "hierarchy of needs" self-actualization of all organizational employees. Thus they are encouraged and abetted by extensive costing data provided by the *Municipal Business System* to institute self-control at all organizational levels.

2. *Behavioral Elements.* Experiments made over ten decades by behavioral scientists and sociologists have proved beyond arguable doubt that the vast majority of workers want to do their best. But they must be educated and motivated, not forced, controlled, or regulated into so performing. Budgetary controls, and the absolute nature of line-item budget rules, abnegate any possibility of achieving self-actualizing self-control on the part of employees and, more important, on the part of line supervisors.

However, well-motivated and organizationally cohesive employees absolutely will act to reduce costs and increase revenues. This was learned by the Author shortly after the revenue-cost matchup and IBS systems were installed and implemented in the City of Inglewood, California, in 1969-70. Quickly, Service Center Managers began complaining about "high rates of central 'supporting' costs". Those were the usual now-internal management service accounts comprising the General Fund. Funds for equipment, benefits, insurance, personnel, building space "rental", central stores, communications, and other charge-backs also were challenged. Thus those "central service" Center Managers were under pressure to reduce costs and improve service. Competition instantly was well underway, between numerous Service Centers and their Managers. Each Service Center Manager had his/her own costs and revenues to tend to. In a subsequent year, in a national economic slump, several Service Center Managers came up with economizing trade-offs with other Service Centers, and greater revenues. Some of the latter were secured literally by "outsourcing" their services to adjacent cities, at prices far below what currently was being provided by those jurisdictions by in-house **or** outsourced activities.

This Book is about how local governments can placate and openly fully disclose services offered and the costs thereof. Accordingly, no further discussions will be here contained relating the assembled encyclopedic knowledge concerning worker behavior.

IMPLEMENTABLE CONTROLS

__The Important Controls.__ In any program-type budget each responsible supervisor/manager must be controlled by the central budget/financial office for four items:

1. Number, classification and pay of employee positions
2. Dollar amount and distribution of benefits, overtime and part-time help
3. Total dollar amount of the program appropriation
4. Total dollar amount of the revenue expected and appropriated.

Controlling, or attempting to limit, by any other line-items or amounts, is duplicative, counterproductive, eliminates any flexibility and initiative to seek better work methods, and is too time consuming to review adequately. However, line-item data must be available in a timely manner to operating Service Center Managers so they might take appropriate actions based on that data. Even more basic, is the need for rational organizational cost analysis to delineate service centers and programs and to reconcile the service center list with the organizational structure. The end result is manageable service centers and appropriate information. The *Municipal Business System* provides all this data.

With one person responsible for and capable of being held fully responsible for the "program" or service center cumulative costs and revenues responsibility and authority are matched as the organization pattern pyramids upward. An appropriately revised budgetary chart of accounts implements the information system.

__Data Monitoring.__ Advocacy of elimination of line-item controls does not imply ignoring of such information by the central budget staff, or single financial officer in small organizations. Rather, such financial output should be reviewed as a part of a whole to be monitored. Such observation will assure early detection of problem situations and spot the potential necessity to remove weak managers who cannot or do not exercise adequate self-control and maintain the values of their assigned service centers. By substituting monitoring for controlling, the central staff does not run the significant risk of substituting its judgment for that of the supervisor, thereby mitigating the authority-responsibility equation. What with the increasing rights of and freedom of action expected of individual employees, at times aided by union representatives, it is going to be increasingly difficult to remove someone from a supervisory position for "inadequate supervision" if the person proposed to be removed has had individual decision-making power usurped by an upstart, uninformed, non-technically qualified central budget analyst/controller.

Thus Integrative Budgeting mated with the *Municipal Business System* relies on careful service center identification and grouping into programs and assignment to responsible supervisors. The inherent service center analysis develops the basis for organizational re-design, chart of account modifications, and service center assignments to the specific developed fund structure. Thus the data handling systemization can provide line service center managers with accurate, adequate and timely information so each may make day-to-day operational decisions and rise or fall on individual merit as results of those decisions. Thus, almost by definition, self-actualizing self-control and initiative will follow – or a supportable and fiscally sound case for removal can be made.

__Cost Center & Program Analysis.__ Depending on the size of the organization, an equally careful job of program analysis will have to be made on instituting an Integrative Budget System. Such is the case of three reasons. First, to have similar activities merged or at least more closely aligned to one another for coordinative and economy reasons. Second, to assure that one supervisor can be held solely responsible for the performance of that particular program. It is important to the concept of Integrative Budgeting to overcome the fear of mass data, which can now be adequately transmitted by electronic means, and to create a program for each identifiable group which has either a first level supervisor or an identifiable function – preferably both. One secret to the *__Municipal Business System__* is thoughtful creation of the budgetary chart of accounts and data handling applications, utilizing appropriate input/output devices and on-line real time data storage and retrieval. Third, and probably most important, is the relation of government revenue and expenditures to the taxpayer/consumer. Each program must be thoughtfully analyzed as to the most equitable way to finance it, so that the function hopefully can be as directly as possible related to an identifiable and benefit-connected revenue source.

__Merit Pay.__ By now it should be apparent that to have an effective budgetary management system supervisorial pay must be set on pure merit principles. Little would be gained were poor managers equally rewarded in traditional government lock-step annual pay increment fashion. Several systems have been devised to provide such merit incentive rewards, ranging from a modified step plan to an almost pure industrial-type point plan. But, however done, self-actualizing entrepreneurial cost-saving and productivity-enhancing program managers must be recognized for their efforts. It is fairly well accepted that self-actualizing self-control is not possible within the present automatic non-merit and longevity/seniority-based governmental pay plan systems. One only has to observe the educational pay system to see the devastating long range results of such a self-perpetuating lock-step methodology to mediocrity.

RELATION TO THE TAXPAPER/CITIZEN/CONSUMER

And now to the way the Integrative Budget System responds to the ubiquitous question: "What am I getting for my tax dollars?" that has been raised so profusely herein.

__Fund Structure.__ Every government has, or should have a formal fund structure. Such an array of funds in effect implement political compacts made with the electorate to expend certain categories of revenues **only** for specified purposes promised at the time the revenue was raised or tax or fee imposed. Bond funds, utilities funds, and highway funds

been challenged by some theorists as being overly restrictive of legislative bodies. It should be remembered, however, that the voters, either through their elected representatives or through direct referenda, decided on such restrictions.

As to budgeting, though, it is important to realize that "computerization" has changed the previous reasons for limiting a jurisdiction to a few funds. A jurisdiction-centric universal fund and account chart, or booklet, provides the goal of service center cost records and program supervisory accountability. IBS is dependent upon a sweeping analysis and major expansion of funds and accounts, on both the revenue and expenditure sides of the budget, so that understandable relationships are established between revenues and the component service centers within the much expanded fund structure. The taxpaying public has a right to that knowledge. The ubiquitous question must always be present: *What am I getting for my money?* That universal query must be answered, revenue source by revenue source; and matching service center by service center. That's marketing.

__Earmarking.__ One of the major criticisms of earmarking of revenue sources to a specific function is the inherent inflexibility of utilizing revenues "excess" to the needs of the fund to which the source is earmarked. But earmarking can and has been used as a restriction to hold down expenditures when revenues decline. Carnegie libraries operating under ancient property tax levy limitations are poverty-ridden attestors to the two edged sword of earmarking. But when an elected official is faced with persistent demand for a service, and an obvious revenue source (like the gas tax-highway equation of the 1920's) the choices are clear: either earmark or do without. So earmarking is a mighty and politically pragmatic device. Such is vital to the operation and inherently necessary inviolability of matching service centers to the revenues generated by each. Practical politics and accounting require the use of service centers grouped into funds, as an alternative to service reduction and ballot box retribution. Adequate explanation and marketing of the match-up of specific services provided with the specific revenue source, in effect, can be an adequate substitute for hard and fast earmarking that has been done by ballot measure.

__Revenue Allocation.__ Revenue allocation currently is not widely used. Specific revenue sources or portions thereof – as differentiated from dollar appropriations from a General Fund – will be allocated annually by the budget document directly to the revenue-generating service center, within a designated fund, thereby giving the policy body the annual power to review and change each of revenue and cost allocations. Such an arrangement relies on allocation of each specific revenue source to the service center which activities generate the revenue. These specific restrictions to revenues obviate the "dip into the General Fund" competition for monies that currently exist. It also automatically acts to sensitize the supervisor of the service centers within the program to which the several specific revenue sources are allocated. Thus the clientele from whom the revenue is extracted know what they are getting for their dollars, be they fee, charge or tax. And can have the information upon which to base an appropriately informed decision as to "whether, and if so, how much revenue, and how much money is necessary"? Probably more important, elected officials will have to come face-to-face with basic economic facts: either revenue must be increased, services curtailed, or the new or upgraded programs or facilities foregone. See the Holmes and Rowe letters herein.

__THAT Question.__ A system of funds, programs, and revenue allocation can go a long way toward establishing an integrated budgeting, accounting and public reporting system capable of providing data needed to answer that unanswered annoying question AGAIN:

"What am I getting for my tax money?"

THE GENERAL FUND "PROBLEM"

The non-earmarked [service center assigned] revenues of most governmental jurisdictions presently fall into the all-encompassing General Fund, which then becomes the battleground between opposing economic, political, ideological and functional forces. Due to the political inability of one group completely to dominate or eliminate the others, the usual political budgetary compromise is to appropriate some – albeit a completely inadequate amount – of General Fund monies to any group which has any voice at all. The General Fund thus has become synonymous with "The Treasury". There is no public or internal relationship to revenues, only to expenditures.

General Fund Division is Unworkable. Three major problems have arisen recently to make the General Fund compromise process less workable than in the past. First, the bottom to the General Fund pit has been found and, between inflation depreciating the purchasing power of the public tax/fee/charge dollar, and the slowness of revenue growth, most General Funds are in a year-to-year deficit position. Second, pressure groups have become more vocal, better organized, and more politically shrewd in their approach. Thus, many can now expect to gain a share of the public dollar from the General Fund. Increasing amounts of General Fund monies are appropriated to obscure programs promoted by pressure groups. The budget officer is thus forced into the unwanted and politically untenable position of being the "watchdog" of the treasury. Third, and potentially most important, are a series of court decisions that possibly indicate a trend. Pressure groups, special interest associations, employees, unions, and citizen lobbies are increasingly resorting to the judiciary to assure that an appropriation is "adequate". For example, implementation of an equal employment program is expensive and, if not done adequately, can subject the delinquent jurisdiction to a court-mandate to conduct a specific program, with specific expenses and fines inherent therein. The same holds true for public health programs, implementation of employee safety, building and operation modifications, and even school busing. There even have been cases in the safety field where both civil and criminal sanctions have been made for, in effect, appropriating inadequate monies. Jail and prison health care and over-crowding are prominent cases.

More court mandates to finance specific programs at higher dollar levels can be expected, in ever-greater detail. The *Municipal Business System* assignment of specific revenue sources to matching services might well serve as a major limitation to this increasingly worrisome trend.

Debilities of the General Fund. It is a major contention of this book that the General Fund suffers from several debilities. Foremost is the inability of any of the political, taxpayer or functional groups to relate to the budgetary decision-making process because they do not relate revenues to expenditures. There is no device within the General Fund structure to establish any such relationship. Next, the General Fund often charges special and enterprise funds either an in-lieu of tax levy or an overhead charge for "services rendered" by the central staff agencies financed through the General Fund. Most such charges are based on no, or at best arbitrary criteria, considerably aggravating both the beneficiaries and operators of the special funds. Also, overreliance on the General Fund as a budgetary vehicle does not make it possible to relate specific services to specific taxes or revenue sources, thus eliminating any possibility of a consumer-type or user-oriented budgetary approach. Such as the *Municipal Business System* in this Book.

CONVERSION OF THE GENERAL FUND

U.S. Federal Office of Management and Budget circular OMB A-87 (now FMC 74-4) establishes a basis for indirect overhead costs to be charged to and made an integral part of many federal grants. The alternative is to either take a set five percent rate, or to charge all costs directly to a grant. The former approach recaptures inadequate indirect charges while the latter is far too complex an accounting procedure. Thus the creation of an *FMC 74-4 Cost Allocation Plan* separates so-called "support and staff" services from direct governmental operations. The process results in an audit-determined, federally-approved percentage figure established by clear guidelines, thus for the most part eliminating arbitrariness and arguability from any overhead charge applied to grants.

It is a short jump of logic from applying this established percentage for indirect overhead charges to a federal grant, to extension of that system to all governmental special funds. It is only an additional short step to separate all General Fund revenue sources, and other than staff and support functions, into a series of special funds. Thus the General Fund would, in effect, be converted into a central staff service and support operation, financed solely by the overhead charges transferred from all the other funds, of whatever category. Or, if you will, conversion of the General Fund into the rough governmental equivalent of the private sector corporate holding company. Several of the more successful corporate conglomerates (ITT, Oracle, Disney, IBM, Google, GE, Microsoft, and especially Berkshire-Hathaway) utilize an analogous corporate approach. Even the late departed Enron did so, but quite sloppily. Hospitals also routinely allocate overhead charges to functional departments and activities, and other facilities in a chain operation.

Overhead as a Concept. Overhead charges have been well accepted in the private sector for decades. If government is ever to adapt business methods to its activities in any meaningful way some system must be devised to inform the governmental voter/tax/service-payer more adequately in consumer-oriented terms. By breaking up the General Fund into a series of special funds, and relating revenues to services provided by each service center or special fund, a consumer-oriented public budget system can be formulated. But without including overhead charges into the special funds, and into each program and service center therein, inadequate costs would be charged for each service. A by-product of such a charging system is generation of considerable internal organizational pressure by the operating agencies to assure that overhead costs – and consequent charges – are reasonable; and that central support services are both adequate and operationally oriented. In practice, such pressures considerably mitigate the almost pervasive conflict between so-called staff and line functionaries. It should be obvious that *The System* outlined in this book, and in some detail for several cities, is necessary.

TRANSFORMATION OF THE GENERAL FUND

Detailed analysis of revenue sources of any governmental jurisdiction, both from the standpoint of the group from whom the tax/fee/charge is extracted, and from the angle of what linkage there is between the revenue source and the potential service benefit to the group taxed, is a relatively easy process. One has only to follow the classification scheme of the National Council on Governmental Accounting's (NCGA) Governmental Accounting, Auditing and Financial Reporting (GAAFR) and Governmental Accounting Standards Board (GASB) guidelines, regulations and volumes, assisted by local laws, ordinances, bond indentures, political commitments and a modicum of knowledge of economic and marketing principles set out in this Book. By so doing one can quickly realize that most governmental revenue sources, save one, can be earmarked or allocated following "*The Municipal Business Sytstem*" process.

The one problematical source is the *sales tax*; another problem area, but *only* of a philosophical nature, is the *income tax*.

Philosophical Problems. It should be apparent by now that the basic thrust of the budgetary system and the underlying revenue and cost distribution and budgeting "Systems" outlined herein is to assist the tax/rate payer to make consumer-oriented decisions. Then communicating those wants to their elected representatives. Put another way, when a government official is faced with the alternative of either eschewing a program, or in effect earmarking a consumer-connected tax/fee/charge, the latter is certainly preferable to telling the consumer (voter) that the service is not available or will deteriorate. This philosophy – of providing governmental services for specified charges and thereby potentially cutting into net disposable income disbursed to the private sector -- obviously will bother those who feel government is already "too big and intrusive". Most local government officials will agree, yet when they are caught between the service demand groups and the taxpayer leagues the retreat into the murkiness of the General Fund is becoming increasingly financially difficult and mightily politically risky. The plethora of techniques to counter these countervailing pressures include "sunset" laws and their handmaiden, zero-base budgeting; "loaded" opinion polls; position freezes; across-the-board dollar or percentage budget cuts accompanied with the admonition "be more efficient"; and an increasing unrealistic usage of long term floating debt. All that huffing and puffing can be superseded by tying the *Municipal Business System* [MBS] into the Integrated Budget System [IBS], outlined in this Chapter.

Thereby local, and maybe even state, governments can enter the era of the **American Consumer** and the **Age of Consumption** they founded.

The income tax creates another philosophical hurdle to cost-revenue connected budgeting. A strong, but controversial case can be made that health, education and welfare programs should be financed exclusively from that revenue source. It is contended that since a person who is unhealthy, in the process of being educated, and/or on welfare is earning at a lower level than "normal" and that once their "problems" are "solved" their income rises. Therefore, the logic proceeds, the income increment should be taxed progressively to repay the improvement in education, condition and earning capacity. Thus the financing of health, education and welfare exclusively from the income tax.

However, few cities receive income taxes directly. If so, usually as a subvention from the State income tax via a League of Cities long-ago lobbied dole, like in Arizona.

Property taxation presents the flip side of this philosophical coinage: that only the direct property-related services of fire and police protection, broad planning and zoning, street cleaning, property maintenance code enforcement, storm drainage, residential street construction and maintenance and lighting, property tax administration, and possibly parks and public building acquisition, construction and maintenance should be financed from such a tax. And even many of the above list could be broken up and re-assembled into logical saleable service centers. For example, special assessment and/or utility funds are being created by which to finance each of street cleaning, storm drainage, street lighting, neighborhood parks and numerous other similar other property-benefitting services.

Agree or not agree, the above arguments obviously would result in earmarking or allocating property tax revenues to property-related services and the income tax to health, education and welfare. That leaves the sales tax among major governmental revenue sources for service "distribution" once removed from the General Fund.

Sales taxes cause added philosophical problems. Since a consumer relation rationale for sales tax proceeds is rather difficult to create, this revenue source could be placed in a service-related substitute for the General Fund in an Integrative Budgeting System. Such allocation would permit the governing body or legislature to utilize that money to subsidize programs which it determines from year-to-year cannot be adequately financed thru direct revenue sources. Thus the problem of the more affluent members of society being able, and possibly willing, to finance higher levels of service for themselves but not others less fortunate would be eliminated, or at least mitigated. There is here even a crude sort of reasoning that those capable of higher levels of consumption would thereby indirectly subsidize programs for those less able to afford the direct consumer-related governmental services. At least some of the theoretical regressivity of the sales tax would be addressed by this approach. The fact that the minimization of the sales tax into its own special purpose fund would facilitate the conversion of the General Fund into the overhead type of fund contemplated by use Systems explained earlier in this Book.

In regard to sales tax, there is one swamp into which no governmental official should fall: Namely, that solely "businesses" should benefit from sales tax collections, since "they/we" generate it. False! Purchasers pay the tax. The business only collects it.

Supplementary Service Levels. Some cities now are creating special assessment or "subscription" districts by which to provide "higher level" police patrol protection. Such usually are proffered to shopping centers and malls. These could, but not necessarily, be subsidized or encouraged by allocation of minor amounts of sales taxes. Thus the battle for "dole" from the current misused General Fund would be mitigated, if not eliminated.

__Matching Revenues to Expenditures.__ By relating each – and every – revenue source to a specific fund, and program or series of service centers within programs in a program-type budget, a recordkeeping and reporting system is thus established whereby revenues must equal expenditures, or vice versa. For example, a Public Safety, or Fire, Police, EMS, and 911 Funds could be created, with fine and appropriate service center revenues, and all other un-earmarked property taxes assigned to those, in proportion to "governing body-decided 'importance'". [See the John Holmes Letter] Many jurisdictions also have libraries and parks operating out of the General Fund. Each should have its revenues allocated to its own special fund, directly supplemented as necessary by the general benefit property taxes and any special fee revenues those might receive.

Sanitation charges, sewer connection fees and service charges, and recreation revenues each should be assigned to their respective operational service centers within the appropriate fund. With program, i.e., functional managers having a vested interest in their assigned revenue sources a rough sort of entrepreneurial equation is established. But potentially more important, the current built-in incentive to spend all one is budgeted is removed. Under present budget systems, surpluses revert to next year's General Fund carryover balance. Following GASBO, GAAFR and AICPA-approved procedures unexpended fund balance, deficit, or overage in revenues is recycled back into the fund of origin. Thus each fund manager can be held truly responsible for over/under expenditures through examination of the array of service centers contained within that specific fund. Or as those could now be termed within the *__Municipal Business System__* – MY business.

The more narrowly focused fund structure mechanically will act to deter the usual "last quarter splurge" or non-husbanding of resources. Such usual bureaucratic machinations would merely amount to penalizing oneself by the fund, i.e. program, manager. For, by spending just to "get rid of the money" to keep from losing it and thereby damaging the basis for succeeding year's appropriations, the manager would be depleting his/her beginning balance for the new fiscal year. A sense of reward and recognition, or at least responsibility, would be built into the budgetary process by the system, something one cannot say of any governmental budget at the present time. But absolutely definitively could be said for the organization of the City of Inglewood, California from 1970 until politically-motivated disassembly in 1975.

__A "Final Fact".__ Think about this one:

> **If ALL revenues are embedded in a fund and/or service center, matched to a specific service, what is there to argue about? Other than 1) service level cuts OR 2) revenue increases?**

As mentioned earlier, a probable result and necessary ingredient would be a true merit pay plan for the middle and top management personnel of the jurisdiction using the combination of *the Municipal Business System* and Integrative Budgeting.

WILL IT WORK?

To varying degrees many of the elements of the above described system have been installed in a few local governmental jurisdictions. The City of Inglewood, California had the most advanced system, although not fully implemented as regards the final degradation of the General Fund. Many of the techniques were transplanted into most of the several hundred clients of MSI, and now RCS.

The political risks have seemed too great, and the desire to maintain the status quo too pervasive until the financial crunch of 2007-20(?). The setting may now be conducive for full implementation over the estimated two to three year period necessary.

MARKETING OF PUBLIC SERVICES

The major problem of public budgeting today is securing revenues to provide services being demanded and to keep abreast of inflation. Federal General Revenue Sharing was killed, and Housing and Community Development grants have been of little benefit, after inflation, due to the requirement of hearings to solicit public desires as to ways to spend the "new" money and/or mandated program area. That effort, too, now appears to be a threatened species, as does any federal financial aid of any type to local governments.

Inflation. Depreciation of the buying power of the public tax dollar by inflation has taken away most of the benefit of any federal revenue sharing approaches, leaving local government with the grant program requirements and the raised expectation insured by public hearings, both to be met by a devalued dollar. Thus most local governmental efforts at marketing of services have been concentrated in defending ways to spend money that still is being depleted by the current 3% or so current national inflation rate. Very few marketing techniques have been aimed at the "consumer society" by public agencies with the intent being to secure specific revenues adequate to provide a specific public service. In fact, it here is again related that NO school of public administration even offers a marketing course, while the now somewhat denigrated graduate schools of business offer a major in the field, without even recognizing local government a seemingly inherent arch enemy, what with "it" being "government".

Consumer-Oriented Budgeting. The above described Integrative Budgeting System operated with the *Municipal Business System*, provides the mechanics for relating every revenue source to a specific service. Some relationships are quite direct, while others – income and sales tax – are somewhat indirect. It is clear that at present there is no possibility of financing promised governmental services and their underlying infrastructure anywhere near adequately. Thus one can reason that a consumer-oriented budget would permit intelligent informed choices to be made by taxpayer-consumers and their elected representatives far better than the present pressure and special interest-ridden process. A decision not to finance, or not to increase, or even to decrease or eliminate a specific revenue source could be a decision that can be openly observed and politically defended. The public demands; elected official promise; appointed officials attempt to deliver; rising costs, inflation and new federal-state requirements act to reduce service levels; and everyone is unhappy. Clearly, the present standard local government budget "system" is not working. And is dying literally almost on the proverbial vine.

Alternative Solutions. The zero-base budgeting concept was put forward, and still is oft-resurrected -- together with its companion concept, "sunset" laws – as an answer to better budgetary decision-making. Yet, by not being directly related to specific revenue sources, the level of understanding is low as to why a program is reduced in scope or eliminated, resulting in significant service delivery, then latent political problems.

Both political and theoretical economic arguments can be raised against relating all ***specific*** revenue sources to ***specific*** programs, and permitting consumer/taxpayer willingness to determine ***specific*** service levels by reacting to ***specific*** tax/fee/charges. But the plain fact is that if governmental services, especially those at the local level, are to do anything but deteriorate into a cloud of obfuscatory criticism, such direct and ***specific*** connections must be made. If the ***specific*** service "sells" then it can be maintained; if not, then so be it – "the public has spoken". Unbridled promises of ***specific*** services, in the face of deteriorating revenues and ***specific*** service levels, and abuse of the bureaucracy simply will not much longer serve the needs of elected officials. One could conclude from the current anti-politician reactions provided in recent polls that candor and openness is the only realistic campaign style. But budgetary and financial information of a reliable nature is prerequisite to such candor. Few such informational systems currently exist in government. The ***Municipal Business System***, coupled with IBS would so provide.

It is a major premise of IBS coupled with and driven by the ***MBS*** that if the electorate is told that a ***specific*** service is to cost so much they will respond – positively if they want it and negatively if not. Then, at least, the elected official and the constituent both will know that the era of having something for nothing is dead and gone; that the "free lunch" never did exist and no longer can be marketed by either elected or appointed officials.

MATRIX BUDGETING

Another concept which can be developed from and work atop the ***Municipal Business System***, combined with the Integrative Budgeting System (IBS) base, can be called "Matrix Budgeting". Thereby taking maximum advantage of advanced computer and communication technology. The diagram that follows shows how such an approach could be related to the neighborhood for certain basic and/or enhanced public services. Thus those who would decentralize government and utilize the indigenous community neighborhood as the basic governmental building block have a practical way to implement their ideas.

Property Tax Centric. Matrix budgeting permits a specific decision to be made by each ***specific*** neighborhood as to the amount of and type of charge for ***specific*** services. But the IBS budgeting system and the ***Municipal Business System*** service center cost-revenue match-ups must be implemented as a prerequisite. With IBS a City or County tax bill could quite easily be produced on either an annual or – preferably – a *monthly* basis similar in appearance to that shown in Table II, for either Neighborhood A or B. Such information about taxes and charges would be a major step to clarify government and, eventually, to make it far more intelligible and responsive to citizen needs.

DISADVANTAGES OF IBS MATRIX BUDGETING

Extension of the *Municipal Business System* for determining full and true costs of each specific servicer, the Integrative Budgeting System concept can encompass the neighborhood or matrix approach. But such has four distinct disadvantages. Of course each individual situation must determine whether the huge advantage of self-determination is either desirable or worth the effort to overcome the negatives of place-ment in the neighborhoods of decision making about *specific* services and levels thereof.

The first disadvantage is that poorer neighborhoods will be unable, and at least theo-retically unwilling to pay as much as a wealthier area. The following Table presents what possibly – and some may say probably – would happen were local neighborhood "home rule" made possible, with Neighborhood A being the wealthier in the example.

A second problem is reconciling geographical areas with functional operations. For-tunately, the IBS computer-reported budgeting technique can resolve those mechanistic difficulties. Personal and behavioral problems will require added effort.

The third difficulty with the Matrix Budget (MB) extension of the *Municipal Business System* coupled with Integrative Budgeting, is securing legal authorization to extend a wide variety of tax and service charge options to the neighborhood level. If one truly believes in local self-determination such can be achieved, but with considerable political effort. Talking of neighborhood government and acceptance of it by local government officials has been divergent. County elected officials, and especially state legislators, have opposed such devolution. In effect, *too much* democracy is just *too much*.[59]

---

[59]   By 1970 Inglewood, California had developed its budgeting, accounting, computer and management systems sufficiently to be able to offer such neighborhood supplemental service levels. Further, the then-precursor of what ten years later would become the fully developed *Municipal Business System* facilitated such direct democratic determinations. Thus the City portion of the **annual** property tax bill compiled and issued by Los Angeles County **could** have been broken down into monthly amounts which **could** have been billed monthly via the City's then sophisticated billing systems. The amounts for all those *specific* services and activities listed on the following potential *City Services Bill* quietly were calculated and, amazingly, resulted in a quite low amount of taxes and charges. These numbers astounded all, particularly when com-paring with corporately-owned Electric, Cable TV, Telephone and other "normal" household or business expenses. And separated from County and Schools property tax levies that were billed annually. But, the "takeover" and conversion of billing to monthly proved to be politically and, perhaps, legally improbable.

When the elected Los Angeles County Assessor was approached to provide the City with assessment valuation computer tapes he refused, stating *"You'll have to take me to the Supreme Court to get them."*

As reported earlier, after six more years of public input, the City Council rejected the concept of public and neighborhood information and inputs, fired Ayres, the Mayor became City Manager and abandoned the IBS software and hardware. As the now-Mayor/City Manager said: "It was just too politically limiting."

MATRIX BUDGET OPTION

CITY OF _____   For Service Call:_____

Address:_____   Year/Month:_____

| Service | - - - - - Neighborhood - | | | | |
	A	B	C	D	E	
Police Protection	$ 10.22	$ 7.35				
Fire Protection	6.89	6.89				
Street Sweeping	.30	.15				AND SO
Refuse Collection*	5.60	4.00				FORTH
Water Service*	18.61	12.00				
Sewer Service*	19.80	14.00				
Storm Drainage	1.27	1.27				
Street Lighting	.48	.12				FOR EACH
Street Landscaping	.46	.24				NEIGHBOR-
Paramedic Service	3.30	3.30				HOOD
Park Const'n/Mainten'ce	1.20	.90				
Library Service	.67	.67				
Planning & Zoning	.22	.22				
Total Community TAX This Month	$24.01	$ 21.11				
Total CHARGES This Month	$ 44.01	$ 30.00				
TOTAL AMOUNT DUE	$ 66.02	$ 51.11			*Due*	*this Month*

*Monthly Service Charge based on volume   (**Note:** 1970 dollar values)

The above is not truly representative. The original computations were not salvaged, since the entirety of the neighborhood choice concept was rejected by the City Council. Thus only generalities of the combined MBS/IBS/Matrix approach can be seen as what is possible with today's level of universal computerization.

Last, the method of securing guidance, acceptance or determination of tax and service charge levels, whether by voting or by indirect representation, will require considerable restructuring of both of municipal organization and prevailing political thought. And especially re-construction and de-centralization of property tax billing. However, like many other governmental concepts, Matrix Budgeting, and its necessary precursors, the *Municipal Business System* and IBS, all deserve to be broached, tried, modified and debugged to make them workable and acceptable. The Author of this *Book* has done so, and the lessons learned are simple: *Full democracy is difficult to achieve and messy to operate; but it works. But, with that said, the tax-paying public deserves better treatment and greater capability to make informed decisions as to how to spend their money.*

CONCLUSION

It has been the intention of this Chapter and of this Book, and indeed the entirety of this attempt to outline a concept and approach that has been partially installed, developed further both in practice and in thought, and expounded in the academic classroom and practitioner workshops. The Author has no doubt that the *Municipal Business System*, with Integrative Budgeting, and its possible extension, Matrix Budgeting, is an idea whose time will come. Whether it is the *Municipal Business System* rather precisely described in this Book, or something lesser or related, it has become all too obvious to any student of government, and reasonably intelligent practitioner, that the one big question constantly and consistently now being asked cannot much longer go begging for a very good answer. That question is the ubiquitous, yet again:

"What am I getting for my money?"

It is the responsibility of theoreticians, teachers and government administrators to work closely with political leaders to provide an answer. If we cannot soon give the public an intelligible response to this question then we deserve to perish rather than to publish.

Acknowledgements for the original IBS Booklet of April 2, 1977 and the resultant base for the revision as Chapter VII of this Book – CONSUMER GOVERNMENT VIA THE ART OF FULL DISCLOSURE
vvvvvvvvvvvvvvvvvvvvvvvvvvvvvvvvvvvvvvvvvvvvvvvvvvvvvvvvvvvvvvvvvvvvvvvvvvvvvvvvvv

Special thanks are extended by the Author to Dick Taylor, Steve Blumberg, "Tug" Tamaru, Dan McGowan, and Mike White for critical review, advice and constructive comment on this paper. The author takes full responsibility for the end result, however.

Mr. Ayres is Visiting Professor of Public Administration at the Graduate Center for Public Policy and Administration of California State University, Long Beach; and Adjunct in the Graduate School of Public Administration of the University of Southern California.

He has been Assistant Town Manager/Town Clerk in Salem, Virginia; City Manager of Melbourne, Florida; Salem, Oregon; Inglewood, California; and CEO of Leisure World/Laguna Hills. Ayres also was on the staff of Public Administration Service, governmental management consultants, acting as a personnel, systems and finance consultant to more than 125 jurisdictions and organizations in many of the United States and other parts of North and South America.

A Conceptual Paper in a Series
©by
Douglas W. Ayres
April 2, 1977
2nd Printing
February, 1978
School of Public Administration
University of Southern California

ILLUSTRATIONS

"The back of the Book"

CITY OF PASADENA   Schedule 9

SUMMARY OF REVENUES, COSTS AND SUBSIDIES

FISCAL YEAR 1992-1993 BUDGET

MSI # (1)	SERVICE CENTER (2)	TOTAL REVENUE (3)	TOTAL COST (4)	TOTAL PROFIT (SUBSIDY) (5)	PERCENT RECOVERY (6)
	COMMUNITY DEVELOPMENT SERVICES				
S-001	Concept Plan Review	$9,600	$104,783	($95,183)	9.2%
S-002	Preliminary Plan Check	$42,062	$88,858	($46,796)	47.3%
S-003	Tentative Parcel Map Review	$36,315	$31,373	$4,942	115.8%
S-004	Tentative Tract Map Review	$58,680	$47,616	$11,064	123.2%
S-005	Construction Staging Plan Review	$0	$9,788	($9,788)	0.0%
S-006	Design Commission Review (Minor)	$3,350	$14,969	($11,619)	22.4%
S-007	Design Commission Review (Major)	$23,750	$99,391	($75,641)	23.9%
S-008	Design Review (Final)	$0	$30,173	($30,173)	0.0%
S-009	Design Review (Seismic)	$0	$5,028	($5,028)	0.0%
S-010	Design Review–City of Gardens	$3,953	$53,665	($49,712)	7.4%
S-011	Design Review (Consolidated)	$10,780	$31,275	($20,495)	34.5%
S-012	Design Review Extension	$0	$446	($446)	0.0%
S-013	Landmark District Review	$0	$8,137	($8,137)	0.0%
S-014	Historic Building Search	$0	$22,072	($22,072)	0.0%
S-015	Master Development Plan Review	$2,799	$17,602	($14,803)	15.9%
S-016	Conditional Use Permit Review	$214,350	$244,635	($30,285)	87.6%
S-017	Minor Conditional Use Permit Review	$11,480	$36,806	($25,326)	31.2%
S-018	Temporary Conditional Use Permit Rvw	$20,020	$26,268	($6,248)	76.2%
S-019	Variance Review	$60,830	$95,105	($34,275)	64.0%
S-020	Minor Variance Review	$9,515	$34,268	($24,753)	27.8%
S-021	Use Permit & Variance Extension	$0	$5,115	($5,115)	0.0%
S-022	Lot Line Adjustment	$13,305	$17,390	($4,085)	76.5%
S-023	Rezoning Request Rvw (Zone Change)	$8,288	$17,591	($9,303)	47.1%
S-024	Subdivision Map Extension Prcssng	$6,152	$8,070	($1,918)	76.2%
S-025	Growth Management Allocation	$32,864	$319,860	($286,996)	10.3%
S-026	Growth Management Allocation Exemption	$0	$19,621	($19,621)	0.0%
S-027	Growth Allocation Appeal	$1,901	$2,064	($163)	92.1%
S-028	Growth Mgt. Conditional Use Permit	$28,580	$30,359	($1,779)	94.1%
S-029	Growth Management Time Extension	$0	$4,603	($4,603)	0.0%
S-031	Environmental Impact Report (Consltnt)	$10,230	$19,236	($9,006)	53.2%
S-032	Fish & Game Environ. Impact Revw	$2,132	$12,543	($10,411)	17.0%
S-033	Env. Impact Mitigation Monitoring	$0	$15,317	($15,317)	0.0%
S-034	Monitoring of Conditions	$0	$277,304	($277,304)	0.0%
S-035	Certificate of Appropriateness	$0	$66,722	($66,722)	0.0%
S-036	Replacement Building Permit Relief	$0	$1,874	($1,874)	0.0%
S-037	Appeal Processing	$18,130	$93,549	($75,419)	19.4%
S-038	Appeal Processing - Staff Decision	$0	$3,111	($3,111)	0.0%

CITY OF PASADENA   Schedule 9

SUMMARY OF REVENUES, COSTS AND SUBSIDIES

FISCAL YEAR 1992–1993 BUDGET

MSI # (1)	SERVICE CENTER (2)	TOTAL REVENUE (3)	TOTAL COST (4)	TOTAL PROFIT (SUBSIDY) (5)	PERCENT RECOVERY (6)
S-039	Vesting Map Review	$16,730	$12,222	$4,508	136.9%
S-040	Final Tract Map Review	$0	$23,095	($23,095)	0.0%
S-041	Final Parcel Map Review	$0	$5,730	($5,730)	0.0%
S-042	Engineering Plan Review	$79,400	$76,644	$2,756	103.6%
S-043	Street Occupation Permit	$207,200	$45,403	$161,797	456.4%
S-044	Public Works Permit	$207,200	$287,508	($80,308)	72.1%
S-045	Street Vacation	$4,144	$45,733	($41,589)	9.1%
S-046	Grading Plan Check	$4,206	$1,422	$2,784	295.8%
S-047	Hillside Grading Plan Check	$6,718	$1,773	$4,945	378.9%
S-048	Grading Inspection	$4,206	$423	$3,783	994.3%
S-049	Hillside Grading Inspection	$0	$4,785	($4,785)	0.0%
S-050	Construction Plan Check	$794,312	$1,555,280	($760,968)	51.1%
S-051	Construction Review and Inspection	$1,455,219	$1,141,048	$314,171	127.5%
S-052	Misc/Special Building Inspection Invstgn	$12,183	$8,219	$3,964	148.2%
S-053	Condominium Conversion	$0	$1,637	($1,637)	0.0%
S-054	Relocation Investigation (House Moves)	$9,324	$7,820	$1,504	119.2%
S-055	Address Change	$966	$716	$250	134.9%
S-056	Address Assignment	$1,650	$8,345	($6,695)	19.8%
S-057	Temporary Certificate of Occupancy	$34,020	$37,007	($2,987)	91.9%
S-058	Occupancy Inspection	$254,384	$680,584	($426,200)	37.4%
S-059	Certificate of Compliance Investigation	$1,955	$7,278	($5,323)	26.9%
S-060	Parkway Usage License Agreement	$3,191	$21,864	($18,673)	14.6%
S-061	Sidewalk Dining Permit	$0	$889	($889)	0.0%
S-062	Building Permit Center	$0	$162,623	($162,623)	0.0%
S-063	Zoning Parking Credit	$2,400	$13,142	($10,742)	18.3%
S-064	Temporary Street Closure (Events)	$1,219	$30,229	($29,010)	4.0%
S-065	Traffic Impact Review	$0	$75,339	($75,339)	0.0%
S-066	Trip Reduction Plan Review	$0	$71,854	($71,854)	0.0%
S-067	Development Agreement Revw	$0	$9,335	($9,335)	0.0%
S-068	Legal Description	$0	$4,387	($4,387)	0.0%
S-069	Planned Development	$0	$4,653	($4,653)	0.0%
S-070	General Plan Amendment	$0	$4,096	($4,096)	0.0%
	SUBTOTAL	$3,779,386	$6,364,054	($2,584,668)	59.4%

CITY OF PASADENA

SUMMARY OF REVENUES, COSTS AND SUBSIDIES

FISCAL YEAR 1992–1993 BUDGET

MSI # (1)	SERVICE CENTER (2)	TOTAL REVENUE (3)	TOTAL COST (4)	TOTAL PROFIT (SUBSIDY) (5)	PERCENT RECOVERY (6)
	PUBLIC SAFETY SERVICES				
S-071	Annual Hm Business Occupancy Permit	$13,000	$24,668	($11,668)	52.7%
S-072	Garage Sale Permit	$7,500	$9,990	($2,490)	75.1%
S-073	Special Business Regulation	$0	$63,207	($63,207)	0.0%
S-074	Wide, Overweight, Overlong Ld Permit	$5,594	$3,337	$2,257	167.6%
S-075	Vehicle Code Enforcement	$240,000	$894,037	($654,037)	26.8%
S-076	Non-Vehicle Code Enforcement	$0	$425,841	($425,841)	0.0%
S-077	Parking Enforcement	$1,625,000	$764,794	$860,206	212.5%
S-078	Parking Permits	$85,988	$145,066	($59,078)	59.3%
S-079	Limited Time Parking Permit	$0	$6,888	($6,888)	0.0%
S-080	Bicycle Registration	$2,132	$3,666	($1,535)	58.1%
S-081	Burglar Alarm Review	$133,500	$34,234	$99,266	390.0%
S-082	Police False Alarm Response	$176,554	$1,069,384	($892,830)	16.5%
S-083	Clearance Letter Processing	$3,000	$3,366	($366)	89.1%
S-084	Police Report Copying	$100,000	$112,243	($12,243)	89.1%
S-085	Police Photograph Reproduction	$3,108	$7,264	($4,156)	42.8%
S-086	Police Photo Lab Services	$0	$59,543	($59,543)	0.0%
S-087	Police Tape & Video Duplication Service	$0	$2,817	($2,817)	0.0%
S-088	Spec. Police Computer Print-Out Service	$1,400	$5,300	($3,900)	26.4%
S-089	Fingerprint Processing	$33,300	$41,531	($8,231)	80.2%
S-090	Vehicle Correction Inspection	$0	$4,658	($4,658)	0.0%
S-091	Removal of Aband/Abated Veh & Release	$0	$91,405	($91,405)	0.0%
S-092	Impound Vehicle Release Service	$0	$60,184	($60,184)	0.0%
S-093	DUI Acc. Response, Invest. & Report	$4,500	$243,933	($239,433)	1.8%
S-094	DUI Arrest Procedure/Non-Accident	$0	$346,891	($346,891)	0.0%
S-095	Noise Disturbance Response Call-back	$0	$11,584	($11,584)	0.0%
S-096	Public Crosswalk Protection	$0	$195,930	($195,930)	0.0%
S-097	One-Day Alcohol Permit Processing	$0	$6,041	($6,041)	0.0%
S-098	Commercial Foot Patrol	$0	$198,704	($198,704)	0.0%
S-099	Rifle Range Use	$25,000	$40,401	($15,401)	61.9%
S-100	Helicopter Pad Landing Use	$4,070	$1,304	$2,766	312.1%
S-101	I.N.S. Prisoner Housing	$391,500	$384,610	$6,890	101.8%
S-102	Trustee Housing	$73,650	$83,247	($9,597)	88.5%
S-103	V.I.N. Verification	$0	$8,280	($8,280)	0.0%
S-104	Hazardous Materials Permit Insp	$766,640	$719,743	$46,897	106.5%

CITY OF PASADENA   Schedule 9

SUMMARY OF REVENUES, COSTS AND SUBSIDIES

FISCAL YEAR 1992–1993 BUDGET

MSI # (1)	SERVICE CENTER (2)	TOTAL REVENUE (3)	TOTAL COST (4)	TOTAL PROFIT (SUBSIDY) (5)	PERCENT RECOVERY (6)
S-105	State Mandated Fire Inspection	$159,360	$185,178	($25,818)	86.1%
S-106	Underground Tank Plan Check/Insp.	$72,505	$62,984	$9,521	115.1%
S-107	Fire False Alarm Response	$0	$99,790	($99,790)	0.0%
S-108	Non-Emergency Service	$0	$19,917	($19,917)	0.0%
S-109	Illegal Burn Response	$0	$11,830	($11,830)	0.0%
S-110	Post-Fire Investigation Analysis	$44,556	$76,272	($31,716)	58.4%
S-111	Fire Report Copying	$1,125	$3,284	($2,159)	34.3%
S-112	Weed Abatement	$33,152	$69,330	($36,178)	47.8%
S-113	Medical Aid Response	$1,600,000	$3,309,171	($1,709,171)	48.4%
S-114	Hazard Abatement Services	$0	$2,838	($2,838)	0.0%
	SUBTOTAL	$5,606,134	$9,914,685	($4,308,551)	56.5%

HEALTH DEPARTMENT SERVICES

MSI # (1)	SERVICE CENTER (2)	TOTAL REVENUE (3)	TOTAL COST (4)	TOTAL PROFIT (SUBSIDY) (5)	PERCENT RECOVERY (6)
S-115	Health Department Plan Check/Insp	$17,000	$23,755	($6,755)	71.6%
S-116	Environmental Health Inspection	$208,432	$140,573	$67,859	148.3%
S-117	Noise Control Permit	$3,200	$15,087	($11,887)	21.2%
S-118	Food Sanitation Inspection	$205,368	$240,468	($35,100)	85.4%
S-119	Mosquito, Fly & Rodent Control	$0	$235,799	($235,799)	0.0%
S-120	Animal Control	$116,264	$425,273	($309,009)	27.3%
S-121	Vital Statistics	$255,408	$255,408	$0	100.0%
S-122	Travel Immmunizations	$181,000	$119,540	$61,460	151.4%
S-123	Water Examination	$99,840	$94,652	$5,188	105.5%
S-124	Alcoholism & Drug Depndncy Prgrm	$269,354	$362,784	($93,430)	74.2%
S-125	First Offender Program	$75,696	$73,491	$2,205	103.0%
S-126	Public Health Laboratory	$246,272	$246,272	$0	100.0%
S-127	Prenatal Clinic	$1,369,582	$1,369,582	$0	100.0%
S-128	Women, Infants & Childrn Voucher	$399,798	$534,954	($135,156)	74.7%
S-129	AIDS Program	$243,223	$294,808	($51,585)	82.5%
S-130	SGV, HIV Early Intervention Program	$255,300	$316,296	($60,996)	80.7%
S-131	Child Health Clinic	$424,713	$424,713	$0	100.0%

CITY OF PASADENA   Schedule 9

SUMMARY OF REVENUES, COSTS AND SUBSIDIES

FISCAL YEAR 1992–1993 BUDGET

MSI # (1)	SERVICE CENTER (2)	TOTAL REVENUE (3)	TOTAL COST (4)	TOTAL PROFIT (SUBSIDY) (5)	PERCENT RECOVERY (6)
S-132	Ambulatory Care Clinic	$16,783	$80,906	($64,123)	20.7%
S-133	Senior Preventive Health Program	$22,427	$112,223	($89,796)	20.0%
S-134	Sexually Transmitted Disease Program	$127,218	$127,218	$0	100.0%
S-135	Tuberculosis Program	$270,649	$313,777	($43,128)	86.3%
S-136	Flu/Pneumonia Immunization	$19,874	$21,943	($2,069)	90.6%
S-137	Immmunization	$57,704	$65,408	($7,704)	88.2%
	SUBTOTAL	$4,885,105	$5,894,930	($1,009,825)	82.9%

LEISURE & CULTURAL SERVICES

MSI #	SERVICE CENTER	TOTAL REVENUE	TOTAL COST	TOTAL PROFIT (SUBSIDY)	PERCENT RECOVERY
S-138	City Youth Sports Programs	$0	$738,658	($738,658)	0.0%
S-139	City Adult Sports Programs	$47,552	$288,392	($240,840)	16.5%
S-140	Private Youth Group Fld Rental Srvc	$0	$59,381	($59,381)	0.0%
S-141	Private Adult Group Fld Rental Svc	$14,947	$63,639	($48,692)	23.5%
S-142	Youth Recreation Classes	$18,217	$230,396	($212,179)	7.9%
S-143	Adult Recreation Classes	$42,372	$72,436	($30,064)	58.5%
S-144	Youth Special Activities	$0	$23,976	($23,976)	0.0%
S-145	Summer Day Camp	$40,000	$236,855	($196,855)	16.9%
S-146	Adaptive Recreation Activities	$21,425	$87,377	($65,952)	24.5%
S-147	Senior Citizen Programs	$6,530	$177,083	($170,553)	3.7%
S-148	Recreational Swimming	$10,464	$167,983	($157,519)	6.2%
S-149	Swimming Lessons	$21,652	$33,601	($11,949)	64.4%
S-150	Recreation Facility Rental	$131,490	$105,716	$25,774	124.4%
S-151	City-Wide Special Events	NA	$489,581	($489,581)	0.0%
S-152	Tournament of Roses Support	$787,577	$1,255,945	($468,368)	62.7%
S-153	Special Event Set-Up/Clean Up	$4,000	$44,598	($40,598)	9.0%
S-154	Overdue Material Processing	$192,461	$28,456	$164,005	676.3%
S-155	Replacing Lost Library Items	$12,897	$19,682	($6,785)	65.5%
S-156	Replacement Of Lost Library Cards	$9,501	$20,448	($10,947)	46.5%
S-157	Book Reservation Service	$5,115	$206,113	($200,998)	2.5%
S-158	Inter Library Loan Processing	$2,060	$51,813	($49,753)	4.0%

CITY OF PASADENA   Schedule 9

SUMMARY OF REVENUES, COSTS AND SUBSIDIES

FISCAL YEAR 1992–1993 BUDGET

MSI # (1)	SERVICE CENTER (2)	TOTAL REVENUE (3)	TOTAL COST (4)	TOTAL PROFIT (SUBSIDY) (5)	PERCENT RECOVERY (6)
S-159	Retrieval & Copying Of Periodicals	$1,734	$2,083	($349)	83.2%
S-160	Reproduction Of Photographs	$100	$510	($410)	19.6%
S-161	Library Media Rental	$5,914	$28,775	($22,861)	20.6%
S-162	Library On-Line Database Search	$12,411	$21,409	($8,998)	58.0%
S-163	Author Program	$5,505	$25,741	($20,236)	21.4%
S-164	Library Facility Rental	$7,500	$110,482	($102,982)	6.8%
	SUBTOTAL	$1,401,425	$4,591,129	($3,189,704)	30.5%

UTILITY & ENTERPRISE SERVICES

S-165	Electrical Power Service	$112,168,115	$117,999,638	($5,831,523)	95.1%
S-166	In-Field Service Spots	$0	$62,944	($62,944)	0.0%
S-167	New Vaults >200 Amps.	$484,334	$147,917	$336,417	327.4%
S-168	Trouble Shooter Service	$0	$252,008	($252,008)	0.0%
S-169	Power Credit Turn Off/On	$35,812	$71,416	($35,604)	50.1%
S-170	Damaged Meter Repair or Replacemnt	$13,350	$49,078	($35,728)	27.2%
S-171	Restore Service Wire Cuts	$2,500	$13,038	($10,538)	19.2%
S-172	Restore Bucket/Underground Cut	$900	$764	$136	117.8%
S-173	Same Day Service Turn-On	$25	$126	($101)	19.8%
S-174	Electric Meter Test	$490	$22,329	($21,839)	2.2%
S-175	Electric Meter Removal & Repl.	$4,150	$52,299	($48,149)	7.9%
S-176	Power Service Relocation	$1,150	$2,478	($1,328)	46.4%
S-177	Power Service Installation	$155,400	$127,120	$28,280	122.2%
S-178	Street Marking for Utility	$0	$163,283	($163,283)	0.0%
S-179	Water Service	$19,126,816	$22,875,219	($3,748,403)	83.6%
S-180	Water Service Installation	$152,100	$174,888	($22,788)	87.0%
S-181	Water Service Cut Off At Street	$200	$537	($337)	37.2%
S-182	Water Credit Turn Off/On	$19,516	$15,271	$4,245	127.8%
S-183	Replacement Of Curb Stop 3/4" & 1"	$11,100	$21,162	($10,062)	52.5%
S-184	Repl. Of 1-1/2" Wheel Gate Valve	$900	$1,708	($808)	52.7%
S-185	Meter Test/Field (5/8" & 1")	$240	$3,784	($3,544)	6.3%
S-186	Water Meter Removal and Replacement	$5,200	$8,438	($3,238)	61.6%
S-187	Water Meter Equipment Upgrade	$0	$21,164	($21,164)	0.0%

CITY OF PASADENA   Schedule 9

SUMMARY OF REVENUES, COSTS AND SUBSIDIES

FISCAL YEAR 1992–1993 BUDGET

MSI # (1)	SERVICE CENTER (2)	TOTAL REVENUE (3)	TOTAL COST (4)	TOTAL PROFIT (SUBSIDY) (5)	PERCENT RECOVERY (6)
S-188	Water Quality Test	$0	$17,192	($17,192)	0.0%
S-189	Flow Test (Low/Leak/Frozen Valve)	$0	$18,158	($18,158)	0.0%
S-190	Hydrant Flow Test	$0	$13,855	($13,855)	0.0%
S-191	Hydrant Portable/Construction Meter	$0	$2,776	($2,776)	0.0%
S-192	Hydrant Installation	$14,112	$4,524	$9,588	311.9%
S-193	Backflow Device Installation	$48,000	$293,726	($245,726)	16.3%
S-194	Utility Billing	$675,000	$524,771	$150,229	128.6%
S-195	Bill Investigation	$0	$16,093	($16,093)	0.0%
S-196	Sewer & Storm Drain Operation & Mtc	$2,598,642	$11,675,856	($9,077,214)	22.3%
S-197	Sewer Stoppage Investigation	$0	$5,422	($5,422)	0.0%
S-198	Utility Excavation Permit	$14,620	$70,448	($55,828)	20.8%
S-199	Residential Refuse Collection	$6,844,500	$7,067,644	($223,144)	96.8%
S-200	Commercial Refuse Service	$1,400,000	$1,423,072	($23,072)	98.4%
S-201	Special Requested Refuse Pick-Up	$45,000	$32,678	$12,322	137.7%
S-202	Street Sweeping	$636,206	$825,836	($189,630)	77.0%
S-203	Right-of-Way Clean-up	$0	$35,777	($35,777)	0.0%
S-204	Rose Bowl Maintenance/Operation	$3,850,292	$6,456,756	($2,606,464)	59.6%
S-205	Golf Course Maintenance/Operation	$1,948,129	$1,367,058	$581,071	142.5%
S-206	Old Pasadena Parking District	$2,492,648	$3,274,759	($782,111)	76.1%
S-207	South Lake Parking District	$135,203	$346,662	($211,459)	39.0%
S-208	Plaza Las Fuentes Parking	$1,950,075	$2,756,310	($806,235)	70.7%
S-209	City Parking Lot Service	$202,451	$604,282	($401,831)	33.5%
	SUBTOTAL	$155,037,176	$178,920,264	($23,883,088)	86.7%

MAINTENANCE SERVICES

S-210	Utility St. Usage (Gas & Elec.)				
S-211	Street Light & Signal Maint & Op'n	$3,900,000	$6,493,336	($2,593,336)	60.1%
S-212	Median & Parkway Maintenance	$0	$440,333	($440,333)	0.0%
S-213	Street Tree Maintenance	$0	$2,218,643	($2,218,643)	0.0%
S-214	Tree Maintenance Contractor Permit Rvw	$320	$1,070	($750)	29.9%
S-215	Barricade Installation	$10,000	$14,253	($4,253)	70.2%

CITY OF PASADENA

SUMMARY OF REVENUES, COSTS AND SUBSIDIES

FISCAL YEAR 1992–1993 BUDGET

MSI # (1)	SERVICE CENTER (2)	TOTAL REVENUE (3)	TOTAL COST (4)	TOTAL PROFIT (SUBSIDY) (5)	PERCENT RECOVERY (6)
S-216	Barric Rental	$2,000	$5,085	($3,085)	39.3%
S-217	Hazardous Materials Clean-up	$0	$39,269	($39,269)	0.0%
S-218	Special Business Services	$0	$238,377	($238,377)	0.0%
S-219	Business Improvement District	$0	$51,033	($51,033)	0.0%
S-220	Alley Maintenance	$0	$440,289	($440,289)	0.0%
S-221	Special Curb Marking	$1,500	$18,169	($16,669)	8.3%
S-222	Neighborhood Park Maintenance	$0	$3,227,138	($3,227,138)	0.0%
S-223	Gasoline Charges	$576,286	$747,615	($171,329)	77.1%
S-224	Smog Check	$1,040	$1,360	($320)	76.5%
S-225	City Property Damage	$56,713	$51,033	$5,680	111.1%
	SUBTOTAL	$5,897,859	$15,419,185	($9,521,326)	38.3%

ADMINISTRATIVE & FINANCE SERVICES

S-226	New/Moved Business Applicatn Rvw	$0	$161,773	($161,773)	0.0%
S-227	Business License Renewal	$0	$462,875	($462,875)	0.0%
S-228	Returned Check (NSF) Processing	$30,000	$47,877	($17,877)	62.7%
S-229	Research Of City Records	NA	NA	NA	NA
S-230	Document Printing and Copying	NA	NA	NA	NA
S-231	Document Certification Charges	$58	$190	($132)	30.7%
S-232	Agenda/Minute Mailing Service	$3,289	$2,975	$314	110.6%
S-233	Facility Rental and Maintenance	$70,000	NA	NA	NA
S-234	Film Permit	$599,480	$246,549	$352,931	243.1%
S-235	Services to Housing & Comm. Dev	$619,000	$823,765	($204,765)	75.1%
	SUBTOTAL	$1,321,828	$1,746,004	($424,176)	75.7%
	TOTALS	$177,928,913	$222,850,251	($44,921,338)	79.8%

CITY OF PASADENA
REVENUE/SERVICE RELATIONSHIP LIST
FISCAL YEAR 1992-93

COMMUNITY DEVELOPMENT SERVICES / COMMUNITY DEVELOPMENT REVENUES

SERVICE PROVIDED (A)	TYPE OF DESIGNATION (B)	SERVICE UNITS 1991-92 EST. ACT. (C)	SERVICE UNITS 1992-93 PROJECTED (D)	REF # (E)	REVENUE TITLE (F)	1991-92 EST. ACT. (G)	1992-93 PROJECTED (H)	PRIMARY DEPARTMENT / Other Departments (I)
Concept Plan Review	Application	40	40	S-001	Concept Plan Review Fees	$9,500	$9,600	PBNS, Public Works, Pol., Water & Power, Fire
Preliminary Plan Check	Application	200	200	S-002	Preliminary Plan Check Fees	$40,600	$42,062	WATER & POWER, Fire, PBNS, PW, Police
Tentative Parcel Map Review	Application	15	15	S-003	Tentative Parcel Map Review Fees	$35,040	$36,315	PBNS, Public Works, Water & Power
Tentative Tract Map Review	Application	20	20	S-004	Tentative Tract Map Review Fees	$44,520	$58,680	PBNS, Public Works, Water & Power
Construction Staging Review	Application	20	20	S-005	Construction Staging Plan Review Fees	$0	$0	PUBLIC WORKS
Design Commission Review (Minor)	Permit	50	50	S-006	Design Commission Review (Minor) Fees	$3,200	$3,350	PBNS
Design Commission Review (Major)	Permit	50	50	S-007	Design Commission Review (Major) Fees	$22,990	$23,750	PBNS
Design Review (Final)	Permit	40	40	S-008	Design Review (Final) Fees	$0	$0	PBNS
Design Review (Seismic)	Permit	30	30	S-009	Design Review (Seismic) Fees	$0	$0	PBNS
Design Review–City of Gardens	Application	24	24	S-010	Design Review–City of Gardens Charges	$3,818	$3,953	PBNS
Design Review (Consolidated)	Permit	20	20	S-011	Design Review ((Consolidated) Fees	$9,160	$10,780	PBNS
Design Review Extension	Application	10	10	S-012	Design Review Extension Fees	$0	$0	PBNS
Landmark District Review	Application	22	22	S-013	Landmark District Review Fees	$0	$0	PBNS
Historic Building Search	Request	360	360	S-014	Historic Building Search Fees	$0	$0	PBNS
Master Development Plan Review	Application	3	3	S-015	Master Development Plan Review Fees	$2,700	$2,789	PBNS, Public Works, Attorney
Conditional Use Permit Review	Application	150	150	S-016	Conditional Use Permit Fees	$206,700	$214,350	PBNS, Public Works
Minor Conditional Use Permit Review	Application	20	20	S-017	Minor Conditional Use Permit Fees	$11,060	$11,480	PBNS, Public Works
Temporary Conditional Use Permit Rvw	Application	70	70	S-018	Temporary Conditional Use Permit Fees	$19,320	$20,020	PBNS, Fire
Variance Review	Application	55	55	S-019	Variance Review Fees	$58,830	$60,830	PBNS, Public Works
Minor Variance Review	Application	20	20	S-020	Minor Variance Review Fees	$9,165	$9,515	PBNS, Public Works
Use Permit & Variance Extension	Request	20	20	S-021	Use Permit & Variance Extension Fees	$0	$0	PBNS
Lot Line Adjustment	Application	15	15	S-022	Lot Line Adjustment Fees	$12,825	$13,365	PBNS, Public Works

CITY OF PASADENA
REVENUE/SERVICE RELATIONSHIP LIST
FISCAL YEAR 1992-93

SERVICE PROVIDED A	TYPE OF DESIGNATION B	SERVICE UNITS 1991-92 EST. ACT. C	1992-93 PROJECTED D	REF # E	REVENUE TITLE F	1991-92 EST. ACT. G	1992-93 PROJECTED H	PRIMARY DEPARTMENT Other Departments I
Rezoning Request Rxw (Zone Change)	Application	4	4	S-023	Rezoning Request Review Fees	$8,000	$8,288	PBNS, Attorney
Subdivision Map Extension Processing	Request	8	8	S-024	Subdivision Map Extension Prcsng Fees	$741	$6,152	PBNS
Growth Management Allocation Review	Application	20	20	S-025	Growth Management Allocation Rxw Fees	$31,722	$32,864	PBNS, Public Works, Finance
Growth Management Allocation Exemption	Application	50	50	S-026	Growth Mgmt Allocation Exemption Fees	$0	$0	PBNS
Growth Allocation Appeal	Project	20	20	S-027	Growth Mgmt. Allocation Appeal Fees	$1,834	$1,901	PBNS, Clerk
Growth Mgt. Conditional Use Permit	Permit	20	20	S-028	Growth Mgt. Conditional Use Permit Fees	$27,560	$28,580	PBNS
Growth Management Time Extension	Application	20	20	S-029	Growth Management Time Extension Fees	$0	$0	PBNS
Initial Environmental Study	Study	82	82	S-030	Initial Environmental Study Fees	$47,888	$49,692	PBNS, Public Works, Police, Water & Power
Environmental Impact Report (Constnt)	Study	3	3	S-031	Environmental Impact Report Fees	$9,873	$10,230	PBNS, Fire, Public Works, Water & Power
Fish & Game Environ. Impact Rxw	Application	82	82	S-032	Fish & Game Environ. Impact Fees	$2,050	$2,132	PBNS
Env. Impact Mitigation Monitoring	Project	24	24	S-033	Environ. Impact Mitigatn Plan Fees	$0	$0	PBNS
Monitoring of Conditions	Project	350	350	S-034	Monitoring of Conditions Fees	$0	$0	PBNS
Certificate of Appropriateness	Permit	50	50	S-035	Certificate of Appropriateness	$0	$0	PBNS
Replacement Building Permit Relief	Application	8	8	S-036	Replacement Building Permit Relief Fees	$0	$0	PBNS
Appeal Processing	Application	25	25	S-037	Appeal Processing Fees	$17,500	$18,130	PBNS, Attorney, Clerk
Appeal Processing -- Staff Decision	Application	5	5	S-038	Appeal Processing -- Staff Decision Fees	$0	$0	PBNS
Vesting Map Review	Application	5	5	S-039	Vesting Map Review Fees	$16,140	$16,790	PBNS, Public Works, Water & Power
Final Tract Map Review	Map	15	15	S-040	Final Tract Map Review Fees	$0	$0	PUBLIC WORKS, Water & Power, Clerk
Final Parcel Map Review	Map	6	6	S-041	Final Parcel Map Fees	$0	$0	PUBLIC WORKS, Water & Power, Clerk
Engineering Plan Review	Plan	47	47	S-042	Engineering Plan Review Fees	$76,640	$79,406	PUBLIC WORKS
Street Occupation Permit	Permit	448	448	S-043	Street Occupation Permit	$200,000	$207,200	PUBLIC WORKS
Public Works Permit	Permit	1,400	1,400	S-044	Public Works Inspection Fees	$200,000	$207,200	PUBLIC WORKS
Street Vacation	Application	8	8	S-045	Street Vacation Fees	$4,000	$4,144	PUBLIC WORKS, PBNS, Water & Power

CITY OF PASADENA
REVENUE/SERVICE RELATIONSHIP LIST
FISCAL YEAR 1992-93

SERVICE PROVIDER (A)	TYPE OF DESIGNATION (B)	SERVICE UNITS 1991-92 EST. ACT. (C)	SERVICE UNITS 1992-93 PROJECTED (D)	REF # (E)	REVENUE TITLE (F)	1991-92 EST. ACT. (G)	1992-93 PROJECTED (H)	PRIMARY DEPARTMENT / Other Department(s) (I)
Grading Plan Check	Plan	8	8	S-046	Grading Plan Check Fees	$4,060	$4,206	PBNS
Hillside Grading Plan Check	Plan	2	4	S-047	Hillside Grading Plan Check Fees	$0	$6,718	PBNS
Grading Inspection	Permit	8	8	S-048	Grading Permit Fees	$4,060	$4,206	PBNS
Hillside Grading Inspection	Permit	2	4	S-049	Hillside Grading Inspection Fees	$0	$0	PBNS
Construction Plan Check	Plan	2,934	2,934	S-050	Construction Plan Check Fees	$768,710	$784,312	PBNS, Public Works, Fire, Water & Power
Construction Review and Inspection	Permit	8,847	8,847	S-051	Construction Permit Fees	$1,404,852	$1,465,219	PBNS, Fire
Misc/Special Building Inspection	Inspection	120	120	S-052	Misc/Special Building Inspection Fees	$11,760	$12,183	PBNS
Condominium Conversion	Application	2	2	S-053	Condominium Conversion Fees	$0	$0	PBNS, Attorney
Relocation Investigation (House Moves)	Permit	12	12	S-054	Relocation Invest. Fees (House Moves)	$9,000	$9,324	PUBLIC WORKS
Address Change	Request	8	8	S-055	Address Change Fees	$870	$966	PBNS
Address Assignment	Project	75	75	S-056	Address Assignment Fees	$1,575	$1,650	PBNS
Temporary Certificate of Occupancy	Application	360	360	S-057	Temporary Certificate of Occupancy Fees	$32,400	$34,020	PBNS
Occupancy Inspection	Inspection	8,408	8,408	S-058	Occupancy Inspection Fees	$245,544	$254,384	PBNS, Finance, Clerk
Certificate of Compliance Investigation	Application	5	5	S-059	Certificate of Compliance Fees	$1,885	$1,955	PBNS, Public Works
Parkway Usage License Agreement	Application	15	15	S-060	Parkway Usage License Agreement Fees	$3,080	$3,191	PUBLIC WORKS, Attorney
Sidewalk Dining Permit	Application	0	5	S-061	Sidewalk Dining Permit Fees	$0	$0	PUBLIC WORKS
Building Permit Center	Permit/App	13,403	13,403	S-062	Building Permit Center Revenues	$0	$0	PBNS, Clerk
Zoning Parking Credit	Application	8	8	S-063	Zoning Parking Credit Fees	$2,400	$2,400	PUBLIC WORKS, PBNS, Attorney
Temporary Street Closure (Events)	Permit	52	52	S-064	Temporary Street Closure Fees	$1,177	$1,219	PUBLIC WORKS
Traffic Impact Review	Study	30	30	S-065	Traffic Impact Review Fees	$0	$0	PUBLIC WORKS, PBNS
Trip Reduction Plan Review	Plan	25	25	S-066	Trip Reduction Plan Review Fees	$0	$0	PUBLIC WORKS
Development Agreement Review	Project	1	1	S-067	Development Agmt Revw Fees	$0	$0	ATTORNEY, PBNS
Legal Description	Project	5	5	S-068	Legal Description Fees	$0	$0	PBNS
Planned Development	Application	1	1	S-069	Planned Development Review Fees	$0	$0	PBNS, Clerk
General Plan Amendment	Application	1	1	S-070	General Plan Amendment Review Fees	$0	$0	PBNS

CITY OF PASADENA
REVENUE/SERVICE RELATIONSHIP LIST
FISCAL YEAR 1992-93

SCHEDULE 2

SERVICE PROVIDED	TYPE OF DESIGNATION	SERVICE UNITS		REF #	REVENUE TITLE			PRIMARY DEPARTMENT
A	B	1991-92 EST. ACT.	1992-93 PROJECTED		F	1991-92 EST. ACT.	1992-93 PROJECTED	Other Departments
		C	D	E		G	H	
PUBLIC SAFETY SERVICES					**PUBLIC SAFETY REVENUES**			
Annual Home Business Occupancy Prmt	Permit	589	589	S-071	Anl. Home Bus. Occupancy Permit Fees	$12,400	$13,000	PBNS, Finance
Garage Sale Permit	Permit	1,000	1,000	S-072	Garage Sale Permit Fees	$7,000	$7,500	FIRE
Special Business Regulation	Application	704	704	S-073	Special Business Permit Regulation Fees	$0	$0	POLICE
Wide, Overweight, Overlong Load Prmt	Permit	196	196	S-074	Wide, Overwght, Overlong Load Pmt Fees	$5,400	$5,594	PUBLIC WORKS
Vehicle Code Enforcement	Citation	50,000	50,000	S-075	Vehicle Code Enforcement Fines	$203,300	$240,000	POLICE
Non-Vehicle Code Enforcement	Citation/Insp.	1,300	1,300	S-076	Non-Vehicle Code Ent. Revenues	$0	$0	ATTORNEY, PBNS, Fire, Police, Health
Parking Enforcement	Citation	115,000	115,000	S-077	Parking Fines	$1,480,933	$1,625,000	POLICE, Finance
Parking Permits	Permit	2,900	2,900	S-078	Parking Permit Fees	$83,000	$85,988	FINANCE, Police
Limited Time Parking Permit	Request	24	24	S-079	Limited Time Parking Permit Revenues	$0	$0	PUBLIC WORKS
Bicycle Registration	License	490	490	S-080	Bicycle License Fees	$2,940	$2,132	POLICE
Burglar Alarm Review	Permit	1,500	1,500	S-081	Burglar Alarm Permit Fees	$127,500	$133,500	FINANCE
Police False Alarm Response	Incident	9,414	9,414	S-082	Police False Alarm Response Charges	$129,819	$176,554	POLICE, Finance
Clearance Letter Processing	Letter	300	300	S-083	Clearance Letter Fees	$2,100	$3,000	POLICE
Police Report Copying	Report Copy	10,000	10,000	S-084	Police Report Copy Charges	$80,000	$100,000	POLICE
Police Photograph Reproduction	Photo	300	300	S-085	Police Photograph Reproduction Fees	$3,080	$3,108	POLICE
Police Photo Lab Services	NA	NA	NA	S-086	Police Photo Lab Charges	$0	$0	POLICE
Police Tape & Video Duplication Service	Tape	60	60	S-087	Police Tape & Video Sales	$0	$0	POLICE
Spec. Police Computer Print-Out Service	Request	175	175	S-088	Special Police Computer Print-Out Fees	$1,400	$1,400	POLICE
Fingerprint Processing	Card	3,700	3,700	S-089	Fingerprint Fees	$25,800	$33,300	POLICE
Vehicle Correction Inspection	Inspection	900	900	S-090	Vehicle Correction Inspection Fees	$0	$0	POLICE
Removal of Aband/Abated Veh & Releases	Vehicle	1,200	1,200	S-091	Abandoned Vehicle Abatement Charges	$0	$0	POLICE
Impound Vehicle Release Service	Vehicle	1,000	1,000	S-092	Impound Vehicle Release Service Fees	$0	$0	POLICE

CITY OF PASADENA
REVENUE/SERVICE RELATIONSHIP LIST
FISCAL YEAR 1992-93

SERVICE PROVIDED	SERVICE UNITS			REF #	REVENUE TITLE	1991-92 EST. ACT.	1992-93 PROJECTED	PRIMARY DEPARTMENT Other Departments
	TYPE OF DESIGNATION	1991-92 EST. ACT.	1992-93 PROJECTED					
A	B	C	D	E	F	G	H	I
DUI Acc. Response, Invest., Report	Incident	525	525	S-093	DUI Accident Response Charges	$4,500	$4,500	POLICE, Fire, Finance, Public Works
DUI Arrest Procedure/Non-Accident	Arrest	1,000	1,000	S-094	DUI Arrest Non-Accident Fees	$0	$0	POLICE
Noise Disturbance Response Call-back	Call-back	100	100	S-095	Noise Disturbance Resp Call-Back Fees	$0	$0	POLICE
Public Crosswalk Protection	Crosswalk	10	10	S-096	Public Crossing Guard Service Fees	$0	$0	POLICE
One-Day Alcohol Permit Processing	Permit	125	125	S-097	One-Day Alcohol Permit Fees	$0	$0	POLICE, City Manager, Recreation
Commercial Foot Patrol	Business	297	297	S-098	Commercial Foot Patrol Charges	$0	$0	POLICE
Rifle Range Use	Customer	4,900	4,900	S-099	Rifle Range Use Charges	$22,157	$25,000	POLICE
Helicopter Pad Landing Use	Permit	10	10	S-100	Helicopter Pad Landing Use Charges	$3,920	$4,070	POLICE
I.N.S. Prisoner Housing	Prisoner	5,220	5,220	S-101	I.N.S. Prisoner Housing Fees	$391,500	$391,500	POLICE
Trustee Housing	Prisoner Day	982	982	S-102	Trustee Housing Fees	$73,650	$73,650	POLICE
V.I.N. Verification	Request	400	400	S-103	V.I.N. Verification Fees	$0	$0	POLICE
Hazardous Materials Permit Inspectn	Inspection	5,000	5,000	S-104	Hazardous Materials Permit Insp Fees	$740,000	$768,840	FIRE
State Mandated Fire Inspection	Inspection	392	392	S-105	State Mandated Fire Inspection Fees	$259,380	$159,360	FIRE
Underground Tank Plan Chk/Insp.	Plan Ck/Insp	1,434	1,434	S-106	Underground Tank Inspection Fees	$69,985	$72,505	FIRE
Fire False Alarm Response	Incident	1,000	1,000	S-107	Fire False Alarm Response Charges	$0	$0	FIRE
Non-Emergency Service	Incident	208	208	S-108	Non-Emergency Service Charges	$0	$0	FIRE
Illegal Burn Response	Response	50	50	S-109	Illegal Burn Response Charges	$0	$0	FIRE
Post-Fire Investigation Analysis	Investigation	224	224	S-110	Post-Fire Investigation Analysis Chg	$43,008	$44,556	FIRE
Fire Report Copying	Report	150	150	S-111	Fire Report Copying Charges	$1,050	$1,125	FIRE
Weed Abatement	Parcel	440	440	S-112	Weed Abatement Assessments	$32,000	$33,152	PUBLIC WORKS, Fire
Medical Aid Response	Avg. Incident	9,500	9,500	S-113	Medical Aid Response Charges	$1,150,000	$1,800,000	FIRE, Finance
Hazard Abatement Services	Incident	10	10	S-114	Hazard Abatement Service Fees	$0	$0	FIRE

CITY OF PASADENA
REVENUE/SERVICE RELATIONSHIP LIST
FISCAL YEAR 1992-93

HEALTH DEPARTMENT SERVICES / HEALTH DEPARTMENT REVENUES

SERVICE PROVIDED	TYPE OF DESIGNATION	SERVICE UNITS 1991-92 EST. ACT.	SERVICE UNITS 1992-93 PROJECTED	REF #	REVENUE TITLE	1991-92 EST. ACT.	1992-93 PROJECTED	PRIMARY DEPARTMENT / Other Departments
A	B	C	D	E	F	G	H	I
Health Department Plan Check	Plan	60	60	S-115	Health Depart Plan Chk/Inspectn Fees	$17,000	$17,000	PUBLIC HEALTH
Environmental Health Inspection	Inspection	8,178	8,178	S-116	Environmental Health Inspection Fees	$201,200	$208,432	PUBLIC HEALTH
Noise Control Permit	Permit	92	92	S-117	Noise Control Permit Fees	$3,200	$3,200	PUBLIC HEALTH
Food Sanitation Inspection	Inspection	6,800	6,949	S-118	Food Sanitation Inspection Fees	$189,000	$205,368	PUBLIC HEALTH
Mosquito, Fly & Rodent Control	Parcel	35,602	35,602	S-119	Vector Control Assessments	$0	$0	PUBLIC HEALTH
Animal Control	License	5,666	5,666	S-120	Animal Control Fees	$100,000	$116,264	PUBLIC HEALTH, Finance
Vital Statistics	Certfict/Prmt	25,939	25,939	S-121	Vital Statistics Fees	$248,396	$255,408	PUBLIC HEALTH
Travel Immunizations	Patient	3,120	3,120	S-122	Travel Immunization Fees	$66,880	$181,000	PUBLIC HEALTH
Water Examination	Specimen	2,424	2,424	S-123	Water Examination Charges	$96,000	$99,840	PUBLIC HEALTH
Alcohol & Drug Dependncy Program	Contact	8,592	8,592	S-124	Alcohol & Drug Depndncy Fees & Charges	$241,339	$269,354	PUBLIC HEALTH
First Offender Program	Client	295	295	S-125	First Offender Program Charges	$68,000	$75,696	PUBLIC HEALTH
Public Health Laboratory	Varies	NA	NA	S-126	Public Health Laboratory	NA	$246,272	PUBLIC HEALTH
Prenatal Clinic	Delivery	1,500	1,500	S-127	Prenatal Clinic Fees	NA	$1,369,582	PUBLIC HEALTH, Finance
Women, Infants & Children Voucher	Recipient	49,000	49,000	S-128	Women, Infants & Children Voucher Fees	NA	$399,798	PUBLIC HEALTH, Finance
AIDS Program	Patient/Contact	4,735	4,735	S-129	AIDS Program Fees	NA	$243,223	PUBLIC HEALTH
SGV, HIV Early Intervention Program	Client	100	100	S-130	SGV, HIV Early Intervention Prgm Fees	NA	$255,300	PUBLIC HEALTH
Child Health Clinic	Patient	6,525	6,525	S-131	Child Health Clinic Fees	NA	$424,713	PUBLIC HEALTH
Ambulatory Care Clinic	Patient	1,922	1,922	S-132	Ambulatory Care Clinic Fees	NA	$16,783	PUBLIC HEALTH
Senior Preventive Health Program	Patient	1,500	1,500	S-133	Senior Preventive Health Revenues	NA	$22,427	PUBLIC HEALTH
Sexually Transmitted Disease Program	Patient	4,160	4,160	S-134	Sexually Trasmitted Disease Prgm Fees	NA	$127,218	PUBLIC HEALTH
Tuberculosis Program	Patient	13,280	13,280	S-135	Tuberculosis Program Fees	NA	$270,649	PUBLIC HEALTH
Flu/Pneumonia Immunization	Patient	4,091	4,091	S-136	Flu/Pneumonia Immunization Revenues	NA	$19,874	PUBLIC HEALTH
Immunization	Patient	5,500	5,500	S-137	Immunization Fees	NA	$57,704	PUBLIC HEALTH

CITY OF PASADENA
REVENUE/SERVICE RELATIONSHIP LIST
FISCAL YEAR 1992-93

LEISURE & CULTURAL SERVICES / LEISURE & CULTURAL REVENUES

SERVICE PROVIDED (A)	TYPE OF DESIGNATION (B)	1991-92 EST. ACT. (C)	1992-93 PROJECTED (D)	REF # (E)	REVENUE TITLE (F)	1991-92 EST. ACT. (G)	1992-93 PROJECTED (H)	PRIMARY DEPARTMENT / Other Departments (I)
City Youth Sports Programs	Participant	2,000	2,000	S-138	Youth Sports Program Fees	$0	$0	RECREATION
City Adult Sports Programs	Team	318	318	S-139	Adult Sports Program Fees	$45,900	$47,552	RECREATION
Private Youth Group Fld Rent Svc	Hour	11,374	11,374	S-140	Private Youth Group Field Rental Fees	$0	$0	RECREATION
Private Adult Group Fld Rent Svc	Hour	5,132	5,132	S-141	Private Adult Group Field Rental Fees	$14,428	$14,947	RECREATION
Youth Recreation Classes	Participant	3,000	3,000	S-142	Youth Contract Recreation Class Fees	$17,584	$18,217	RECREATION
Adult Recreation Classes	Participant	7,000	7,000	S-143	Adult Contract Recreation Class Fees	$40,900	$42,372	RECREATION
Youth Special Activities	Participant	NA	NA	S-144	Youth Special Activities Fees	$0	$0	RECREATION, Human Services
Summer Day Camp	Participant	400	400	S-145	Summer Daycamp Program Fees	$40,000	$40,000	RECREATION
Adaptive Recreation Activities	Participant	145	145	S-146	Adaptive Recreation Activity Fees	$21,425	$21,425	RECREATION
Senior Citizen Programs	Total Particpnt	1,258	1,258	S-147	Senior Citizen Program Fees	$6,530	$6,530	HUMAN SERVICES, Recreation
Recreational Swimming	Swimmer	17,150	17,150	S-148	Recreational Swimming Fees	$10,100	$10,464	RECREATION
Swimming Lessons	Student	9,030	9,030	S-149	Swimming Lesson Fees	$20,b30	$21,652	RECREATION
Recreation Facility Rental	Hour	14,691	14,691	S-150	Facility Rental Revenues	$126,921	$131,490	RECREATION, Human Services
City-Wide Special Events	Participant	NA	NA	S-151	City-Wide Special Event Fees	NA	NA	POLICE, Recreation, Human Services, City Mgr
Tournament of Roses Support	Est. Attend	1,000,000	1,000,000	S-152	Tournament of Roses Revenues	$696,553	$787,577	PW,W&P,Rec,R.B.,PBNS,Fire,Pol,Hlth,A.S.,Tran
Special Event Set-Up/Clean	Request	25	25	S-153	Special Event Set-Up/Clean Up Fees	$0	$4,000	PUBLIC WORKS
Overdue Material Processing	NA	33,250	33,250	S-154	Overdue Material Processing Charges	$192,461	$192,461	INFORMATION SERVICES
Replacing Lost Library Items	Item	575	575	S-155	Lost Library Item Charges	$12,897	$12,897	INFORMATION SERVICES
Replacement Of Lost Library Cards	Card	3,800	3,800	S-156	Lost Library Card Charges	$9,501	$9,501	INFORMATION SERVICES
Book Reservation Service	Reservation	29,979	29,979	S-157	Book Reserve Service Fees	$5,115	$5,115	INFORMATION SERVICES
Inter Library Loan Processing	Request	3,678	3,678	S-158	Inter Library Loan Fees	$2,060	$2,060	INFORMATION SERVICES
Retrieval & Copying Of Periodicals	Request	150	150	S-159	Periodical Copying Service Fees	$1,734	$1,734	INFORMATION SERVICES

CITY OF PASADENA
REVENUE/SERVICE RELATIONSHIP LIST
FISCAL YEAR 1992-93

UTILITY & ENTERPRISE SERVICES / UTILITY & ENTERPRISE REVENUES

SERVICE PROVIDED	TYPE OF DESIGNATION	SERVICE UNITS		REF #	REVENUE TITLE		PRIMARY DEPARTMENT Other Departments
		1991-92 EST. ACT.	1992-93 PROJECTED			1991-92 EST. ACT. / 1992-93 PROJECTED	
A	B	C	D	E	F	G / H	I
Reproduction Of Photographs	Photograph	50	50	S-160	Reproduction of Photographs Charges	$100 / $100	INFORMATION SERVICES
Library Media Rental	Item	5,150	5,150	S-161	Library Media Rental Fees	$5,914 / $5,914	INFORMATION SERVICES
Library On–Line Database Search	Request	350	350	S-162	On–Line Records Search Charges	$12,411 / $12,411	INFORMATION SERVICES
Author Program	Ticket	1,092	1,092	S-163	Author Program Charges	$5,505 / $5,505	INFORMATION SERVICES
Library Facility Rental	Rental	1,315	1,315	S-164	Library Facility Rental Charges	$7,500 / $7,500	INFORMATION SERVICES
Electrical Power Service	Customers	57,084	57,084	S-165	Electrical Power Service Fees	$101,019,137 / $112,168,115	WATER & POWER, Finance, Public Works
In-Field Service Spots	Incident	217	217	S-166	In-Field Service Spot Fees	$0 / $0	WATER & POWER
New Vaults >200 Amps.	Vault	60	60	S-167	New Vaults >200 Amps. Fees	$484,334 / $484,334	WATER & POWER
Trouble Shooter Service	Incident	3,640	3,640	S-168	Trouble Shooter Service Fees	$0 / $0	WATER & POWER
Power Credit Turn Off/On	Credit Off/On	2,941	2,941	S-169	Power Credit Turn Off/On Fees	$35,812 / $35,812	WATER & POWER
Damaged Meter Repair or Replacement	Meter	267	267	S-170	Damaged Meter Repair (1 Phase) Fees	$13,000 / $13,350	WATER & POWER
Restore Service Wire Cuts	Incident	100	100	S-171	Restore Service Wire Cuts Fees	$2,500 / $2,500	WATER & POWER
Restore Bucket/Underground Cut	Incident	8	8	S-172	Restore Bucket/Underground Cut Fees	$900 / $900	WATER & POWER
Same Day Service Turn-On	Incident	1	1	S-173	Same Day Turn-On Fees	$25 / $25	WATER & POWER
Electric Meter Test	Meter	14	14	S-174	Electric Meter Test Fees	$490 / $490	WATER & POWER
Electric Meter Removal & Repl.	Meter	166	166	S-175	Electric Meter Removal & Repl. Fees	$4,150 / $4,150	WATER & POWER
Service Relocation	Project	10	10	S-176	Service Relocation Charges	$1,150 / $1,150	WATER & POWER
Power Service Installation	Installation	777	777	S-177	Power Service Installation Fees	$155,400 / $155,400	WATER & POWER
Street Marking for Utility	Request	2,340	2,340	S-178	Street Marking for Utility Charges	$0 / $0	WATER & POWER
Water Service	Customer	36,234	36,234	S-179	Water Service Charges	$14,886,898 / $19,126,816	WATER & POWER, Finance, Public Works
Water Service Installation	Incident	169	169	S-180	Water Service Installation Fees	$152,100 / $152,100	WATER & POWER
Water Service Cut Off At Street	Incident	2	2	S-181	Water Service Cut Off At Street Fees	$200 / $200	WATER & POWER

CITY OF PASADENA
REVENUE/SERVICE RELATIONSHIP LIST
FISCAL YEAR 1992-93

| SERVICE PROVIDED | SERVICE UNITS | | | REF # | REVENUE TITLE | 1991-92 | 1992-93 | PRIMARY DEPARTMENT |
| | TYPE OF DESIGNATION | 1991-92 EST. ACT. | 1992-93 PROJECTED | | | EST. ACT. | PROJECTED | Other Departments |
A	B	C	D	E	F	G	H	I
Water Credit Turn Off/On	Credit Off/On	1,583	1,583	S-182	Water Credit Turn Off/On Fees	$19,516	$19,516	WATER & POWER
Replacement Of Curb Stop 3/4" & 1"	Incident	185	185	S-183	Repl. Of Curb Stop 3/4" & 1" Fees	$11,100	$11,100	WATER & POWER
Repl. Of 1-1/2" Wheel Gate Valve	Incident	12	12	S-184	Repl. Of 1-1/2" Wheel Gate Valve Fees	$900	$900	WATER & POWER
Meter Test/Field (5/8" & 1")	Test	24	24	S-185	Meter Test/Field (5/8" & 1") Fees	$240	$240	WATER & POWER
Water Meter Removal and Replacement	Meter	104	104	S-186	Water Meter Removal and Repl. Fees	$5,200	$5,200	WATER & POWER
Water Meter Equipment Upgrade	Meter	148	148	S-187	Water Meter Equipment Upgrade Fees	$0	$0	WATER & POWER
Water Quality Test	Test	90	90	S-188	Water Quality Test Fees	$0	$0	WATER & POWER
Flow Test (Low/Leak/Frozen Valve)	Test	200	200	S-189	Flow Test (Low/Leak/Frozen Valve) Fees	$0	$0	WATER & POWER
Hydrant Flow Test	Test	52	52	S-190	Hydrant Flow Test Fees	$0	$0	WATER & POWER
Hydrant Portable/Construction Meter	Meter	79	79	S-191	Hydrant Portable/Const. Meter Fees	$0	$0	WATER & POWER
Hydrant Installation	Hydrant	1	1	S-192	Hydrant Installation Fees	$14,112	$14,112	WATER & POWER
Backflow Device Installation	Device	2,000	2,000	S-193	Backflow Device Installation Fees	$48,000	$48,000	WATER & POWER, Public Health
Utility Billing	Varies	204,040	204,040	S-194	Utility Billing Administration Charges	$25,000	$675,000	FINANCE
Bill Investigation	Investigation	2,788	2,788	S-195	Bill Investigation Charges	$0	$0	WATER & POWER
Sewer & Storm Drain Operation & Mtc	City H2O Cust	29,839	29,839	S-196	Swr & Storm Drain Operation & Mtc Chgs	$2,991,931	$2,598,642	PUBLIC WORKS, Finance
Sewer Stoppage Investigation	Request	20	20	S-197	Sewer Stoppage Investigation Fees	$0	$0	PUBLIC WORKS
Utility Excavation Permit	Permit	450	450	S-198	Utility Excavation Permit	$14,620	$14,620	PUBLIC WORKS
Residential Refuse Collection	Account	26,740	26,740	S-199	Residential Refuse Collection Charges	$6,469,313	$6,844,500	PUBLIC WORKS, Finance, Transportation
Commercial Refuse Service	Customer	1,343	1,343	S-200	Commercial Refuse Service Charges	$1,615,353	$1,400,000	PUBLIC WORKS, Finance, Transportation
Special Requested Refuse Pick-Up	Pick-up	918	918	S-201	Special Refuse Pick-Up Fees	$45,000	$45,000	PUBLIC WORKS
Street Sweeping	Power Custmr	57,084	57,084	S-202	Street Sweeping Fines	$593,206	$636,206	PUBLIC WORKS, Finance
Right-of-Way Clean-up	Power Custmr	57,084	57,084	S-203	Right-of-Way Clean-up Fees	$0	$0	PUBLIC WORKS
Rose Bowl Maintenance/Operation	Varies	NA	NA	S-204	Rose Bowl Maintenance/Operation Fees	$3,850,292	$3,850,292	ROSE BOWL, Finance, P.W., Arroyo Seco

CITY OF PASADENA
REVENUE/SERVICE RELATIONSHIP LIST
FISCAL YEAR 1992-93

| SERVICE PROVIDED | TYPE OF DESIGNATION | SERVICE UNITS 1991-92 EST. ACT. | 1992-93 PROJECTED | REF # | REVENUE TITLE | 1991-92 EST. ACT. | 1992-93 PROJECTED | PRIMARY DEPARTMENT / Other Departments |
A	B	C	D	E	F	G	H	I
Golf Course Maintenance/Operation	Round	190,000	190,000	S-205	Golf Course Revenues	$1,556,046	$1,948,129	ARROYO SECO, Rose Bowl, Finance
Old Pasadena Parking District	Space	1,450	1,450	S-206	Old Pasadena Parking Fees	$1,112,837	$2,492,648	PUBLIC WORKS
South Lake Parking District	Space	750	750	S-207	South Lake Business Assessment (Pkg)	$132,845	$135,203	PUBLIC WORKS, Finance
Plaza Las Fuentes Parking	Space	850	850	S-208	Plaza Las Fuentes Parking Fees	$1,679,738	$1,950,075	PUBLIC WORKS
City Parking Lot Service	Space	1,753	1,753	S-209	City Parking Lot Revenues	$191,044	$202,451	PUBLIC WORKS
MAINTENANCE SERVICES					*MAINTENANCE REVENUES*			
Utility St. Usage (Gas & CATV)	Miles R-O-W	330	330	S-210	Franchise Fees	$1,050,000	$1,350,000	PUBLIC WORKS
Street Light & Signal Maint & Op'n	Power Custmr	57,084	57,084	S-211	Street Light & Traffic Signal Tax	$3,849,533	$3,900,000	PUBLIC WORKS
Median & Parkway Maintenance	Parcel	35,602	35,602	S-212	Median & Parkway Assessments	$0	$0	PUBLIC WORKS
Street Tree Maintenance	Parcel	35,602	35,602	S-213	Street Tree Maintenance Assessments	$0	$0	PUBLIC WORKS
Tree Maintenance Contractor Permit Rvw	Permit	20	20	S-214	Tree Maint. Contractor Permit Fees	$320	$320	PUBLIC WORKS
Barricade Installation	Request	40	40	S-215	Barricade Installation Fees	$9,640	$10,000	PUBLIC WORKS
Barricade Rental	Request	40	40	S-216	Barricade Rental Fees	$0	$2,000	PUBLIC WORKS
Hazardous Materials Clean-up	Incident	15	15	S-217	Hazardous Materials Clean-up Fees	$0	$0	PUBLIC WORKS
Special Business Services	Various	NA	NA	S-218	Special Business Service Charges	$0	$0	PUBLIC WORKS
Business Improvement District	Parcel	3,231	3,231	S-219	Business Improvement Dist. Assessments	$0	$0	FINANCE
Alley Maintenance	Parcel	2,400	2,400	S-220	Alley Maintenance Assessments	$0	$0	PUBLIC WORKS
Special Curb Marking	Request	105	105	S-221	Spot Curb Mrkng (Incl Valet Pkg) Fees	$1,500	$1,500	PUBLIC WORKS
Neighborhood Park Maintenance	Res'l Parcel	20,849	20,849	S-222	Neighborhood Park Assessments	$0	$0	PUBLIC WORKS, Recreation
Gasoline Charges	Gallons	NA	NA	S-223	Gasoline Revenues	$578,286	$578,286	GENERAL SERVICES
Smog Check	Certificate	50	50	S-224	Smog Check Fees	$1,040	$1,040	GENERAL SERVICES
City Property Damage	Incident	NA	NA	S-225	City Property Damage Fees	$56,713	$56,713	FINANCE

PAGE 11 OF 11

SCHEDULE 2

CITY OF PASADENA

REVENUE/SERVICE RELATIONSHIP LIST

FISCAL YEAR 1992-93

ADMINISTRATIVE & FINANCE SERVICES / ADMINISTRATIVE & FINANCE REVENUES

| SERVICE PROVIDED | SERVICE UNITS | | | REF # | REVENUE TITLE | 1991-92 EST. ACT. | 1992-93 PROJECTED | PRIMARY DEPARTMENT / Other Departments |
| | TYPE OF DESIGNATION | 1991-92 EST. ACT. | 1992-93 PROJECTED | | | | | |
A	B	C	D	E	F	G	H	I
New/Moved Business Applicn Review	Application	1,797	1,797	S-226	New/Moved Bus. Appl. Revw Fees	$0	$0	PBNS, Finance
Business License Renewal	Business	10,621	10,621	S-227	Business License Renewal Fees	$0	$0	FINANCE
Returned Check (NSF) Processing	Check	3,000	3,000	S-228	Returned Check (NSF) Charges	$30,000	$30,000	FINANCE
Research Of City Records	NA	NA	NA	S-229	Research Fees	$0	$0	PUBLIC WORKS, Clerk
Document Printing and Copying	Page	NA	NA	S-230	Document Printing and Copying Fees	NA	NA	Various
Document Certification Charge	Document	16	16	S-231	Document Certification Charges	$56	$56	CLERK
Agenda/Minute Mailing Service	Subscription	25	25	S-232	Agenda/Minute Mailing Charges	$3,175	$3,289	CLERK
Facility Rental and Maintenan	Hour/Reservtn	36	36	S-233	Facility Rental Charges	$44,395	$70,000	VARIOUS
Film Permit	Permit	360	360	S-234	Film Permit Fees	$599,480	$599,480	PBNS, Fire, Public Works, Police
Services to Housing & Comm. Dev.	Varies	NA	NA	S-235	Svcs to Housing & Comm. Dev. Revenues	$453,842	$619,000	FINANCE, PBNS

CITY OF PASADENA   SCHEDULE 6
FRINGE BENEFIT RATES
FISCAL YEAR 1992–1993 BUDGET

PROGRAM	BENEFIT BASE RATE	BURDEN RATE	TOTAL RATE
City Council	39.7%	0.6%	40.3%
City Manager	39.7%	3.8%	43.5%
City Manager – Communications	39.7%	0.7%	40.4%
City Attorney	39.7%	5.0%	44.7%
City Clerk	39.7%	3.2%	42.9%
Affirmative Action	39.7%	4.1%	43.7%
Human Resources	39.7%	7.2%	46.9%
Risk Management	39.7%	0.9%	40.6%
Finance	39.7%	3.3%	43.0%
Police Department – FPRS	47.4%	18.8%	66.1%
Police Department – SPERS	41.6%	18.8%	60.4%
Police Department – Other	39.7%	18.8%	58.4%
Fire Department – FPRS	47.4%	13.8%	61.2%
Fire Department – SPERS	41.6%	13.8%	55.5%
Fire Department – Other	39.7%	13.8%	53.5%
Planning, Building & Neighborhood Services	39.7%	2.4%	42.0%
Information Services	39.7%	1.0%	40.7%
Health	39.7%	3.3%	43.0%
Women, Infants & Children	44.0%		44.0%
Human Services	39.7%	19.2%	58.9%
Recreation	39.7%	9.9%	49.6%
Rose Bowl	39.7%	5.2%	44.9%
Golf Course	39.7%	5.2%	44.9%
Public Works – Administration, Engineering & Transportation	39.7%	7.3%	47.0%
Public Works – Field Operations & Parks Maintenance	39.7%	6.2%	45.9%
Public Works – Refuse Collection	39.7%	19.5%	59.2%
Public Works – Sewer & Storm Drain Maintenance	39.7%	1.5%	41.2%
General Services	39.7%	11.9%	51.6%
Water & Power – Power	39.7%	5.1%	44.7%
Water & Power – Water	39.7%	5.8%	45.4%
Affiliated Agencies - PCDC, CDBG & Housing	39.7%	0.6%	40.3%
Affiliated Agencies - Job Training & Partnership Act	39.7%	1.9%	41.6%

NOTES:

1. Benefit Base Rate includes all Benefit Fund Expenses except various holiday, vacation and sick expenses. The MSI calculated sick leave and vacation accural rate has also been included here.

2. Burden Rate includes Workers Compensation, Liability Claims, and Long Term Disability.

3. For purposes of cost calculations, Fiscal Year 1992–1993 Budget amounts as of 5/18/92 were used.

CITY OF PASADENA
FIXED ASSET CHARGES SUMMARIZED BY DEPARTMENT/PROGRAM
FISCAL YEAR 1992–1993

Department/Program/Facility	Estimated Repl. Cost	Annual Fixed Asset Exp.
City Council	$175,001	$21,140
City Manger:		
Administration	$110,797	$14,390
Management Systems	$44,383	$8,880
Nothwest Management	$17,384	$2,920
KPAS–Cable Television Operations	$480,239	$96,050
Public Affairs	$18,061	$2,880
City Attorney:		
City Attorney	$166,641	$24,100
City Prosecutor	$136,426	$26,280
City Clerk:		
Official Records	$48,285	$5,930
Records Management	$32,025	$4,200
Finance:		
Administration	$56,005	$7,960
Accounting & Analysis	$101,121	$15,510
Budget	$41,590	$7,100
Financial Services	$109,986	$16,150
Financial Systems Support	$41,601	$6,930
Municipal Services:		
Administration	$31,410	$4,070
Parking	$117,941	$15,310
Cash/Credit	$86,418	$11,210
Utility Services	$164,983	$21,420
Treasury	$47,285	$7,090
Purchasing	$58,978	$9,740
Planning,Building & Neighborhood Services:		
PBNS Administration	$262,104	$32,390
Building Division:		
Building Division Administration	$12,828	$2,520
Building Code Enforcement	$12,552	$2,510
Development Processing	$51,127	$10,010
Housing & Neighborhood Svcs:		
Administration	$8,712	$1,750
Code Compliance	$73,463	$14,030
MASH	$95,006	$15,130
Facility–Civil Defense Center	$235,000	$7,830
Neighborhood Connections	$16,425	$2,110
Planning Division:		
Administraion	$17,308	$2,630
Planning & Research	$86,881	$13,610
Urban Conservation	$78,607	$10,910
Zoning Administration	$69,394	$13,660
Growth Management	$26,375	$4,080
Arts Division	$19,519	$2,760

CITY OF PASADENA
FIXED ASSET CHARGES SUMMARIZED BY DEPARTMENT/PROGRAM
FISCAL YEAR 1992–1993

Department/Program/Facility	Estimated Repl. Cost	Annual Fixed Asset Exp.
Public Works:		
Administration	$54,346	$7,780
Engineering Services	$28,506	$4,530
Design Engineering:		
Administration	$14,480	$2,540
Civil Engineering	$31,344	$4,970
Parks & Landscape	$11,406	$1,340
Lights & Signals	$19,956	$3,170
Multi–Discipline	$19,955	$3,170
Construction Engineering	$51,300	$8,150
Transportation:		
Administration	$17,719	$2,840
Traffic Commuter Services	$35,447	$5,670
Traffic Invest. & Planning	$22,156	$4,430
Off–Street Parking	$8,863	$1,410
Operations:		
Administration	$4,719	$470
Traffic Control Admininistration	$1,174	$120
St. Lighting/Traffic Signals	$14,163	$1,420
Roadway Maintenance	$10,626	$1,060
Street Maintenance Admininistration	$1,174	$120
Street Cleaning	$18,890	$1,890
Street Signs & Traffic Painting	$11,800	$1,180
Sewer/Storm Drain Maintenance	$14,163	$1,420
Parks:		
Administration	$73,562	$11,560
Brookside Park & Lower Arroyo Maintenance	$11,363	$1,140
Central Services	$9,944	$990
Park Maintenance Admininistration	$2,839	$280
Street Tree Maintenance Administration	$4,220	$420
Street Tree Maintenance (Force)	$15,629	$1,560
Street Tree Maintenance (Contract)	$5,685	$570
Maintenance Area I	$15,629	$1,560
Maintenance Area II	$11,363	$1,140
Solid Waste:		$0
Administration	$61,380	$6,140
Residential Sanitation	$7,672	$770
Commercial Sanitation	$7,672	$770
General Services:		
Administration	$55,664	$7,400
Communications Systems:		
Radio & Data Communication Services	$1,609,223	$312,210
Telephone Services	$1,862,105	$371,300

SCHEDULE 4

CITY OF PASADENA
FIXED ASSET CHARGES SUMMARIZED BY ITEM
FISCAL YEAR 1992–93

ITEM	AV. LIFE	ESTIMATED REPL. COST	ANNUAL FIXED ASSET EXP.
Alleys	20	$7,464,540	$373,230
Automotive--General	5	$2,990,127	$598,030
Automotive--Police	3	$4,511,998	$1,504,000
Automotive--Special Purpose	15	$12,992,330	$866,170
Bridges	30	$56,900,000	$1,896,670
Buildings	30	$214,806,266	$7,160,200
Communication Equipment	5	$2,615,373	$523,100
Computer Equipment	5	$8,507,865	$1,701,620
Curbs, Gutters & Sidewalks	20	$157,450,000	$7,872,500
Electrical Power System	50	$679,631,002	$13,592,620
Golf Course	20	$16,923,973	$846,200
Helicopters	20	$1,400,000	$70,000
Library Books	VAR	$12,837,001	$855,801
Medians	20	$6,380,800	$319,040
Office Equipment	5	$759,805	$152,020
Office Furniture	10	$5,303,459	$519,960
Other Equipment	10	$4,287,906	$428,830
Parks Landscaping & Equipment	VAR	$44,281,245	$2,565,895
Parking Lots	20	$7,009,999	$350,500
Parking Structures	50	$32,134,400	$642,690
Sewer System	40	$298,125,000	$7,453,130
Storm Drain System	50	$124,382,000	$2,487,600
Street Lights	20	$39,549,000	$1,977,450
Street Trees	50	$7,275,150	$145,500
Streets	20	$162,600,000	$8,130,000
Traffic Signals	10	$13,750,000	$1,375,000
Traffic Signs	8	$339,500	$42,440
Water System	50	$318,394,063	$6,367,880
TOTAL		$2,243,602,803	$70,818,116

CITY OF PASADENA

DETAIL OF BUILDING OCCUPANCY CHARGES

FISCAL YEAR 1992–1993 BUDGET

BUILDING/DEPARTMENT	% OF BLDG (1)	ASSET REPLCMNT CHARGE (2)	DEBT SVC OR RENT (3)	CUSTDL & LNDSCPE MNTC (4)	INSURANCE (5)	UTILITIES (6)	TOTAL (7)
CITY HALL							
City Council	3.8%	$22,246		$11,688	$865	$6,245	$41,044
City Manager:							
Administration	4.2%	$24,588		$12,918	$957	$6,903	$45,366
Management Systems	0.5%	$2,927		$1,538	$114	$822	$5,401
Northwest Management	0.5%	$2,927		$1,538	$114	$822	$5,401
Cable TV	0.5%	$2,927		$1,538	$114	$822	$5,401
Public Affairs/Information	0.6%	$3,513		$1,845	$137	$986	$6,481
City Attorney	6.0%	$35,126		$18,454	$1,366	$9,861	$64,807
City Clerk:							
Official Records	1.6%	$9,367		$4,921	$364	$2,630	$17,282
Records Management	2.6%	$15,221		$7,997	$592	$4,273	$28,083
Finance:							
Administration	2.5%	$14,636		$7,689	$569	$4,109	$27,003
Accounting & Analysis:							
Financial Analysis/Gen Acctg	1.2%	$7,025		$3,691	$273	$1,972	$12,961
Grants Accounting	0.6%	$3,513		$1,845	$137	$986	$6,481
Utility Accounting	0.3%	$1,756		$923	$68	$493	$3,240
Budget	1.3%	$7,611		$3,998	$296	$2,136	$14,041
Financial Services:							
Accounts Payable	0.6%	$3,513		$1,845	$137	$986	$6,481
Accounts Receivable	0.8%	$4,683		$2,461	$182	$1,315	$8,641
Payroll	1.0%	$5,854		$3,076	$228	$1,643	$10,801
Financial Systems Support:							
Credit Collections	0.2%	$1,171		$615	$46	$331	$2,163
Municipal Services	0.5%	$2,927		$1,538	$114	$822	$5,401
Business License	1.0%	$5,854		$3,076	$228	$1,643	$10,801
Cashiers	0.6%	$3,513		$1,845	$137	$986	$6,481
Credit	0.6%	$3,513		$1,845	$137	$986	$6,481
Parking Citations	0.4%	$2,342		$1,230	$91	$657	$4,320
Utility Billing	3.1%	$18,148		$9,535	$706	$5,095	$33,484
Treasury	1.1%	$6,440		$3,383	$251	$1,808	$11,882
Plng, Bldg & Neighborhood Svcs:							
PBNS Administration	2.6%	$15,221		$7,997	$592	$4,273	$28,083
Building:							
Bldg & Dev Services Admn	0.3%	$1,756		$923	$68	$493	$3,240
Bldg Code Enforcement	1.2%	$7,025		$3,691	$273	$1,972	$12,961
Development Processing	1.7%	$9,952		$5,229	$387	$2,794	$18,362
Housing & Neighbrhood Svcs:							
Hsng & Neigh Srvcs Admn	0.4%	$2,342		$1,230	$91	$657	$4,320
Code Enforcement	1.4%	$8,196		$4,306	$319	$2,301	$15,122
Planning:							
Administration	0.8%	$4,683		$2,461	$182	$1,315	$8,641
Planning & Research	3.4%	$19,905		$10,457	$774	$5,588	$36,724
Urban Conservation	2.0%	$11,709		$6,151	$455	$3,287	$21,602
Zoning Administration	1.2%	$7,025		$3,691	$273	$1,972	$12,961
Growth Management	1.4%	$8,196		$4,306	$319	$2,301	$15,122

CITY OF PASADENA   SCHEDULE 5
DETAIL OF BUILDING OCCUPANCY CHARGES
FISCAL YEAR 1992–1993 BUDGET

BUILDING/DEPARTMENT	% OF BLDG (1)	ASSET REPLCMNT CHARGE (2)	DEBT SVC OR RENT (3)	CUSTDL & LNDSCPE MNTC (4)	INSURANCE (5)	UTILITIES (6)	TOTAL (7)
CITY YARD – (349 W. MOUNTAIN)							
General Services:							
Building Systems:							
Building Maintenance	81.2%	$53,405			$1,600	$9,006	$64,011
Housekeeping	18.8%	$12,365			$370	$2,085	$14,820
TOTAL	100.0%	$65,770			$1,970	$11,091	$78,831
CENTRAL LIBRARY							
Information Services:							
Administration	7.8%	$29,725		$12,762	$5,880	$12,966	$61,333
Public Services	37.4%	$142,528		$61,190	$28,196	$62,170	$294,084
Reference Services	39.1%	$149,005		$63,972	$29,478	$64,996	$307,451
Support Services	11.1%	$42,301		$18,161	$8,368	$18,452	$87,282
Rental – Paid	1.9%	$7,241		$3,109	$1,432	$3,158	$14,940
Rental – Tax	0.9%	$3,430		$1,472	$680	$1,496	$7,078
Non-Departmental:							
Pasadena – City Use	1.8%	$6,860		$2,944	$1,357	$2,992	$14,153
TOTAL	100.0%	$381,090		$163,610	$75,391	$166,230	$786,321
ALLENDALE BRANCH LIBRARY							
Public Services	99.1%	$5,450		$4,074	$100	$8,714	$18,338
Rental – Paid	0.8%	$44		$33	$1	$70	$148
Non-Departmental:							
Pasadena City Use	0.1%	$6		$4	$0	$9	$19
TOTAL	100.0%	$5,500		$4,111	$101	$8,793	$18,505

CITY OF PASADENA
DETAIL OF BUILDING OCCUPANCY CHARGES
FISCAL YEAR 1992–1993 BUDGET

BUILDING/DEPARTMENT	% OF BLDG (1)	ASSET REPLCMNT CHARGE (2)	DEBT SVC OR RENT (3)	CUSTDL & LNDSCPE MNTC (4)	INSURANCE (5)	UTILITIES (6)	TOTAL (7)
VICTORY PARK							
Recreation Department:							
Recreation Programs Administratn	4.0%	$1,248		$869	$19	$1,520	$3,656
Program Registration	1.3%	$406		$282	$6	$494	$1,188
Special Interest Programs	1.3%	$406		$282	$6	$494	$1,188
Youth Sports Programs	3.5%	$1,092		$760	$17	$1,330	$3,199
Adult Sports Programs	0.3%	$94		$65	$1	$114	$274
Youth Recreation Programs	23.8%	$7,424		$5,171	$113	$9,044	$21,752
Adult Recreation Programs	1.2%	$374		$261	$6	$456	$1,097
Adult Fitness Classes	12.8%	$3,994		$2,781	$61	$4,864	$11,700
Handicapped Citizen Activities	12.2%	$3,806		$2,651	$58	$4,636	$11,151
Senior Citizen Classes	1.4%	$437		$304	$7	$532	$1,280
Tax Programs – Drop In	3.2%	$998		$695	$15	$1,216	$2,924
Recreation Facilities Mngmnt	4.6%	$1,435		$999	$22	$1,748	$4,204
Facility Rental Reservation	1.8%	$562		$391	$9	$684	$1,646
Rental – Paid	8.5%	$2,652		$1,847	$40	$3,230	$7,769
Rental – Tax	4.8%	$1,498		$1,043	$23	$1,824	$4,388
Non-Departmental:							
Pasadena City Use	15.3%	$4,774		$3,325	$73	$5,812	$13,984
TOTAL	100.0%	$31,200		$21,726	$476	$37,998	$91,400
LA CASITA DEL ARROYO							
Recreation:							
Rental – Paid	80.0%	$4,000		$6,106	$64	$1,354	$11,524
Rental – Tax	12.0%	$600		$916	$10	$203	$1,729
Non-Departmental:							
Pasadena City Use	8.0%	$400		$610	$6	$135	$1,151
TOTAL	100.0%	$5,000		$7,632	$80	$1,692	$14,404
SENIOR CITIZEN CENTER							
Human Services:							
Senior Services	100.0%	$15,330			$235	$19,974	$35,539

NOTES TO SCHEDULE 5:
  Columns 2 through 6 are allocated by the percentage of building in Column 1.

CITY OF PASADENA   SCHEDULE 8A

OVERHEAD–DEPARTMENTAL EXPENSE DETAIL

FISCAL YEAR 1992--1993 BUDGET

DEPARTMENT	SALARIES (1)	BENEFITS (2)	OPERATING EXPENSES (3)	BUILDING OCCUPANCY CHARGE (4)	INTERNAL SERVICE CHARGE (5)	FIXED ASSET CHARGE (6)	TOTAL (7)
Human Services	$165,228	$97,319	$13,322	$17,032	$36,250	$445	$329,596
Fire Department	$287,860	$159,763	$318,698	$53,846	$23,611	$20,876	$864,654
Police Department	$1,081,815	$642,342	$293,983	$227,548	$130,830	$25,547	$2,402,065
Plng,Bldg,Neighbrhd Svcs	$367,853	$150,934	$91,644	$63,165	$47,770	$27,714	$749,080
Public Health	$253,251	$108,898	$68,657	$12,842	$31,299	$4,125	$479,072
Information Services	$227,434	$92,566	$86,960	$44,976	$137,421	$3,285	$592,642
Recreation	$180,356	$89,457	$16,987	$10,733	$32,426	$4,263	$334,222
Public Works	$224,955	$95,840	$111,474	$20,767	$73,932	$6,847	$533,815
Water and Power	$554,962	$248,068	$40,596	$66,137	$115,858	$29,206	$1,054,827
Housing and Development	$172,531	$67,848	$56,985	$14,606	$17,161	$1,252	$330,383
TOTALS	$3,516,245	$1,753,035	$1,099,306	$531,652	$646,558	$123,560	$7,670,356

CITY OF PASADENA   SCHEDULE 8B

ADMINISTRATION EXPENSE DETAIL

FISCAL YEAR 1992---1993 BUDGET

DEPARTMENT/PROGRAM	ACTUAL BUDGET (1)	ADDITIONS BLDG.OCCUP. CHARGE (2)	FIXED ASSET CHGE. (3)	SUBTOTAL (4)	DEDUCT DIRECT CHARGES (5)	TOTAL (6)
City Council	$774,809	$43,483	$21,140	$839,432		$839,432
City Manager	$1,016,180	$45,367	$14,390	$1,075,937	($558)	$1,075,379
Management Systems	$293,971	$5,401	$8,880	$308,252		$308,252
Public Information	$357,175	$6,481	$2,880	$366,536	($30,970)	$335,566
Cable Television	$327,529	$86,632	$96,050	$510,211		$510,211
City Clerk	$955,280	$17,282	$5,931	$978,493	($374,279)	$604,214
Records Management	$189,384	$28,083	$4,199	$221,666	($19,126)	$202,540
City Attorney	$1,767,337	$64,809	$24,099	$1,856,245	($125,466)	$1,730,779
Contract Legal Services	$743,280	$0	$0	$743,280		$743,280
Human Resources	$2,725,466	$57,246	$36,060	$2,818,772		$2,818,772
Affirmative Action	$456,025	$12,962	$7,860	$476,847		$476,847
Finance	$348,855	$27,004	$7,961	$383,820	($2,787)	$381,033
Accounting & Analysis	$1,541,032	$22,682	$15,510	$1,579,224	($824,717)	$754,507
Budget	$393,794	$14,041	$7,100	$414,935		$414,935
Financial Services	$903,996	$25,925	$16,149	$946,070	($296,130)	$649,940
Treasury	$486,234	$11,881	$7,090	$505,205	($240,501)	$264,704
Financial Systems Suppt	$728,272	$2,163	$6,932	$737,367	($185,181)	$552,186
Municipal Svcs-Cashier	$565,541	$12,962	$11,210	$589,713	($563,828)	$25,885
Purchasing	$403,431	$35,502	$9,740	$448,673		$448,673
Information Svcs-Bldg Use	$742,365	$113,221	$4,478	$860,064	($844,726)	$15,338
Recreation-Building Use	$340,280	$25,937	$4,270	$370,487	($355,352)	$15,135
TOTALS	$16,060,236	$659,064	$311,929	$17,031,229	($3,863,621)	$13,167,608

CITY OF PASADENA
OVERHEAD AND ADMINISTRATION EXPENSE
FISCAL YEAR 1992–1993 BUDGET

SCHEDULE 7

	ADJ. BUDGET (1)	COSTING ADJ. (2)	TOTAL BASE (3)	LESS OVERHEAD (4)	OVERHEAD BASE (5)	OVERHEAD — OVERHEAD AMOUNT (6)	OVERHEAD — DEPT. RATE (7)	OVERHEAD — GENERAL RATE (8)
GENERAL GOVERNMENT	$22,517,480	$311,929	$22,829,409	$13,167,608	$9,661,801	$13,167,608		8.5%
DEPARTMENTS:								
Human Services	$3,332,461	$445	$3,332,906	$329,596	$3,003,310	$329,596	11.0%	
Fire Department	$16,483,177	$20,876	$16,504,053	$864,654	$15,639,399	$864,654	5.5%	
Police Department	$28,281,860	$25,547	$28,307,407	$2,402,065	$25,905,342	$2,402,065	9.3%	
Planning,Bldg,Neighbrhd	$6,968,508	$27,714	$6,996,222	$749,080	$6,247,142	$749,080	12.0%	
Public Health	$5,750,468	$4,125	$5,754,593	$479,072	$5,275,521	$479,072	9.1%	
Information Services	$6,558,617	$3,285	$6,561,902	$592,642	$5,969,260	$592,642	9.9%	
Recreation	$1,949,534	$4,263	$1,953,797	$334,222	$1,619,575	$334,222	20.6%	
Public Works	$35,234,378	$6,847	$35,241,225	$533,815	$34,707,410	$533,815	1.5%	
Water and Power	$41,469,610	$29,206	$41,498,816	$1,054,827	$40,443,989	$1,054,827	2.6%	
Housing and Development	$6,165,567	$1,252	$6,166,819	$330,383	$5,836,436	$330,383	5.7%	
	$174,711,660	$435,489	$175,147,149	$20,837,964	$154,309,185	$20,837,964		
Budget Adjustments	$122,297,696							
Total Budget	$297,009,356							

Combined General & Departmental Rate: 13.5%

==================

NOTES TO SCHEDULE:

"BUDGET ADJUSTMENTS" — additions for capital outlay, contingency appropriations, appropriations estimated to be unspent, transfers, PCDC non–operating expenditures, Pasadena Center Operating Company, and depreciation & debt service not included in the cost of services for overhead calculations.

"ADJUSTED BUDGET" — additions for building occupancy costs and capital projects included for overhead calculations.

"COSTING ADJUSTMENTS" (col. 2) — additions for costs related to fixed assets in overhead.

CITY OF PASADENA   Schedule 11

SUMMARY OF REVENUES, COSTS AND SUBSIDIES BY ORDER OF SUBSIDY

FISCAL YEAR 1992–1993 BUDGET

SEQ. # (1)	SERVICE CENTER (2)	MSI # (3)	TOTAL REVENUE (4)	TOTAL COST (5)	TOTAL PROFIT (SUBSIDY) (6)	PERCENT RECOVERY ACTUAL (7)	PERCENT RECOVERY SUGGEST (8)	POSSIBLE NEW REVENUE (9)
1	Sewer & Storm Drain Operation & Mtc	S–196	$2,598,642	$11,675,856	($9,077,214)	22.3%	100.0%	$9,077,200 *
2	Electrical Power Service	S–165	$112,168,115	$117,999,638	($5,831,523)	95.1%	100.0%	$23,859,376 *
3	Water Service	S–179	$19,126,816	$22,875,219	($3,748,403)	83.6%	100.0%	$7,318,924 *
4	Neighborhood Park Maintenance	S–222	$0	$3,227,138	($3,227,138)	0.0%	100.0%	$3,227,100 *
5	Rose Bowl Maintenance/Operation	S–204	$3,850,292	$6,456,756	($2,606,464)	59.6%	100.0%	$2,606,500 *
6	Street Light & Signal Maint & Op'n	S–211	$3,900,000	$6,493,336	($2,593,336)	60.1%	100.0%	$2,593,300 *
7	Street Tree Maintenance	S–213	$0	$2,218,643	($2,218,643)	0.0%	100.0%	$2,218,600 *
8	Medical Aid Response	S–113	$1,600,000	$3,309,171	($1,709,171)	48.4%	100.0%	$256,000 */**
9	Police False Alarm Response	S–082	$176,554	$1,069,384	($892,830)	16.5%	100.0%	$44,600 */**
10	Plaza Las Fuentes Parking	S–208	$1,950,075	$2,756,310	($806,235)	70.7%	100.0%	$806,200 *
11	Old Pasadena Parking District	S–206	$2,492,648	$3,274,759	($782,111)	76.1%	100.0%	$782,100 *
12	Construction Plan Check	S–050	$794,312	$1,555,280	($760,968)	51.1%	100.0%	$761,000 *
13	City Youth Sports Programs	S–138	$0	$738,658	($738,658)	0.0%	50.0%	$92,000 */**
14	Vehicle Code Enforcement	S–075	$240,000	$894,037	($654,037)	26.8%	100.0%	SEE TEXT
15	City–Wide Special Events	S–151	NA	$489,561	($489,581)	0.0%	10.0%	$10,000 */**
16	Tournament of Roses Support	S–152	$787,577	$1,255,945	($468,368)	62.7%	100.0%	$468,400 *
17	Business License Renewal	S–227	$0	$462,875	($462,875)	0.0%	100.0%	$462,900 *
18	Median & Parkway Maintenance	S–212	$0	$440,333	($440,333)	0.0%	100.0%	$440,300 *
19	Alley Maintenance	S–220	$0	$440,289	($440,289)	0.0%	100.0%	$440,300 *
20	Occupancy Inspection	S–058	$254,384	$680,584	($426,200)	37.4%	100.0%	$426,200 *
21	Non–Vehicle Code Enforcement	S–076	$0	$425,841	($425,841)	0.0%	50.0%	SEE TEXT
22	City Parking Lot Service	S–209	$202,451	$604,282	($401,831)	33.5%	100.0%	$401,800 *
23	DUI Arrest Procedure/Non–Accident	S–094	$0	$346,891	($346,891)	0.0%	100.0%	$52,000 */**
24	Animal Control	S–120	$116,264	$425,273	($309,009)	27.3%	50.0%	$46,300 *
25	Growth Management Allocation	S–025	$32,864	$319,860	($286,996)	10.3%	100.0%	$287,000 *
26	Monitoring of Conditions	S–034	$0	$277,304	($277,304)	0.0%	100.0%	$277,300 *
27	Trouble Shooter Service	S–168	$0	$252,008	($252,008)	0.0%	100.0%	$252,000
28	Backflow Device Installation	S–193	$48,000	$293,726	($245,726)	16.3%	100.0%	$245,700
29	City Adult Sports Programs	S–139	$47,552	$288,392	($240,840)	16.5%	75.0%	$120,000 */**
30	DUI Acc. Response, Invest. & Report	S–093	$4,500	$243,933	($239,433)	1.8%	100.0%	$35,900 */**
31	Special Business Services	S–218	$0	$238,377	($238,377)	0.0%	100.0%	$238,400 *
32	Mosquito, Fly & Rodent Control	S–119	$0	$235,799	($235,799)	0.0%	100.0%	$235,800 *
33	Residential Refuse Collection	S–199	$6,844,500	$7,067,644	($223,144)	96.8%	100.0%	$223,100 *
34	Youth Recreation Classes	S–142	$18,217	$230,396	($212,179)	7.9%	50.0%	$26,500 */**
35	South Lake Parking District	S–207	$135,203	$346,662	($211,459)	39.0%	100.0%	$211,500 *
36	Services to Housing & Comm. Dev	S–235	$619,000	$823,765	($204,765)	75.1%	100.0%	$204,800 *
37	Book Reservation Service	S–157	$5,115	$206,113	($200,998)	2.5%	100.0%	$5,000 */**

CITY OF PASADENA   Schedule 11

SUMMARY OF REVENUES, COSTS AND SUBSIDIES BY ORDER OF SUBSIDY

FISCAL YEAR 1992–1993 BUDGET

SEQ. # (1)	SERVICE CENTER (2)	MSI # (3)	TOTAL REVENUE (4)	TOTAL COST (5)	TOTAL PROFIT (SUBSIDY) (6)	PERCENT RECOVERY ACTUAL (7)	PERCENT RECOVERY SUGGEST (8)	POSSIBLE NEW REVENUE (9)	
38	Commercial Foot Patrol	S-098	$0	$198,704	($198,704)	0.0%	100.0%	$99,300	*
39	Summer Day Camp	S-145	$40,000	$236,855	($196,855)	16.9%	50.0%	$9,800	*/**
40	Public Crosswalk Protection	S-096	$0	$195,930	($195,930)	0.0%	100.0%	$0	*
41	Street Sweeping	S-202	$636,206	$825,836	($189,630)	77.0%	100.0%	$189,600	*
42	Gasoline Charges	S-223	$576,286	$747,615	($171,329)	77.1%	100.0%	$171,300	*
43	Senior Citizen Programs	S-147	$6,530	$177,083	($170,553)	3.7%	25.0%	$2,000	*/**
44	Street Marking for Utility	S-178	$0	$163,283	($163,283)	0.0%	100.0%	$163,300	
45	Building Permit Center	S-062	$0	$162,623	($162,623)	0.0%	100.0%	$162,600	*
46	New/Moved Business Applicatn Rvw	S-226	$0	$161,773	($161,773)	0.0%	100.0%	$161,800	*
47	Recreational Swimming	S-148	$10,464	$167,983	($157,519)	6.2%	50.0%	$5,000	*/**
48	Women, Infants & Childrn Voucher	S-128	$399,798	$534,954	($135,156)	74.7%	100.0%	$0	*
49	Library Facility Rental	S-164	$7,500	$110,482	($102,982)	6.8%	100.0%	$10,000	**
50	Fire False Alarm Response	S-107	$0	$99,790	($99,790)	0.0%	100.0%	$10,000	*/**
51	Concept Plan Review	S-001	$9,600	$104,783	($95,183)	9.2%	100.0%	$57,100	*/**.
52	Alcoholism & Drug Depndncy Prgrm	S-124	$269,354	$362,784	($93,430)	74.2%	100.0%	$46,700	*
53	Removal of Aband/Abated Veh & Release	S-091	$0	$91,405	($91,405)	0.0%	100.0%	$9,100	*/**
54	Senior Preventive Health Program	S-133	$22,427	$112,223	($89,796)	20.0%	100.0%	$9,000	*
55	Utility St. Usage (Gas & CATV)	S-210	$1,350,000	$1,432,182	($82,182)	94.3%	100.0%	$82,200	*
56	Public Works Permit	S-044	$207,200	$287,508	($80,308)	72.1%	100.0%	$80,300	*
57	Design Commission Review (Major)	S-007	$23,750	$99,391	($75,641)	23.9%	100.0%	$75,600	*
58	Appeal Processing	S-037	$18,130	$93,549	($75,419)	19.4%	100.0%	$37,700	**
59	Traffic Impact Review	S-065	$0	$75,339	($75,339)	0.0%	100.0%	$75,300	*
60	Trip Reduction Plan Review	S-066	$0	$71,854	($71,854)	0.0%	100.0%	$71,900	*
61	Certificate of Appropriateness	S-035	$0	$66,722	($66,722)	0.0%	100.0%	$66,700	*
62	Adaptive Recreation Activities	S-146	$21,425	$87,377	($65,952)	24.5%	25.0%	$500	*/**
63	Ambulatory Care Clinic	S-132	$16,783	$80,906	($64,123)	20.7%	100.0%	$13,000	*
64	Special Business Regulation	S-073	$0	$63,207	($63,207)	0.0%	100.0%	$63,200	*
65	In–Field Service Spots	S-166	$0	$62,944	($62,944)	0.0%	100.0%	$62,900	
66	SGV, HIV Early Intervention Program	S-130	$255,300	$316,296	($60,996)	80.7%	100.0%	$61,000	*
67	Impound Vehicle Release Service	S-092	$0	$60,184	($60,184)	0.0%	100.0%	$36,000	**
68	Police Photo Lab Services	S-086	$0	$59,543	($59,543)	0.0%	100.0%	$20,800	*
69	Private Youth Group Fld Rental Srvc	S-140	$0	$59,381	($59,381)	0.0%	50.0%	$15,000	*/**
70	Parking Permits	S-078	$85,988	$145,066	($59,078)	59.3%	100.0%	$47,200	**
71	Utility Excavation Permit	S-198	$14,620	$70,448	($55,828)	20.8%	100.0%	$55,800	
72	AIDS Program	S-129	$243,223	$294,808	($51,585)	82.5%	100.0%	$51,600	*
73	Business Improvement District	S-219	$0	$51,033	($51,033)	0.0%	100.0%	$51,000	*
74	Inter Library Loan Processing	S-158	$2,060	$51,813	($49,753)	4.0%	50.0%	$2,500	*/**

CITY OF PASADENA   Schedule 11

SUMMARY OF REVENUES, COSTS AND SUBSIDIES BY ORDER OF SUBSIDY

FISCAL YEAR 1992-1993 BUDGET

SEQ. # (1)	SERVICE CENTER (2)	MSI # (3)	TOTAL REVENUE (4)	TOTAL COST (5)	TOTAL PROFIT (SUBSIDY) (6)	PERCENT RECOVERY ACTUAL (7)	PERCENT RECOVERY SUGGEST (8)	POSSIBLE NEW REVENUE (9)	
75	Design Review–City of Gardens	S–010	$3,953	$53,665	($49,712)	7.4%	100.0%	$49,700	
76	Private Adult Group Fld Rental Svc	S–141	$14,947	$63,639	($48,692)	23.5%	75.0%	$24,000	*/**
77	Electric Meter Removal & Repl.	S–175	$4,150	$52,299	($48,149)	7.9%	100.0%	$48,100	
78	Preliminary Plan Check	S–002	$42,062	$88,858	($46,796)	47.3%	100.0%	$46,800	*
79	Initial Environmental Study	S–030	$49,692	$96,384	($46,692)	51.6%	100.0%	$46,700	
80	Tuberculosis Program	S–135	$270,649	$313,777	($43,128)	86.3%	100.0%	$11,000	*
81	Street Vacation	S–045	$4,144	$45,733	($41,589)	9.1%	100.0%	$41,600	
82	Special Event Set–Up/Clean Up	S–153	$4,000	$44,598	($40,598)	9.0%	100.0%	$4,000	*
83	Hazardous Materials Clean–up	S–217	$0	$39,269	($39,269)	0.0%	100.0%	$9,800	**
84	Weed Abatement	S–112	$33,152	$69,330	($36,178)	47.8%	100.0%	$18,000	**
85	Right–of–Way Clean–up	S–203	$0	$35,777	($35,777)	0.0%	100.0%	$0	*
86	Damaged Meter Repair or Replacement	S–170	$13,350	$49,078	($35,728)	27.2%	100.0%	$35,700	
87	Power Credit Turn Off/On	S–169	$35,812	$71,416	($35,604)	50.1%	100.0%	$35,600	
88	Food Sanitation Inspection	S–118	$205,368	$240,468	($35,100)	85.4%	100.0%	$35,100	*
89	Variance Review	S–019	$60,830	$95,105	($34,275)	64.0%	100.0%	$34,300	
90	Post–Fire Investigation Analysis	S–110	$44,556	$76,272	($31,716)	58.4%	100.0%	$31,700	
91	Conditional Use Permit Review	S–016	$214,350	$244,635	($30,285)	87.6%	100.0%	$21,200	**
92	Design Review (Final)	S–008	$0	$30,173	($30,173)	0.0%	100.0%	$30,200	*
93	Adult Recreation Classes	S–143	$42,372	$72,436	($30,064)	58.5%	75.0%	$11,900	*/**
94	Temporary Street Closure (Events)	S–064	$1,219	$30,229	($29,010)	4.0%	100.0%	$14,500	**
95	State Mandated Fire Inspection	S–105	$159,360	$185,178	($25,818)	86.1%	100.0%	$25,800	*
96	Minor Conditional Use Permit Review	S–017	$11,480	$36,806	($25,326)	31.2%	100.0%	$17,700	**
97	Minor Variance Review	S–020	$9,515	$34,268	($24,753)	27.8%	100.0%	$24,800	
98	Youth Special Activities	S–144	$0	$23,976	($23,976)	0.0%	50.0%	$2,400	*/**
99	Final Tract Map Review	S–040	$0	$23,095	($23,095)	0.0%	100.0%	$23,100	
100	Commercial Refuse Service	S–200	$1,400,000	$1,423,072	($23,072)	98.4%	100.0%	$23,100	*
101	Library Media Rental	S–161	$5,914	$28,775	($22,861)	20.6%	75.0%	$5,700	*/**
102	Water Service Installation	S–180	$152,100	$174,888	($22,788)	87.0%	100.0%	$22,800	
103	Historic Building Search	S–014	$0	$22,072	($22,072)	0.0%	100.0%	$16,500	**
104	Electric Meter Test	S–174	$490	$22,329	($21,839)	2.2%	100.0%	$21,800	
105	Water Meter Equipment Upgrade	S–187	$0	$21,164	($21,164)	0.0%	100.0%	$21,200	
106	Design Review (Consolidated)	S–011	$10,780	$31,275	($20,495)	34.5%	100.0%	$20,500	*
107	Author Program	S–163	$5,505	$25,741	($20,236)	21.4%	100.0%	$17,000	**
108	Non–Emergency Service	S–108	$0	$19,917	($19,917)	0.0%	100.0%	$5,000	**
109	Growth Management Allocation Exemption	S–026	$0	$19,621	($19,621)	0.0%	100.0%	$19,600	
110	Parkway Usage License Agreement	S–060	$3,191	$21,864	($18,673)	14.6%	100.0%	$18,700	
111	Flow Test (Low/Leak/Frozen Valve)	S–189	$0	$18,158	($18,158)	0.0%	100.0%	$18,200	

CITY OF PASADENA

Schedule 11

SUMMARY OF REVENUES, COSTS AND SUBSIDIES BY ORDER OF SUBSIDY

FISCAL YEAR 1992–1993 BUDGET

SEQ. # (1)	SERVICE CENTER (2)	MSI # (3)	TOTAL REVENUE (4)	TOTAL COST (5)	TOTAL PROFIT (SUBSIDY) (6)	PERCENT RECOVERY ACTUAL (7)	PERCENT RECOVERY SUGGEST (8)	POSSIBLE NEW REVENUE (9)
112	Returned Check (NSF) Processing	S-228	$30,000	$47,877	($17,877)	62.7%	100.0%	$8,900 *
113	Water Quality Test	S-188	$0	$17,192	($17,192)	0.0%	100.0%	$17,200
114	Special Curb Marking	S-221	$1,500	$18,169	($16,669)	8.3%	100.0%	$16,700
115	Bill Investigation	S-195	$0	$16,093	($16,093)	0.0%	100.0%	$27,900
116	Rifle Range Use	S-099	$25,000	$40,401	($15,401)	61.9%	100.0%	$15,400
117	Env. Impact Mitigation Monitoring	S-033	$0	$15,317	($15,317)	0.0%	100.0%	$15,300 *
118	Master Development Plan Review	S-015	$2,799	$17,602	($14,803)	15.9%	100.0%	$14,800
119	Hydrant Flow Test	S-190	$0	$13,855	($13,855)	0.0%	100.0%	$13,900
120	Police Report Copying	S-084	$100,000	$112,243	($12,243)	89.1%	100.0%	$12,200
121	Swimming Lessons	S-149	$21,652	$33,601	($11,949)	64.4%	75.0%	$3,500 */**
122	Noise Control Permit	S-117	$3,200	$15,087	($11,887)	21.2%	100.0%	$5,900 */**
123	Illegal Burn Response	S-109	$0	$11,830	($11,830)	0.0%	100.0%	$11,800
124	Annual Hm Business Occupancy Prmt	S-071	$13,000	$24,668	($11,668)	52.7%	100.0%	$11,700
125	Design Commission Review (Minor)	S-008	$3,350	$14,969	($11,619)	22.4%	100.0%	$11,600 *
126	Noise Disturbance Response Call-back	S-095	$0	$11,584	($11,584)	0.0%	100.0%	$1,700 **
127	Replacement Of Lost Library Cards	S-156	$9,501	$20,448	($10,947)	46.5%	100.0%	$3,800 */**
128	Zoning Parking Credit	S-063	$2,400	$13,142	($10,742)	18.3%	100.0%	$10,700
129	Restore Service Wire Cuts	S-171	$2,500	$13,038	($10,538)	19.2%	100.0%	$10,500
130	Fish & Game Environ. impact Revw	S-032	$2,132	$12,543	($10,411)	17.0%	100.0%	$10,400
131	Replacement Of Curb Stop 3/4" & 1"	S-183	$11,100	$21,162	($10,062)	52.5%	100.0%	$10,100
132	Construction Staging Plan Review	S-005	$0	$9,788	($9,788)	0.0%	100.0%	$9,800
133	Trustee Housing	S-102	$73,650	$83,247	($9,597)	88.5%	100.0%	$9,600
134	Development Agreement Revw	S-067	$0	$9,335	($9,335)	0.0%	100.0%	$0 #
135	Rezoning Request Rvw (Zone Change)	S-023	$8,288	$17,591	($9,303)	47.1%	100.0%	$9,300
136	Environmental Impact Report (Consltnt)	S-031	$10,230	$19,236	($9,006)	53.2%	100.0%	$9,000
137	Library On-Line Database Search	S-162	$12,411	$21,409	($8,998)	58.0%	100.0%	$5,000 **
138	V.I.N. Verification	S-103	$0	$8,280	($8,280)	0.0%	100.0%	$4,100 **
139	Fingerprint Processing	S-089	$33,300	$41,531	($8,231)	80.2%	100.0%	$7,000 **
140	Landmark District Review	S-013	$0	$8,137	($8,137)	0.0%	100.0%	$8,100
142	Limited Time Parking Permit	S-079	$0	$6,888	($6,888)	0.0%	100.0%	$6,900
143	Replacing Lost Library Items	S-155	$12,897	$19,682	($6,785)	65.5%	100.0%	$6,800
144	Health Department Plan Check/Insp	S-115	$17,000	$23,755	($6,755)	71.6%	100.0%	$6,800 *
145	Address Assignment	S-056	$1,650	$8,345	($6,695)	19.8%	100.0%	$6,700
146	Temporary Conditional Use Permit Rvw	S-018	$20,020	$26,268	($6,248)	76.2%	100.0%	$4,700 **
147	One-Day Alcohol Permit Processing	S-097	$0	$6,041	($6,041)	0.0%	100.0%	$6,000
148	Final Parcel Map Review	S-041	$0	$5,730	($5,730)	0.0%	100.0%	$5,700

CITY OF PASADENA　　　　　　　　　　　Schedule 11

SUMMARY OF REVENUES, COSTS AND SUBSIDIES BY ORDER OF SUBSIDY

FISCAL YEAR 1992–1993 BUDGET

SEQ. # (1)	SERVICE CENTER (2)	MSI # (3)	TOTAL REVENUE (4)	TOTAL COST (5)	TOTAL PROFIT (SUBSIDY) (6)	PERCENT RECOVERY ACTUAL (7)	SUGGEST (8)	POSSIBLE NEW REVENUE (9)
149	Sewer Stoppage Investigation	S–197	$0	$5,422	($5,422)	0.0%	100.0%	$5,400
150	Certificate of Compliance Investigation	S–059	$1,955	$7,278	($5,323)	26.9%	100.0%	$5,300
151	Use Permit & Variance Extension	S–021	$0	$5,115	($5,115)	0.0%	100.0%	$5,100
152	Design Review (Seismic)	S–009	$0	$5,028	($5,028)	0.0%	100.0%	$5,000 *
153	Hillside Grading Inspection	S–049	$0	$4,785	($4,785)	0.0%	100.0%	$4,800 *
154	Vehicle Correction Inspection	S–090	$0	$4,658	($4,658)	0.0%	100.0%	$3,000 **
155	Planned Development	S–089	$0	$4,653	($4,653)	0.0%	100.0%	$0 #
156	Growth Management Time Extension	S–029	$0	$4,603	($4,603)	0.0%	100.0%	$4,600
157	Legal Description	S–068	$0	$4,387	($4,387)	0.0%	100.0%	$4,400
158	Barricade Installation	S–215	$10,000	$14,253	($4,253)	70.2%	100.0%	$3,000 **
159	Police Photograph Reproduction	S–085	$3,108	$7,264	($4,156)	42.8%	100.0%	$4,200
160	General Plan Amendment	S–070	$0	$4,096	($4,096)	0.0%	100.0%	$0 #
161	Lot Line Adjustment	S–022	$13,305	$17,390	($4,085)	76.5%	100.0%	$4,100
162	Spec. Police Computer Print–Out Service	S–088	$1,400	$5,300	($3,900)	26.4%	100.0%	$3,900
163	Meter Test/Field (5/8" & 1")	S–185	$240	$3,784	($3,544)	6.3%	100.0%	$3,500
164	Water Meter Removal and Replacement	S–186	$5,200	$8,438	($3,238)	61.6%	100.0%	$3,200
165	Appeal Processing – Staff Decision	S–038	$0	$3,111	($3,111)	0.0%	100.0%	$1,500 **
166	Barricade Rental	S–216	$2,000	$5,085	($3,085)	39.3%	100.0%	$1,500 **
167	Temporary Certificate of Occupancy	S–057	$34,020	$37,007	($2,987)	91.9%	100.0%	$3,000
168	Hazard Abatement Services	S–114	$0	$2,838	($2,838)	0.0%	100.0%	$800 **
169	Police Tape & Video Duplication Service	S–087	$0	$2,817	($2,817)	0.0%	100.0%	$2,800
170	Hydrant Portable/Construction Meter	S–191	$0	$2,776	($2,776)	0.0%	100.0%	$2,800
171	Garage Sale Permit	S–072	$7,500	$9,990	($2,490)	75.1%	100.0%	$1,900 **
172	Fire Report Copying	S–111	$1,125	$3,284	($2,159)	34.3%	100.0%	$2,200
173	Flu/Pneumonia Immunization	S–136	$19,874	$21,943	($2,069)	90.6%	100.0%	$2,100 *
174	Subdivision Map Extension Prcssng	S–024	$6,152	$8,070	($1,918)	76.2%	100.0%	$1,900
175	Replacement Building Permit Relief	S–036	$0	$1,874	($1,874)	0.0%	100.0%	$1,900
176	Growth Mgmnt Conditional Use Permit	S–028	$28,580	$30,359	($1,779)	94.1%	100.0%	$1,800
177	Condominium Conversion	S–053	$0	$1,637	($1,637)	0.0%	100.0%	$1,600
178	Bicycle Registration	S–080	$2,132	$3,666	($1,535)	58.1%	100.0%	$1,500
179	Power Service Relocation	S–176	$1,150	$2,478	($1,328)	46.4%	100.0%	$1,300
180	Sidewalk Dining Permit	S–061	$0	$889	($889)	0.0%	100.0%	$900
181	Repl. Of 1–1/2" Wheel Gate Valve	S–184	$900	$1,708	($808)	52.7%	100.0%	$800
182	Tree Maintenence Contractor Permit Rvw	S–214	$320	$1,070	($750)	29.9%	100.0%	$800
183	Design Review Extension	S–012	$0	$446	($446)	0.0%	100.0%	$400
184	Reproduction Of Photographs	S–160	$100	$510	($410)	19.6%	100.0%	$200 **
185	Clearance Letter Processing	S–083	$3,000	$3,366	($366)	89.1%	100.0%	$400

CITY OF PASADENA

Schedule 11

SUMMARY OF REVENUES, COSTS AND SUBSIDIES BY ORDER OF SUBSIDY

FISCAL YEAR 1992-1993 BUDGET

SEQ. # (1)	SERVICE CENTER (2)	MSI # (3)	TOTAL REVENUE (4)	TOTAL COST (5)	TOTAL PROFIT (SUBSIDY) (6)	PERCENT RECOVERY ACTUAL (7)	PERCENT RECOVERY SUGGEST (8)	POSSIBLE NEW REVENUE (9)
186	Retrieval & Copying Of Periodicals	S-159	$1,734	$2,083	($349)	83.2%	100.0%	$200 **
187	Water Service Cut Off At Street	S-181	$200	$537	($337)	37.2%	100.0%	$300
188	Smog Check	S-224	$1,040	$1,360	($320)	76.5%	100.0%	$300 *
189	Growth Allocation Appeal	S-027	$1,901	$2,064	($163)	92.1%	100.0%	$200
190	Document Certification Charges	S-231	$58	$190	($132)	30.7%	100.0%	$100 **
191	Same Day Service Turn-On	S-173	$25	$126	($101)	19.8%	100.0%	$100
	SUBTOTAL — SUBSIDY		$165,654,970	$213,998,285	($48,343,315)	77.4%	100.0%	$62,121,000

192	Vital Statistics	S-121	$255,408	$255,408	$0	100.0%	100.0%	$0 *
193	Public Health Laboratory	S-126	$246,272	$246,272	$0	100.0%	100.0%	$0 *
194	Prenatal Clinic	S-127	$1,369,582	$1,369,582	$0	100.0%	100.0%	$0 *
195	Child Health Clinic	S-131	$424,713	$424,713	$0	100.0%	100.0%	$0 *
196	Sexually Transmitted Disease Program	S-134	$127,218	$127,218	$0	100.0%	100.0%	$0 *
197	Address Change	S-055	$966	$716	$250	134.9%	100.0%	($300)
198	Agenda/Minute Mailing Service	S-232	$3,289	$2,975	$314	110.6%	100.0%	($300)
199	Relocation Investigation (House Moves)	S-054	$9,324	$7,820	$1,504	119.2%	100.0%	($1,500)
200	First Offender Program	S-125	$75,696	$73,491	$2,205	103.0%	100.0%	$0 *
201	Wide, Overweight, Overlong Ld Prmt	S-074	$5,594	$3,337	$2,257	167.6%	100.0%	($2,300)
202	Engineering Plan Review	S-042	$79,400	$76,644	$2,756	103.6%	100.0%	($2,800)
203	Helicopter Pad Landing Use	S-100	$4,070	$1,304	$2,766	312.1%	100.0%	$0 *
204	Grading Plan Check	S-046	$4,206	$1,422	$2,784	295.8%	100.0%	($2,800) *
205	Grading Inspection	S-048	$4,206	$423	$3,783	994.3%	100.0%	($3,800) *
206	Misc/Special Building Inspection Invstgn	S-052	$12,183	$8,219	$3,964	148.2%	100.0%	($4,000)
207	Water Credit Turn Off/On	S-182	$19,516	$15,271	$4,245	127.8%	100.0%	$0 *
208	Vesting Map Review	S-039	$16,730	$12,222	$4,508	136.9%	100.0%	($4,500)
209	Tentative Parcel Map Review	S-003	$36,315	$31,373	$4,942	115.8%	100.0%	($4,900)
210	Hillside Grading Plan Check	S-047	$6,718	$1,773	$4,945	378.9%	100.0%	($4,900) *
211	Water Examination	S-123	$99,840	$94,652	$5,188	105.5%	100.0%	($5,200) *
212	I.N.S. Prisoner Housing	S-101	$391,500	$384,610	$6,890	101.8%	100.0%	$0 *
213	Underground Tank Plan Check/Insp.	S-106	$72,505	$62,984	$9,521	115.1%	100.0%	($9,500)
214	Hydrant Installation	S-192	$14,112	$4,524	$9,588	311.9%	100.0%	$0 *
215	Tentative Tract Map Review	S-004	$58,680	$47,616	$11,064	123.2%	100.0%	($11,100)
216	Special Requested Refuse Pick-Up	S-201	$45,000	$32,878	$12,322	137.7%	100.0%	$0 *
217	Recreation Facility Rental	S-150	$131,490	$105,716	$25,774	124.4%	100.0%	$0 *
218	Hazardous Materials Permit Insp	S-104	$766,640	$719,743	$46,897	106.5%	100.0%	$0 *
219	Travel Immmunizations	S-122	$181,000	$119,540	$61,460	151.4%	100.0%	$0 *

CITY OF PASADENA   Schedule 11

SUMMARY OF REVENUES, COSTS AND SUBSIDIES BY ORDER OF SUBSIDY

FISCAL YEAR 1992–1993 BUDGET

SEQ # (1)	SERVICE CENTER (2)	MSI # (3)	TOTAL REVENUE (4)	TOTAL COST (5)	TOTAL PROFIT (SUBSIDY) (6)	PERCENT RECOVERY ACTUAL (7)	SUGGEST (8)	POSSIBLE NEW REVENUE (9)
220	Environmental Health Inspection	S–116	$208,432	$140,573	$67,859	148.3%	100.0%	($67,900) *
221	Burglar Alarm Review	S–061	$133,500	$34,234	$99,266	390.0%	100.0%	SEE TEXT
222	Utility Billing	S–194	$675,000	$524,771	$150,229	128.6%	100.0%	$0 *
223	Street Occupation Permit	S–043	$207,200	$45,403	$161,797	456.4%	100.0%	$0 *
224	Overdue Material Processing	S–154	$192,461	$28,456	$164,005	676.3%	100.0%	$0 *
225	Construction Review and Inspection	S–051	$1,455,219	$1,141,048	$314,171	127.5%	100.0%	SEE TEXT *
226	Film Permit	S–234	$599,480	$246,549	$352,931	243.1%	100.0%	$0 *
227	Golf Course Maintenance/Operation	S–205	$1,948,129	$1,367,058	$581,071	142.5%	100.0%	$0 *
228	Parking Enforcement	S–077	$1,625,000	$764,794	$860,206	212.5%	100.0%	SEE TEXT
	SUBTOTAL — PROFIT		$11,506,596	$8,525,132	$2,981,464	135.0%	100.0%	($125,800)

SEQ #	SERVICE CENTER	MSI #	TOTAL REVENUE	TOTAL COST	TOTAL PROFIT (SUBSIDY)	ACTUAL	SUGGEST	POSSIBLE NEW REVENUE
229	Research Of City Records	S–229	NA	NA	NA	NA	100.0%	NA */**
230	Document Printing and Copying	S–230	NA	NA	NA	NA	100.0%	NA */**
231	Facility Rental and Maintenance	S–233	$70,000	NA	NA	NA	100.0%	NA *
232	Restore Bucket/Underground Cut	S–172	$900	$764	$136	117.8%	100.0%	$0 *
233	City Property Damage	S–225	$56,713	$51,033	$5,680	111.1%	100.0%	$0 *
234	Power Service Installation	S–177	$155,400	$127,120	$28,280	122.2%	100.0%	$0 *
235	New Vaults >200 Amps.	S–167	$484,334	$147,917	$336,417	327.4%	100.0%	$0 *
	SUBTOTAL – INSUFFICIENT DATA		$767,347	$326,834	$440,513	234.8%	100.0%	$0

	TOTALS		$177,928,913	$222,850,251	($44,921,338)	79.8%	100.0%	$61,995,200

NOTES:

*   * – See Text
*   ** – Market Sensititve
*   # – Frequency of Service Unknown

CITY OF PASADENA

REVENUE/SERVICE RELATIONSHIP LIST, BY SERVICE TYPE

FISCAL YEAR 1992-93

REF # (1)	SERVICE PROVIDED (2)	TYPE OF DESIGNATION (3)	UNITS 1992-93 PROJECTED (4)	COSTS 1992-93 PROJECTED (5)	REVENUE 1992-93 PROJECTED (6)	USE OF TAX $ OR (PROFIT) (7)
SPECIAL BENEFIT SERVICES						
S-001	Concept Plan Review	Application	40	$104,783	$9,600	$95,183
S-002	Preliminary Plan Check	Application	200	$88,858	$42,062	$46,796
S-003	Tentative Parcel Map Review	Application	15	$31,373	$36,315	($4,942) *
S-004	Tentative Tract Map Review	Application	20	$47,616	$58,680	($11,064) *
S-005	Construction Staging Plan Review	Application	20	$9,788	$0	$9,788
S-006	Design Commission Review (Minor)	Permit	50	$14,969	$3,350	$11,619
S-007	Design Commission Review (Major)	Permit	50	$99,391	$23,750	$75,641
S-008	Design Review (Final)	Permit	40	$30,173	$0	$30,173
S-009	Design Review (Seismic)	Permit	30	$5,028	$0	$5,028
S-010	Design Review–City of Gardens	Application	24	$53,665	$3,953	$49,712
S-011	Design Review (Consolidated)	Permit	20	$31,275	$10,780	$20,495
S-012	Design Review Extension	Application	10	$446	$0	$446
S-013	Landmark District Review	Application	22	$8,137	$0	$8,137
S-014	Historic Building Search	Request	360	$22,072	$0	$22,072
S-015	Master Development Plan Review	Application	3	$17,602	$2,799	$14,803
S-016	Conditional Use Permit Review	Application	150	$244,635	$214,350	$30,285
S-017	Minor Conditional Use Permit Review	Application	20	$36,806	$11,480	$25,326
S-018	Temporary Conditional Use Permit Rvw	Application	70	$26,268	$20,020	$6,248
S-019	Variance Review	Application	55	$95,105	$60,830	$34,275
S-020	Minor Variance Review	Application	20	$34,268	$9,515	$24,753
S-021	Use Permit & Variance Extension	Request	20	$5,115	$0	$5,115
S-022	Lot Line Adjustment	Application	15	$17,390	$13,305	$4,085
S-023	Rezoning Request Rvw (Zone Change)	Application	4	$17,591	$8,288	$9,303
S-024	Subdivision Map Extension Processing	Request	8	$8,070	$6,152	$1,918
S-025	Growth Management Allocation	Application	20	$319,860	$32,864	$286,996
S-026	Growth Management Allocation Exemption	Application	50	$19,621	$0	$19,621
S-027	Growth Allocation Appeal	Project	20	$2,064	$1,901	$183
S-028	Growth Mgt. Conditional Use Permit	Permit	20	$30,359	$28,580	$1,779
S-029	Growth Management Time Extension	Application	20	$4,603	$0	$4,603
S-030	Initial Environmental Study	Study	82	$96,384	$49,692	$46,692
S-031	Environmental Impact Report (Consltnt)	Study	3	$19,236	$10,230	$9,006
S-032	Fish & Game Environ. Impact Revw	Permit	82	$12,543	$2,132	$10,411
S-033	Env. Impact Mitigation Monitoring	Project	24	$15,317	$0	$15,317
S-034	Monitoring of Conditions	Project	350	$277,304	$0	$277,304
S-035	Certificate of Appropriateness	Permit	50	$66,722	$0	$66,722
S-036	Replacement Building Permit Relief	Application	8	$1,874	$0	$1,874
S-037	Appeal Processing	Application	25	$93,549	$18,130	$75,419

CITY OF PASADENA
REVENUE/SERVICE RELATIONSHIP LIST, BY SERVICE TYPE
FISCAL YEAR 1992-93

REF # (1)	SERVICE PROVIDED (2)	TYPE OF DESIGNATION (3)	UNITS 1992-93 PROJECTED (4)	COSTS 1992-93 PROJECTED (5)	REVENUE 1992-93 PROJECTED (6)	USE OF TAX $ OR (PROFIT) (7)
S-038	Appeal Processing – Staff Decision	Application	5	$3,111	$0	$3,111
S-039	Vesting Map Review	Application	5	$12,222	$16,730	($4,508) *
S-040	Final Tract Map Review	Map	15	$23,095	$0	$23,095
S-041	Final Parcel Map Review	Map	6	$5,730	$0	$5,730
S-042	Engineering Plan Review	Plan	47	$76,644	$79,400	($2,756) *
S-043	Street Occupation Permit	Permit	448	$45,403	$207,200	($161,797) *
S-044	Public Works Permit	Permit	1,400	$287,508	$207,200	$80,308
S-045	Street Vacation	Application	8	$45,733	$4,144	$41,589
S-046	Grading Plan Check	Plan	8	$1,422	$4,206	($2,784) *
S-047	Hillside Grading Plan Check	Plan	4	$1,773	$6,718	($4,945) *
S-048	Grading Inspection	Permit	8	$423	$4,206	($3,783) *
S-049	Hillside Grading Inspection	Permit	4	$4,785	$0	$4,785
S-050	Construction Plan Check	Plan	2,934	$1,555,280	$794,312	$760,968
S-051	Construction Review and Inspection	Permit	8,847	$1,141,048	$1,455,219	($314,171) *
S-052	Misc/Special Building Inspection Invstgn	Inspection	120	$8,219	$12,183	($3,964) *
S-053	Condominium Conversion	Application	2	$1,637	$0	$1,637
S-054	Relocation Investigation (House Moves)	Permit	12	$7,820	$9,324	($1,504) *
S-055	Address Change	Request	6	$716	$966	($250) *
S-056	Address Assignment	Project	75	$8,345	$1,650	$6,695
S-057	Temporary Certificate of Occupancy	Application	380	$37,007	$34,020	$2,987
S-058	Occupancy Inspection	Inspection	8,408	$680,584	$254,384	$426,200
S-059	Certificate of Compliance Investigation	Application	5	$7,278	$1,955	$5,323
S-060	Parkway Usage License Agreement	Application	15	$21,864	$3,191	$18,673
S-061	Sidewalk Dining Permit	Application	5	$889	$0	$889
S-062	Building Permit Center	Permit/App	13,403	$162,623	$0	$162,623
S-063	Zoning Parking Credit	Application	8	$13,142	$2,400	$10,742
S-064	Temporary Street Closure (Events)	Application	52	$30,229	$1,219	$29,010
S-065	Traffic Impact Review	Study	30	$75,339	$0	$75,339
S-066	Trip Reduction Plan Review	Plan	25	$71,854	$0	$71,854
S-067	Development Agreement Revw	Project	1	$9,335	$0	$9,335
S-068	Legal Description	Project	5	$4,387	$0	$4,387
S-069	Planned Development	Application	1	$4,653	$0	$4,653
S-070	General Plan Amendment	Application	1	$4,096	$0	$4,096
S-071	Annual Home Business Occupancy PerMIT	Permit	589	$24,668	$13,000	$11,668
S-072	Garage Sale Permit	Permit	1,000	$9,990	$7,500	$2,490
S-073	Special Business Regulation	Application	704	$63,207	$0	$63,207
S-074	Wide, Overweight, Overlong Load PerMIT	Permit	196	$3,337	$5,594	($2,257) *
S-076	Non-Vehicle Code Enforcement	Citation/Insp.	1,300	$425,841	$0	$425,841
S-077	Parking Enforcement	Citation	115,000	$764,794	$1,625,000	($860,206) *

CITY OF PASADENA
REVENUE/SERVICE RELATIONSHIP LIST, BY SERVICE TYPE
FISCAL YEAR 1992-93

REF # (1)	SERVICE PROVIDED (2)	TYPE OF DESIGNATION (3)	UNITS 1992-93 PROJECTED (4)	COSTS 1992-93 PROJECTED (5)	REVENUE 1992-93 PROJECTED (6)	USE OF TAX $ OR (PROFIT) (7)
S-078	Parking Permits	Permit	2,900	$145,066	$85,988	$59,078
S-079	Limited Time Parking Permit	Request	24	$6,888	$0	$6,888
S-080	Bicycle Registration	License	490	$3,666	$2,132	$1,535
S-081	Burglar Alarm Review	Permit	1,500	$34,234	$133,500	($99,266) *
S-082	Police False Alarm	Incident	9,414	$1,069,384	$176,554	$892,830
S-083	Clearance Letter Processing	Letter	300	$3,366	$3,000	$366
S-084	Police Report Copying	Report Copy	10,000	$112,243	$100,000	$12,243
S-085	Police Photograph Reproduction	Photo	300	$7,264	$3,108	$4,156
S-086	Police Photo Lab Services	NA	NA	$59,543	$0	$59,543
S-087	Police Tape & Video Duplication Service	Tape	60	$2,817	$0	$2,817
S-088	Spec. Police Computer Print-Out Service	Request	175	$5,300	$1,400	$3,900
S-089	Fingerprint Processing	Card	3,700	$41,531	$33,300	$8,231
S-090	Vehicle Correction Inspection	Inspection	900	$4,658	$0	$4,658
S-092	Impound Vehicle Release Service	Vehicle	1,000	$60,184	$0	$60,184
S-093	DUI Acc. Response, Invest. & Report	Incident	525	$243,933	$4,500	$239,433
S-094	DUI Arrest Procedure/Non-Accident	Arrest	1,000	$346,891	$0	$346,891
S-095	Noise Disturbance Response Call-back	Call-back	100	$11,584	$0	$11,584
S-096	Public Crosswalk Protection	Crosswalk	10	$195,930	$0	$195,930
S-097	One-Day Alcohol Permit Processing	Permit	125	$6,041	$0	$6,041
S-098	Commercial Foot Patrol	Business	297	$198,704	$0	$198,704
S-099	Rifle Range Use	Customer	4,900	$40,401	$25,000	$15,401
S-100	Helicopter Pad Landing Use	Permit	10	$1,304	$4,070	($2,766) *
S-101	I.N.S. Prisoner Housing	Prisoner	5,220	$384,610	$391,500	($6,890)
S-102	Trustee Housing	Prisoner Day	982	$83,247	$73,650	$9,597
S-103	V.I.N. Verification	Request	400	$8,280	$0	$8,280
S-104	Hazardous Materials Permit Inspectn	Inspection	5,000	$719,743	$766,640	($46,897) *
S-106	Underground Tank Plan Check/Insp.	Plan Ck/Insp	1,434	$62,984	$72,505	($9,521) *
S-107	Fire False Alarm Response	Incident	1,000	$99,790	$0	$99,790
S-108	Non-Emergency Service	Incident	208	$19,917	$0	$19,917
S-109	Illegal Burn Response	Response	50	$11,830	$0	$11,830
S-110	Post-Fire Investigation Analysis	Investigation	224	$76,272	$44,556	$31,716
S-111	Fire Report Copying	Report	150	$3,284	$1,125	$2,159
S-112	Weed Abatement	Parcel	440	$69,330	$33,152	$36,178
S-113	Medical Aid Response	Avg. Incident	9,500	$3,309,171	$1,600,000	$1,709,171
S-114	Hazard Abatement Services	Incident	10	$2,838	$0	$2,838
S-115	Health Department Plan Check/Insp	Plan	60	$23,755	$17,000	$6,755
S-116	Environmental Health Inspection	Inspection	8,178	$140,573	$208,432	($67,859) *
S-117	Noise Control Permit	Permit	92	$15,087	$3,200	$11,887
S-118	Food Sanitation Inspection	Inspection	6,949	$240,468	$205,368	$35,100

MSI SERVICE CENTER WORKSHEET FOR FEES AND CHARGES

SERVICE PROVIDED	CITY	REF.NO.
TENTATIVE TRACT MAP REVIEW	**PASADENA**	S-004

SERVICES PRIMARILY PERFORMED BY	FUND	EXP.ACCT.
PBNS-Zoning Administration	General	350116

REVENUE RECEIVED [Actual - Potential]	FUND	REV.ACCT.
TENTATIVE TRACT MAP REVIEW FEES	General	05-3955

REVENUE AUTHORIZATION	
Resolution 6761	DATE LAST REVISED: 6/30/92
	SUBSIDY RATIONALE: None

DESCRIPTION OF SERVICE	
Reviewing tentative tract map to identify any special conditions and determine extent to which it complies with appropriate Code requirements.	REVENUE COLLECTION SCHEDULE: At time of filing map
	REVENUE COLLECTED BY: PBNS-Zoning Administration
	UNIT OF SERVICE DESIGNATION: Application

CURRENT FEE STRUCTURE

$1,754 plus $57 per land and/or air parcel
$ 496 Notification Fee

FISCAL YEAR 1992-1993 REVENUE AND COST COMPARISON

TOTAL EST. REVENUE	:	$58,680	UNIT REVENUE	:	$2,934.00
TOTAL COST	:	$47,616	UNIT COST	:	$2,380.80
PROFIT (SUBSIDY)	:	$11,064	PROFIT (SUBSIDY)	:	$553.20
% of COST RECOVERED	:	123.2%	UNITS OF SERVICE	:	20

SUGGESTED % RECOVERY AND FEE STRUCTURE

PERCENT: 100%   **SPECIAL CONDITIONS:** None

$2,380 plus $50 per land and/or air parcel (includes notification)

[T-003]

MSI SERVICE CENTER WORKSHEET FOR COST DETAIL

SERVICE PROVIDED					CITY	REF.NO.
Tentative Tract Map Review					PASADENA	S-004

TOTAL UNITS: 20

KEY	FILE	DEPARTMENT	DIVISION	SECTION	ACCOUNT	TYPE	UNITS
A	DESG_PRK	Public Works	Engineering	Design Eng – Parks	460352		20
B	DESG_CVL	Public Works	Engineering	Design Eng – Civil	460329		20
C	P_ENG	Water & Power	Power	Engineering			20
D	TRNS_PLN	Public Works	Transportation	Invest'N/Planning	259911		20
E	DESG_LGT	Public Works	Engineering	Design Eng – Lght/Signals	460337		20
F	ENG_SVCS	Public Works	Engineering	Engineering Services	460451		20
G	PBNSZONE	PBNS	Planning	Zoning Administration	350116		20

EXPENSE TYPE	TOTAL	A	B	C	D	E	F	G
SALARIES & WAGES	$23,218	$360	$664	$673	$636	$1,328	$10,007	$9,550
FRINGE BENEFITS	$10,419	$169	$312	$301	$299	$624	$4,703	$4,011
SERVICES AND SUPPLIES	$2,876			$77	$223	$253	$831	$1,492
BUILDING OCCUPANCY	$1,114	$40	$12	$52	$28	$127	$657	$198
GENERAL SERVICES	$1,695			$51	$11		$423	$1,210
GENERAL OVERHEAD	$3,342	$48	$84	$98	$102	$198	$1,413	$1,399
DEPARTMENT OVERHEAD	$2,331	$9	$15	$30	$18	$35	$249	$1,975
SUPERVISION & INDIRECTS	$2,258			$139	$107			$2,012
FIXED ASSET REPLACEMENT	$363	$2	$6	$8	$11	$12	$115	$209
TOTAL	$47,616	$628	$1,093	$1,429	$1,435	$2,577	$18,398	$22,056

EXPENSE TYPE	PER UNIT	A	B	C	D	E	F	G
SALARIES & WAGES	$1,160.90	$18.00	$33.20	$33.65	$31.80	$66.40	$500.35	$477.50
FRINGE BENEFITS	$520.95	$8.45	$15.60	$15.05	$14.95	$31.20	$235.15	$200.55
SERVICES AND SUPPLIES	$143.80			$3.85	$11.15	$12.65	$41.55	$74.60
BUILDING OCCUPANCY	$55.70	$2.00	$0.60	$2.60	$1.40	$6.35	$32.85	$9.90
GENERAL SERVICES	$84.75			$2.55	$0.55		$21.15	$60.50
GENERAL OVERHEAD	$167.10	$2.40	$4.20	$4.90	$5.10	$9.90	$70.65	$69.95
DEPARTMENT OVERHEAD	$116.55	$0.45	$0.75	$1.50	$0.90	$1.75	$12.45	$98.75
SUPERVISION & INDIRECTS	$112.90			$6.95	$5.35			$100.60
FIXED ASSET REPLACEMENT	$18.15	$0.10	$0.30	$0.40	$0.55	$0.60	$5.75	$10.45
TOTAL	$2,380.80	$31.40	$54.65	$71.45	$71.75	$128.85	$919.90	$1,102.80

MSI SERVICE CENTER WORKSHEET FOR FEES AND CHARGES

SERVICE PROVIDED	CITY	REF.NO.
CONSTRUCTION REVIEW AND INSPECTION	**PASADENA**	S-051

SERVICES PRIMARILY PERFORMED BY	FUND	EXP.ACCT.
PBNS-Building Code Enforcement	General	350140

REVENUE RECEIVED [Actual - Potential]	FUND	REV.ACCT.
CONSTRUCTION PERMIT FEES	General	05-3240

REVENUE AUTHORIZATION		
Resolution 6761	DATE LAST REVISED:	6/30/92
	SUBSIDY RATIONALE:	None

DESCRIPTION OF SERVICE	REVENUE COLLECTION SCHEDULE:
Reviewing and inspecting building construction and remodeling to assure compliance with appropriate code requirements.	At time of application
	REVENUE COLLECTED BY:
	PBNS-Development Proc.
	UNIT OF SERVICE DESIGNATION:
	Permit

CURRENT FEE STRUCTURE   Based on valuation. Examples:

```
$     1 -    $500 - $ 17
$   501 - $2,000 - $ 17 1st $500 + $3.80 ea add'l $100 or fraction
$ 2,001 - $25,000 - $ 75 1st $2,000 + $12.00 ea add'l $1,000 or frac.
$ 25,001 - $50,000 - $349 1st $25,000 + $11.00 ea add'l $1,000 or fract.
$100,000 and over   - $931 1st $100,000 + $4.95 ea add'l $1,000 or
                            fraction
Sunday/Night Work   - $652
Processing Fee      - $ 22
Fees vary for plumbing, mechanical, electrical, solar and are charged
by fixtures, appliances, installations, etc.
```

FISCAL YEAR 1992-1993 REVENUE AND COST COMPARISON

TOTAL EST. REVENUE	:	$1,455,219	UNIT REVENUE	:	$164.49
TOTAL COST	:	$1,141,048	UNIT COST	:	$128.98
PROFIT (SUBSIDY)	:	$314,171	PROFIT (SUBSIDY)	:	$35.51
% of COST RECOVERED	:	127.5%	UNITS OF SERVICE	:	8,847

SUGGESTED % RECOVERY AND FEE STRUCTURE

  PERCENT: 100%   **SPECIAL CONDITIONS:** None

No change.

See text, Chapter V, page 120, for discussion

[T-037]

MSI SERVICE CENTER WORKSHEET FOR COST DETAIL

SERVICE PROVIDED						CITY		REF.NO.
Construction Review and Inspection						PASADENA		S–051
								TOTAL UNITS 8847

KEY	FILE	DEPARTMENT	DIVISION	SECTION	ACCOUNT	TYPE	UNITS
A	PBNSCODE	PBNS	Neighborhood Svcs	Code Compliance	350157	partial	208
B	FD_PREV	Fire	Prevention		259770	partial	2100
C	PBNSBDCE	PBNS	Building	Code Enforcement	350140		8847
D							
E							
F							
G							

EXPENSE TYPE	TOTAL	A	B	C	D	E	F	G
SALARIES & WAGES	$544,526	$20,784	$48,358	$475,384				
FRINGE BENEFITS	$234,263	$8,729	$26,839	$198,695				
SERVICES AND SUPPLIES	$37,007	$1,642	$1,039	$34,326				
BUILDING OCCUPANCY	$16,356	$462	$4,425	$11,469				
GENERAL SERVICES	$10,196	$1,375	$2,849	$5,972				
GENERAL OVERHEAD	$71,599	$2,804	$7,098	$61,697				
DEPARTMENT OVERHEAD	$95,654	$3,959	$4,593	$87,102				
SUPERVISION & INDIRECTS	$128,029	$5,864	$27,481	$94,684				
FIXED ASSET REPLACEMENT	$3,418	$429	$768	$2,221				
TOTAL	$1,141,048	$46,048	$123,450	$971,550				

EXPENSE TYPE	PER UNIT	A	B	C	D	E	F	G
SALARIES & WAGES	$61.55	$99.92	$23.03	$53.73				
FRINGE BENEFITS	$26.48	$41.97	$12.78	$22.46				
SERVICES AND SUPPLIES	$4.18	$7.89	$0.49	$3.88				
BUILDING OCCUPANCY	$1.85	$2.22	$2.11	$1.30				
GENERAL SERVICES	$1.15	$6.61	$1.36	$0.68				
GENERAL OVERHEAD	$8.09	$13.48	$3.38	$6.97				
DEPARTMENT OVERHEAD	$10.81	$19.03	$2.19	$9.85				
SUPERVISION & INDIRECTS	$14.47	$28.19	$13.09	$10.70				
FIXED ASSET REPLACEMENT	$0.39	$2.06	$0.37	$0.25				
TOTAL	$128.98	$221.38	$58.79	$109.82				

NOTE: "PER UNIT" column is based upon "TOTAL UNITS" and represents an average cost per total units.

(c) Management Services Institute, Inc., Anaheim, CA; March, 1990 & June, 1992

MSI SERVICE CENTER WORKSHEET FOR FEES AND CHARGES

SERVICE PROVIDED	CITY	REF.NO.
POLICE FALSE ALARM RESPONSE	**PASADENA**	S-082

SERVICES PRIMARILY PERFORMED BY	FUND	EXP.ACCT.
Police-Support	General	300129

REVENUE RECEIVED [Actual - Potential]	FUND	REV.ACCT.
POLICE FALSE ALARM RESPONSE CHARGES	General	05-4308

REVENUE AUTHORIZATION		
Resolution 6761	DATE LAST REVISED:	6/30/92
	SUBSIDY RATIONALE:	None

DESCRIPTION OF SERVICE	REVENUE COLLECTION SCHEDULE:
Responding to false alarms given by private alarm systems, and generating a list of false alarm activities each month to send to the Finance Department for billing.	Upon receipt of bill
	REVENUE COLLECTED BY:
	Finance-Municipal Services
	UNIT OF SERVICE DESIGNATION:
	Incident

CURRENT FEE STRUCTURE

Fourth and Subsequent False Alarms - $82 each

FISCAL YEAR 1992-1993 REVENUE AND COST COMPARISON

TOTAL EST. REVENUE	:	$176,554	UNIT REVENUE	:	$18.75
TOTAL COST	:	$1,069,384	UNIT COST	:	$113.60
PROFIT (SUBSIDY)	:	<$892,830>	PROFIT (SUBSIDY)	:	<$94.84>
% of COST RECOVERED	:	16.5%	UNITS OF SERVICE	:	9,414

SUGGESTED % RECOVERY AND FEE STRUCTURE

PERCENT: 100%   **SPECIAL CONDITIONS:** Market

In any 12-month period:
  Third false alarm   - $50
  Fourth false alarm   - $75
  Fifth false alarm   - $100
  Each additional false alarm - $500
    (without extenuating circumstances approved by Police Chief)

See text, Chapter V, page 126, for further discussion.

[T-072]

MSI SERVICE CENTER WORKSHEET FOR COST DETAIL

SERVICE PROVIDED					CITY	REF.NO.
Police False Alarm Response					PASADENA	S–082
						TOTAL UNITS 9414

KEY	FILE	DEPARTMENT	DIVISION	SECTION	ACCOUNT	TYPE	UNITS
A	FIN_SPRT	Finance	Financial Systems Support			partial	100
B	FIN_SVCS	Finance	Financial Services		259507		9414
C	PD_SUPPT	Police	Support Services	Support Operations	300129		9414
D	PD_HELI	Police	Field Services	Helicopter Patrol	300111	response	7531
E	PD_PAT	Police	Field Services	N.C.T.F.	300137		9414
F							
G							

EXPENSE TYPE	TOTAL	A	B	C	D	E	F	G
SALARIES & WAGES	$418,729	$3,946	$14,602	$33,386	$77,077	$289,818		
FRINGE BENEFITS	$249,169	$1,654	$6,170	$19,740	$46,555	$175,050		
SERVICES AND SUPPLIES	$68,092	$8,932	$1,394	$6,068	$50,528	$3,170		
BUILDING OCCUPANCY	$15,078	$59	$736	$4,872	$3,023	$6,386		
GENERAL SERVICES	$82,553	$1,938	$3,989	$3,879	$13,525	$59,222		
GENERAL OVERHEAD	$70,857	$1,226	$2,286	$5,775	$16,210	$45,360		
DEPARTMENT OVERHEAD	$73,884			$6,319	$17,736	$49,829		
SUPERVISION & INDIRECTS	$76,177		$5,516	$5,289	$24,255	$41,117		
FIXED ASSET REPLACEMENT	$15,045	$189	$494	$239	$12,854	$1,269		
TOTAL	$1,069,384	$15,844	$35,189	$85,567	$261,783	$671,021		

EXPENSE TYPE	PER UNIT	A	B	C	D	E	F	G
SALARIES & WAGES	$44.48	$39.46	$1.55	$3.55	$10.23	$30.79		
FRINGE BENEFITS	$26.47	$16.54	$0.66	$2.10	$6.18	$18.59		
SERVICES AND SUPPLIES	$7.23	$89.32	$0.15	$0.64	$6.71	$0.34		
BUILDING OCCUPANCY	$1.60	$0.59	$0.08	$0.52	$0.40	$0.68		
GENERAL SERVICES	$8.77	$19.38	$0.42	$0.41	$1.80	$6.29		
GENERAL OVERHEAD	$7.53	$12.26	$0.24	$0.61	$2.15	$4.82		
DEPARTMENT OVERHEAD	$7.83			$0.67	$2.38	$5.27		
SUPERVISION & INDIRECTS	$8.09		$0.59	$0.56	$3.22	$4.37		
FIXED ASSET REPLACEMENT	$1.60	$1.89	$0.05	$0.03	$1.71	$0.13		
TOTAL	$113.60	$156.44	$3.74	$9.09	$34.76	$71.28		

NOTE: "PER UNIT" column is based upon "TOTAL UNITS" and represents an average cost per total units.

MSI SERVICE CENTER WORKSHEET FOR FEES AND CHARGES

SERVICE PROVIDED	CITY	REF.NO.
TOURNAMENT OF ROSES SUPPORT	**PASADENA**	S-152

SERVICES PRIMARILY PERFORMED BY	FUND	EXP.ACCT.
Various	Various	Various

REVENUE RECEIVED [Actual - Potential]	FUND	REV.ACCT.
TOURNAMENT OF ROSES SUPPORT FEES	Rose Bowl	44-3380, 3390

REVENUE AUTHORIZATION		
Services Contract 12,195	DATE LAST REVISED:	12/11/84
	SUBSIDY RATIONALE:	None

DESCRIPTION OF SERVICE	REVENUE COLLECTION SCHEDULE:
Meeting with Tournament of Roses to plan and coordinate various support services prior to, during and after the Tournament of Roses Parade and Rose Bowl game.	Various
	REVENUE COLLECTED BY:
	Finance
	UNIT OF SERVICE DESIGNATION:
	Estimated Attendance

CURRENT FEE STRUCTURE

Revenue collected by the City consists of:

Grand Stand Seat Tax	- $173,937
Grand Stand Permits	- $ 20,935
Miscellaneous Licenses and Permits	- $ 20,935
Various Concessions	- $117,142
Admissions Tax	- $ 77,383
RV Overnight Parking	- $ 34,240
Miscellaneous "Billable Costs"	- $ 27,872

These revenues are combined with revenues collected by the Tournament of Roses & "distributed" to the City and the Tournament Ass'n resulting in:
Payment from Tournament of Roses Association - $787,577

FISCAL YEAR 1992-1993 REVENUE AND COST COMPARISON

TOTAL EST. REVENUE	:	$787,577	UNIT REVENUE	:	$0.79
TOTAL COST	:	$1,255,945	UNIT COST	:	$1.26
PROFIT (SUBSIDY)	:	<$468,368>	PROFIT (SUBSIDY)	:	<$0.47>
% of COST RECOVERED	:	62.7%	UNITS OF SERVICE	:	1,000,000

SUGGESTED % RECOVERY AND FEE STRUCTURE

PERCENT: 100%   **SPECIAL CONDITIONS:** Contract

See text, Chapter V, page 151, for discussion.

[T-198]

MSI SERVICE CENTER WORKSHEET FOR COST DETAIL

SERVICE PROVIDED: Tournament of Roses Support

CITY OF: PASADENA

REF.NO. S-152.1

UNITS: 1000000

KEY	FILE	DEPT	DIVISION	SECTION	ACCOUNT	TYPE	UNITS
A	P_TESTER	Water/Pow	Power	Power Dist	269911	parade	
B	TRNS_PLN	Public Wor	Transport'n	Invest'N/Plan	269911	parade	
C	FD.MGMT	Fire	Management		269788	parade	
D	P_TESTER	Water/Pow	Power	Power Dist		parade	
E	REC.WEST	Recreation	Rec Facilities	West Area	405241	parade	
F	P_TRBLST	Water/Pow	Power	Power Dist		parade	
G	TRNS_ADM	Public Wor	Transport'n		460410	parade	

KEY	FILE	DEPT	DIVISION	SECTION	ACCOUNT	TYPE	UNITS
H	ENG_SVCS	Public Works	Engineering	Eng Svcs	480461	parade	
I	P_TESTER	Water/Power	Power	Power Dist		parade	
J	P_UNDGRD	Water/Power	Power	Distribution		parade	
K	P_TRBLST	Water/Power	Power	Power Dist		parade	
L	PD_JAIL	Police	Support Svcs	Jail	300210	parade	
M	RADIO	General Svcs	Comp & Com	Radio	500216	parade	

EXPENSE TYPE	TOTAL	A	B	C	D	E	F	G	H	I	J	K	L	M
SALARIES & WAGES	$457,375	$58	$189	$268	$464	$295	$749	$748	$1,147	$750	$810	$943	$704	$667
FRINGE BENEFITS	$228,441	$28	$76	$149	$207	$128	$335	$351	$31	$335	$582	$422	$411	$344
SERVICE & SUPPLIES	$163,413	$8	$58	$37	$80	$233	$43	$26	$96	$98	$94	$105	$218	$196
BUILDING OCCUPANCY	$31,770	$1	$7	$55	$8		$1	$41	$75	$13	$1	$1	$219	$6
GENERAL SERVICES	$115,569	$5	$3	$17	$40	$214	$55	$74	$46	$65	$62	$69	$97	
GENERAL OVERHEAD	$94,463	$8	$28	$45	$66	$73	$104	$105	$119	$107	$113	$131	$140	$103
DEPARTMENT OVERHEAD	$43,293	$3	$5	$29	$20	$177	$32	$19	$21	$33	$35	$40	$163	$44
SUPERVISION & INDIRECTS	$122,880	$12	$27	$22	$94	$104	$66	$111	$182	$152	$105	$71	$217	$76
FIXED ASSET REPLACEMENT	$9,496		$3		$1	$17	$2	$11	$13	$2	$2	$2	$16	$774
FACILITY MAINT & REPL	$2,236													
TOTAL	$1,255,945	$121	$361	$622	$960	$1,291	$1,417	$1,463	$1,549	$1,555	$1,584	$1,764	$2,176	$2,209

EXPENSE TYPE	PER UNIT	A	B	C	D	E	F	G	H	I	J	K	L	M
SALARIES & WAGES	$0.46													
FRINGE BENEFITS	$0.23													
SERVICE & SUPPLIES	$0.16													
BUILDING OCCUPANCY	$0.03													
GENERAL SERVICES	$0.12													
GENERAL OVERHEAD	$0.08													
DEPARTMENT OVERHEAD	$0.04													
SUPERVISION & INDIRECTS	$0.12													
FIXED ASSET REPLACEMENT	$0.01													
FACILITY MAINT & REPL														
TOTAL BY UNIT	$1.28													

NOTE: "PER UNIT" column is based upon "TOTAL UNITS" and represents an average cost per total units.
(c) Management Services Institu... Inc., Anaheim, CA; March, 1990 & June, 1992

MSI SERVICE CENTER WORKSHEET FOR COST DETAIL

CITY OF **PASADENA**   REF. NO. **S-152.2**   UNITS **1000000**

SERVICE PROVIDED: **Tournament of Roses Support**

KEY	FILE	DEPT	DIVISION	SECTION	ACCOUNT	TYPE	UNITS
A	DES_PRK	Public Works	Engineering	Design Eng	480362	gens	
B	PK.ENRN	Public Health	Env Health		498216	gens	
C	RADIO	General Svcs	Comp & Com	Radio	498216	gens	
D	FD.EMS	Fire	EMS		420408	gens	
E	PD.EMS	Police	Field Service	Traffic	260217	gens	
F	PD.TRRF	Police	Field Service	Traffic	260111	gens	
G	FD.MGMT	Fire	Management	Helicopter	268748	gens	

KEY	FILE	DEPT	DIVISION	SECTION	ACCOUNT	TYPE	UNITS
H	FD_PREV	Fire	Prevention		268779	gens	
I	ENG_BVDS	Public Works	Engineering	Eng Bus	480451	gens	
J	GOLF	Arroyo Seco	Golf Course		405014	gens	
K	pk_rwcom	Public Works	Solid Waste	Commercial		gens	
L	P_OVERHD	Water/Power	Power	Power Dist	808312	gens	
M	FLT_MTE	General Svcs	Flt Mte			gens	

EXPENSE TYPE	TOTAL	A	B	C	D	E	F	G	H	I	J	K	L	M
SALARIES & WAGES		$188	$215	$372	$557	$470	$439	$663	$453	$1,790	$646	$737	$1,663	$1,224
FRINGE BENEFITS		$66	$83	$192	$209	$240	$227	$279	$582	$248	$646	$434	$826	$632
SERVICE & SUPPLIES		$21	$13	$106	$452	$111	$201	$84	$14	$148	$1,534	$1,467	$202	$1,061
BUILDING OCCUPANCY		$21	$9	$3	$43	$11	$18	$138	$90	$118		$12	$2	$81
GENERAL SERVICES		$25	$13	$57	$117	$47	$51	$343	$36		$113	$422	$134	
GENERAL OVERHEAD		$25	$30	$57	$92	$96	$96	$114	$96	$74	$207	$265	$267	$259
DEPARTMENT OVERHEAD		$4	$52	$24	$59	$105	$105	$74	$82	$179	$549	$75	$109	
SUPERVISION & INDIRECTS			$18	$42	$29	$69	$143		$371	$31	$227	$227	$224	$276
FIXED ASSET REPLACEMENT*		$1	$4	$432	$11	$7	$77	$66	$10	$26		$66	$4	$66
FACILITY MAINT & REPL														
TOTAL		$229	$505	$1,231	$1,269	$1,405	$1,561	$1,661	$1,685	$2,326	$2,447	$2,562	$2,462	$2,618

EXPENSE TYPE	PER UNIT	A	B	C	D	E	F	G	H	I	J	K	L	M
SALARIES & WAGES														
FRINGE BENEFITS														
SERVICE & SUPPLIES														
BUILDING OCCUPANCY														
GENERAL SERVICES														
GENERAL OVERHEAD														
DEPARTMENT OVERHEAD														
SUPERVISION & INDIRECTS														
FIXED ASSET REPLACEMENT														
FACILITY MAINT & REPL														
TOTAL BY UNIT														

NOTE: "PER UNIT" column is based upon "TOTAL UNITS" and represents an average cost per total units.

(c) Management Services Institute, Inc., Anaheim, CA, March, 1990 & June, 1992

MSI SERVICE CENTER WORKSHEET FOR COST DETAIL

SERVICE PROVIDED: Tournament of Roses Support
CITY OF: PASADENA
REF. NO.: S-152.2
UNITS: 1000000

Identification

KEY	DEPT	FILE	DIVISION	SECTION	ACCOUNT	TYPE	UNITS
N	Wtr/Power	W. MTSHOP	Water	Const & Prod	320002	game	
O	FD	FD_OPS	Operations	Community S	300194	game	
P	Po	PD_COMSV	Staff Svcs	Build Mte	600074	game	
Q	Ga	BUILD MTE	Build Sys	Code Comp	350157	game	
R	PB	PBMSCODE	Neigh Svcs	Detectives	300145	game	
S	Po	PD_INV	Investigative	Detectives	300137	game	
T	Po	PD_PAT	Field Services	N.C.T.F.		game	

KEY	FILE	DEPT	DIVISION	SECTION	ACCOUNT	TYPE	UNITS
U	BOWL_OPS	Rose Bowl	Operations		256872	game	
V							
W							
X							
Y							
Z							

Cost Detail

EXPENSE TYPE	TOTAL	N	O	P	Q	R	S	T	U	V	W	X	Y	Z
SALARIES & WAGES		$2,622	$3,373	$4,232	$7,555	$8,611	$12,787	$13,958	$44,837					
FRINGE BENEFITS		$1,281	$1,872	$2,471	$2,366	$3,700	$7,629	$6,407	$20,042					
SERVICE & SUPPLIES		$1,096	$592	$647	$4,155	$696	$189	$153	$82,786					
BUILDING OCCUPANC			$120	$437	$561	$196	$1,119	$306						
GENERAL SERVICES		$326	$488	$723		$663	$1,129	$2,692	$25,234					
GENERAL OVERHEAD		$489	$694	$719	$1,285	$1,199	$1,942	$2,193	$12,278					
DEPARTMENT OVERHE		$144	$326	$787	$546	$1,678	$2,125	$2,338						
SUPERVISION & INDIRE		$741	$243	$4,337	$1,648	$2,488	$1,020	$1,976						
FIXED ASSET REPLACE		$9	$70	$434	$95	$182	$679	$61	$858					
FACILITY MAINT & REP														
TOTAL		$9,888	$7,058	$14,737	$14,688	$16,521	$26,693	$32,288	$104,318					

EXPENSE TYPE	PER UNIT	N	O	P	Q	R	S	T	U	V	W	X	Y	Z
SALARIES & WAGES														
FRINGE BENEFITS														
SERVICE & SUPPLIES														
BUILDING OCCUPANC														
GENERAL SERVICES														
GENERAL OVERHEAD														
DEPARTMENT OVERHE														
SUPERVISION & INDIRE														
FIXED ASSET REPLACE														
FACILITY MAINT & REP														
TOTAL BY UNIT														

NOTE: "PER UNIT" column is based upon "TOTAL UNITS" and represents an average cost per total units.
(c) Management Services Institute, Inc., Anaheim, CA; March, 1990 & June, 1992

MSI SERVICE CENTER WORKSHEET FOR FEES AND CHARGES

SERVICE PROVIDED	CITY	REF.NO.
WATER SERVICE	**PASADENA**	S-179

SERVICES PRIMARILY PERFORMED BY	FUND	EXP.ACCT.
WP-Water	Water	250720

REVENUE RECEIVED [Actual - Potential]	FUND	REV.ACCT.
WATER SERVICE FEES	Water	41-5070, 5090

REVENUE AUTHORIZATION		
Resolution 6308	DATE LAST REVISED:	02/90
	SUBSIDY RATIONALE:	None

DESCRIPTION OF SERVICE	REVENUE COLLECTION SCHEDULE:
Providing water service to consumers.	Monthly
	REVENUE COLLECTED BY:
	Finance
	UNIT OF SERVICE DESIGNATION:
	Customer

CURRENT FEE STRUCTURE

```
Inside City:   5/8" & 3/4" - $   5.32 standby svc + $.407 1st 15,000 cf
               5/8" & 3/4" - $   5.32 standby svc + $.549 all other cf
               1"          - $  10.11 standby svc + $.407 1st 15,000 cf
               4"          - $180.90 standby svc + $.407 1st 400,000 cf
               6"          - $276.68 standby svc + $.407 1st 400,000 cf
Outside City:  5/8" & 3/4" - $   7.18 standby svc + $.872 1st 15,000 cf
               1"          - $  13.65 standby svc + $.872 1st 15,000 cf
```

FISCAL YEAR 1992-1993 REVENUE AND COST COMPARISON				
TOTAL EST. REVENUE	:	$19,126,816	UNIT REVENUE :	$527.87
TOTAL COST	:	$22,875,219	UNIT COST :	$631.32
PROFIT (SUBSIDY)	:	<$3,748,403>	PROFIT (SUBSIDY) :	<$103.45>
% of COST RECOVERED	:	83.6%	UNITS OF SERVICE :	36,234

SUGGESTED % RECOVERY AND FEE STRUCTURE

PERCENT: 100%   **SPECIAL CONDITIONS:** None

Refer to text, Chapter V page 148, for further discussion.

Note that to the extent other "special" Water services (Identified in cost centers S-180 through S-193) are not recovered by user fees, these rates must be increased. The Total Cost above DOES NOT include costs of other "special" services.

[W-001]

MSI SERVICE CENTER WORKSHEET FOR COST DETAIL

SERVICE PROVIDED: Water Service
CITY OF: PASADENA
REF. NO.: S-179
UNITS: 36234

KEY	FILE	DEPT	DIVISION	SECTION	TYPE	UNITS
A	MUNI_ADM	Finance	Muni Svce	Administration		36234
B	MUNI_CSH	Finance	Muni Svce	Cash/Credit		36234
C	WP-METER	Water/Pow	Business Ops	Meter Rdng		36234
D	WP-METER	Water/Pow	Business Ops	Meter Rdng	customer svc	36234
E	MUNI_ADM	Finance	Muni Svce	Administration		36234
F	W_ENGDS	Water/Pow	Water	Engineering		36234
G	MUNI_CSH	Finance	Muni Svce	Cash/Credit		36234

KEY	FILE	DEPT	DIVISION	SECTION	ACCOUNT	TYPE	UNITS
H	WP-METER	Water/Pow	Business Ops	Meter Rdng		meter reads	36234
I	MUNI_UTL	Finance	Muni Svce	Utility Billing			36234
J	FIN_TRSY	Finance	Treasury				36234
K	FIN_ACCT	Finance	Acct & Anlys				36234
L	WP-CSTMR	Water/Pow	Business Ops	Cost Svc			36234
M	W_FIRE	Water/Pow	Water	Const & Prod			36234

Notes on "OTHER COSTS": ( ) Bond Interest, (T) Street Costs, (X) Transfer to the General Fund, (Y) Purchased Water($6,367,880)+Infrastructure Replacement($7,183,506).

EXPENSE TYPE	TOTAL	A	B	C	D	E	F	G	H	I	J	K	L	M
SALARIES & WAGES	$2,616,649	$1,434	$3,371	$4,113	$9,201	$8,692	$13,760	$16,728	$17,723	$10,560	$31,047	$85,457	$36,034	$99,293
FRINGE BENEFITS	$1,193,888	$617	$1,450	$1,887	$4,177	$2,678	$6,247	$6,763	$8,046	$4,541	$13,737	$31,499	$16,359	$45,079
SERVICE & SUPPLIES	$1,166,505	$187	$442	$934	$2,089	$873	$5,332	$2,083	$4,023	$31,852	$10,248	$8,750	$61,223	$32,479
BUILDING OCCUPANCY	$58,874	$45	$136	$40	$90	$208	$1,154	$638	$174	$433	$1,397	$2,243	$3,710	
GENERAL SERVICES	$320,718	$2,841	$39	$787	$1,760	$13,259	$1,584	$183	$3,389	$248	$911	$16,457	$8,891	$11,654
GENERAL OVERHEAD	$456,161	$436	$462	$858	$1,472	$2,032	$2,387	$2,187	$2,635	$4,088	$4,950	$10,747	$9,708	$16,014
DEPARTMENT OVERHEAD	$126,124			$201	$450		$730		$857				$2,970	$4,899
SUPERVISION & INDIRECTS	$711,822	$738	$1,874	$1,390	$3,110	$3,445	$3,276	$7,811	$5,991	$8,743			$39,636	$26,299
FIXED ASSET REPLACEMENT	$27,371	$34	$118	$87	$160	$167	$247	$550	$288	$405	$434	$1,230	$2,380	$336
OTHER COSTS	$16,187,009													
TOTAL	$22,875,219	$6,332	$7,892	$10,057	$22,499	$29,544	$34,718	$35,691	$43,336	$61,078	$64,024	$136,413	$168,911	$234,955

EXPENSE TYPE	PER UNIT	A	B	C	D	E	F	G	H	I	J	K	L	M
SALARIES & WAGES	$72.22	$0.04	$0.09	$0.11	$0.25	$0.18	$0.38	$0.43	$0.49	$0.29	$0.86	$1.81	$0.99	$2.74
FRINGE BENEFITS	$32.95	$0.02	$0.04	$0.06	$0.12	$0.08	$0.17	$0.19	$0.22	$0.13	$0.38	$0.87	$0.45	$1.24
SERVICE & SUPPLIES	$32.19	$0.01	$0.01	$0.03	$0.06	$0.02	$0.15	$0.06	$0.11	$0.88	$0.28	$0.24	$1.41	$0.90
BUILDING OCCUPANCY	$1.90					$0.01	$0.03	$0.02		$0.02	$0.04	$0.06	$0.10	
GENERAL SERVICES	$8.85	$0.08		$0.02	$0.05	$0.37	$0.04	$0.01	$0.09	$0.01	$0.03	$0.06	$0.10	$0.32
GENERAL OVERHEAD	$12.59	$0.01	$0.01	$0.02	$0.04	$0.06	$0.07	$0.06	$0.08	$0.11	$0.14	$0.51	$0.19	$0.44
DEPARTMENT OVERHEAD	$3.48			$0.01	$0.01		$0.02		$0.02				$0.08	$0.14
SUPERVISION & INDIRECTS	$19.65	$0.02	$0.05	$0.04	$0.09	$0.10	$0.09	$0.22	$0.17	$0.24			$1.09	$0.70
FIXED ASSET REPLACEMENT	$0.76						$0.01	$0.02	$0.01	$0.01	$0.02	$0.03	$0.07	$0.01
OTHER COSTS	$446.74													
TOTAL BY UNIT	$631.32	$0.17	$0.21	$0.28	$0.62	$0.82	$0.96	$0.99	$1.20	$1.69	$1.77	$3.62	$4.66	$5.45

NOTE: "PER UNIT" column is t[...] based upon "TOTAL UNITS" and represents an average cost per total units.
(c) Management Services Institu[te], Inc., Anaheim, CA; March, 1990 & June, 1992

MSI SERVICE CENTER WORKSHEET FOR COST DETAIL

SERVICE PROVIDED: Water Service

CITY OF	REF NO.
PASADENA	S-179
	UNITS 36234

KEY	FILE	DEPT	DIVISION	SECTION	ACCOUNT	TYPE	UNITS
N	MUN.UTL	Finance	Municipal Ser	Utility Billing			
O	W.PLANT	Water/Power	Water	Const & Prod			36234
P	W.OPER	Water/Power	Water	Const & Prod			36234
Q	W.ENGDS	Water/Power	Water	Engineering			36234
R	W.ENGPF	Water/Power	Water	Engineering			36234
S	W.SERVC	Water/Power	Water				
T	ST_COSTS	Public Works	Street Const	Const & Prod	Interest		36234

KEY	FILE	DEPT	DIVISION	SECTION	ACCOUNT	TYPE	UNITS
U	W_MAIN	Water/Power	Water	Const & Prod			36234
V	W_ENG03	Water/Power	Engineering	Const & Prod			36234
W	W_MTSHOP	Water/Power	Water	Engineering			36234
X	W_ENGPF	Water/Power	Water	Engineering	transfer		36234
Y	W_ENGPF	Water/Power	Water	Engineering	Infra & watr		36234
Z							

Notes on "OTHER COSTS": (R) Bond Interest, (T) Street Costs, (X) Transfer to the General Fund, (Y) Purchased Water($6,397,880)+Infrastructure Replacement($7,163,508).

EXPENSE TYPE	TOTAL	N	O	P	Q	R	S	T	U	V	W	X	Y	Z
		UNITS	UNITS											UNITS
SALARIES & WAGES		$49,278	$151,638	$184,100	$280,608	$332,997	$161,181		$342,085	$332,224	$429,165		$218,445	
FRINGE BENEFITS		$21,189	$66,796	$83,561	$115,544				$148,098	$167,773	$194,936		$99,628	
SERVICE & SUPPLIES		$148,732	$58,527	$71,487	$100,939	$129,289			$132,451	$122,520	$196,587		$85,188	
BUILDING OCCUPANCY		$2,952			$21,838				$14,098				$19,620	
GENERAL SERVICES		$1,150	$17,478	$21,233	$29,990	$30,406	$33,406		$39,352	$36,402	$49,494		$25,310	
GENERAL OVERHEAD		$18,980	$25,214	$30,632	$44,949	$55,408			$65,267	$57,206	$71,608		$38,173	
DEPARTMENT OVERHEAD			$7,713	$9,376	$13,749	$16,948			$17,211	$17,496	$21,842		$11,676	
SUPERVISION & INDIRECTS		$40,793	$39,833	$43,392	$61,683	$67,530			$88,888	$75,603	$112,804		$52,384	
FIXED ASSET REPLACEMENT		$1,889	$462	$580	$4,676		$1,208		$1,290	$6,300	$1,440		$3,730	
OTHER COSTS						$687,235		$413,000				$1,135,388	$13,551,388	
TOTAL		$264,961	$569,663	$449,355	$653,874	$687,235	$812,945	$413,000	$925,622	$831,524	$1,047,554	$1,135,388	$14,106,440	

EXPENSE TYPE	PER UNIT	N	O	P	Q	R	S	T	U	V	W	X	Y	Z
SALARIES & WAGES		$1.36	$4.18	$5.08	$7.19		$9.19		$9.44	$9.17	$11.84		$6.06	
FRINGE BENEFITS		$0.58	$1.90	$2.31	$3.18		$4.17		$4.09	$4.63	$5.38		$2.76	
SERVICE & SUPPLIES		$4.10	$1.62	$1.97	$2.79		$3.57		$3.66	$3.38	$4.60		$2.35	
BUILDING OCCUPANCY		$0.08			$0.60				$0.39				$0.54	
GENERAL SERVICES		$0.03	$0.48	$0.59	$0.83		$1.08		$1.09	$1.00	$1.37		$0.70	
GENERAL OVERHEAD		$0.52	$0.70	$0.85	$1.24		$1.53		$1.55	$1.58	$1.97		$1.05	
DEPARTMENT OVERHEAD			$0.21	$0.26	$0.38		$0.47		$0.47	$0.48	$0.60		$0.32	
SUPERVISION & INDIRECTS		$1.13	$1.10	$1.34	$1.70		$2.42		$2.45	$2.17	$3.11		$1.45	
FIXED ASSET REPLACEMENT		$0.05	$0.01	$0.02	$0.13		$0.03		$0.04	$0.15	$0.04		$0.10	
OTHER COSTS						$16.97		$22.44				$31.33	$374.00	
TOTAL BY UNIT		$7.85	$10.21	$12.40	$18.05	$16.97	$22.44	$22.44	$23.79	$22.95	$28.91	$31.33	$389.32	

NOTE: "PER UNIT" column is based upon "TOTAL UNITS" and represents an average cost per total units.

(c) Management Services Institute, inc., Anaheim, CA, March, 1990 & June, 1992

MSI SERVICE CENTER WORKSHEET FOR COST DETAIL

SERVICE PROVIDED						CITY	REF.NO.
Patrol Services						PASADENA	S-248

TOTAL UNITS
96662

KEY	FILE	DEPARTMENT	DIVISION	SECTION	ACCOUNT	TYPE	UNITS
A	PD_HELI	Police	Field Services	Helicopter Patrol	300111	flight hours	
B	PD_TRAFF	Police	Field Services	Traffic	300277		
C	PD_NCTF	Police	Field Services	N.C.T.F.	300238	hours	
D	PD_SUPPT	Police	Support Services	Support Operations	300129	service call	
E	PD_PAT	Police	Field Services	N.C.T.F.	300137	service call	
F							
G							

EXPENSE TYPE	TOTAL	A	B	C	D	E	F	G
SALARIES & WAGES	$7,427,968	$447,185	$728,882	$806,217	$712,837	$4,732,867		
FRINGE BENEFITS	$4,196,273	$261,655	$433,827	$448,585	$393,008	$2,659,198		
SERVICES AND SUPPLIES	$480,661	$293,140	$241	$4,740	$129,568	$52,972		
BUILDING OCCUPANCY	$257,699	$17,536	$11,491	$16,303	$104,020	$108,349		
GENERAL SERVICES	$1,185,180	$78,466	$51,150	$5,623	$82,815	$967,126		
GENERAL OVERHEAD	$1,151,562	$93,327	$104,175	$108,925	$120,891	$724,244		
DEPARTMENT OVERHEAD	$1,259,944	$102,110	$113,980	$119,177	$132,269	$792,408		
SUPERVISION & INDIRECTS	$1,058,526	$139,838	$68,711	$82,948	$110,716	$856,513		
FIXED ASSET REPLACEMENT	$117,799	$74,571	$7,623	$9,775	$5,104	$20,726		
TOTAL	$17,135,612	$1,507,608	$1,520,080	$1,602,293	$1,791,228	$10,714,403		

EXPENSE TYPE	PER UNIT	A	B	C	D	E	F	G
SALARIES & WAGES	$76.84							
FRINGE BENEFITS	$43.41							
SERVICES AND SUPPLIES	$4.97							
BUILDING OCCUPANCY	$2.67							
GENERAL SERVICES	$12.26							
GENERAL OVERHEAD	$11.91							
DEPARTMENT OVERHEAD	$13.03							
FIXED ASSET REPLACEMENT	$1.22							
TOTAL	$177.27							

NOTE: "PER UNIT" column is based upon "TOTAL UNITS" and represents an average cost per total units.

(c) Management Services Institute, Inc., Anaheim, CA; March,1990 & June,1992

MSI GENERAL BENEFIT CENTER WORKSHEET

SERVICE PROVIDED	CITY	REF.NO.
CRIMINAL INVESTIGATION & ANALYSIS	**PASADENA**	S-249

SERVICES PRIMARILY PERFORMED BY	FUND	EXP.ACCT.
POLICE-Detectives	General	Various

DISCUSSION OF SERVICE

This service center compiles the costs of completing investigations and following-up investigations of reported criminal offenses. This includes:

- Identifying suspects

- Taking suspects into custody

- Seeking complaints and/or warrants against suspects

- Securing search warrants

- Gathering, analyzing, and processing physical evidence

- Interviewing suspects, witnesses, and victims of crimes

- Coordinating courtroom prosecutions

- Processing subpoenas

- Locating, identifying, storing, and returning property and evidence

- Processing impounded vehicles

- Processing, analyzing, and storing latent fingerprints for suspect identification

[T-334]

MSI SERVICE CENTER WORKSHEET FOR COST DETAIL

SERVICE PROVIDED					CITY	REF.NO.
Criminal Investigation & Analysis					PASADENA	S-249
						TOTAL UNITS 13232

KEY	FILE	DEPARTMENT	DIVISION	SECTION	ACCOUNT	TYPE	UNITS
A	PD_PHOTO	Police	Support Services	Photo Lab	300228		
B	PD_SPINV	Police	Investigative	Special Investigations	300152	vice	
C	PD_TRAFF	Police	Field Services	Traffic	300277		
D	PD_R&D	Police	Research & Dev		300293		
E	PD_SUPPT	Police	Support Services	Support Operations	300129	reprtd offns	
F	PD_SPINV	Police	Investigative	Special Investigations	300152	narcotics	
G	PD_INV	Police	Investigative	Detectives	300145		

EXPENSE TYPE	TOTAL	A	B	C	D	E	F	G
SALARIES & WAGES	$2,137,604	$1,653	$43,054	$56,741	$97,669	$227,503	$363,599	$1,347,385
FRINGE BENEFITS	$1,186,426	$965	$22,944	$34,272	$58,309	$125,719	$192,065	$752,152
SERVICES AND SUPPLIES	$133,354	$1,547	$4,013	$19	$30,529	$41,352	$36,028	$19,866
BUILDING OCCUPANCY	$169,548	$1,079	$1,585	$895	$1,449	$33,198	$13,387	$117,955
GENERAL SERVICES	$178,478	$425	$3,088	$3,982	$94	$26,431	$26,075	$118,383
GENERAL OVERHEAD	$323,459	$482	$6,348	$8,152	$15,984	$38,607	$53,648	$200,238
DEPARTMENT OVERHEAD	$353,904	$527	$6,946	$8,920	$17,489	$42,241	$58,697	$219,084
SUPERVISION & INDIRECTS	$328,270	$747	$18,954	$5,377	$4,573	$35,358	$160,182	$103,079
FIXED ASSET REPLACEMENT	$122,633	$862	$5,079	$593		$1,829	$42,889	$71,581
TOTAL	$4,933,676	$8,287	$112,011	$118,951	$226,096	$572,038	$946,570	$2,949,723

EXPENSE TYPE	PER UNIT	A	B	C	D	E	F	G
SALARIES & WAGES	$161.55							
FRINGE BENEFITS	$89.66							
SERVICES AND SUPPLIES	$10.08							
BUILDING OCCUPANCY	$12.81							
GENERAL SERVICES	$13.49							
GENERAL OVERHEAD	$24.45							
DEPARTMENT OVERHEAD	$26.75							
SUPERVISION & INDIRECTS	$24.81							
FIXED ASSET REPLACEMENT	$9.27							
TOTAL	$372.86							

NOTE: "PER UNIT" column is based upon "TOTAL UNITS" and represents an average cost per total units.

(c) Management Services Institute, Inc., Anaheim, CA; March,1990 & June,1992

```
┌─────────────────────────────────────────────────────────────────────────┐
│              MSI GENERAL BENEFIT CENTER WORKSHEET                         │
├──────────────────────────────────────┬─────────────┬────────────────────┤
│ SERVICE PROVIDED                     │ CITY        │ REF.NO.            │
│ LIBRARY SERVICES & SPECIAL PROGRAMS  │ PASADENA    │   S-257            │
├──────────────────────────────────────┼─────────────┼────────────────────┤
│ SERVICES PRIMARILY PERFORMED BY      │ FUND        │ EXP.ACCT.          │
│  Information Services                │ General     │                    │
├──────────────────────────────────────┴─────────────┴────────────────────┤
│ DISCUSSION OF SERVICE                                                    │
└─────────────────────────────────────────────────────────────────────────┘
```

DISCUSSION OF SERVICE

The cost of providing general library services to City of Pasadena and surrounding communities is shown on the facing page.   Services include

- Children's library services

- Adult library services

- Reference services

- Communicating with the community through the "In the Know" newsletter

- Tax form availability

- Literacy services

- Maintaining the Pasadena library collection

[T-359

MSI SERVICE CENTER WORKSHEET FOR COST DETAIL

SERVICE PROVIDED: Library Services & Special Program

CITY OF: PASADENA   **REF.NO.:** S-257   **UNITS:** 131000

KEY	FILE	DEPT	DIVISION	SECTION	ACCOUNT	TYPE	UNITS
A	REF_SVC	Info Svcs	Ref Svcs		402024		
B	SUPT_SVC	Info Svcs	Support Svcs		402032		
C	LIBR_ADM	Info Svcs	Administration		402008		
D	PBLC_SVC	Info Svcs	Public Service		402016		
E	FIN_SPRT	Finance	Financial Systems Support			document	
F	REF_SVC	Info Svcs	Ref Svcs		402024		
G	LIBR_ADM	Info Svcs	Administration		402008		

KEY	FILE	DEPT	DIVISION	SECTION	ACCOUNT	TYPE	UNITS
H	LIBR_ADM	Info Svcs	Administration		402008		
I	PBLC_SVC	Info Svcs	Public Svcs		402016		
J	REF_SVC	Info Svcs	Ref Svcs		402024		
K	PBLC_SVC	Info Svcs	Public Svcs		402016		
L	REF_SVC	Info Svcs	Ref Svcs		402024		
M	PBLC_SVC	Info Svcs	Public Svcs		402016		

EXPENSE TYPE	TOTAL	A	B	C	D	E	F	G	H	I	J	K	L	M
SALARIES & WAGES	$2,651,709	$615	$624	$1,560	$3,174	$2,436	$8,130	$5,909	$56,150	$142,386	$288,994	$206,183	$806,373	$418,980
FRINGE BENEFITS	$950,498	$360	$264	$668	$1,292	$1,047	$2,495	$2,405	$22,883	$67,952	$99,273	$100,037	$219,067	$147,957
SERVICE & SUPPLIES	$361,100	$40	$122	$646	$178	$4,581	$401	$2,259	$21,408	$7,964	$17,557	$117,158	$120,885	$23,381
BUILDING OCCUPANCY	$802,618	$168	$56	$534	$1,733	$37	$1,871	$1,169	$11,104	$77,795	$573,291	$167,190	$186,221	$227,996
GENERAL SERVICES	$510,612	$77	$42	$1,021	$1,108	$1,227	$771	$3,670	$33,818	$49,716	$53,618	$106,690	$978,238	$145,535
GENERAL OVERHEAD	$451,048	$98	$93	$372	$898	$777	$975	$1,902	$12,085	$28,643	$41,897	$90,074	$101,030	$81,734
DEPARTMENT OVERHEAD	$524,434	$114	$109	$434	$741		$1,135	$1,816	$14,405	$33,244	$45,708	$69,989	$117,870	$326,126
SUPERVISION & INDIRECTS	$388,045	$78	$86	$24	$525		$778	$85		$23,585	$33,344	$45,508	$80,411	$87,480
FIXED ASSET REPLACEMENT	$1,143,624	$37	$128	$24	$258	$110	$966	$95	$811	$11,579	$16,159	$982,629	$96,413	$545,955
TOTAL	$7,793,468	$1,477	$1,514	$5,208	$9,645	$10,034	$14,722	$18,215	$173,087	$432,727	$633,101	$1,249,327	$1,624,109	$1,748,943

EXPENSE TYPE	PER UNIT	A	B	C	D	E	F	G	H	I	J	K	L	M
SALARIES & WAGES	$20.32													
FRINGE BENEFITS	$7.26													
SERVICE & SUPPLIES	$2.91													
BUILDING OCCUPANCY	$6.13													
GENERAL SERVICES	$3.90													
GENERAL OVERHEAD	$4.00													
DEPARTMENT OVERHEAD	$2.81													
SUPERVISION & INDIRECTS	$3.73													
FIXED ASSET REPLACEMENT														
TOTAL BY UNIT	$59.40													

NOTE: *PER UNIT* column is based upon *TOTAL UNITS* and represents an average cost per total units.
(c) Management Services Institute, Inc., Anaheim, CA; March,1990 & June, 1992

MSI SERVICE CENTER WORKSHEET FOR COST DETAIL

CITY OF **PASADENA** REF. NO. **S-257** UNITS **131000**

SERVICE PROVIDED

Library Services & Special Program

KEY	FILE	DEPT	DIVISION	SECTION	ACCOUNT	TYPE	UNITS
N	SUPT. SVC	Info Svcs	Support Svcs		4020/32		
O							
P							
Q							
R							
S							
T							

KEY	FILE	DEPT	DIVISION	SECTION	ACCOUNT	TYPE	UNITS
U							
V							
W							
X							
Y							
Z							

EXPENSE TYPE	TOTAL	N	O	P	Q	R	S	T	U	V	W	X	Y	Z
SALARIES & WAGES	$864,250													
FRINGE BENEFITS	$204,728													
SERVICE & SUPPLIES	$164,628													
BUILDING OCCUPANCY	$75,091													
GENERAL SERVICES	$55,813													
GENERAL OVERHEAD	$121,149													
DEPARTMENT OVERHEAD	$141,105													
SUPERVISION & INDIRECTS	$112,163													
FIXED ASSET REPLACEMENT	$173,856													
TOTAL	**$1,973,379**													

EXPENSE TYPE	PER UNIT	N	O	P	Q	R	S	T	U	V	W	X	Y	Z
SALARIES & WAGES														
FRINGE BENEFITS														
SERVICE & SUPPLIES														
BUILDING OCCUPANCY														
GENERAL SERVICES														
GENERAL OVERHEAD														
DEPARTMENT OVERHEAD														
SUPERVISION & INDIRECTS														
FIXED ASSET REPLACEMENT														
TOTAL BY UNIT														

NOTE: "PER UNIT" column is based upon "TOTAL UNITS" and represents an average cost per total units.

(c) Management Services Institute, Inc., Anaheim, CA; March, 1990 & June, 1992.

MSI GENERAL BENEFIT CENTER WORKSHEET

SERVICE PROVIDED	CITY	REF.NO.
CRIME PREVENTION & INVEST. SUPPORT	**PASADENA**	S-250
SERVICES PRIMARILY PERFORMED BY	FUND	EXP.ACCT.
POLICE-Records	General	300160

DISCUSSION OF SERVICE

The Support Services Division supports crime prevention and investigation through the use of the Records program. The functions included in this program are:

- Operating, supervising, and controlling the warrant system

- Disseminating records data within the Department and other local, State, and Federal agencies as well as the public

- Maintaining, calculating, and distributing mandated and supplemental statistical information.

[T-3383]

MSI SERVICE CENTER WORKSHEET FOR COST DETAIL

SERVICE PROVIDED					CITY		REF.NO.
Crime Prevention & Invstigative Support					PASADENA		S–250
							TOTAL UNITS 2000000

KEY	FILE	DEPARTMENT	DIVISION	SECTION	ACCOUNT	TYPE	UNITS
A	PD_SUPPT	Police	Support Services	Support Operations	300129		
B	PD_RECOR	Police	Support Services	Records	300160	documents	
C							
D							
E							
F							
G							

EXPENSE TYPE	TOTAL	A	B	C	D	E	F	G
SALARIES & WAGES	$551,403	$107,271	$444,132					
FRINGE BENEFITS	$250,008	$59,385	$190,623					
SERVICES AND SUPPLIES	$30,071	$19,498	$10,573					
BUILDING OCCUPANCY	$78,038	$15,653	$62,385					
GENERAL SERVICES	$153,187	$12,482	$140,705					
GENERAL OVERHEAD	$90,329	$18,213	$72,116					
DEPARTMENT OVERHEAD	$98,830	$19,927	$78,903					
SUPERVISION & INDIRECTS	$123,454	$16,680	$106,774					
FIXED ASSET REPLACEMENT	$6,843	$768	$6,075					
TOTAL	$1,382,143	$269,857	$1,112,286					

EXPENSE TYPE	PER UNIT	A	B	C	D	E	F	G
SALARIES & WAGES	$0.28							
FRINGE BENEFITS	$0.13							
SERVICES AND SUPPLIES	$0.02							
BUILDING OCCUPANCY	$0.04							
GENERAL SERVICES	$0.08							
GENERAL OVERHEAD	$0.05							
DEPARTMENT OVERHEAD	$0.05							
SUPERVISION & INDIRECTS	$0.06							
FIXED ASSET REPLACEMENT								
TOTAL	$0.69							

NOTE: "PER UNIT" column is based upon "TOTAL UNITS" and represents an average cost per total units.

(c) Management Services Institute, Inc., Anaheim, CA; March,1990 & June,1992

MSI SERVICE CENTER WORKSHEET FOR FEES AND CHARGES

SERVICE PROVIDED	CITY	REF.NO.
NEIGHBORHOOD PARK MAINTENANCE	**PASADENA**	S-222

SERVICES PRIMARILY PERFORMED BY	FUND	EXP.ACCT.
PW-Parks	General	461-111,127,103

REVENUE RECEIVED [Actual - Potential]	FUND	REV.ACCT.
NEIGHBORHOOD PARK ASSESSMENTS	None	NA

REVENUE AUTHORIZATION		
None	DATE LAST REVISED:	NA
	SUBSIDY RATIONALE:	None

DESCRIPTION OF SERVICE	REVENUE COLLECTION SCHEDULE:
Maintaining, operating, repairing and replacing landscaping and equipment within City neighborhood parks.	NA
	REVENUE COLLECTED BY:
	None
	UNIT OF SERVICE DESIGNATION:
	Residential Parcel

CURRENT FEE STRUCTURE

None

FISCAL YEAR 1992-1993 REVENUE AND COST COMPARISON

TOTAL EST. REVENUE	:	$0	UNIT REVENUE	:	$0.00
TOTAL COST	:	$3,227,138	UNIT COST	:	$156.29
PROFIT (SUBSIDY)	:	<$3,227,138>	PROFIT (SUBSIDY)	:	<$156.29>
% of COST RECOVERED	:	0.0%	UNITS OF SERVICE	:	20,649

SUGGESTED % RECOVERY AND FEE STRUCTURE

PERCENT: 100%   **SPECIAL CONDITIONS:** None

$13.02/parcel/month on utility bill

See text, Chapter V, page 157, for further discussion.

The City may want to phase in the fees over 3-5 years. Actual assessments to be determined after required Engineer's study.

[T-265]

MSI SERVICE CENTER WORKSHEET FOR COST DETAIL

SERVICE PROVIDED						CITY		REF.NO.
Neighborhood Park Maintenance						PASADENA		S-222
								TOTAL UNITS 20649

KEY	FILE	DEPARTMENT	DIVISION	SECTION	ACCOUNT	TYPE	UNITS
A	TREE_MTC	Public Works	Parks	Street Tree Mtce	461210		20649
B	REC_FADM	Recreation	Rec Facilities Admin		405217		20649
C	TREE_ADM	Public Works	Parks	Street Tree Admin	461202		20649
D	PKMTC_RP	Public Works	Parks	Central Services	461137		20649
E	PKMTC_II	Public Works	Parks	Park Mtce -- Area II	461129		20649
F	PKMTC_I	Public Works	Parks	Park Mtce -- Area I	461111		20649
G	PKMTC_AD	Public Works	Parks	Park Mtce Supv'N	461103		20649

EXPENSE TYPE	TOTAL	A	B	C	D	E	F	G
SALARIES & WAGES	$241,807	$631	$12,764	$22,968	$54,984	$53,683	$96,777	
FRINGE BENEFITS	$108,729	$290	$6,331	$10,542	$24,987	$23,333	$43,246	
SERVICES AND SUPPLIES	$342,952	$93	$1,185	$1,208	$11,622	$17,980	$40,864	$270,000
BUILDING OCCUPANCY	$16,622	$24	$885	$829	$2,612	$5,014	$7,258	
GENERAL SERVICES	$89,309	$405	$2,355	$336	$22,597	$22,645	$40,971	
GENERAL OVERHEAD	$67,951	$123	$1,999	$3,050	$9,928	$10,426	$19,475	$22,950
DEPARTMENT OVERHEAD	$16,484	$22	$4,845	$538	$1,752	$1,840	$3,437	$4,050
SUPERVISION & INDIRECTS	$240,858	$85	$1,747	$2,110	$6,869	$45,381	$84,770	$99,896
FIXED ASSET REPLACEMENT	$1,073	$3	$25	$80	$241	$243	$481	
FACILITY MAINT & REPL	$2,101,353							$2,101,353
TOTAL	$3,227,138	$1,676	$32,136	$41,661	$135,592	$180,545	$337,279	$2,498,249

EXPENSE TYPE	PER UNIT	A	B	C	D	E	F	G
SALARIES & WAGES	$11.71	$0.03	$0.62	$1.11	$2.66	$2.60	$4.69	
FRINGE BENEFITS	$5.27	$0.01	$0.31	$0.51	$1.21	$1.13	$2.09	
SERVICES AND SUPPLIES	$16.61		$0.06	$0.06	$0.56	$0.87	$1.98	$13.08
BUILDING OCCUPANCY	$0.80		$0.04	$0.04	$0.13	$0.24	$0.35	
GENERAL SERVICES	$4.33	$0.02	$0.11	$0.02	$1.09	$1.10	$1.98	
GENERAL OVERHEAD	$3.29	$0.01	$0.10	$0.15	$0.48	$0.50	$0.94	$1.11
DEPARTMENT OVERHEAD	$0.80		$0.23	$0.03	$0.08	$0.09	$0.17	$0.20
SUPERVISION & INDIRECTS	$11.66		$0.08	$0.10	$0.33	$2.20	$4.11	$4.84
FIXED ASSET REPLACEMENT	$0.05				$0.01	$0.01	$0.02	
FACILITY MAINT & REPL	$101.77							$101.77
TOTAL	$156.29	$0.08	$1.56	$2.02	$6.57	$8.74	$16.33	$120.99

FIXED ASSET EXPENSE CALCULATION FORM -- CITY OF PASADENA

DEPARTMENT: RECREATION
PROGRAM/DIVISION: NEIGHBORHOOD PARKS

ITEM	AV. LIFE	ESTIMATED REPL. COST	ANNUAL FIXED ASSET EXP.
Alleys	20		$0
Automotive--General	5		$0
Automotive--Police	3		$0
Automotive--Special Purpose	15		$0
Bridges	30		$0
Buildings	30		$0
Communication Equipment	5		$0
Computer Equipment	5		$0
Curbs, Gutters & Sidewalks	20		$0
Electr. System - Distribution	50		$0
Golf Course	20		$0
Helicopters	20		
Library Books	VAR		$0
Medians	20		
Office Equipment	5		$0
Office Furniture	10		
Other Equipment	10		$0
Parks Landscaping & Equipment	VAR	$32,656,245	$2,101,353
Parking Lots	20		$0
Parking Structures	50		
Sewer System	40		$0
Storm Drain System	50		
Street Lights	20		$0
Street Trees	50		
Streets	20		$0
Streets - Parking	20		
Traffic Signals	10		$0
Traffic Signs	8		
Water - Distribution System	40		$0
TOTAL		$32,656,245	$2,101,353

MSI REVENUE DATA WORKSHEET

REVENUE TITLE	CITY	REF. NO.
SALES AND USE TAX	PASADENA	TAX–1

REVENUE COLLECTED BY	FUND	REV. ACCT.
State Board of Equalization	General	05–3020 thru 3021

LEGAL AUTHORIZATION	DATE ENACTED:	NA
Gov Code S. 37101, Rev & Tax Code 7702 et seq	DATE LAST REVISED:	March, 1990

DESCRIPTION	REMITTANCE SCHEDULE
The City's share of the standardized 8.25% sales tax.	Collected by State Board of Equalization and remitted monthly, based on quarterly computations followed by a "clean-up" fourth payment; e.g., 22 1/2 on 3/20 22 1/2 on 4/20 45% on 5/20 & 10% on 6/20

REMITTANCE BASIS	ANALYSIS OF TREND
1/8 of the 8.25% retail sales since tax collected within the City limits. City's share is 1% of the total 8.25% tax State's share is 4 3/4% County's share is 1 1/4% Local Transportation's share is 1 1/4%	Small increase due to an expected increase in sales revenue, within the City.

FISCAL YEAR:	86–87	87–88	88–89	89–90	90–91	91–92	92–93
EST. ACTUAL REV:	$17,722,004	$18,316,642	$19,249,716	$20,522,293	$22,339,119	$20,246,590	$21,760,015

MSI REVENUE DATA WORKSHEET

REVENUE TITLE	CITY	REF. NO.
PROPERTY/TRANSFER/EXEMPTION TAXES	PASADENA	TAX–2

REVENUE COLLECTED BY	FUND	REV. ACCT.
Finance	General	05–3000 thru 3002

LEGAL AUTHORIZATION		
Article XIIIA, California Constitution	DATE ENACTED:	1978
	DATE LAST REVISED:	Not Known

DESCRIPTION	REMITTANCE SCHEDULE
Tax on valuation of real property and certain limited classes of personal property, for general City purposes. Includes property tax exemption, transfer tax and delinquent taxes and penalties from prior year delinquent payments. Secured Tax – on value of real property Unsecured Tax – on movable industrial, commercial, and other personal property	Monthly partial payments from the County Tax Collector.

REMITTANCE BASIS	ANALYSIS OF TREND
The basic property tax is based on the property's assessed value as of March 1, 1986, with an annual inflation factor of 2%, or current market value if the property is sold. The tax rate is 1% of the assessed value, plus debt service, with the allocation between governmental agencies determined by the County based on Government Code Section 26912. The rate for transfer tax is $0.275 per $500 sales value of property transferred, exclusive of any lien or encumbrance.	Future decrease expected due to current legislative action.

FISCAL YEAR:	86–87	87–88	88–89	89–90	90–91	91–92	92–93
EST. ACTUAL REV:	$12,422,396	$15,526,431	$17,173,964	$18,031,369	$19,990,169	$21,025,704	$21,592,812

MSI REVENUE DATA WORKSHEET

REVENUE TITLE	CITY	REF. NO.
MOTOR VEHICLE IN–LIEU TAX	PASADENA	TAX–4
REVENUE COLLECTED BY	FUND	REV. ACCT.
State Department of Motor Vehicles	General	05–3660
LEGAL AUTHORIZATION	DATE ENACTED:	NA
Revenue and Taxation Code, Section 11005	DATE LAST REVISED:	1984

DESCRIPTION	REMITTANCE SCHEDULE
Tax collected by the State Department of Motor Vehicles through its vehicle registration program in lieu of a City personal property tax on motor vehicles.	Monthly, about the 10th, from the State Controller.

REMITTANCE BASIS	ANALYSIS OF TREND
Apportioned equally between cities and counties on the basis of population. SB 201 of 1982 reduced the amount, with the balance retained by the State for its purposes. The 1982 State budget bill further reduced the local government share, which was reinstated in 1983, and made "permanent" by Legislative action in 1984.	Anticipate future decrease due to reduced governmant payouts.

FISCAL YEAR:	86–87	87–88	88–89	89–90	90–91	91–92	92–93
EST. ACTUAL REV:	$3,833,992	$4,090,739	$4,566,247	$4,682,304	$4,680,270	$4,548,606	$4,587,525

CITY OF BEVERLY HILLS
COST DETAIL WORKSHEET
FY 2006-2007

SERVICE				REFERENCE NO.		
LIBRARY SERVICES				**TAX-31**		
NOTE				TOTAL UNITS		
Unit Costs are an Average of Total Units				1		

DEPARTMENT	POSITION	TYPE	UNIT TIME	UNIT COST	ANN. UNITS	TOTAL COST
LITERACY SERVICES	LIBRARY TECH - TEMP	55 HR/WK	2,949.00	$153,701.88	1	$153,702
LITERACY SERVICES	LIBRARY CLERK I - TEMP	63 HR/WK	3,150.00	$82,845.00	1	$82,845
LITERACY SERVICES	SENIOR LIBRARY CLERK	100%	3,308.00	$224,083.92	1	$224,084
LITERACY SERVICES	SR LIBRARY CLERK	100%	1,654.00	$106,831.86	1	$106,832
REFERENCE SERVICES	LIBRARIAN III	1.44 FTE	2,381.76	$262,898.67	1	$262,899
REFERENCE SERVICES	LIBRARIAN II		6,996.42	$729,096.93	1	$729,097
REFERENCE SERVICES	LIBRARIAN II - TEMP		8,500.00	$454,410.00	1	$454,410
REFERENCE SERVICES	SENIOR LIBRARIAN	75%	1,240.50	$154,963.26	1	$154,963
REFERENCE SERVICES	LIBRARIAN I -TEMP	45 HR/WK	2,250.00	$70,335.00	1	$70,335
REFERENCE SERVICES	LIBRARY CLERK II - PT	25% OF 1,750 HRS	440.00	$23,751.20	1	$23,751
REFERENCE SERVICES	LIBRARY CLERK II - TEMP	62% OF 27 HR/WK	840.00	$27,997.20	1	$27,997
REFERENCE SERVICES	SENIOR LIBRARY CLERK	100% OF 1.5 FTE	2,481.00	$192,748.89	1	$192,749
REFERENCE SERVICES	SR LIBRARY CLERK - PT	25 HR/WK	1,250.00	$114,312.50	1	$114,313
LIBRARY PROGRAMS	LIBRARIAN III	1.08 FTE	1,786.32	$213,929.68	1	$213,930
LIBRARY PROGRAMS	LIBRARIAN II		1,141.26	$128,403.16	1	$128,403
LIBRARY PROGRAMS	LIBRARIAN II - TEMP	35% OF 78 HR/WK	1,360.00	$70,597.60	1	$70,598
LIBRARY PROGRAMS	LIBRARY CLERK II - PT	25% OF 1,750 HRS	440.00	$25,907.20	1	$25,907
LIBRARY PROGRAMS	LIBRARY CLERK II - TEMP	75% OF 11 HR/WK	410.00	$22,578.70	1	$22,579
LIBRARY PROGRAMS	SENIOR LIBRARY CLERK	50%	827.00	$69,716.10	1	$69,716
LIBRARY PROGRAMS		Prof/Contract Svcs	0.00	$3,000.00	1	$3,000
LIBRARY PROGRAMS		Print/Graph/Cable TV	0.00	$17,570.00	1	$17,570
CIRCULATION SVCS	SENIOR LIBRARIAN	25%	413.50	$53,395.26	1	$53,395
CIRCULATION SVCS	LIBRARY TECHNICIAN	100% OF 1	1,654.00	$139,597.60	1	$139,598
CIRCULATION SVCS	LIBRARY CLERK I - PT	90 HR/WK	4,500.00	$191,970.00	1	$191,970
CIRCULATION SVCS	LIBRARY CLERK I - TEMP	177 HR/WK	8,850.00	$339,574.50	1	$339,575
CIRCULATION SVCS	LIBRARY CLERK II	Remainder Of 4.5	5,917.70	$445,129.39	1	$445,129
CIRCULATION SVCS	LIBRARY CLERK II - PT	100% OF 35 HR/WK	1,325.00	$72,066.75	1	$72,067
CIRCULATION SVCS	LIBRARY CLERK II - TEMP	28 HR/WK	1,400.00	$54,712.00	1	$54,712
CIRCULATION SVCS		50% Of Facil Charges	0.00	$235,350.00	1	$235,350
SHELVING MATERIALS	LIBRARY PAGE II - PT	57.75 HR/WK	2,890.00	$93,462.60	1	$93,463

CITY OF BEVERLY HILLS
COST DETAIL WORKSHEET
FY 2006-2007

SERVICE		REFERENCE NO.
LIBRARY SERVICES		**TAX-31**

NOTE	TOTAL UNITS
Unit Costs are an Average of Total Units	1

DEPARTMENT	POSITION	TYPE	UNIT TIME	UNIT COST	ANN. UNITS	TOTAL COST
SHELVING MATERIALS	LIBRARY PAGE II - TEMP	16 HR/WK	800.00	$21,928.00	1	$21,928
SHELVING MATERIALS	SR LIBRARY PAGE	100% OF 2	3,308.00	$141,582.40	1	$141,582
SHELVING MATERIALS	SR LIBRARY PAGE - PT	35 HR/WK	1,750.00	$60,742.50	1	$60,743
SHELVING MATERIALS	LIBRARY PAGE I - TEMP	228 HR/WK	11,400.00	$182,172.00	1	$182,172
SHELVING MATERIALS		Facility Charges	0.00	$354,778.00	1	$354,778
COLLECTION DEVELOP	LIBRARIAN III	1.48 FTE	2,447.92	$280,702.99	1	$280,703
COLLECTION DEVELOP	LIBRARIAN II		2,778.72	$300,601.93	1	$300,602
COLLECTION DEVELOP	LIBRARIAN II - TEMP	10% OF 132.5 HR/WK	660.00	$38,695.80	1	$38,696
COLLECTION DEVELOP	SENIOR LIBRARIAN	25%	413.50	$53,659.90	1	$53,660
COLLECTION DEVELOP		Materials	0.00	$935,139.00	1	$935,139
MATERIALS ACQUIS.	SENIOR LIBRARIAN	25%	413.50	$52,266.40	1	$52,266
MATERIALS ACQUIS.	LIBRARY TECHNICIAN	Remainder Of 1.25	1,907.50	$153,897.10	1	$153,897
MATERIALS ACQUIS.	LIBRARY CLERK II - PT		2,800.00	$153,692.00	1	$153,692
MATERIALS ACQUIS.	SENIOR LIBRARY CLERK	75% OF 1	1,240.50	$94,650.15	1	$94,650
LIB. DATABASE MNT	LIBRARIAN II		661.60	$71,949.00	1	$71,949
LIB. DATABASE MNT	SENIOR LIBRARIAN	50%	827.00	$108,345.27	1	$108,345
LIB. DATABASE MNT	LIBRARY TECHNICIAN	Rem Of 75% & 25%	1,494.00	$126,990.00	1	$126,990
LIB. DATABASE MNT	LIBRARY TECH - TEMP	3 HR/WK	150.00	$6,117.00	1	$6,117
LIB. DATABASE MNT	LIBRARY CLERK II	100% OF 1.25 FTE	2,067.50	$151,878.55	1	$151,879
LIB. DATABASE MNT	LIBRARY CLERK II - PT	50% OF 25 HR/WK	625.00	$37,025.00	1	$37,025
LIB. DATABASE MNT	LIBRARY CLERK II - TEMP	3 HR/WK	150.00	$5,437.50	1	$5,438
LIB. DATABASE MNT	SENIOR LIBRARY CLERK	25% OF 1	413.50	$32,703.72	1	$32,704
LIB. DATABASE MNT		Contract Svcs	0.00	$31,050.00	1	$31,050
MATERIAL PROCESS.	LIBRARY TECHNICIAN	75% OF 1	1,240.50	$116,904.72	1	$116,905
MATERIAL PROCESS.	LIBRARY PAGE II - PT	35% OF 35 HR/WK	610.00	$24,058.40	1	$24,058
MATERIAL PROCESS.	LIBRARY CLERK I - PT	Remainder 70 HR/WK	3,340.00	$182,230.40	1	$182,230
MATERIAL PROCESS.	LIBRARY CLERK II	25% OF 1	413.50	$35,283.96	1	$35,284
MATERIAL PROCESS.	LIBRARY CLERK II - TEMP	38% OF 27 HR/WK	510.00	$20,885.60	1	$20,686
MATERIAL PROCESS.		Supplies/Printing	0.00	$67,310.00	1	$67,310
LIB. SECURITY SVCS	LIBRARY CLERK I - TEMP	38 HR/WK	1,900.00	$74,062.00	1	$74,062

CITY OF BEVERLY HILLS
COST DETAIL WORKSHEET
FY 2006-2007

SERVICE				REFERENCE NO.			
LIBRARY SERVICES				**TAX-31**			

NOTE				TOTAL UNITS			
Unit Costs are an Average of Total Units				1			

DEPARTMENT	POSITION	TYPE	UNIT TIME	UNIT COST	ANN. UNITS	TOTAL COST
LIB. SECURITY SVCS	LIBRARY CLERK II	100% OF 1	1,654.00	$131,410.30	1	$131,410
LIB. SECURITY SVCS	LIBRARY CLERK II - PT	2,375 HRS	2,370.00	$162,747.90	1	$162,748
LIB. SECURITY SVCS	LIBRARY CLERK II - TEMP	25% OF 11 HR/WK	140.00	$7,690.20	1	$7,690
		TYPE SUBTOTAL	118,841.70	$8,993,324.54		$8,993,325
April 10, 2007		TOTALS	118,841.70	$8,993,325.00		$8,993,325

Serving Local Governments Since 1975

Revenue & Cost Specialists (RCS), originally formed as Management Services Institute (MSI), was established to calculate the full cost and benefit of all public services provided by local government.

In the wake of Proposition 13 in California in 1978, the founders of MSI (Doug Ayres, Rick Kermer, and Lee Weber) realized that public agencies would need to be able to identify their full costs just like a business would. City councils around the State, faced with lower property tax revenues, were forced to make hard decisions about which public services should be financed with tax dollars and which services should either be cut or financed from user fees.

MSI created the Municipal Business System to provide public agencies with a systematic and detailed method for calculating the full business-like costs of providing all public services. This costing system, which has been updated by RCS, then allows the city council to concentrate on the policy decisions about who should be subsidized with limited tax dollars and who should not.

In the last thirty years MSI, and then RCS, has provided these services to over 250 public agencies in six states.

Rick Kermer
President

Scott Thorpe
Senior Vice President

Eric Johnson
Vice President

APPENDIX A

The following suggested Ordinance was developed at the request of numerous entities. The reason was simple: Any outsourcing or contracting-out of municipal functions, activities and projects should be subjected to a full revenue-cost and beneficiary analysis. Such would assure that prior to displacement of municipal employees by a private sector contract both of municipal and contractor costs and quality would be assessed and assured to be known and included. All such "costs reasonably borne", including the costs of securing and monitoring any such outsourcing contract, must be included. And equal quality assured. Other terms to be met by both of contractor and municipality are enumerated and should be implemented.

This model ordinance variously has been titled as: The Level Playing Field Ordinance, The Outsourcing Guidelines Ordinance, and The Anti-Corruption Ordinance

---

AN ORDINANCE ESTABLISHING STANDARDS BY WHICH SERVICES MAY BE CONTRACTED TO PRIVATE PARTIES BY THE CITY

ORDINANCE NO. _____

Purpose and Intent. *This Ordinance specifically is designed and intended to assure the public, citizens, visitors, and tax, rate, license and fee payers that services, products and projects provided directly by employees and contractors of the City have been analyzed, costed and reviewed for quality and quantity with what has been offered by potential alternate outsourcing, thus achieving the best and highest quality services for the least possible cost, be such costs incurred by City employees or outsourced contractors.*

Section 1. The provisions of this Ordinance shall be applied to all procedures, whether by competitive bid, request for proposals, request for quotations, informal bid, sealed bid, or any other process whereby any service presently provided by or potentially provided by City employees is proposed to be contracted to any private party, be it an individual, association, partnership, corporation or any other profit-making or non-profit organization.

A) All City officials shall apply the provisions of this Ordinance to all bid or proposal documents, preliminary proposals and actual quotation, bid or proposal documents.

(B) The provisions of this Ordinance also shall be applicable and applied to any contract for services of any nature or kind under any existing or future contract or agreement issued by the City in amount of $2,500 or more.

Contracting Standards Ordinance – continued – page 2

Section 2. Each and every bidder or proposer on any such work as hereinbefore in Section 1 described shall, as part of the bid or proposal documents, include the following materials, on forms provided and supplied by the City Finance Director and approved as to form by the City Attorney:

Section 2.1   Donations. (A) A statement, sworn under penalty of perjury, that none of the principals in the firm or any shareholder thereof who holds more than five (5%) percent of the stock or partnership points of any proposing or bidding corporation, partnership or subsidiary thereof, has made a contribution, either directly or indirectly, in excess of $100 to the campaign of, or any amount to the personal benefit of any City employee, City official or elected City official within the last four years.

(B) A statement, sworn under penalty of perjury, that none of those enumerated in Sub-Section (A) will make or cause to be made either directly or indirectly, any contribution of any amount, in cash or goods or services, to the election campaign of, or for the personal benefit of any City employee, City official or elected City official, or to any candidate for election to any City office, for the duration of any contract which might be awarded by the City ,and for four years after the termination of such contract, for whatever reason such contract may be terminated.

Section 2.2   Jobs. (A) A statement, sworn under penalty of perjury, that the bidder or proposer has not employed in any paid capacity, be it as an employee, attorney, consultant, or in any other paid engagement, any present City elected official, City department head, City official, administrative or management employee, or operational or other employee at any time during the four years immediately prior to the submission of the bid or proposal.

(B) A statement, sworn under penalty of perjury, that the bidder or proposer will not employ in any capacity any of those positions or persons enumerated in (A) for a period of four years after the termination of that person's employment with the City or after the termination of the contract, whichever comes last.

Section 2.3   Citizenship. **(A)** A statement, sworn under penalty of perjury, that all persons employed by the bidder or proposer who will be utilized, in whole or in part, on any work involved in any City contract, if awarded, will be a citizen of the United States or documented alien resident of the United States. Such status also will be certified by utilization of the e-Verify system of the United States Department of Homeland Security.

(B) "Documented alien" shall possess the appropriate registration forms issued by the United States Department of Homeland Security, which documents will be examined by the appropriate law enforcement agency, and certified by an official thereof, in writing, as being genuine, complete and currently valid, and valid for the probable length of any awarded contract. Such status also will be certified by utilization of the e-Verify system of the United States Department of Homeland Security.

Section 2.4   Financial Statement.   (A) A financial statement, sworn under penalty of perjury, and approved and verified in writing by a CPA employed by the currently contracted City Auditor, as correct and adequate to illustrate that the proposer or bidder has sufficient financial capacity, resources or readily available resources and appropriately knowledgeable and skilled personnel to execute the contract should it be awarded, for the duration of the contract.

(B) A performance bond, in form approved by the City Attorney, in amount equal to one-and-one-half (1½) times the dollar amount or value of the contract for which the bid or proposal is made.

Section 3.   For each contract proposed to be awarded, prior to its award, the Police Chief or County Sheriff shall review the list of positions proposed to be utilized in the execution of the work to be performed under the contract and make a determination, in writing, as to whether the work to be performed and the locus of the work by the contract employee or employees is such that a background investigation of each proposed and/or involved person should be conducted.

Section 3.1   Positions.   The positions reviewed shall be those estimated by City staff and/or by the proposer or bidder to be utilized in the conduct of the work or services included in the bid or request for proposal documents.

Section 3.2   Criteria.   Any position determined by the Police Chief or County Sheriff to have considerable contact with the public, to be conducting work alone in or on City premises, facilities or equipment, to have contact with youths under the age of eighteen (18) years of age, or persons over the age of seventy (70) years, or to require a background check were the position to be filled by a City employee rather than a contract-provided person, shall have a comprehensive background check performed by the Police Chief or County Sheriff prior to the contractor-provided employee being permitted to perform work under the contract.

Section 3.3   Background Check. The Police Chief or County Sheriff shall cause the Police Department or County Sheriff Department to conduct the appropriate background check determined by him/her to be necessary, including but not restricted to (A) criminal record check (B) fingerprint check, (C) driving record check, (D) personal background investigation, and   (E) which other appropriate legal methods and techniques the Police Chief or County Sheriff may require should the Police Chief or County Sheriff find under Section 3.2 hereof that such background check is necessary.

Section 3.4   Restrictions. No contract-provided employee shall work on or in City-owned, leased or rented property, be provided or work with City information until the determinations and any background checks required by Section 3 are completed.

Section 4.   (A) All staff reports and studies and all cost estimates provided the City Council concerning any proposed, vendor/contractor provided, or recommended contracted service shall have included in the cost estimates all "costs reasonably borne" as set out and defined in Section 5 hereof in drawing the specifications, bid documents, and in considering, processing and awarding any contract.

(B) Included in the computed "costs reasonably borne" by the City Finance Director shall be all costs of drawing the specifications and bid documents, and in reviewing, discussing, processing and awarding any contract. Also included shall be all direct and indirect costs of contract preparation, contract administration, contract service monitoring, and contract enforcement.

Section 4.1 Annual "Costs Reasonably Borne" Report.   Annually, pursuant to the procedure and definitions set out in Section 5 hereof, the City Finance Director shall make a report to the elected governing body providing all "costs reasonably borne" for the services enumerated in (A) and (B) of this Section 4. In addition, the report shall include the "costs reasonably borne" for each and every service contracted for or by the City, payments made under each contract for the past two years, those budgeted and estimated for the current year, and those estimated for the subsequent year.

(A) Such contracts as required by Section 4 hereof to be reported to the City Council shall be listed by type of service and by vendor or contractor.

(B)   The estimated expenses required to be reported by Section 4 and 4.1 shall be considered a "cost" and used in all comparative studies and reports prepared by and utilized by the City Council or its contractors when comparing costs of providing services by City employees with providing the same service by contract.

Section 5. "Costs Reasonably Borne". The purpose of calculating and reporting the costs of services shall be definitive and validated comparative information for both of City and private contractor-supplied services so decisions can be made relative to privatization, outsourcing, contracting, abandonment, tax-subsidized, tax-financed, and fee and charge-financed services so service consumer, tax and rate payers may be aware of the relative merits and costs of alternate methods of service delivery. Full "costs reasonably borne" as defined herein shall be equitably and validly compared by applying common definitions to both of government and private contract services, goods or projects, as set out in this Ordinance.

Section 5.1. Elements and Definition of Costs Reasonably Borne. All reasonable costs appropriate for the continuation of the service over time shall be compiled by calculating and applying the following costs to identified specific services per procedures set out herein.

(A) The following costs shall be allocated over all services, goods and projects.
  (1) Personnel costs of:
    (a) salaries and wages
    (b) employee benefits
    (c) employee insurance and retirement expense
  (2) All applicable maintenance and operation costs, including insurance
  (3) Overhead and administration expenses, including insurance
  (4) Start-up costs
  (5) Costs for future capacity
  (6) Capital replacement expenses
  (7) Expansion of service costs
  (8) Repayment of related bond issuances and interest and amortized underwriting costs thereof

Section 5.2 Revenues. The separation of taxes from licenses, fees and charges shall be made to assure that taxes are exclusively utilized for services provided the community at large, and fees, charges and license revenues exclusively shall be used to pay for direct benefit services, goods and projects. Total amounts of revenue generated by fees or charges for specific identified and specified services provided must:

(A) Be a governmental imposition exacted in exchange for a direct benefit received by the payer.

Contracting Standards Ordinance – continued – page 6

(B) Be for a service or for products provided directly to the payer and not for a service or product generally enjoyed by the community at large.

(C) Taxes are a general imposition on a broad cross-section of the citizenry for a general governmental purpose, and shall be utilized to provide such direct benefit services benefitting the community at large.

Section 6. (A) Any staff study proposing, and all recommendations made to the City Council by City staff shall contain a signed statement that the services proposed to be outsourced by contract, which services currently are provided by City employees, are to be strictly comparable in both quality and quantity. Such statement shall be supplied to the City Council annually for each and every service contract in force.

(B) A signed statement that specific identifiable services currently provided by City employees shall be provided stating that such services are being provided at less than comparable contract cost and also are comparable in both quality and quantity to those which are, or have been or potentially could be provided by private contractors.

(C) All contracts awarded by the City Council shall contain a one year cancellation provision, which provision shall be invoked automatically and mandatorily in the event the statement required by each of Section 6 (A) and 6 (B) is not filed or states that the service provided by contract is of lesser quality, quantity and/or are at higher cost than could be provided by City employees at the same or lower cost.

Section 7. All other bid and proposal requirements shall be met and fully complied with by proposers or bidders falling under the purview of this Ordinance. This Ordinance shall be supplementary to all other State Code provisions, City Codes and Ordinances, City Resolutions, and City Rules and Regulations.

Section 8. No contract for any service shall be awarded for longer than four years unless approved and authorized by recorded vote of three-fourths (¾ ths) of the City Council.

Section 9. Any violation of this Ordinance shall be a misdemeanor and, further, shall upon conviction thereof act to revoke automatically, without further notice, the contract held by any person, firm or corporation convicted under the provision for which the misdemeanor action was brought.

Any violation of this Ordinance, and misdemeanor conviction thereunder, by any City employee, shall result in automatic termination of the convicted employee.

Contracting Standards Ordinance – continued – page 7

Section 10. If any provision, clause or phrase of this Ordinance is held to be unconstitutional or contrary to State law by decision of the State Supreme Court, then the remainder of this Ordinance shall remain in full force and effect.

Adopted this _____ day of _____, 201__ by the City Council of the City of _____

Ayes:

Nays:

_____
                         /s/ Mayor

Attest:

_____
/s/ City Clerk

Approved as to form:

_____
/s/ City Attorney

Approved as to financial integrity and accuracy:

_____
/s/ City Finance Director

Approved as to financial accuracy and compliance with Governmental Accounting Standards Board provisions, rules and regulations:

_____,CPA
/s/ City Auditor

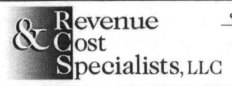

consulting   software   articles   **about us**

Home | Ordering | Contact Us

History

"Doug Ayres, who owns a company that helps California governments determine their true costs, says that only 4 percent of local governments know the direct cost of each service they provide, only 2 percent know the total cost of each service they provide, and only 10 percent can even tell you what services they provide!"

- Gaebler & Osborne, Reinventing Government, p.217, 1992

Early History

Around 1980, three professionals combined their talents to create Management Services Institute (MSI). Doug Ayres had been a consultant with Public Administration Service (PAS) in Chicago, a finance director and a city manager of several cities including Salem, Oregon, and Inglewood, California. Lee Weber had also been a consultant with PAS and had been a city manager in Texas. Rick Kermer had been an independent financial consultant and finance director of three cities including Buena Park, Compton and Lynwood, California.

Doug had prepared a seminal study for Kansas City while at PAS where revenues were linked to costs. Both Doug and Rick had worked in their respective cities to use data processing to show the revenues associated with budgeted activities. Their first study together was for Doug Dunlop, city manager of Villa Park, California. Over the years, their work grew to include studies for over one-quarter of the cities in California.

Present Time

In the early '90s, Doug and Lee retired and Ted Gaebler recommended to Rick and his new partners that MSI change its name to something that reflected what we did. This was the rebirth of MSI as Revenue & Cost Specialists, L.L.C. As our software grew in importance, we created Government Software Systems, L.L.C., to better identify the software side of our business.

About Us

*"This may strike many readers as odd, but most governments have **no idea how much it costs** to deliver the services they offer. Even if they can give you a budget figure for each service, it **typically excludes** indirect costs, such as administrative overhead, capital costs and employee fringe benefits. How can one even establish an appropriate subsidy if one doesn't know the cost of a service?"*

- Gaebler & Osborne, Reinventing Government, pp.216-217, 1992

Our principals have been helping public agencies with their financial planning **since 1975**.

In 1975 Ayres recognized the considerable advantages of incorporating, rather than taking a salary. So *DWA, Inc.* was created. Thereafter all his time and activities, save for the USC Professor appointment, literally were "rented" to his other subsidiary organizations. *DWA, Inc.* provided a retirement plan and other significant tax advantages. In 1985 the CEO of *DWA, Inc.* acquired an Executive Vice-President – Pamela Swift Ayres. Both *DWA, Inc.* and a remaining subsidiary, *Ayres & Ayres, Inc.,* were dissolved at the end of the 20th century. In 2001 another entity, *Ayres Fiduciary Services, Inc.* was needed, lasting until 2009.

APPENDIX B

Clients of REVENUE COST SPECIALISTS (RCS) & its predecessor
MANAGEMENT SERVICES INSTITUTE, Inc. (MSI)

January 2012

Arizona
City of Goodyear
Lake Havasu City
County of Mohave
City of Peoria
City of Sedona
County of Yavapai

California
City of Alhambra
City of American Canyon
City of Anaheim
Antelope Valley Fire Protection District
Town of Apple Valley
Apple Valley Fire Protection District
City of Arcadia
City of Atascadero
City of Avalon
City of Azusa
City of Bakersfield
City of Banning
City of Barstow
City of Bell Gardens
City of Bellflower
City of Beverly Hills
City of Big Bear Lake
City of Brea
Bridgeport Fire Protection District
City of Buena Park
City of California City
City of Calimesa
City of Canyon Lake
City of Carlsbad
City of Carpinteria
Carpinteria Sanitary District
Carpinteria-Summerland Fire District
City of Carson
Central & West Basin Water Replenishment
District
Central Basin Municipal Water District
Chalfant Public Services (Fire) District
City of Ceres
City of Chino
Chino Valley Independent Fire District
City of Chula Vista

California (continued)
City of Claremont
City of Coachella
Coachella Valley Association of
Governments
City of Colton
City of Commerce
Commerce Redevelopment Agency
City of Compton
City of Concord
County of Contra Costa
City of Corona
City of Coronado
City of Costa Mesa
City of Cotati
City of Covina
City of Cudahy
City of Cypress
Cypress Parks & Recreation District
City of Del Rey Oaks
City of Desert Hot Springs
City of Dinuba
City of Duarte
City of El Cajon
El Dorado Hills Community Services District
City of El Monte
City of El Segundo
City of Elk Grove
City of Eureka
Feather River Recreation and Park District
City of Fillmore
City of Folsom
City of Fontana
City of Foster City
City of Fountain Valley
City of Fullerton
City of Garden Grove
City of Gilroy
City of Glendale
City of Glendora
City of Gonzales
City of Grand Terrace
City of Grass Valley
City of Greenfield
City of Hawthorne

California (continued)
City of Hemet
City of Hermosa Beach
City of Hesperia
Hesperia Water District
City of Highland
City of Hollister
City of Huntington Beach
City of Huntington Park
County of Imperial
City of Irwindale
June Lake Fire Protection District
City of King City
City of La Canada-Flintridge
City of La Habra
La Habra Heights Mutual Water Company
City of La Mirada
City of La Palma
City of La Puente
City of Lake Elsinore
City of Lake Forest
City of Lakewood
City of Lancaster
City of Lathrop
City of Lawndale
City of Lemoore
City of Lincoln
City of Lindsay
City of Loma Linda
City of Long Beach Marine Bureau
Long Valley Fire Protection District
City of Los Altos
Los Angeles Mission College
County of Los Angeles - San Dimas Civic
Center Authority
City of Los Angeles Fire/Police Retirement
Systems
City of Lynwood
Town of Mammoth Lakes
City of Manhattan Beach
City of Marina
City of Merced
City of Milpitas
City of Monrovia
City of Montclair
City of Monterey
County of Monterey
City of Moreno Valley
City of Morgan Hill
City of Morro Bay
City of Murrieta

California (continued)
City of Needles
City of Newport Beach
City of Norco
North Central Fire Protection District
City of Norwalk
City of Oakdale
City of Oakland
City of Oceanside
Oceanside Harbor District
City of Ontario
Ontario-Montclair School District
City of Orange
City of Oroville
City of Oxnard
City of Pacific Grove
City of Palm Desert
City of Palm Springs
City of Palmdale
Town of Paradise
City of Pasadena
City of Paso Robles
City of Petaluma
City of Pico Rivera
City of Pismo Beach
City of Pittsburg
Placer County Water Agency
City of Pomona
City of Port Hueneme
City of Porterville
City of Poway
City of Rancho Cordova
City of Rancho Cucamonga
City of Rancho Mirage
City of Rancho Palos Verdes
City of Red Bluff
City of Redlands
City of Reedley
City of Rialto
City of Richmond
City of Riverside
Riverside County Transportation
Commission
City of Rocklin
City of Salinas
City of San Bernardino
San Bernardino Associated Governments
San Bernardino Mountain Community
Hospital District
County of San Bernardino Special Districts
City of San Clemente

California (continued)
City of San Diego
County of San Diego
San Dimas-Laverne Recreational Authority
City of San Juan Capistrano
City of San Rafael
City of Sand City
City of Sanger
City of Santa Clarita
City of Santa Monica
City of Santa Paula
City of Scotts Valley
City of Seal Beach
City of Seaside
City of Selma
City of Shafter
City of Sierra Madre
City of Solana Beach
City of Solvang
City of South Gate
City of South Lake Tahoe
City of South Pasadena
Southeast Recreation & Park District
City of Stanton
City of Stockton
City of Suisun City
Summerland Sanitary District
City of Taft
City of Thousand Oaks
Town of Tiburon
City of Tracy
Town of Truckee
City of Tulare
County of Tulare
City of Turlock
City of Upland
City of Vallejo
County of Ventura Fire District
City of Villa Park
Visalia Redevelopment Agency
City of Vista
City of West Covina
City of Westminster
City of Wheatland
Wheeler Crest Fire Protection District
City of Whittier
Town of Windsor
City of Yuba City
City of Yucca Valley

Georgia
County of Cobb
City of Winder

Florida
City of Sarasota

Ohio
City of Dublin

Oregon
City of Bend

North Carolina
City of Cary
City of Durham
City of Wilmington

South Carolina
City of Aiken
City of Columbia
City of Florence
City of Georgetown
City of Goose Creek
City of Mt. Pleasant
City of North Augusta
City of North Myrtle Beach
City of Orangeburg
City of Rock Hill
City of Spartanburg
City of Sumter
City of York

Utah
Brigham City
North Ogden City
North View Fire Department
City of South Jordan
South Ogden City
City of Springville
Washington Terrace City
City of West Jordan

Virginia
City of Norfolk

Washington
City of Kennewick

Additional Consulting Clients and Engagements

Douglas W. Ayres conducted consulting, research, writing, organizational design, and organizational forensic examinations, and installation studies of widely varying types for approximately 100 additional clients scattered throughout the United States, Canada and Venezuela. These engagements were performed by him personally, his DWA, Inc.; while with Public Administration Service of the National Governmental Center of the University of Chicago; through the Western Region of PAS when it was attached to California State University – Long Beach or the University of Southern California Graduate School of Public Administration, and by the former PAS Western Regional Office after Ayres purchased this Region from PAS, as the nucleus of his DWA, Inc.

These clients ranged from the Territory, *nee* State of Alaska; the State of Hawai'i; the 35 government corporations and autonomous institutes of the Republic of Venezuela; formation of the Corporaciòn Venezolana de Guayana; the Isla Vista (California) Incorporation Study Commission; Charter Bank of Culver City, California; Beverly Hills Cab Company; LPG of Melbourne, Florida; the City of Eau Gallie, Florida; the San Bernardino County Local Agency Formation Commission for incorporation of each of the Cities of Hesperia and Grand Terrace; on and on.

Doug often was engaged multiple times by the above listed clients, and others. Ayres also had 100+ clients that retained him for capital financing advisory service, or separately, selecting and leading all participants literally to "take it off our hands". That Ayres-select "team" proceeded with the required financing instruments, multiple times for many clients. Somewhere north of a billion, or five or so, of tax exempts resulted. When total "involved engagements" hit 500 he quit counting.

It seems that I took to the bond issuance thing like a duck to water. What the "industry" had made "complicated", to me, at least, was straightforward and simple. The issuances I guided always beat the market by at least .20% EVERY time, and at about 70% of the expenses incurred by others. That "easy and quickly done" type of work made me draw the conclusion early that the "financial services industry" was massively ripping off municipal governments. Some of the things I saw done – prior to my retention to "clean up" subsequent financings – verged on criminality. The fees and processes were so one-sided for the underwriter, bond counsel, underwriter counsel, trustee, printer, and rating agencies they all were "crooked" and "thieves" by my lights. That is why I got so many personal engagements. I was honest and forthright and thus trusted. It was really easy to get debt service and expenses reduced by around 75% or so over the 20 to 30 year duration of the issuance. I could "turn around" a large issue in one day, and did so often. The City of Beaumont was the leader in literally being taken over and massively exploited by the so-called "Financial Advisory Firms".

SPECIAL PERSONAL APPRECIATION

Spouse for 25 years and beloved for 30, Pamela Swift Ayres is a fantastic support system, co-consultant, airplane co-pilot, boat co-captain, and the captain of my life, for which I am deeply grateful. During the research, compilation and writing of this **CONSUMER GOVERNMENT** book she gracefully bailed me out of all sorts of computer and data glitches and otherwise potentially embarrassing situations. She accomplished innumerable vital "things", gently condoning and facilitating my latest passion: explaining and spreading the gospel about local government revenue-costing systems that now has become my retirement endeavor. The nation's local and state governments need the **Municipal Business System**. More important, all of government needs far greater transparency, understanding, much improved program and revenue explanation, and great amounts of competent "product and service" mass marketing. The **Municipal Business System** provides and illustrates how to accomplish the basics for those nationally necessary goals.

Additionally, Pam is the only person I have ever seen who could smooze a 500 person assemblage for an hour and recall everyone's first and last names, their position and organization, and have all remember her grace.

With Pam a publishable manuscript was achieved. She hopes it just might sell. And we both believe the "System" laid out in detail herein can well lead to the financial salvation of local government and, perhaps, even the individual states of our revered United States.

APPENDIX C

EXPOSITORY & EXPANSIONARY ARTICLES

The following articles are extracted from the RCS website www.revenuecost.com. They were written by the most academically qualified and experienced municipal cost analysts in America. Their work has consumed the latter two thirds of the career of each. Each has experience helping at least 100 revenue-starved and thus troubled jurisdictions.* Name the situation and they have not only discovered it, but solved it. It was a joy to have recruited, trained, worked with, and now to observe the groundbreaking outpourings of this group. The salvation of local government in the United States, Canada and English speaking governments is within their systemic and personal capabilities. All needed is for the message purveyed by this Book to be spread and truly understood.

---

* Doug Ayres completed around 50 'other' consulting studies prior to and subsequent to the formation of MSI and its retitling to RCS. His 'personal' consulting project count is somewhere north of 300.

----

1. Capitalism and Local Government

Rick Kermer, CPA on October 11, 2010

One of the many nice features of our capitalist system is the ability to vote with our dollars to get the products that we want in the market place. When we go into a grocery store we have many choices in the products that we buy and we can buy one item or many. The grocer does not tell us that if we want to buy milk that we also have to buy apples. If he did, we would go to another grocery store that let us buy what we wanted.

When we consume government services, we try to get as close to capitalism as possible. We pay taxes to get what we perceive as tax services: primarily public safety and improved quality of life. We also understand that governments will aid those less fortunate than ourselves but we often question the efficacy of those services because we only want to subsidize individuals who deserve to be subsidized.

The bottom line for me, personally, is that when I pay my taxes I expect to get police, fire, and park services. I don't expect to be subsidizing my neighbor who is adding an addition to his house. I don't expect to be subsidizing the guy down the street who wants the city to organize a softball league so that he and his buddies have someplace to play. All of my judgments are subjective. Others will have their own list of what they think should be included in tax services and what should and should not be subsidized by taxes.

All decisions on how local taxes are spent should be determined by local taxpayers and voters. The perceived failure to do this led to the voter backlash in California where several voter initiatives were adopted to force the issue. Authors of the "tightest" national initiative, Proposition 4 (the Gann Initiative, now *California Constittuion Article XIIIB)*, wanted to know several things which seemed commonsense to them: (1) What was the State and local government doing? (2) Who on staff was doing it? (3) What did it cost to do it? (4) Who was paying for it? And, (5) From whence did the money come for these things?

These questions seem so straightforward. Every business asks them and must know the answers. But, at that time they were foreign concepts to local governments. They budgeted and accounted for expenditures (flow of cash) not expenses (accruals). They worked a normal workday with minimal consideration given to what or how many products or services were produced. Fees were determined by either "That's what we always charged" or by calling around to other governments to ask what they charged. Taxes were raised as necessary to balance the budget with little consideration given to how taxes were used.

The capitalist marketplace addressed some needs with niche companies that were formed to answer these questions for local governments using the kinds of tools the private sector had developed many decades ago. That the private sector jumped into the information and marketing gap was logical given that the taxpayer revolt was underwritten by realtor associations and chambers of commerce.

The result was that more and more local governments began to understand the private sector approach. As tax revenues were reduced and as more accurate costs for "personal choice" services were identified, fees that benefited small groups of individuals were increased so that the taxes that were formerly subsidizing them could be used to provide tax services to the general community.

The natural bias before the taxpayer revolt was to keep fees artificially low so that the customer would be happy. The unintended consequence of the taxpayer revolt was that it was now possible – and literally required -- to identify the cost of individual services and to charge accordingly. That, along with the reduced level of taxes, made it essential for the remaining tax revenues to be more precisely focused on traditional tax services.

"Whoa – that's not what I wanted! I wanted my taxes to be spent 'better' but *my* subsidies to remain." Maybe those were not the words used but they certainly seem to be the attitudes expressed once fees started rising.

Now what? Well that old saw, "location, location, location" is still true. I can show an example of two cities of identical population within miles of each other. One has a lot of vacant commercial space and courts more development by discounting all its fees. The other has done everything possible, with the exception of digging a moat, to discourage developers, including the cost of additional development reviews, yet developers still fight to get into that city.

Well then, maybe all cities should have the same fees mandated by the state legislature? It seems logical as all cities have the same basic laws that have to be met. If they all had to work within the limits of a mandated fee, wouldn't they become more efficient? Let's take that concept to its logical conclusion: Shouldn't all gas stations charge the same amount per gallon? After all, gas is gas is gas! Shouldn't all housing have the same price per square foot? "Whoa – that's socialism! I only want socialism for government? Arrrgh. What did I just say?!!"

Capitalism is capitalism and socialism is socialism. Decide what you want but I'm happy with our capitalist system with the least number of tweaks. So, for the sake of argument, can we agree that capitalism is also "good" for government? If so, the issue becomes how to insure that the calculation of fees is legitimate.

Business people may not know government (Schwarzenegger proved that in California) but they certainly know when a fee makes sense. Since we are in a transition stage from the old *("what are the neighboring cities charging?")* to the new *("here's how we calculated our costs")*, there are going to be errors made by local governments.

A classic error comes from a city experiencing rapid growth. Their grading fee structure was established in formerly quiet times. As their growth turned to the rolling hills that were formerly pasture land, a developer submitted a project that involved a tremendous amount of dirt being moved from one spot to another. When the city calculated the grading fee, it penciled out to over $1 million. Staff should have immediately recognized the problem and adjusted the fee. However, government staff like to fall back to the "that's the way we've always done it" mode. It took the developer threatening to sue and a call from staff to RCS before the fee was changed to actual cost of staff time and directly allied, provable costs.

There were two lessons from this example: First, government staff needs to think like the consumers of their services. If something doesn't "smell" right, resolve it as quickly as possible. Notice that I said "resolve it". The other problem I see is the vigilante staff person who will change the fee without authority because they believe the change is "just." Vigilante justice is no more appropriate in government than it is in the "new" west.

Second is the lesson that mistakes have been and will continue to be made. I don't walk on water. I don't know of any other cost consultant who walks across the swimming pool. And, although they may claim otherwise, governmental staff don't walk on water either. If government staff and customers approach the obvious errors with the attitude of "Wow, that's really weird. I'm surprised no one saw this before," we can dispel the defensiveness that would have occurred with the "how could you be so stupid" approach.

In case you haven't noticed, this has segued into discussing development service fees for the same reason Willie Sutton robbed banks. Police services that can be charged for generate little revenue. Fire prevention fees are a growing source of fees but they also impact the development and business community. Recreation fees, "can we talk" should be raised but cannot practically be increased if the community wants a recreation program.

So, focusing on development fees, the goal of appropriate charges is that the revenue is sufficient to insure adequate, well-trained staff to perform the application review process in a timely manner. Developers have consistently said that the fees are not unreasonable if he/she would be able to get through the process quickly and without hassles. The real cost to a developer has usually been the interest on construction loans that pile up while staff dithers with the application.

The alternative is to have low fees which pay for low-skilled and overworked staff that slowly process the application such that the fee savings are spent on interest payments. Either way, the developer pays, but it's my expectation that correctly calculated higher fees supporting a skilled staff will ultimately cost less to the developer.

----

2. There Are No More Rabbits

Scott Thorpe on April 17, 2010

As a child I remember a number of instances of being with my Dad and watching magicians pull rabbits out their hat. I generally found it entertaining, but after a few times began to wonder why my Dad always watched so intently, as I would have thought he understood the trick by now. Later in life I asked him why he always seemed to enjoy it every time. He told me that it wasn't the act of watching rabbits being pulled out of a hat. He said it was only an illusion; simply a hat filled with rabbits and anyone can learn to do that. But as a result, they all eventually are going to run out of rabbits, because they simply, by the laws of physics, will have to. He said it was a matter of style and that he was more interested in *what they did when they ran out of their finite number of rabbits*. He said the good magicians don't leave you disappointed when they run out of rabbits.

I use an analogy of magicians, but please don't take this badly as it's a time-honored and respected skill. Just think of it as marketing. Now don't take that badly either, as many of you still have PIO's! Well, since the passage of Proposition 13 (Jarvis) and the follow-up Proposition 4 (Gann), many local officials, like magicians, annually have had to pull rabbits out of hats. They have had to create the illusion of a balanced budget where no one's services have been adversely affected, or one that is somehow exactly what the community needs. Except now there are fewer rabbits, they seem to be smaller, and no one is willing to refill your magician's hat. To generate a balanced budget suitable for City Council adoption over the roughly 35 years since the passage of Propositions 13 and 4, City Managers, department heads, finance and administrative types, and other rabbit pulling magicians, have probably had to do the following things -- and this is a *very* partial list:

- Close the libraries to maybe 50% of what they had once been open. We won't even mention the book budget.

- Contract out many services no one ever thought would happen, like park mowing and maintenance, sometimes with good results; and sometimes not. Cost be-damned.

- Increase the number of hours expected out of public safety vehicles before replacing them, or simply reduce the number of vehicles.

- Increase all fees for fee-based services to the "cost reasonably borne" standard of the Gann Article XIIIB of the *California Constitution*.

- Institute hiring freezes on replacement of public safety personnel, dropping the service level even if the approved number of trained personnel has not changed.

- Decrease the amount of financial reserves to lower percentages than comfortable.

- Eliminate replacement reserves and maintenance of public facilities to absolute minimums, or sadly, less than minimum and watch them deteriorate faster.

- Pass on grants because they would build a facility that cannot be staffed or maintained, or requires matching monies.

- Reduce maintenance of streets and storm drainage systems to the point where any dysfunction can cause other more costly events, like lawsuits.

- Utility systems with the more lenient rate-setting capabilities still cannot seem to get the support for revenue increases needed to properly replace continually aging systems. Then wait for the failures.

You can see where this is going. [WARNING: you are beginning to run out of rabbits or already have an empty hat]. The illusion of budget reduction without some sort of corresponding significant service reduction cannot continue. Actual service reductions with actual consequences are going to have to happen. I expect we will start seeing some actual municipal bankruptcies within a year or two. There have been some agencies close to or in this drastic process (Vallejo) in the recent past.

So, the audience comes to the act expecting to see rabbits pulled out of a hat (we knew you could!). How can you not leave the public disappointed when you have to admit there are no more rabbits and have to start making service reductions that are significant and noticeable to all residents and business owners? Well if other agencies continue to pull rabbits out of their hats (or out of yours, but that's a different story) it will be hard to end the magic act with crowd applause.

A few suggestions come to mind, and they all relate to information. Start planning for this end of the rabbit-from-the-hat-pulling act. Generate data and compile a list of services that were once available in the mid-70's that no longer exist. Also, identify the major cost saving processes that have been instituted during that time. The lack of revenue is NOT your fault. You have stretched it as far as it can go. It is time to say that out loud and then make suggestions as to what reductions in service can or need to be undertaken.

Appointed city officials have to be advocates, and the City Council's advocate, on what already has been done. Act as if it was your money. What would you do? Over the last 35 years I have seen government change in so many positive ways.

Don't keep what you have done a secret!

----

3. Long-Range Financial Plans -- How to Simplify the Process

Rick Kermer, CPA on June 8, 2008

I got a call recently from a California city interested in consultants that did long-range financial plans (LRFP). I couldn't remember the last time I had a similar call even though LRFPs had once been the rage. I mumbled something about how our approach was completely different than the historical LRFP process and left it there for the city to decide whether to pursue our approach.

Nevertheless, the call got me thinking about how we used to do LRFPs and how our approach simplified the process. It went like this:

Step #1 – Establish Internal Service Funds to allocate the types of indirect costs that could be purchased in the marketplace. Use the market price as a maximum for the internal service cost. If it exceeds that cost, eliminate the internal service and replace it with a contracted service. The city can now ignore indirect costs as they are part of each line department's operating budget.

Step #2 – Prepare a cost allocation plan or a simplified percentage overhead to distribute general government to the line departments. Based on the results, the city could establish a standard percentage overhead that it would use as a maximum for the cost of general government. The city can now ignore general government as this known cost is also charged to each line department.

Step #3 – Conduct a cost of services study for fee and potential fee services. Work with staff and the city council to establish the subsidy that these services should receive from general taxes, if any. Openly, not by budget burial. Treat the whole group of fee services as one tax service similar in nature to the services provided by line departments. The city can now ignore the cost of individual fee services as the group can be treated as a whole.

Step #4 – Expand the coverage of the cost of services study to include all tax services. This is necessary to break out of the organizational model to the program model of local government finance. The city now knows the cost of each tax-supported service provided to the public of which the subsidy to fee services is just one more tax draining device.

Step #5 – If the city is growing, prepare a development impact analysis so that the cost of future infrastructure required by new development is covered by the developers of that new real estate venture. This also identifies any city liability for cost sharing in the necessary infrastructure.

RECAP: At this point, the city has general revenues (mostly taxes and subventions) to match against the full cost of tax services. There will only be four to six significant revenues that will need projection as the rest can be lumped together for trend analysis. Since cities cannot print money, this general revenue total will be the maximum that can be budgeted for all of the tax services (including the fee subsidies) that the city wants to provide. Some cities have gone so far as to allow increases or require decreases to the tax services that are in line with the growth or decline of the general revenues.

Notice how much simpler the financial picture is when it is possible to ignore indirect costs, general overhead and individual fee services. Notice how much simpler it is to forecast general revenues when the city focuses on the major revenues and lumps the others together. Notice how much simpler it is to forecast expenditures when the available revenues determine the level of expenditure.

----

4. Cost Allocation Plan vs. Internal Service Fund

Eric Johnson on April 6, 2008

What happens when you write a Program Budget and no one cares? In other words, identify the full costs of providing various services to the community but it does not affect funding decisions. So depending on resources, ask: "What do we hope to achieve by allocating administrative costs?" Let's explore a couple of different scenarios:

We only want to recover administrative costs from the Enterprise Funds --

If this is the only motivation, then a Cost Allocation Plan (CAP) is the best bet because it does not create the on-going accounting work that an Internal Service Fund does. But if already allocating administrative positions to the Enterprise Funds in the budget, then those positions cannot be included in the CAP. Unfortunately, as preparing the budget it is easier to allocate all or parts of positions to Enterprise Funds than to use an administrative charge supported by a CAP. An abbreviated CAP that only allocates to the Enterprise Funds also can be prepared. Although it is not that much extra work to allocate to all funds once the CAP process is set up for the Enterprise Funds.

We want to identify administrative costs for fee recovery --

Since most agencies do not calculate costs for fee recovery on an annual budgetary basis, a process that allocates costs on an annual basis is not needed. Therefore a CAP fits those needs perfectly. Of course now there is a need to make sure that allocations are made to all funds and departments, as it is most likely to want to look at every fund or department for possible fee recovery. Does that require annual updates?

We want to prepare a Program Budget to identify full costs for all services provided to the public --

While a CAP can certainly allocate all administrative costs to all funds and departments on an annual basis, Internal Service Funds (ISFs) should be considered if creating a program budget. This is because ISFs typically are an institutionalized part of the budget and accounting process, whereas a CAP is not. Therefore, it usually is easier to determine what exactly is being charged to each fund or department if ISF charges show up as line items in each departmental budget. But for a program budget to have credibility, time and effort should be spent to review with each department how and why they are being charged for various administrative costs. So internal "protests" could be considered.

Traditionally, ISFs have not included general administrative departments, such as Finance and Human Resources. But to create a complete program budget it is necessary to add all administrative and support departments into various ISFs. Otherwise, the ISF approach covers only part of the costs of a CAP.

So, depending on the goals for cost allocation there are certain methods that are more efficient than others. But even when trying to determine how to best use limited resources, it is important to keep in mind the following thoughts from an articulate Finance Director, which came in response to me lately:

"You are right that [elected officials] may still choose to [ignore the costs] if given that option, but they sure can't claim ignorance if they are given the information and ignore it. Change can be difficult and it can mean more work initially, but the information can also be a powerful tool that will allow the City Council to make decisions and use the information to support the decisions rather than just succumbing to the influence/pressure of public safety or other "politically immune" operations.

5. Prioritizing Within The Budget

Eric Johnson on September 8, 2008

As the California State Legislature and Governor once again conclude their annual kabuki dance over the budget, it reminds me of the fact that no one in State government is setting priorities for the budget. Instead they are demanding across-the-board cuts for every area or producing a series of inadequate stopgap measures. The State is looking at the budget process exactly backwards. (Of course, that may not be irrational in California.)

Instead of doing everything poorly, the State should decide what it has the political will and the money, at whatever revenue level, to provide well. The State of Washington has gone through this process, as well as a great number of, if not the vast majority of cities and counties in the United States.

The point is to use the budget as a conscious prioritization tool. That is, after all, what the budget process is supposed to be. Of course, any budget reflects what that agency spends money on, but does not always really reflect what is important to that agency.

The only way to prioritize a budget effectively is to cost out all of the services that your agency provides and put them in order of priority. And if everything is number one then you or your elected officials are not taking the process seriously. As you go down the priority list, the point when you run out of money means that everything below that spot does not get funded, barring any new revenue source.

Of course, some deserving programs will get cut. But it is much better to do that and provide other more deserving programs full funding than providing all programs half a loaf. And then watch them wallow through an excruciating death.

Obviously setting priorities are political decisions, but these decisions cannot be made until the data exists as to what every service costs. This is where the *Costing Process* inherent in a ***Municipal Business System*** comes in. What does the police helicopter program cost versus the police DARE program? Where in the priority list should each program lie? These are separate steps in the process, but equally important. If one tries to make prioritization decisions without complete and accurate costing data then decisions are being made in a vacuum, and more important, no one will know when the line has been crossed and the money runs out. Mid-year, maybe?

The first step in the *Costing Process* is to define what level of detail is wanted to provide for the various services. Costing police patrol service is not that meaningful, but costing the various components of police patrol will allow for real budget decisions to be made.

The prioritization step is the harder and more time consuming part, because value decisions need to be made as to what services are more important than others. There will be different voices that will have different ideas about what is important. The community, either through the City Council or through a larger Budget Task Force, should be the ones making this determination because they will be the ones that will be most affected by these decisions.

But after the priorities are set, the community will have bought into the City's budget and its priorities. And if some programs require a revenue increase, the community will be able to tell exactly what they are getting for that extra revenue. Of course, there is always the intransigent that must be dealt with, somehow.

Every budget involves trade-offs, but those should at least be based on full information and be conscious decisions. Maybe if enough local agencies prioritize their budgets the State government will someday follow suit.

Another issue is that all services are not created equal. If a program has its own separate funding source, such as fees or grants, should it be treated differently?

----

6. Prioritizing The Budget – Part II

Rick Kermer, CPA on October 11, 2008

The above article ended with the question whether programs with their own funding source should be treated differently in the prioritization process. The best answer to that question is *Yes and No*.

The prioritization process, as discussed above, is useful for the allocation of tax dollars to programs. If a program is TOTALLY financed by fees or grants, then it gets no tax dollars and should be excluded from the prioritization process. However, to the extent that it is subsidized by taxes, it should be included.

If governments were to adopt this approach, it would have the following positive effects:

- The budget process would be simpler as fewer programs would require review.
- A simpler budget process would allow for more analysis of the tax programs.
- Departments would see an advantage in reducing their dependence on taxes by instituting fees for services.
- Departments would have a greater incentive to match staffing with the projected workload.

If the fact that the budget process is a game can be accepted, then this last point should suggest an amendment to the Proposition: Projecting that the operation is going to be 100% financed from fees is nice but actually having that operation 100% financed from fees should be the criteria. The only way this can practically happen, is to account for fee-supported operations in a special revenue or enterprise fund where the annual profits and losses can balance each other over time. This amendment addresses the *It's Free* budget game identified by Chris Argyris in his book, *The Hidden Ball Game*.

Overcoming Organizational Defenses

Is there a risk that customers will be gouged by government fees under this proposition? In my experience, departments typically undercharge for services because they have to deal directly with the customer and, therefore, are the most sensitive to complaints. The private sector has the marketplace for pricing discipline. The surrogate in governments is the tension created when the department has the legislative pressure to charge full-cost on one side and the customer complaining about high fees on the other side.

To make this approach work, the free programs need the *Municipal Business System* Costing Process to insure that they are truly free. O.K. now that fee and grant-financed programs have been considered, focus now can be exclusively on tax programs.

----

7. Prioritizing Tax Programs

Eric Johnson on July 4, 2010

Given that the budget process is a game, prioritizing programs requires more information than just the name of the program. An explainable and defensible Costing Process is necessary to provide the data for prioritizing; and, the first step in the Costing Process – after identifying all services offered -- is to define the level of detail needed to provide for various services. For example: park maintenance. What is needed to know in order to prioritize this program? The following would be a good start:

- How often are the parks mowed?
- What grass height are they mowed to?
- How many acres can be mowed by one worker in a day?
- Would the number of acres mowed in a day increase with a different mower?
- A favorite -- What would be the consequence of not mowing?

The issues raised are: (1) maintenance standards, and (2) productivity. It would be hard to prioritize park maintenance without knowing the answer to the above issues. And, once the answers are known, there might be multiple cost options for park maintenance which would lead to multiple priority options.

By taking the MSI/RCS costing process down to the lowest level possible, also addressed is Chris Argyris' *The Hidden Ball Game* where an unattractive program is concealed within an attractive one. Also dealt with is the "It Can't Be Measured Game" by showing that the program really can be measured.

In summary, the **Municipal Business System** Costing Process can help simplify the budget process by focusing effort on the allocation of tax dollars. That focus is essential in the prioritization process to thwart the game players in the budget process.

----

8. Achieving the Potential of GASB 34

Rick Kermer, CPA on March 16, 2010

Statement 34 was adopted with much fanfare by the Governmental Accounting Standards Board (GASB) in June of 1999. By the end of 2004, more than 84,000 governmental units were required to include the *estimated* historical cost of infrastructure in their comprehensive annual financial reports. This statement had been circulating in various forms almost since the inception of the Board in 1984. By that time, Management Services Inc. (MSI), the predecessor to RCS, had been preparing cost of services studies for four years assisting California local governments with the twin *California Constitution* citizen initiative body-blows of Proposition 13 and Proposition 4.

MSI Founder, Chairman and CEO, USC Professor, former Salem, Oregon Finance Director/Treasurer, and City Manager of three cities, Doug Ayres had been preaching such an accounting change and requirement for two decades. A two-class USC (Public Finance and Public Budgeting) MPA student of Doug's, Barbara Henderson, a quite prominent California municipal Finance Director, subsequently was appointed to the GASBoard. She soon proposed and achieved adoption of Doug's ideas, now known as GASB Statement 34. The time was right. The concept and proposal had been talked about enough. It passed!

Fortunately, the authors of Proposition 4, which was sold to voters as finishing the job of Proposition 13, opined that an appropriate cost of government was "…reasonable allocations for capital replacement." Since these authors were members of the California Chamber of Commerce and the California Board of Realtors, they would have assumed that everyone knew that assets are replaced at their current cost and not their historical cost. In an attempt to influence GASB's fixed asset research, MSI sent a voluminous packet of information that showed the significant difference we had found between historical cost and current replacement cost for clients to that date. Barbara Henderson utilized that data in her presentations. She won the battle to secure the Statement, but lost the skirmish requesting a reasonable "private sector" level of asset definition.

In defense of Barbara and the Board, MSI/RCS accepted the fact that historical cost was a traditional element of financial practices and statements in the private sector, and that changing to replacement cost for government financials would be a hard sell. Such would have been especially difficult as representatives of the Governmental Finance Officers Association (GFOA) were already opposed to incurring the cost to provide information many felt would be of 'no demonstrative value'. Although "replacement cost" in fact does have demonstrative value, GFOA was mum on the concept at the time and only recently (post 2000) has discussed it as a budgetary "best practice".

Today, governments have a GASB 34 report. The Statement's authors expect that people will want to compare the current maintenance of infrastructure groups with the depreciation of those groups as would be done in the private sector. The problem is that few private companies have infrastructure that is between 50 and 100 years or more old. Unfortunately, that "problem" is too common for governments. Each agency should on its own determine if its infrastructure maintenance effort is adequate. Most municipal engineers say that catastrophe is just a tiny bit away. Engineering Associations strongly agree.

Most GASB 34 reports prepared by professional consultants have an estimated replacement cost. Therefore, it is possible to calculate the average age of an infrastructure category using the historical information and apply that factor to the estimated replacement cost. Most municipal officials will have to do this on their own since reports that take that next step of comparing current maintenance expenditures with the annual expiration of infrastructure value are rare.

Intergenerational Equity is the reason that this is an issue. To the extent that governments are blithely going on their way, sure that compliance with GASB 34 is the *last* word, they are spending too much on current operations and not enough on infrastructure maintenance. Today's kids and grandkids are the ones who will have to pay the piper for poor decisions now being made. Unfortunately, today that unfulfilled saying comes up often.

Historically, Cost of Services studies included estimated infrastructure replacement cost and show the annual "expiration of infrastructure value" as a tax expense. This was very helpful for managers and council members as fee for service increases could be justified to free up tax revenues to partially cover that expense.

Unfortunately, Gresham's Law also applies to Cost of Services studies. Due to asymmetry of information, municipal officials did not understand the value of the infrastructure information and chose consultants who provided a less expensive and expansive product. Accordingly, RCS stopped providing this information unless specifically requested. Naturally, we push for inclusion of such vital information, but more often fail in that insistence. Now, government staffs are facing the question of why fees should be increased? The answer is to pull out your GASB 34 report and compare current maintenance expenditures with the annual amount of infrastructure expiration at current cost, thereby achieving the full potential of GASB 34.

9. When is a Fee a Tax?

Scott Thorpe -- on August 18, 2009 (After the mortgage 'crash' was well underway)

Short answer: When it's not collected as a fee!

This may be preaching to the choir a bit, but sometimes the choir likes some attention too. All RCS Staff have been in public hearings regarding changes to development impact fees (DIFs) and heard some developer claim: "It's a tax, it walks like a duck and quacks like a duck." Well, you know the rest. Well, it's true! For the existing public, an impact fee becomes a tax when the DIF **isn't adopted and maintained.**

Many cities are now struggling with the issue of DIFs. The Building Industry Association, national and local Realtors Associations, and other allied organizations orchestrate statewide campaigns to have these important fees reduced or eliminated, with successes in some states and local agencies. If California local government officials calculated DIFs according to California State Law (Gov't Code 66000 *et. seq.*), the fees are limited to an amount that merely accommodates new development. So it follows that if not imposed and collected, DIFs, by definition, are not accommodating new development. But clearly new development creates increased demands for (among others): public safety services, circulation system travel space, and storm drainage/utilities capacity. So, the capital needs still exist, but to be paid for at whose expense?

Thus, uncollected DIFs become an unrecognized or delayed tax on the general public, and they take the form of longer commutes, longer police/fire responses, and more crowded public facilities. If not adopted, they also require diversion of taxes from general benefit to the benefit, costs and profit of the developers and/or the purchasers in the development. The latter ultimately will pay with future taxes. Or in the current climate, it will simply not ever get constructed and the resulting infrastructure problem will just become a part of the perpetually frayed fabric of the community.

I recently was asked to sit in on a meeting with the staff of a client city and four developers. I thought I was invited to defend that City's DIFs. What I saw was a City defense of DIFs in general. The City Council and staff simply "got it". The City Council policy is that new development must pay its own way, period, and that they will accommodate, but not subsidize development. Development does not define them, but it could break them. They are paying more attention to the operational needs of the existing community and less to the developers asking for subsidies to enhance a profit. The city officials rejected the argument that development for the sake of development is somehow a good or necessary thing. Oh, they did review their DIFs to see where actual reductions to project costs (mostly for land acquisition) have occurred and will act on those.

So, what to do? It's probably best to ask: Does the city need to subsidize development; and is there any substantive benefit to the existing community from such subsidy? The following discussion assumes a suspension of DIFs and the roll-on impact through the three major land-uses.

RESIDENTIAL – There does not seem to be any plausible explanation of how the approval of twenty residential dwellings without any DIFs imposed improves the economy of a community. It may merely increase the currently high vacancy rate and be a drag on the current General Fund taxes. It might be wise to check with the many homeowners with homes for sale now on how they would feel about that. There also is a long-held shibboleth coming from cities: "single family residential development does not 'carry' itself by taxes paid by their owners."

COMMERCIAL – This type of development is one of the highest demand land-uses and there no doubt are many existing struggling businesses and current vacancies there also. However, if the new development is in an urban area already containing the required hard infrastructure, further commercial building may be beneficial.

INDUSTRIAL/MANUFACTURING – For these new buildings such a subsidy may make some sense, especially if it's a new business that creates jobs that increase the average wage in the community (check the local U.S. census numbers). But if it reduces the average wage, why should that be subsidize?

That's the point. A community needs to have a policy and consider that large gray area in the middle of that continuum. Avoid the knee-jerk reaction of assuming that the DIFs are somehow a bonus revenue. They are real, they are important, and they represent what the community will be in the future. If there is a real desire to reduce the DIFs to stimulate building, have those reductions sunset at a certain date. When it comes time for the elected body to have this DIF discussion (and perhaps that point can be controlled), preparation with a cognizant and logical policy that makes sense for your community is wise. That policy ought to meet some sort of group objective other than the fairly vague "partnership" with the construction industry to "get the economy going". That will happen when the number of vacant and/or foreclosed residential and business structures decreases significantly enough to have a housing/store shortage.

Count on it?

----

10. Ensuring Utilities Pay Their Way

Rick Kermer, CPA on April 15, 2009

In the early 1980s, MSI pioneered the use of the Franchise Fee as a charge for the use of city or county rights-of-way by municipal and government-owned utilities. (Also see Article 16 of this Appendix C.) Insistence on the franchise fee as a charge and not a tax flew in the face of conventional wisdom at the time, which considered it a tax. There is a large body of case law defining franchise fees as a distinctly different type of municipal revenue. These fall more closely to the category of "land rental" than either of a fee or tax. The MSI approach gained greater acceptance after the passage of California Proposition 4, which required that cities calculate their proceeds of taxes, fees and charges.

Nevertheless, just as the municipal finance profession was getting used to the idea of a franchise fee, California voters retaliated with the passage of Proposition 218, which required that any transfer of monies from a utility fund to the general fund be based on a calculation of the services provided by the general fund. This issue was returned to consciousness recently when a California finance director asked the California State Municipal Finance Officer member forum whether anyone was applying franchise fees to municipally-owned utilities.

The League of California Cities publication, "Proposition 218 Implementation Guide", dated January of 1997 is explicit in stating, on page 59, that the drafters of Proposition 218 have asserted that such transfers violate article XIIID, section 6(b)(1) and (2). It goes on to debate on the same page whether the drafters were correct, but concludes by saying that even if that interpretation does apply there would be no violation of Prop. 218 to the extent that "…a public agency is able to articulate why the transfer is justified as part of the cost of providing the service, based on the enterprise's or utility's fair share of the costs incurred in receiving services from the agency's general fund operations." Consequently, franchise fees are now referred to as charges, not transfers.

Bad Charges: Over the years, there have been several charges that could not pass the giggle test (i.e. can you make the case without starting to giggle at how silly it is). The worst examples were charges for police and/or fire services. Unless there is something unusual about a utility, there is little chance for it to be stolen or burnt down.

Good Charges: General Administration. A charge for general city administration supported by a Total Cost Allocation Plan (CAP) is a basic first step in recovering general fund costs from utilities. The Total Cost CAP includes the legislative body and administrative staff that support the legislative body, and the utility operation either directly or indirectly. The A-87 Compliant CAP excludes legislative costs and should only be used for utility charges if local laws require it.

Specific Departmental Services. The following are common general fund services provided to utility funds:

- Utility billing and payment processing by the finance department
- Engineering services performed in-house for system repairs or expansion
- Facility maintenance on utility buildings
- Fleet maintenance on utility equipment
- Corporate yard costs not covered above

It should be insured that the utility funds have paid for these services.

Miscellaneous Benefits. Some cities still treat some or all staff related benefits in non-departmental activities. All employee benefits including retiree benefits paid by the City should have their proportionate share paid by the utility funds as part of a full cost franchise charge, and/or use permit.

Infrastructure Repair. This is the most difficult cost to calculate as most utility lines are under the streets. Since it is rare for utility line repairs to be performed only when streets are being resurfaced, there is an impact to the integrity of streets whenever the surface is cut into. If you have a capital projects engineer who is responsible for street maintenance, that person should be able to identify the impact on the life of a street whenever utility maintenance is performed. This is a cost that is only beginning to be recognized. The former finance director of Garden Grove, Tony Andrade, did such a study before retiring. Also see Article 16 of this Appendix C for much more justification of franchise 'fees'.

It is still possible to recover general fund costs from utility funds, only now the recovery must be based, at least in California, on quantifiable costs. Such detailed calculations are good practice wherever publicly-owned utilities are operated.

----

11. Using a Program Budget to Restore Trust

Eric Johnson on May 16, 2009

As the drama unfolds, with every passing day the California State budget deficit seems to grow deeper. So what do the voters say to Sacramento? "We don't believe you." The voters think that they are sending enough revenue to the State for the Legislature and Governor to be able to provide all of the services that the State provides. Of course, the voters are wrong, but that is a whole other article. But they are taking out that anger on

State government but channeling it to their own local governments, which are the only readily available agencies to which to vent. Cities and counties hold meetings weekly, and the public speaks and expresses their disgust at each session.

How can local agencies gain the trust of voters?

One thing that local agencies can do to diminish that anger is to try to restore the connection between revenues received and services provided. The best way that a local agency can do this is through a program budget. This process involves identifying all of the services that are provided to the public down to the lowest functional level that makes sense. Then the revenues associated with that service are identified and any difference is made up from general taxes.

This process is similar to stacking building blocks, with each service being a separate block. If total costs exceed total revenues, then blocks either need to be removed or they need to be made smaller. But until all of the blocks are identified and stacked up before the community, it is impossible for the community and its governing body to make informed decisions about what services they truly can afford. If the community says they still want all the services, then the groundwork has been laid for a discussion about revenue increases. Of any or, most probably, of each of fees, charges and taxes.

But until the trust with the community is restored about what it truly costs to provide all of the services that it receives, and that revenue is being utilized to meet ONLY those defined specific needs, any discussion about cutting services or increasing revenues will be very difficult and open to great earned criticism.

Much has been written in more detail about program budgets in past RCS newsletters. Go to www.revenuecost.com/newsletter.php and look at the newsletter articles for September and October 2008. (*And at the body of this Book.*)   See also CHAPTER VII -- BUDGETING of this Book.

----

12. To Outsource or Not to Outsource

Eric Johnson on May 18, 2011

In these days of budget angst and woe pressure is on from elected officials or community on city staff to outsource services currently provided by city personnel. But will this actually save the city money while providing the same level of service to the community?

To determine whether that is the case one must look at not only the direct cost of providing the service, but any ancillary costs that go along with that service that might be outsourced. Here is an example: outsourcing tree trimming services.

Direct Costs

It could be relatively simple to determine the direct cost of providing tree trimming services in a city, if there were discrete individuals who only do tree trimming. But if the parks staff does tree trimming <u>and</u> other services, such as park mowing, then it gets more complicated. There is a need to determine what each employee does and how much time they spend doing it. Then look at the employee mix if tree trimming were no longer provided by city staff. How many employees and supervisors are needed to provide the remaining services? If there are minimal layoffs, chances are the cost savings will be less than hoped for because you will likely be laying-off newer and cheaper employees.

Indirect Costs

While looking at the full costs of providing a service when comparing that service with a private contractor, including overhead costs, it is important to understand what costs the city will be saving and what costs will just be reallocated to other services. For instance, part of the overhead cost is a portion of the city manager and city council cost. Obviously, even after contracting out tree trimming services, there will still be a need for both. These costs will just be reallocated to other services, and there is no cost savings to the city. But if contracting out tree trimming services means there will be less vehicle maintenance costs, then there will be that cost savings to the city. So now the same questions asked of the park maintenance staff above will need to be asked of the vehicle maintenance staff and everyone else who provides administrative support to parks maintenance. How would job responsibilities change based on tree trimming being contracted. Only then can it be determined what are fixed costs and what marginal costs are.

Contract Administration and Conversion Costs

Finally, it needs to be determined what costs would be added to city staff if tree trimming is outsourced. There is now a new contract that needs to be developed, legally prepared, advertised, reviewed, and potentially awarded. Then there is the cost of administering, supervising, and inspection as to quality. There should be performance measures in the contract that would need to be spot-checked. Who would do contract administration and how will that affect the other services currently provided by that specific contract administration employee? And what is the cost of the above development, review and review processes?

Are there one-time conversion costs, such as pay outs to laid-off employees or costs associated with transferring maintenance vehicles to the contractor. Are those costs going to be front-loaded in the first year or amortized over the length of the contract? Also, are there any off-setting revenues that would accrue to the city by contracting out, or would the city lose any revenues by contracting?

This overview shows that deciding whether to outsource a service is not a simple process. More important, it reinforces the idea that decisions of this type cannot made in a vacuum. Good decisions come from good information. Information is needed about what services are being provided to the public, what services are being provided to other departments, and who is providing those services. Without this information it is not possible to know whether outsourcing a service is economical or not.

Then there always are the quality and continuity issues.

----

13. The Costa Mesa, California Experiment

Scott Thorpe on July 26, 2011

As many California local government officials probably know, the City of Costa Mesa has pink-slipped nearly half of its employees. Considering that as-of-yet none of those pink-slipped have included firefighters, and only eight out of the existing 139 police positions were involved. Thus it is understood that the cuts primarily came from the ranks of general employees and the services they provide(d).

Regardless of what one may think, it is hard to know for sure if the changes are more politically, ideologically, or fiscally motivated. Given that all current City Council members consider themselves fiscal conservatives, politics would be hard to ignore. But, given that the City also has had a significant downturn in General Fund tax receipts, combined with escalating retirement costs, fiscal prudence needs cannot be eliminated either.

Municipal service delivery changes that are being considered include sharing service delivery with other nearby local agencies, as well as fully contracting out to other levels of government or private sector contractors. Also, numerous services deemed as not being worth the cost are being eliminated. These changes are not unheard of in municipal government. Many newly incorporated cities employ such practices with great success. And hey, we all get it; the public elects a City Council, the City Council makes policy, and staff, at least the remaining ones, carry out that policy to the best of their ability. If an appointed city official doesn't understand this, they probably are in the wrong line of work.

So what are a few ways that make any actions more fiscally prudent and less politically motivated? Here are some suggestions:

Recognize the twin principles of efficiency and effectiveness. Sure, they differ. The former relates to cost, the latter relates to how well the service is provided. Savings can always be made, but at what cost to the level of service (or LOS)? The City could easily hire a bunch of monkeys (officially called a "troop") and give them a hundred typewriters to write the City's press releases. No doubt it will be efficient, but the monkeys would probably fail on effectiveness. Who knows, eventually they might even come up with something sensible. On the other hand, hiring ten fully tenured literature professors to carry out the same task would probably be effective, but not efficient. A balance needs to be struck between the two.

Measure the delivery of municipal services. This process is known by many names, including Management by Objectives, Quality Circles, and Zero-Based Budgeting. But whatever the name, they all require the measurement of the provided service, identifying the resources it takes to provide the service, and then measuring the quality of the actual service. Though it seems counter-productive to spend more time on record-keeping (or as some call it, "management") when resources are limited, to make changes just for the sake of saving money, is as some used to call it, just whistling past the cemetery. Everyone in the room is just pretending the decision was for the better.

Distribute Resources and Responsibility. Rather than micro-manage how a service is provided, the city council could simply allocate the available resources (or the revenue pie) to the departments and then let the professionals responsible for that service determine how to best use those limited resources. The police chief should be the professional the council expects to look for law enforcement delivery decisions. If they don't, then its time they get the city manager to choose one that delivers. If the council makes the staffing decisions, how can the chief be held responsible for the outcome? He simply can't be.

Discuss these major changes above-board. No one should fault any city council for reviewing service delivery options. But sweeping statements like, "the private sector can do it better" does not make for better decisions. "Better" needs to be defined, as does the task and the follow-up review of the results. For instance, did the change in source of service delivery actually provide for the complete needs of the public, and was it cheaper? Thus "costs" need to be identified, and assembled. Again the effectiveness/efficiency thing raises its head. If the service is to be outsourced to a private sector firm there must be a profit. Further, public cost must be sure to include the costs of developing, and then monitoring the contract work to insure that the terms of the contract are met.

That Constant Social Spectre

There always is another spectre in outsourcing an existing municipal service: Namely, is lesser cost being achieved by the contractor employing considerably lower wage personnel, without any benefits, assuming those people are physically, mentally, and honest enough to be fully capable of providing the service? This portion of the decision tree often is referred to as "the Community Social Element."

What is most helpful to all local government is that the members of the City Council of the City of Costa Mesa, California have placed themselves individually and as an elected group in the public laboratory Petri dish for all to observe. They have become the biggest experiment going, and frankly, all should take advantage of open and often viewing of this noble experiment. Provided, of course, that the contracts are properly and ethically rewarded, all costs are enumerated and included, and service level quality is agreed-to, monitored and reported. And those procedures can be confirmed. See Appendix A for a partial "solution" to the above-mentioned 'social' factors.

---

14. Should Across-the-Board Cuts Affect All Departments?

Eric Johnson on January 13, 2009

In this time of financial uncertainty it has become common for cities, and even the State, to call for across-the-board reductions in expenditures. But what if a department or function is entirely fee supported? This could apply to Building & Safety, Current Planning, and Development Engineering. Should those departments have to reduce staffing even if their funding comes from user fees and not general taxes? And, naturally, the contra would require staff layoffs were development fee income to drop below budgeted levels.

Under Article XIIIB of the *California State Constitution*, fees are only allowed to recover up to the "costs reasonably borne" of providing the service. So, if expenditures are reduced without alignment with the needs of the customers, it could lead to lower fees and therefore lower revenues, even though there may still be unfinished work to be done.

The building cycle will tend to reduce development-related expenditures at its own pace. As there is less development during an economic downturn there will be less need for development-supported services. So a reduction in expenses, whether contract or actual staffing, should follow to fit the new workload.

But the ups and downs of the building cycle don't go in lockstep with the ups and downs of tax revenues. By applying an across-the-board reduction to the departments involved in development there may still be work to be done that was previously funded by fees. At the other end of the cycle, building tends to ramp back up before the rest of the economy and before new tax dollars start flowing in. (But not necessarily in early 2012, *yet.*)

All in all, this makes the case that these development-supported departments and all the services provided should be individual Service Centers isolated in enterprise or special revenue funds, and allowed to act independently of the variations in general taxes. The bottom line should be the fund balance for those development-related funds. As development increases, expenses need to keep pace. As development slows, expenses need to also contract. It becomes the responsibility of the fund manager(s) (Service Center Managers and department head) to insure that the revenues are always around the costs and that the fund balance is not too large or negative.

This should not have a large impact on the amount that individual applicants pay in fees. But it should insure that there is the right amount of staff on hand to process the project in a timely manner, always a major goal of the developer.

To treat these development-supported departments in the same manner as general tax-supported departments creates unneeded management and customer service problems.

----

15. Development Winners and Losers

Rick Kermer on June 22, 2010

There are four players in the development game:

1. Developers

2. Contractors

3. Land owners

4. Current residents.

Each plays a critical role and each has goals that are not necessarily shared by the others.

Developers are the entrepreneurs who see potential in the development of a parcel of property. The developer is the risk taker who bets that he or she can buy the rights to develop a parcel, hire a contractor to build the development and sell/lease it to buyers/tenants at a profit. As the risk taker, the developer can lose everything, win big, or end up somewhere in between. Or, as of 2007 and later – have to choose between bankruptcy or foreclosure by lenders.

Costs are extremely important to developers as they come out of their pockets or a leveraged loan. Some develop to leave a legacy, others to acquire a fortune, but most because developing is what they know how to do to make a living. Often the developer goes where opportunity is the greatest, which can make association with a community a tenuous relationship at best.

Contractors are local workers who construct development conceived by the developer. Their livelihood is based on the existence of development. Anything that threatens development is perceived as a personal threat, so consequently, they are allies of developers.

Land owners of developable land can be realtors or the rancher/farmer who is ready to retire or move to an area more remote from civilization. Often they are the long-term speculator who sees potential in property where others see dust. Land owners and developers will court each other until a match is found that meets the needs of both parties. But not necessarily of the local residents or the local governing body.

These three groups are obviously pro-development as that is their career and/or it affects their financial well-being. The fourth group is comprised of a community's current residents, who have a conflicted view of development.

The current resident is someone who already lives in the community and, along with the business community, pays taxes for current services. The individual resident may have limited clout in the local legislative body where businesses and other special interests often contribute money and time to elect candidates for office, and lobby to curry favors. Only when sufficient numbers of residents are aggravated about an issue can the strength of their electoral numbers overcome the financial advantage of their perceived adversaries.

In the early stages of a community's growth, open land is plentiful and development is scattered and sparse. Developers who work in this environment rarely encounter opposition for modest developments or for developments that meet a particular need of the community. However, at some point in the growth of a community, it becomes more and more apparent that new developments are impacting the existing residents. The signs are subtle at first: a longer commute to work or to the store because of the volume of cars on the road or because an intersection takes so long to maneuver through. That open space across the street or down the block that the kids could play in is now filled with homes or stores and the kids have to find a new place to play. Where's the park, is now the question. The little Carnegie Library that served the community so well in its early days is now overwhelmed by local school children seeking books or website resources that their school libraries can no longer afford.

At this point generally it is when the professional staff of the community – be it a town, city or even an unincorporated county area -- recommends development fees to the legislative body. The impetus can be financial or "quality of life." From a financial standpoint, the community may not have the monies to construct the infrastructure that a development requires to avoid impacting the current residents. From a "quality of life" standpoint, the empty lots which were used as unofficial parks are now full of homes and alternatives need to be found for youth recreation.

What has happened is that a community has reached a "tipping point." Obviously, every development that has occurred in the past has had an impact. But, suddenly: "It's my development that is going to be charged. Whereas the guy who developed before the impact fees made lots of money, I may now go broke from having to pay these fees."

No one questions that there is an impact from building thousands of new homes in a small community. But, it is a lot harder to see the impact of building three homes on a small parcel.

The Development Agreement process was the initial method used to obtain infrastructure funding from a developer. However, the development agreement was not always the fairest way to mitigate the impacts of a development. Many communities found that the facilities constructed using the development agreement were perceived as "belonging" to the neighborhood and not to the community as a whole. At the same time, other impacts were too small to be addressed in the development agreement, such as library books, or else they were too large to be thought of as impacts, such as the need for a larger sewer trunk line or creek/river bridge servicing the entire community.

Believe it or not, the development impact fee process was designed to be the fairest for all developments: neither overcharging the large development nor undercharging the small development. The process is simple: (1) identify the cost of additional infrastructure that will be necessary to support the total community at build-out; (2) split the cost of the additional infrastructure between what the existing community requires and what new development requires; (3) identify what new development will occur between "now" and build-out; (4) Identify a "use" factor for how the new development "uses" the infrastructure; and, (5) spread the cost of the additional infrastructure over all new development based on how the new development will use the infrastructure.

If it can be agreed that development impact fees are, conceptually, the fairest way to allocate impacts to developments, why is the development community often seen as opposed to them? The obvious answer is that the cost of the impact fees is coming out of the developer's pocket, or more likely, out of the construction loan. But, ultimately, will have to be either added to the asking price for the structure, or taken from profit. Therefore, if a community is at the "tipping point," the rational developer would like to be the last to develop before impact fees are imposed.

An argument is often made that impact fees increase the price of homes. In a perfect world, that would be true as every home being built has an impact on its community's infrastructure. However, we don't have a perfect world. Some communities have established impact fees while neighboring communities have not. Since the value of a home is determined by the marketplace, the home in a community that has established impact fees may not be marketable at a price such that the impact fee is in addition to the developer's costs. In such cases, the developer pays the fees out of his/her own pocket, or loan.

Nevertheless, once the tipping point is in the past, new developments all will be paying the impact fees, and these costs will then be included in the price of homes. Is this bad? Probably not, for the costs will have to be paid by someone. If it isn't the owner of the new home, it is everyone else in the community who is paying, either overtly by having some of the taxes that would have been used for police and fire diverted to capital projects; or covertly such as a longer commute time with increasing road rage. What this means is that a community that has rejected development impact fees has made a decision to have the entire community pay for the impacts caused by new development. In a democracy, that is perfectly okay as long as it's understood that the non-decision is actually a decision that the existing community is going to pay.

So, are all development impact fees wonderful? Of course not! Often when staff develops, and the governing body adopts the list of projects required by build-out, the list includes projects that inflate the cost and are unnecessary. Or, projects that the existing community needs are attributed to new development. Members of the development community should carefully review the projects to understand why, or if, they are needed and whether the cost-sharing is fair. Then again, some state legislatures, such as Arizona, have interfered in the process and have statutorily limited both of what fees can be applied, and a limit for each. Thus the State has decided to add to local tax rates.

The positive side of development impact fees for developers and land owners is that projects and land in a community where the infrastructure has kept pace with development will command a higher price than in a community where residents are unhappy with their facilities. Unfortunately, the marketplace does not immediately make that adjustment so those at the "tipping point" will not see the benefit.

Impact fees are another price of civilization. It is no different from paying taxes to have a professional firefighter standing by rather than depending on neighbors to put out the fire with garden hoses. Nevertheless, at each tipping point, there are winners and losers. All need to understand that when the development community fights to develop without paying its fair share of infrastructure, it's similar to the "open range" philosophy that all grazing land and water should be free.

In case you haven't noticed, the times they are a-changin'.

----

16. Do Utilities Affect Street Costs? (Part 1 of 3 Parts)

Doug Ayres & Rick Kermer in 1995 (based on Ayres in each of 1957 and 1980)

This summarizing article is backed up by two other research studies and resultant thought pieces which offer significantly greater detailed facts and discussions. Only the first is here provided. At issue is a literal battle between public and private utility owners/operators on one hand, and municipal public works street maintenance executives on the other. That bitter war has been waged from the late 1940's until the present day. There have been winners – mainly the utilities, especially the investor-owned corporate entities -- over the streets maintenance people.

Ayres participated in a major study conducted jointly by the American Public Works Association (APWA) and the American Water Works Association (AWWA). That was back in the 1950's when both organizations were housed at the University of Chicago's National Governmental Center, or as it was commonly referred to: **1313** – East 60th Street, on the south side of Chicago, on the Midway where 'da Bears practiced, leading to the still very convenient original Chicago airport -- Midway.

Sufficient explanation is provided in this Article to image the "war", its battles and the results, stand-offs, and non-results. And the consequent steady and enhanced deterioration of the nation's street system.

The other two Parts are:

Part II -- **"There Is a Need to Calculate the Costs Utilities Inflict on Streets"**

Part III – **"Did Influential Public Works Leaders Skew Research Results?"**

Copies of Parts II and III are available to purchasers of this Book, with documentation of purchase. Contact the Author at

Douglas W. Ayres
10 Thunder Road
Sedona, AZ 86351-9205

OTHER BOOKS BY DOUGLAS W. AYRES:|

All can be ordered at: http://bookstore.Trafford.com OR at the above address
www.Amazon.com

RIGHT IN THE CITY – A Dog's Tale (VOLUME I)

RIGHT IN THE CITY – More Bizarre Tales (VOLUME II)

THE LOCAL GOVERNMENT JOKE BOX

UNDAUNTED CURIOSITY – BOATING AMERICA'S COASTS AND WATERWAYS
     (VOLUME I)—British Columbia to New York City

UNDAUNTED CURIOSITY – BOATING AMERICA'S COASTS AND WATERWAYS
     (VOLUME II)—New York City to Mississippi via Canada

CONSUMER GOVERNMENT – VIA THE ART OF FULL DISCLOSURE

LATE NOTE RE: CORRUPTION

Those who might question, or even challenge the "flat out statement" made on page 103 about **CORRUPTION**, the Author refers you to a book I discovered while this Book – *CONSUMER GOVERNMENT* -- was in the final throes of "correction editing and alleviation". The term "**CORRUPTION**" used on page 143 was specifically applied to "outsourcing of governmental activities". The following intensely researched and annotated reference work greatly expands both the definition and coverage of **CORRUPTION**.

THROW THEM ALL OUT by Peter Schweizer -- 2011

Houghton Mifflin Harcourt Publishing Company
215 Park Avenue South, New York, New York 10003
ISBN 978-0-547-57314-4

DO UTILITIES AFFECT STREET COSTS?

by Douglas W. Ayres
and Albert R. "Rick" Kermer, Jr., CPA
February 15, 1995

The maintenance of public roads is the most ancient of governmental services. The genesis of taxation was to defray the cost of maintaining those public roads. The existence of public roads and streets assures the flow of commerce and the transit of persons, a basic prerequisite of civilization.

Another Major Beneficiary of Streets

Other than the movement of persons and goods, streets and roads also provide the route by which public utilities can emanate from or to their respective sources or destinations, to and from customers. Water distribution, refuse collection, storm drainage routing, gas distribution, sanitary sewage collection, electric power distribution, telephone wire and cable routing, product pipeline stringing, TV cable installation and, lately, multi-media cable laying all have, do and will benefit mightily from the very existence of those public rights-of-ways on which streets are constructed.

Streets as an Expensive Investment. In 1913, University of Illinois civil engineering professor Ira O. Baker summarized the future of streets thusly:

> "In no other branch of civil engineering is there expended so large an amount of money in so unsystematic a manner, and generally with such unsatisfactory results. .... Street pavements are by far the most expensive single improvement that the municipality undertakes; yet in hardly any of the cities of this country are there suitable laws, proper organization, or sufficient public spirit adequate to care for the investment after it is once made...." 1/

Unfortunately, it appears that little has changed in the 80 years since Dr. Baker opined.

A Goal. The goal of this article is to present and to analyze what should be, but isn't basic knowledge about urban roadways in the United States, and why they are in such a state of disrepair and disrepute. This article will attempt to lay the groundwork for determining the **exact** and true total annual cost of the amount of monies which **should be but is not** provided by public utilities to be expended on major street maintenance to repair the damage done by the utilities.

1/ Baker, Ira O.; Roads and Pavements, 3rd edition; New York, 1913; quoted in History of Public Works in the United States -- 1776 - 1976; American Public Works Association; Chicago, 1976; page 67.

"Do Utilities Affect Street Costs?" by Ayres & Kermer   Page 2

The Second Major Beneficiary.   Utilities, whether publicly or
investor-owned, have two choices for placement of their lines and
appurtenances. A utility can either purchase easements or fee rights
in properties to secure the necessary rights-of-ways, OR it can "nego-
tiate" a franchise with the local government. The procedure is simpler
when the utility is owned by the same government which legally controls access to and use of the street rights-of-way.

The Municipal Right-Of-Way. The utilities have taken the least
complicated and, by far, the least expensive of the two alternate
physical routes. It is well known, and accepted, that the investor-
owned utilities (and some publicly-owned utilities as well) long ago
developed, have retained, and possess "political clout" completely
disproportionate to their size. The utilities are "important" because
they provide "essential" services and, for the most part, are govern-
mentally-approved monopolies, complete with governmentally-assigned
exclusive service territories, and governmentally-guaranteed profits,
or "rates of return". Thus utilities generally meet the criteria of
the old saw of being "the only act in town".

That many utilities possess lengthy (30 to 99 years, and even some
perpetual) franchises, on such favorable terms to the utility, and exercise such influence is no surprise to those who are familiar with
the history of local government. The very eagerness of a community,
and consequently, its elected representatives, to possess the latest
"technological advancement", be it coal gas, Mr. Bell's telephone,
Thomas Alva Edison's electric lights, natural gas, CATV, or the newer
"multi-media information superhighway" of optic fiber cable, has acted
to keep the cities in an economic and political position of both physical and especially financial subservience to the utilities, be they
investor or publicly owned.

The Cost to the Public

One of the earlier fully-developed urban areas in the nation, New
York City, recognized early that it had permitted a monster in its
midst when it provided unlimited access to the street rights-of-ways
by the public utilities. The New York City results are reported:

> "The practice of tearing up pavements to install and re-
> pair gas, water, and sewer lines was particularly de-
> structive to the life of street pavements. The magni-
> tude of the problem was well illustrated in an 1896
> report of the New York City Department of Public Works.
> It indicated that one in every four miles of paved
>
> year. The lack of care in refilling trenches and the
> carelessness in replacing pavements often presented
> serious problems for city officials." 2/

2/ Ibid.; page 68.

"Do Utilities Affect Street Costs?" by Ayres & Kermer   Page 3

Chronic Lack of Money. The problem, of course, is that the
decried "lack of care" and "carelessness" continue in far too many --
if not most -- municipalities. The general cause is most often cited
as "lack of money" with which to hire inspectors or to make repairs.

To the end of eliminating that excuse, an article companion to
this will propose a major new, but basically old and overlooked, revenue source to assure that "lack of care" and "carelessness" are removed from the maintenance of public streets.   And another connected
piece will provide some heretofore little known, only partially realized, and some suspected downright suppressed knowledge about why
cities still allow utilities to have almost complete sway over their
little appreciated, but most precious rights-of-ways.

An Early Physical Solution. The 1896 New York City solution was to
require either the pre-placement of utility conduits in streets as
they were being constructed or re-constructed, or to require that:

> "...no excavations of any nature, except for emergency
> repairs of existing pipes and fixtures, shall be per-
> mitted in any street except upon written application of
> the individual or corporation desiring to make such ex-
> cavation, and the filing of a proper indemnity bond." 3/

The Conventional Solution. Added revenue sources beyond the
traditional "road tax" -- a portion of the property tax -- to both
construct and to maintain the growing national system of roads and
streets was needed, so:

> "Oregon in 1919 became the first state to enact a gaso-
> line tax and provide income to be used for highway pur-
> poses. This practice quickly received widespread accep-
> tance. Local roads [city streets] ...were considered the
> responsibility of the property owners and were financed
> largely from real estate taxes." 4/

So taxation financing for roads and streets was continued, and is
still being expanded, with which to finance public roads and city
street construction, maintenance and, presently, re-construction due
to age, failure and obsolescence.

Research, Standards and Yet More Research

Civil engineering research has been conducted on road construction
methodologies since the Roman roads and the era of John L. McAdam, 5/
mostly by the trial and error method. National and local road and
street construction standards were gradually developed during the
----
3/ Ibid.; quoted on pages 68 and 69.
4/ Ibid.; page 80.
5/ Ibid.; page 59.

"Do Utilities Affect Street Costs?" by Ayres & Kermer   Page 4

1920's and 30's, mostly under the auspices of what became the Federal Bureau of Public Roads (BPR), the American Association of State High-way Officials (AASHO), and the American Public Works Association (APWksA). Utilities officials and utility facilities accommodations were a major component of those standards and their development.

Beginning Street Research. It was not until the mid-1940's that any meaningful coordinative street research was conducted, financed by significant amounts of federal highway monies. National highway legis-lation passed in each of 1944 and 1954 for the first time required, first, origin and destination studies of traffic, and; next, "certifi-cation" of the use of the previously developed street and highway con-struction "standards".6/

Diversity of Street Use. The U.S. Bureau of Public Roads did studies and provided grant monies in the 1950's under the "TOPICS" (Traffic Operations Program to Increase Capacity and Safety) program. Those efforts, according to the authoritative history of streets in this country:

> "...clearly revealed the diversity of public and private
> interests involved and affected by the design of streets
> to serve the people living and working in an urban envi-
> ronment." 7/

Genesis of The Study of Utility Cost Impacts on Streets. In either 1952 or 1953 the Eugene Water and Electric Board (EWEB), the utility arm of the City of Eugene, Oregon, conducted field research for a study which resulted in a Report which received some notoriety in the field of public works administration and costing. That document determined what apparently now seems to be so obvious as to be unargu-able. But, the early 1950's was a time of great awakenings and initial and basic research in local governmental matters, World War II being ended only seven years.

The EWEB report drew the conclusion that were all utilities in-stalled in raw ground and the street then built over and around those facilities, that the cost of both construction and of long term (20 years or longer) street maintenance could be reduced by two-thirds.

Eugene was growing and, apparently, EWEB was trying to convince its Board and the City Council that they should make the joint commit-ment and forward capital expenditure to require that subdivisions be built with complete facilities underground, rather than following the then-prevailing national practice of building utilities and streets piecemeal, in a relatively uncoordinated manner.

6/ Ibid.; pages 81 through 98, especially pages 85 and 96.
7/ Ibid.; page 90.

"Do Utilities Affect Street Costs?" by Ayres & Kermer   Page 5

   <u>Recollections.</u> As Ayres recalls -- and, not having a copy of the
Report, which has disappeared into the maw of "records management and
document disposal" -- that's all there is, recollection of the EWEB
document. It also made a plea for what at that time was considered to
be an evolving theme: that the subdivider be required to pay for or
install the utilities and streets, rather than the general tax and
utility rate payer absorbing the costs from the City's tax rate and
the utility's capital accounts.

   <u>Committee Theme.</u> Several years later, in 1956, a Joint Committee
formed by the American Water Works Association (AWWA) and the American
Public Works Association to study the costs of utility construction on
streets picked up on this thrust from Eugene. One initial sub-theme
of the Joint Committee, which apparently had resulted in its being
joint between AWWA and APWA, was an idea about how street cut expenses
could be reduced on both of existing and new streets.

   The idea was that were the major water distribution line installed
under the parking strip on one side of the street and a 2" house distribution line under the other strip, and the two connected by 2" lat-
erals mid-block, that street cuts for house connections could all but
be eliminated. The thought of the Joint Committee apparently was to
prove the cost effectiveness of this technique and of the EWEB theme,
so that it could be recommended to the members of both organizations.

   <u>A Theory Overwhelmed by Facts.</u> As is often the case, however, a
good theory was overwhelmed by the facts. Ayres' initial assignment
was to work with one of the AWWA staff engineers (who might have well
been from Alvord, Burdick and Howson [ABH]) to establish the costs of
the two water line approach. 8/

   The engineers did the engineering calculations and construction
and street repair estimates while Ayres did the costing calculations
derived from the engineering numbers. The physical "two line" theory
was applied to a number of actual situations in and around the Mid-
West, of both older and newly constructed neighborhoods. The city circumstances came from the files of the cities in the area, derived by
telephone call, and from Committee member and ABH client files. This
effort took about two or three days to accomplish.

   It took only that short time before it became apparent that the
costs of installing and maintaining the two lines required under this
scheme, coupled with another then-current theme of street space allocation, plus the practicalities of periodic water service connection
renewal, made the two line idea impracticably expensive.

8/ Telephone conversation on December 29, 1993 with Don Eckmann of
Alvord, Burdick and Howson, Engineers, of Chicago, Illinois.

"Do Utilities Affect Street Costs?" by Ayres & Kermer   Page 6

A Different Direction. So the Joint Committee Study took a different direction. The members decided to determine to what extent the
very existence of utility lines within street rights-of-way would have
on the heavy maintenance and life expectancy of streets.

A Basic Determination. The Study consumed only a short time to
compile a lot of field work, from a questionnaire instrument and from
interviews by telephone and in person with Public Works Street Engineers from all over the country, but primarily the Mid-West.

The results and conclusions were based on the costs derived from
two sets of numbers, drawn from two distinctly different situations.
First, the cost of utility location on long-established streets. And
second, data about streets which had been constructed since 1950 [Five
years after the end of World War II].

Remarkable Conclusions. The conclusions were absolute. The data,
and both the utility and street engineers agreed, showed definitively
that in both circumstances, over a twenty year period, the costs of
street cutting, reconstruction and rehabilitation caused by ditch subsidence, cut spalling and water intrusion, base failure over utility
facilities and the like, were double the costs incurred in maintaining
a street containing no utilities, and suffering no soil invasions.

The numbers for the non-utility street were "backed into", in that
the cumulative amounts for such repairs and rebuilding were compared
to the life expectancy of 20 years of a newly built street constructed
on undisturbed soil. The only cost incurred in the 20 years for the
theoretical "new" street was periodic pavement surface sealing.

Double the Costs. The maintenance and reconstruction incidence and
costs of the streets in which utilities were located were twice those
of the theoretical "control" street, where no utilities existed. Or,
put another way, the capital life of the street was halved by the very
existence of utilities in, on and under the street surface.

But the costs incurred in repairing and rebuilding both "old" and
"new" streets in which utilities were located were nearly identical.
The trend line had been set on the "new" streets to follow the cut and
consequent failure and maintenance and reconstruction requirements
found to exist on the "old" streets. Thus the data showed that:

> Universally, the existence of utilities within street
> rights-of-ways act over time to double the costs of
> street maintenance, thus halving the life expectancy of
> the street prior to its requiring major reconstruction.

How Are Street Maintenance Costs Recouped From Utilities?

There really are only two ways in which to defray the costs of
major street maintenance, as follows:

"Do Utilities Affect Street Costs?" by Ayres & Kermer   Page 7

       1. Utility Franchise Fees

       2. General Fuel or Property Taxes

   Utility Franchises. Public utilities, whether publicly or investor-owned, once having made the decision to utilize public rights-of-
way rather than incurring the expense of acquiring private properties,
must have a franchise of some type. For the former it is relatively
simple; for the latter a formal franchise is required. But

       "All utility facilities must have some form of govern-
       mental authorization to utilize space in, on, and over
       rights-of-way in public streets, highways, lanes and
       other public areas. This authorization is given by var-
       ious types of statutes, ordinances or resolutions
       granted by various levels of government." 9/

   Backfilling. Street solidity, be it from initial installation of
utilities or their subsequent repair, comes in for much discussion in
a major APWKs Report relative to the accommodation of utility lines
within street rights-of-way. Germane quotes follow:

       "Reference must be made to the rare instances where
       backfilling is carried out by the municipality - a
       minority circumstance in the national practice scene -
       and to the motivation therefor. The reason for city
       intervention in a practice which is in most cases a
       responsibility of the permittee-utility is all too
       clear: improper backfill methods can result in eventual
       failure of the underground utility, produce need for
       later reopening of the trench at such points, and pro-
       duce unstable surface paving conditions which will
       result in road depressions and progressive failure of
       the entire street or road surface." 10/

   The only mentions of actual costs in this entire process and
Accommodation Report are as follows:

*   "East Kildonan, a community which has been taken into
*   Winnipeg, estimated that over a pavement's lifetime
*   about one-half of the capital costs of street construc-
*   tion were required to repair settlements, due to poor
*   construction and backfilling practices by utilities."
         11/

9/   Accommodation of Utility Plant Within the Rights-of-Way of Urban
Streets and Highways; American Public Works Association; Chicago, July
1974; pages iii - ix.
10/ Ibid.; page 30.
11/ Ibid.; page 30.

"Do Utilities Affect Street Costs?" by Ayres & Kermer   Page 8

To further support the above-reported local experience,

*   "The City of Oakland, Calif. experience indicates that
*   street resurfacing is required twice as frequently on
*   areas where cuts have been made and restored than on
*   streets where no utility cuts have been made. While
*   some municipal agencies believe that utility cuts, prop-
*   erly replaced, do not shorten the effective life of
*   pavements, a majority of respondees to the mail survey
*   and of the officials interviewed during the field inves-
*   tigation tend to feel that the pavement's life span is
*   affected by such work. This explains why the vast ma-
*   jority of communities attempt to ban cuts in recently
*   installed road structures." 12/

Control and Regulation? The Accommodation Report presents the
following solution to the backfill subsidence and pavement failure
problems caused by utilities:

"Additional control and regulation of right-of-way cuts
is evolving from poor backfill and temporary surfaces
for trenches cut by privately-owned utilities, contractors, plumbers and drainlayers." 13/

To those experienced and intimately familiar with urban governments of late recognize two major problems inherent in the above simplistic "solution".

First, publicly-owned utilities are as guilty of shoddy practices
as are private parties.

Second, all public agencies, be they utilities or public works
inspection and street maintenance operations, have been cut far below
even minimum staffing and appropriations levels in recent years sufficient to be able even to inspect, much less to correct or to charge
anyone with correcting backfill and pavement failures.

A Perverse Rationale. The Accommodation Report reports a significant element of the street engineering community apparently adheres to
the "ignore it and it'll go away" approach, as follows:

"Concern over inadequate and ineffective inspection programs is often allayed by the claim that defects in
right-of-way excavation, backfill and surface restora-
~~tion cannot be hidden, that they are eventually dis~~
closed by pavement and trench failures....By the time
evidence of improper backfill methods and material, com-

12/ Ibid.; page 34.
13/ Ibid.; page 34.

"Do Utilities Affect Street Costs?" by Ayres & Kermer   Page 9

> paction and surface restoration appears as trench de-
> pressions, damage has been done to adjoining surface
> areas, traffic has been affected, and the impedences of
> right-of-way re-digging and replacement operations must
> be expected." 14/

The above also could be cynically responded to by saying that by
the time the surface damage appears the person who should have in-
spected it will be retired, the current generation of utility rate
payers and utility shareholders will be off the financial hook, the
cumulative damage to the streets will be a major and noticeable financial burden, and the self-fulfilling prophesy of "poor government services" will have come totally true.

Operational Problems. Fortunately, for the credibility of the
Accommodations Report, numerous city street maintenance supervisory
personnel are quoted as universally having inadequate resources and
procedures to prevent major street failures due to utility damage.

And this Report is based on practices followed in 1974, long before the massive budget, personnel and resultant public maintenance
and service quality cuts of the 1990s. It also should be noted that
the inspectional laxities of the past are now resulting in the need
for street reconstruction in the present. The time which has passed
since the following reports having been issued is exactly the generally recognized life span of a street pavement -- 20 years.

Some select quotes germane to the assignment of street costs to
utilities follow.

> "Privately-owned utilities in Austin, Tex., provide
> their own inspection of projects but this procedure is
> deemed unsatisfactory by the regulating agency because
> backfilling requirements are not consistently met. No
> charges are made for inspection work under the city's
> non-inspectional policy." 15/

> [Wichita] "Officials have expressed objections to the
> lack of inspectional uniformity on utility work but they
> have not succeeded in obtaining adequate appropriations
> to increase their single-man capabilities." 16/

> "Kalamazoo utilizes no formal utility inspection force,
> but depends on informal spot checks of utility construc-
> tion sites by several city agencies. Inspection of
> trench restoration work is not carried out on an organ-
> ized or systematic basis." 16/

14/ Ibid.; page 44.
15/ Ibid.; page 46
16/ Ibid.; page 47.

"Do Utilities Affect Street Costs?" by Ayres & Kermer   Page 10

A Remarkable Conclusion. A startling admission, the basic facts underlying it having been discovered nearly 20 years earlier in the Joint Committee study, is literally buried in Chapter VIII of the Accommodations Study. The Chapter is entitled "Location Practices and Standards". 17/

The conclusion is buried even deeper -- on the fifth page of a section entitled "Excerpts From A Summary - Comparison of Practices (Covering observed conditions in five Metropolitan Areas)":

* "4. The consensus is that pavement cuts affect the ulti-
* mate life of roadways, regardless of how effectively
* backfill and resurfacing operations are carried out. The
* better the work, the less the detrimental effect." 18/

Other Germane Findings. Further Accommodations Report findings are hereinbelow quoted:

"Underground utility facilities experience more or less frequent failures, due to various causes, some of which might be attributed load, shock and other impacts on roads and streets and abutting properties." 19/

"Economics and the determination of cost to each user (utility) may restrict the use of the best practice for the overall interests of the public." 20/

"Many of the problems which have been reviewed in this report appear to be the result of insufficient permit and inspection services by many public agencies. Few agencies have had adequate funds to enforce permit and inspection programs. In a large measure this appears to be the result of low fee schedules which do not cover the cost of the service provided, and the inability of agencies to convince their legislative bodies of their manpower and equipment needs." 20/

Stopping Short. The Accommodations Report comes close to reaching an inescapable conclusion -- which was reached nearly 20 years earlier by the lost Joint Committee Report of 1956. But when tested, the conclusion was blunted and, typically, more research -- and the passage of yet another 20 or 40 or 60 or 80 years of a "reduced fare ride" by the utilities -- was assured. The salient Report quote is as follows, after which the Accommodations Report ducked out on the entire issue.

17/ Ibid.; pages 81, 94 and 98.
18/ Ibid.; page 98.
19/ Ibid.; page 100.
20/ Ibid.; page 115.

"Do Utilities Affect Street Costs?" by Ayres & Kermer   Page 11

"The ultimate goal of this aspect [data interpretation
and appraisal] of the research project was to determine
the degree of motorist and vehicle costs associated with
utility construction and maintenance activities. Once
these costs were determined they would be evaluated with
costs associated with other utility-related activities
and serve as a significant element in arriving at opti-
mum locations for utilities within the public rights-of-
way." 21/

How To Improve Practice. A companion APWksA and ASCE Report,
also published in 1974, shared the "Accommodation of Utility Plant..."
title, only it is labelled as a Manual of Improved Practice. The
Manual contains a few insights as to why utility cost reimbursement
for street reconstruction has never gotten "off the ground."

First, the sponsors, Steering Committee and staff were identical
to the State of the Art Report; utility executives dominated.

Second, successful accommodation of utilities needs these identified elements, among others:

"1. Enabling legislation to establish rights of local
agencies to control use of right-of-way;
 2. Provision of adequate staff and budget to protect
the public's investment in its streets and highways.
 3. Establishment and implementation of adequate permit,
inspection, and pavement restoration controls;..." 22/

Third, the field survey found, again in 1974 as was found in 1956:

"1. The cost of permits does not provide sufficient
funds to administer a permit and record operation;
 2. Enforcement of requiring permits varies greatly,
generally due to lack of personnel and budget;
 3. Inadequate inspection fees often result in inadequate funds and personnel to provide [inspection and
street repair] service;
 4. Pavement restoration practices vary widely, and the
public investment [read taxes] to repair and replace
street surfaces due to utility openings and to correct
their long term deleterious effect is high;..." 23/

21/ Ibid.; page 147.
22/ Accommodation of Utility Plant Within the Rights-of-Way of Urban
Streets and Highways - Manual of Improved Practice; American Public
Works Association, Chicago; 1974.
23/ Ibid.; page 2.

Fourth, keying off the previous quote, the circular process followed in the regulation of utilities to assure adequate street condition can be summarized by the following quote:

> "Despite this right [franchises] of privately-owned utilities to utilize right-of-way space, they do not possess the right to use their franchise privileges where, when and how they wish. [Try to tell a utility that, in practice]....
>
> "The method used by local government to control and regulate the operations of utilities within the public right-of-way is to require applications for all proposed work involving the cutting, obstruction, disturbance and restoration of road and street areas, and by the issuance of permits to carry out such work under specific conditions that will protect the integrity of the right-of-way, assure the protection of other structures, and guarantee the optimum safety and public convenience.
>
> "Regulation of such utility functions can be made effective by carefully established rules and regulations, review and issuance of permits in accordance with such provisions, and inspection and control of all right-of-way operations." 24/

Last, the political and economic power of the utilities, compared to others, and the common acceptance that a franchise is a license to do anything unfettered by regulation, is illustrated by a simple statement contained in the Manual:

> "Few governmental agencies assign full-time inspectors to in-city [utility] projects, even if they involve large areas and long periods of time. However, many regulating agencies provide full-time inspection coverage of subdivision development work on utility installations in road and street rights-of-way, all constructed and installed in conformity with city specifications. The developer is charged for these services." 25/

A Muddy Model. The Manual then, in 21 pages, built around a complex mathematical formula, attempts to develop a costing "model" to distribute costs of street reconstruction and maintenance to each of:

1. Utility company
2. Roadway user
3. Utility user
4. Municipality

24/ Ibid.; page 5.
25/ Ibid.; page 13.

"Do Utilities Affect Street Costs?" by Ayres & Kermer   Page 13

Each of safety, economic impact on abutting property owners, aesthetic impact, social ramification, and other factors are acknowledged and recognized. 26/

Negation of the Model. The Manual then goes on to negate its own model by admitting as follows:

> "It should be noted that when computing the total system cost...all expenses (both actual and perceived)...are treated equally dollar for dollar [Note: what that means I know not] In actual practice the burden of these expenses is allocated according to the economic and political power of the participants....Political power, emotional reactions..., or simply the lack of accurate cost data may lead to the choice of an alternative which is less costly to one or more of the parties involved but more costly to society [read taxpayer] when the total system costs are considered." 27/

Yet Another Joint Utility - Street Committee Report. In 1977 APWA issued a monograph on forming utility location and coordination committees. A few quotes from that provides further insight into both the mind fix of the public officials involved, and the significant influence of the utilities on street use, maintenance, costs, repair, and who pays those expenses.

The "Task Force" that developed the guide consisted of six investor-owned utility executives, one consulting engineer, and one rural county public works director.

The Guide identifies 16 distinct underground and nine overhead utilities utilizing public street rights-of-way. Some utilities, like telephone and CATV, fall into both groups. A few choice quotes follow:

> "The need for improved coordination among all parties involved in the accommodation of utility plant within the public rights-of-way surfaced as a national concern in the U. S. in the late 1960s and early 1970s." 28/

There is no argument about the need and usefulness of such committees in each locality. However, in reading the charge of such groups, the major issue of cost allocation and sharing is totally absent.

26/ Ibid.; pages 56 thru 76, with the mathematical model being on page 59.
27/ Ibid.; page 56.
28/ How to Form Utility Location and Coordination Committees; American Public Works Association; Chicago; August, 1977; page 3.

"Do Utilities Affect Street Costs?" by Ayres & Kermer   Page 14

> "Major goals of utility location and coordination com-
> mittees are to:
>
>> 1. Improve communication and exchange informa-
>> tion among all responsible parties, trade and
>> professional associations, and the general
>> public.
>> 2. Minimize damage to utility and street
>> structures.
>> 3. Coordinate scheduling of capital improve-
>> ment and maintenance projects.
>> 4. Minimize inconvenience and cost to the pub-
>> lic in providing services.
>> 5. Improve safety conditions.
>> 6. Develop suggested standards for accommodat-
>> ing utilities within common corridors." 29/

Obviously, the decision to charge utilities for both of current
services and damage done to street surfaces will have to be discussed
and made at a much higher level than the local coordinating committee.

Some Progress? Yet another APWksA Federal Highway Administration-
financed effort, published in 1985, contains a few mentions of some
progress being made in recognition of the extraordinary and generally
uncompensated damage done to streets by utilities.

For a change, four of the members of the Project Advisory Committee for this Manual were public employees, one a consulting civil
engineer, and four industry/association representatives. No utilities
persons were involved.

The first significant quote is as follows:

> "For streets in Rochester [New York] that have recently
> been reconstructed (within the past six years), or re-
> surfaced (in the past four years), an extended mainte-
> nance fee [read "utility street service charge"] is im-
> posed in addition to the pavement-cut permit fee. This
> extended maintenance fee is designed to cover the cost
> of street maintenance that may be needed after the two-
> year guarantee period is up and before the city is pre-
> pared to rehabilitate the street again." 30/

This Manual, once again, makes the point made by the missing 1956
Joint Committee Study, and citations in those studies performed since

----
29/ Ibid.; page 10.
30/ Street & Highway Maintenance Manual; American Public Works
Association; Chicago; 1985; page 121.

> "...one of the major causes of pavement degradation, particularly in urban areas, is cutting of pavement for utility additions or relocations." 31/

A Rationale for A Utility Street Service Charges and Further Research.

The thrust of this article has been aimed at exposing the thesis that utilities which occupy street rights-of-way have for more than a century been given what, in effect, amounts to a significant public tax subsidy for their use of public street properties, and that a full examination -- both technically and politically -- should be had of the entire subject of who pays for street repairs and reconstruction.

The property and gas tax payers have been disadvantaged long enough. Perhaps it is time to spread the cost burden per the earlier cited "grand accounting".

Conclusion

The missing 1956 Joint Committee Report raised a major challenge to the utilities, be they publicly-owned or investor-owned. Every year, or as it has worked out, every decade that all costs of street replacement can be put off onto the property and gas tax payers, rather than being more fairly distributed among the utilities, is another decade in which literally BILLIONS of dollars are improperly charged to those taxpayers. Much of those billions find their way into utility investor accounts.

Utilities Pay? The utilities -- be they publicly owned or investor-owned, should pay for the actual cost of damage which they inflict -- both short and long term -- on public streets and roads.

To that end, more definitive **objective and unbiased engineering** studies need to be performed to **absolutely and definitively** ascertain the costs of such damage.

It is the contention of one of the authors of this article, Douglas W. Ayres, who participated in a major joint AWWA/APWksA study of the impact of utilities on streets, that the resultant Draft Joint Committee Report was "lost" on purpose. On purpose so that utilities, both publicly-owned and investor-owned, wouldn't have to increase their rates to recompense streets for the damages rendered; to prevent a more equitable distribution of street costs so that taxes could be either mitigated or used for matters which benefit all society.

END

31/ Ibid.; page 158.

KEY PHRASE & ISSUES INDEX

GENERAL FUND

THE CURRENT IDEOLOGICAL HORRIBLY FALSE VIEW of GOVERNMENT

The above empty-headed engorged fat man illustrates the all-consuming nature of LOCAL and STATE GOVERNMENT GENERAL FUNDS. Everything goes in: taxes, fees, charges, & anything and all things monetary are sucked up and disappear into the yawning maw of the gigantic GENERAL FUND. Individual, corporate CEOs, lobbyists, "general public", poor, rich, middle class and all those expectant citizen/taxpayers who seek output in the form of unlimited and high quality services and facilities stand waiting for their personal cornucopia. But too little comes out. ALL are greatly disappointed, disillusioned, and ANGRY at the wasteful, lazy, ignorant, and overpaid socialist bureaucratic slacker 'public servants' who typify ALL government employees. And the elected officials who created and condone this MESS. So the outrageously high pay, FAT retirement, health care, sick leave, vacation, overtime, vehicles, and "many other lucrative benefits" MUST be slashed–NOW! ABSOLUTELY! Without thought, analysis, consideration, care or empathy.

There is no reason __WE__ should pay for __THEM__ -- So the cry goes out --

ALL GOVERNMENT IS USELESS, WASTEFUL AND CORRUPT !!!
'IT' must be gut and cut! NOW! RIGHT NOW!!!!

THE WAVE OF THE FUTURE IS *NO TAXES – NONE, NONE, NONE!!*